PLANT SELECTOR

A MARSHALL GARDEN GUIDE

PLANT SELECTOR

*Instant visual reference
for planning your garden*

Jenny Hendy
Photography Peter Stiles

MARSHALL PUBLISHING · LONDON

A QUARTO BOOK

First published in the UK in 1998 by
Marshall Publishing Ltd
170 Piccadilly
London W1V 9DD

ISBN 1 84028 111 1

This book was designed and produced by
Quarto Publishing plc
6 Blundell Street,
London N7 9 BH

CONSULTANTS Frances Hutchison (Australia),
Peter Kruger (South Africa), Sally Roth (USA)
TEXT EDITOR Sally Roth
SENIOR EDITOR Sally MacEachern
DESIGNERS Jennie Dooge, Sally Bond
ART EDITOR Sally Bond
PHOTOGRAPHER Peter Stiles
PICTURE RESEARCHER Miriam Hyman
ASSISTANT ART DIRECTOR Penny Cobb
EDITORIAL DIRECTOR Pippa Rubinstein
ART DIRECTOR Moira Clinch

Typeset by Central Southern Typesetters,
Eastbourne
Manufactured by United Graphics (Pte) Ltd,
Singapore
Printed by Star Standard Industries (Pte) Ltd

East
DUNBARTONSHIRE
Council

CONTENTS

INTRODUCTION

GREEN

BLUE

YELLOW

PINK

ORANGE

RED

WHITE

PURPLE

INDEX

CREDITS

How to use this book

Simple color schemes like the one shown here—blocks of pastel blue pansies edged with pink *Begonia semperflorens*—are particularly eye-catching.

DESIGNING WITH COLOR

Plantings where the use of color is restricted are usually far more striking and effective than those that incorporate many different shades. This book is designed to help you create color-themed borders with ease. You'll find plenty of ideas in the chapter openers for single-color schemes and combinations, but it's important to realize that your main color will come and go in a mixed planting depending on the time of year. For instance, it is difficult to maintain a blue border year-round because of the lack of blue-flowering plants in winter. This is where blending with another color, such as yellow, will be

useful. The dynamics of a two-color border create far more interest in other seasons, too.

Annuals are great for experimenting with different color schemes - if something doesn't work out, you can always try again next season. But for permanent plantings in a mixed border, it's wise to have some kind of evergreen framework or backbone planting to provide continuity. Foliage is just as important a consideration as flower, and even if it is not quite as colorful, it is far more enduring. It comes in a wide variety of tints and serves to enhance blooms in specific color schemes.

There are of course other factors to consider when designing a border, such as blending different shapes and textures for maximum contrast. The close-up and general view photographs and descriptive text should give you a good idea of the form of the plant. Try to imagine your scheme in black and white to ensure that there is sufficient variety of form. Flowering time is also important. For a scheme to work well, plants that are in bloom at the same time must combine satisfactorily. And there's no point putting a group of plants together because they make a pleasing combination on paper, if they all bloom at different times.

Finally, there's no reason why you have to stick to a particular color scheme year-round. You can choose a main color to link the seasons, and then weave in contrasting or complementary shades as the year unfolds. Bulbs and annuals are particularly useful for bringing about the changes.

SEASONAL VARIETY

Each color chapter opens with plants for springtime and gradually takes you through the seasons, ending in winter. Some plants remain attractive for many months but only appear once in the chapter - usually at the time when they are most useful or effective. In warmer climates where the winter is very mild or nonexistent, plants may continue to flower virtually year-round. A good example is impatiens, which in frost-free areas not only flowers almost continuously but also self-seeds. Roses also perform well under mild conditions, coming into flower in spring and continuing to late autumn.

Where there is a marked difference in flowering time, this is indicated in brackets in the description.

The ideal border has something of interest all through the year, but in practice this is hard to achieve, particularly if you're trying to maintain a narrow color scheme. It is often better to go for a series of peaks throughout the season. Use annuals and tender perennials as fillers to add color when the border enters a quiet phase.

PLANTING BY SIZE

The top row of each page contains back-of-the-border plants that grow taller than 4ft (1.2m); the middle row, plants which generally speaking fall into the 2 to 4ft (0.6-1.2m) category; and the bottom row, front-of-the-border plants which on average don't grow any taller than 2ft (0.6m). In warmer climates, especially in frost-free areas where growth is unchecked, plants may grow to a larger size than listed. This is especially true of climbers, shrubs, and trees.

Use the height ranking to get an idea of relative sizes. For instance, if the border is very narrow or small, you may not want to use any plant over 4ft(1.2m). Don't be too rigid about keeping taller plants at the back: It's far more interesting visually to bring some forward as

Shown below is an example of a typical directory page and a detail showing one of the plant entries (below right).

Close-up of plant

Symbols for information on hardiness and whether the plant likes sun or shade (see pp.8-9)

General view of plant

Color grouping

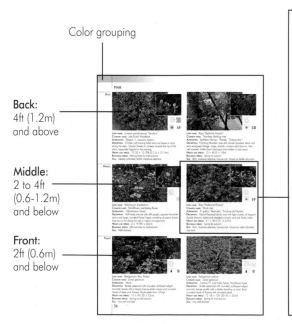

Back:
4ft (1.2m)
and above

Middle:
2 to 4ft
(0.6-1.2m)
and below

Front:
2ft (0.6m)
and below

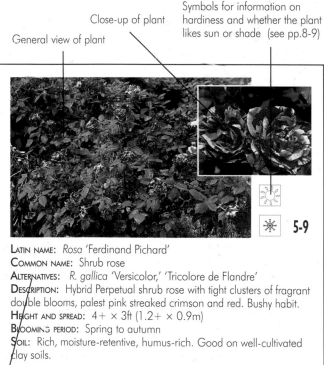

LATIN NAME: *Rosa 'Ferdinand Pichard'*
COMMON NAME: Shrub rose
ALTERNATIVES: *R. gallica* 'Versicolor,' 'Tricolore de Flandre'
DESCRIPTION: Hybrid Perpetual shrub rose with tight clusters of fragrant double blooms, palest pink streaked crimson and red. Bushy habit.
HEIGHT AND SPREAD: 4+ × 3ft (1.2+ × 0.9m)
BLOOMING PERIOD: Spring to autumn
SOIL: Rich, moisture-retentive, humus-rich. Good on well-cultivated clay soils.

Ideas for other species or varieties which give a similar effect to that of the plant illustrated.

INTRODUCTION

Lavenders are herbs from the Mediterranean region and, like many silver or gray-leaved plants, must have a position in full sunshine to keep growth compact and healthy and to maximize flowering potential.

accents and to break up low, front-of-the-border plantings. Choose plants with a fairly narrow, sculptural profile or with an open, airy habit, so that you can still see the plants behind.

SUN OR SHADE?

Some plants thrive in full sun and others prefer some shade. Many fall into the category of being shade-tolerant - they can put up with dappled shade from trees or a spot in the border that only gets sun for part of the day. A few plants will tolerate full shade, i.e., a position that receives no direct sunlight. To enable you to choose plants appropriate to the light conditions, we've devised the following key:

 Requires full sun

 Likes a sunny spot but also does well in partial shade

 Requires partial shade and will suffer if subjected to full sun or full shade

 Cannot tolerate full sun. Does well in partial or full shade

 Thrives in full shade

 Tolerates any light conditions

SOIL TYPE

A brief guide to the kind of soil required is given for each plant. Often the key to success is drainage - too wet or too dry, and the plant will suffer. Plants that enjoy a well-drained site will often tolerate dry conditions for short periods. Many plants like to have moisture at their roots, particularly through the growing season, but will suffer if

the ground is wet or waterlogged. You can keep roots moist by digging in plenty of organic matter (humus) and also by mulching the surface to conserve moisture. A position in partial shade will also help relieve pressure when the soil is on the dry side. Few border plants need wet or boggy positions, but some ornamentals have been included to cater to waterlogged or constantly wet sites.

Soil acidity or alkalinity is measured on a pH scale from 1 to 14, where 7 is neutral, numbers less than 7 denote acidity, and above 7, alkalinity. It's essential to know what your soil pH is before you begin planting in earnest, as some plants have very specific requirements and you could end up wasting a lot of time and money. You can buy an inexpensive and easy to use kit from most garden centers. Acid-loving plants like rhododendrons, azaleas, and camellias must have a pH of 7 or below and generally require moisture-retentive, humus-rich soil. Most plants tolerate slightly acid, neutral, or slightly alkaline conditions, in which case pH is not mentioned in the text. A few plants do best on quite alkaline or lime-rich soils with a pH above 7.

Another factor to consider is soil fertility. Happily, there are plants to suit any conditions. On poor, dry, stony soils, "hungry" plants like shrub roses produce poor growth unless conditions are improved by cultivation. Drought-tolerant, sun-loving Mediterranean plants, including many aromatic herbs and silver-leaved shrubs, thrive in these same conditions. It is important to maintain soil fertility through additions of fertilizers and manure or garden compost, but bear in mind that a rich, well-fed soil can cause certain plants like hardy annuals to produce too much leaf at the expense of flower. Overfeeding also encourages soft, sappy growth that is vulnerable to insect pests and frost damage.

Rhododendrons, azaleas and other ericaceous plants, including pieris and many heaths and heathers, must have acid soil to thrive. Any lime in the soil causes the foliage to turn yellow (chlorosis) and the plant may die.

8

HARDINESS

Each plant has a number or range of numbers that corresponds with the zone maps (below). Once you know what climate zone you live in, you can tell at a glance whether or not a particular plant will thrive in your garden or if it needs winter protection. Annual plants that die once they've finished flowering are marked with a flower symbol and can be grown in any zone.

5-7   Example of climate zone range (see key right)

❀   Annual plant

Hardiness is not just a question of minimum temperature, however. Poor drainage often contributes markedly to the failure of plants to survive the winter. Exposure to wind during freezing conditions can also be highly destructive. If you can provide shelter and protect the roots from freezing solid by covering the ground with a thick mulch in autumn, many vulnerable plants can be coaxed through the winter months.

KEY TO ZONES ON MAP

1 =		below -10° C (-50° F)
2 =		-9 to -10° C (-40 to -50° F)
3 =		-8 to -9° C (-30 to -40° F)
4 =		-6 to -8° C (-20 to -30° F)
5 =		-5 to -6° C (-10 to -20° F)
6 =		-4 to -5° C (0 to -10° F)
7 =		-3 to -4° C (10 to 0° F)
8 =		-1 to -3° C (20 to 10° F)
9 =		0 to -1° C (30 to 20° F)
10 =		1 to 0° C (40 to 30° F)

For countries that don't use zone maps, hardiness is indicated as follows:

💧   Half hardy to 0° C (30° F)

❄   Frost hardy to -5° C (-10° F)

❅   Fully hardy to -6° C or below (-20° F or below)

PINK

PURE PINKS ARE A BLEND OF TRUE PRIMARY RED AND WHITE, BUT THE RANGE OF COLORS WE CALL PINK IS MUCH GREATER. THE COOLER BLUE-PINKS EVENTUALLY MERGE INTO LILAC AND THE WARMER YELLOW-PINKS INTO SOFT PEACH. GENERALLY SPEAKING, PINKS AT THESE EXTREMES DO NOT SIT WELL NEXT TO EACH OTHER IN THE BORDER. BRIGHT SALMON-PINKS ARE OFTEN DIFFICULT TO PLACE, BUT THEY LOOK WELL WHEN SURROUNDED BY COOL SHADES - WHITE, CLEAR BLUE, AND LIME-GREEN. IT USED TO BE A CARDINAL SIN TO MIX PINK WITH YELLOW, BUT SALMON-PINKS CAN LOOK STUNNING WITH THE RIGHT YELLOW. IT'S JUST A MATTER OF EXPERIMENTATION!

SOFT PINKS ARE GENTLE ON THE EYE AND HELP TO CREATE A RESTFUL AND HARMONIOUS EFFECT IN THE GARDEN. WHAT'S MORE, PINK BORDERS ARE RELATIVELY EASY TO CREATE AND CAN LOOK BEAUTIFUL WHEN SET AGAINST THE SIMPLE BACKDROP OF A CLIPPED EVERGREEN HEDGE. WATCH OUT FOR BRICK AND TERRACOTTA, HOWEVER. ORANGE AND PINK REALLY DO SHOUT AT EACH OTHER!

PINK MAKES A ROMANTIC STATEMENT WHEN BLENDED WITH DIAPHANOUS WHITE FLOWERS AND SILVER FILIGREE FOLIAGE. BLUE-PINKS BLEND PERFECTLY WITH LIGHT PURPLES AND BLUES FOR A PASTEL EFFECT. BUT TRY NOT TO GET CARRIED AWAY OR YOU MIGHT END UP WITH AN INSIPID SCHEME LACKING IN DEPTH. SPRINKLE IN GLOWING CERISE OR DEEP VELVETY CRIMSON FOR CONTRAST.

LEFT: *This simple scheme of pink rhododendrons underplanted with foxgloves is wonderfully romantic.*

BACK

☀️ ❄️ **5-7**

LATIN NAME: *Rhododendron* 'Christmas Cheer'
COMMON NAME: Known by Latin name
ALTERNATIVES: 'Pink Pearl'
DESCRIPTION: Evergreen shrub with dense rounded heads of light pink, funnel-shaped blooms. This rhododendron flowers in late winter or early spring and in cold climates can be forced for earlier flowering.
HEIGHT AND SPREAD: 4 × 5ft (1.2 × 1.5m)
BLOOMING PERIOD: Winter to early spring
SOIL: Acid, humus-rich, moisture-retentive.

☀️ ❄️ **4-9**

LATIN NAME: *Prunus* × *subhirtella* 'Autumnalis Rosea'
COMMON NAME: Winter-flowering cherry, Higan cherry
ALTERNATIVES: *P. mume* 'Beni-chidori'
DESCRIPTION: Tree of light, airy habit with oval-shaped leaves giving good yellow autumn color. Clusters of rosy pink blossoms on bare branches during mild winters.
HEIGHT AND SPREAD: 24 × 24ft (7 × 7m)
BLOOMING PERIOD: Late autumn to early spring
SOIL: Any well-drained.

MIDDLE

☀️ ❄️ **4-9**

LATIN NAME: *Daphne mezereum*
COMMON NAME: February daphne
ALTERNATIVES: *D. odora* 'Aureomarginata'
DESCRIPTION: Shrub with a goblet-shaped habit. The bare stems are smothered in purple-pink, four-petalled blooms which are highly fragrant. Poisonous red berries sometimes follow. Leaves small, lance-shaped.
HEIGHT AND SPREAD: 2½ × 3ft (0.75 × 0.9m)
BLOOMING PERIOD: Late winter to early spring
SOIL: Deep, fertile, well-drained but moisture-retentive. Humus-rich.

☀️ ❄️ **8-10**

LATIN NAME: *Erica erigena* 'Superba' syn. *E. mediterranea*
COMMON NAME: Mediterranean heath, Irish heath
ALTERNATIVES: 'Brightness,' 'Irish Salmon'
DESCRIPTION: Evergreen shrub with green, needle-like leaves darkening in winter and spikes of tiny, fragrant bell flowers. Must have acid soil and plentiful summer moisture to thrive.
HEIGHT AND SPREAD: 4 × 4ft (1.2 × 1.2m)
BLOOMING PERIOD: Late winter to spring
SOIL: Acid, humus-rich, moisture-retentive.

FRONT

☀️ ❄️ **7-9**

LATIN NAME: *Cyclamen coum*
COMMON NAME: Known by Latin name
ALTERNATIVES: *C. persicum* cultivars
DESCRIPTION: Tuberous perennial having attractive, leathery-textured, heart-shaped leaves with silver patterning. Mauve-pink shaded blooms. Good groundcover under deciduous trees and shrubs.
HEIGHT AND SPREAD: 4 × 2–4in (10 × 5–10cm)
BLOOMING PERIOD: Winter
SOIL: Humus-rich, moisture-retentive but well-drained.

☀️ ❄️ **3-9**

LATIN NAME: *Primula* × *polyantha* 'Crescendo Rose'
COMMON NAME: Polyanthus
ALTERNATIVES: Rainbow strain, Wanda hybrids, Hercules strain
DESCRIPTION: Hardy perennial grown as a biennial for spring bedding. Forms a basal rosette of green, crinkled leaves from which stout flower stems arise. Deadhead and remove yellowing leaves.
HEIGHT AND SPREAD: 9–12 × 12in (23–30 × 30cm)
BLOOMING PERIOD: Spring
SOIL: Moisture-retentive.

4-9

4-9

LATIN NAME: *Magnolia stellata* 'Rosea'
COMMON NAME: Star magnolia
ALTERNATIVES: 'King Rose,' 'Susan'
DESCRIPTION: Dome-shaped shrub, with branches upright at first then becoming spreading. Oval leaves expand after flowering. Starry blooms with many strap-shaped petals. Fragrant.
HEIGHT AND SPREAD: 8 × 12ft (2.5 × 3.5m)
BLOOMING PERIOD: Early spring
SOIL: Avoid extreme alkalinity.

LATIN NAME: *Magnolia × soulangiana*
COMMON NAME: Tulip magnolia, saucer magnolia
ALTERNATIVES: *M. × loebneri* 'Leonard Messel'
DESCRIPTION: Large shrub with upright branches. Large broadly oval leaves. Goblet-shaped blooms, light pink shaded purple, appear before the leaves.
HEIGHT AND SPREAD: 13 × 13ft (4 × 4m)
BLOOMING PERIOD: Spring
SOIL: Humus-rich, moisture-retentive. Does well on clay.

7-8

2-7

LATIN NAME: *Rhododendron × cilpinense*
COMMON NAME: Known by Latin name
ALTERNATIVES: *R. williamsianum, R.* 'Praecox,' *R. yakushimanum*
DESCRIPTION: Semi-evergreen shrub of compact habit with dark, glossy green leaves and clusters of pale pink, bell-shaped blooms with dark brown anthers. Deeper pink shading on buds and reverse of flowers.
HEIGHT AND SPREAD: 4 × 4ft (1.2 × 1.2m)
BLOOMING PERIOD: Early spring
SOIL: Acid, humus-rich and moisture retentive.

LATIN NAME: *Prunus tenella* 'Fire Hill'
COMMON NAME: Dwarf Russian almond
ALTERNATIVES: None
DESCRIPTION: Suckering shrub with upright stems which become clothed in vibrant pink blooms all along the length before the leaves open. 'Fire Hill' is a shorter-growing form of the species.
HEIGHT AND SPREAD: 4 × 3ft (1.2 × 0.9m)
BLOOMING PERIOD: Early spring
SOIL: Any well-drained, avoiding extreme alkalinity.

5-9

9-10

LATIN NAME: *Veltheimia bracteata* syn. *V. undulata, V. viridifolia*
COMMON NAME: Known by Latin name
ALTERNATIVES: None
DESCRIPTION: Bulbous plant, member of the lily family, with a basal rosette of broad, glossy, strap-shaped leaves and poker-shaped spikes of pink, red or orange, green-tipped tubular flowers.
HEIGHT AND SPREAD: 12–18 × 10–15in (30–45 × 25–38cm)
BLOOMING PERIOD: Late winter
SOIL: Well-drained.

LATIN NAME: *Primula vulgaris* subsp. *sibthorpii*
COMMON NAME: Hardy primrose
ALTERNATIVES: *P.* Wanda hybrids
DESCRIPTION: Hardy perennial with a basal rosette of crinkled leaves and central clusters of lilac-pink, rounded blooms produced singly on short stems. Greenish yellow "eye."
HEIGHT AND SPREAD: 6 × 6in (15 × 15cm)
BLOOMING PERIOD: Early to mid-spring
SOIL: Well-drained, moisture-retentive.

13

BACK

8-9

LATIN NAME: *Camellia × williamsii* 'Bow Bells'
COMMON NAME: Known by Latin name
ALTERNATIVES: 'Donation,' 'November Pink'
DESCRIPTION: Evergreen shrub with oblong to lance-shaped, glossy green leaves and rose-pink, semi-double, funnel-shaped blooms over a long period.
HEIGHT AND SPREAD: 10 × 10ft (3 × 3m)
BLOOMING PERIOD: Late autumn to early spring
SOIL: Acid, humus-rich, moisture retentive.

5-9

LATIN NAME: *Rhododendron racemosum*
COMMON NAME: Known by Latin name
ALTERNATIVES: None
DESCRIPTION: Evergreen shrub, vigorous, with a strongly upright, stiff-branched habit and small, dark green, aromatic leaves. Profusion of small, pale pink, funnel-shaped flowers in clusters.
HEIGHT AND SPREAD: 8 × 8ft (2.5 × 2.5m)
BLOOMING PERIOD: Spring
SOIL: Acid, humus-rich, moisture retentive.

MIDDLE

6-9

LATIN NAME: *Rhododendron* 'Kirin'
COMMON NAME: Evergreen azalea, Kurume azalea
ALTERNATIVES: 'Blaauw's Pink,' 'Hino-mayo'
DESCRIPTION: Evergreen azalea of dense, bushy habit with small, oval, dark green leaves and numerous small, funnel-shaped flowers which are deep rose-pink shaded paler pink.
HEIGHT AND SPREAD: 4 × 4ft (1.2 × 1.2m)
BLOOMING PERIOD: Spring
SOIL: Acid, humus-rich, moisture-retentive.

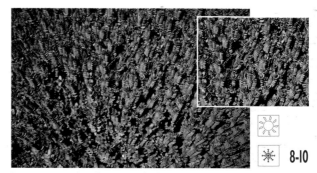

8-10

LATIN NAME: *Hebe albicans* 'Red Edge'
COMMON NAME: Known by Latin name
ALTERNATIVES: 'Candy'
DESCRIPTION: Evergreen shrub making a perfect dome shape. The small, gray-green leaves have a thin red margin and the shoot tips are pink-shaded. Short white flower spikes. Clip back lightly after flowering.
HEIGHT AND SPREAD: 2 × 3ft (0.6 × 0.9m)
BLOOMING PERIOD: Early summer
SOIL: Well-drained.

FRONT

5-9

LATIN NAME: *Erica carnea* 'Myretoun Ruby'
COMMON NAME: Heather, winter heath
ALTERNATIVES: 'December Red,' 'King George,' 'Pink Spangles'
DESCRIPTION: Evergreen shrublet forming good groundcover with dark green, needle-like leaves and tiny bell-shaped blooms of carmine-pink in dense clusters. Clip back lightly after flowering.
HEIGHT AND SPREAD: 8 × 18+in (20 × 45+cm)
BLOOMING PERIOD: Late winter to early spring
SOIL: Well-drained, humus-rich. Tolerates alkalinity.

LATIN NAME: *Bellis perennis* 'Robella'
COMMON NAME: English daisy
ALTERNATIVES: 'Monstrosa,' Goliath and Radar series
DESCRIPTION: Short-lived perennial usually grown as a biennial for spring bedding, making a rosette of leaves above which the large, fully double blooms on slender stems appear.
HEIGHT AND SPREAD: 3–6 × 6in (7.5 × 15cm)
BLOOMING PERIOD: Mid-spring to mid-summer
SOIL: Any reasonably well-drained.

3-10

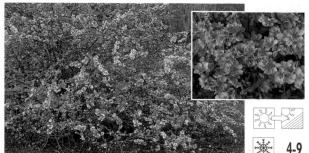

5-8

4-9

LATIN NAME: *Pieris* 'Flamingo'
COMMON NAME: Lily-of-the-valley shrub, andromeda
ALTERNATIVES: 'Pink Delight', 'Christmas Cheer,' 'Valley Rose'
DESCRIPTION: Evergreen shrub with small, pointed, dull green leaves and bushy, upright habit. Attractive overwintering buds open to hanging tresses of deep pink bell flowers.
HEIGHT AND SPREAD: 6 × 10–12ft (1.8 × 3–3.5m)
BLOOMING PERIOD: Mid-spring to late spring
SOIL: Acid, humus-rich, moisture retentive.

LATIN NAME: *Chaenomeles speciosa* 'Moerloosii' ('Appleblossom')
COMMON NAME: Flowering quince
ALTERNATIVES: *C. × superba* 'Pink Lady'
DESCRIPTION: Shrub of open habit with thorny stems and small, dark green leaves. Appleblossom-like flowers open directly from the stem. Small aromatic fruits sometimes produced.
HEIGHT AND SPREAD: 10 × 10ft (3 × 3m)
BLOOMING PERIOD: Winter to spring
SOIL: Any well-drained but avoiding strongly alkaline.

3-10

LATIN NAME: *Dicentra spectabilis*
COMMON NAME: Bleeding heart, lady's locket, lyre flower
ALTERNATIVES: None
DESCRIPTION: Herbaceous perennial with fern-like foliage and arching sprays of heart-shaped crimson-pink and white blooms which are excellent for cutting.
HEIGHT AND SPREAD: 2 × 1½ft (0.6 × 0.45m)
BLOOMING PERIOD: Late spring to early summer
SOIL: Moisture-retentive, humus-rich.

LATIN NAME: *Daphne odora* 'Aureomarginata'
COMMON NAME: Winter daphne
ALTERNATIVES: *D. odora, D. bholua* and cultivars
DESCRIPTION: Evergreen shrub with dark green glossy leaves edged with a fine margin of yellow. Highly fragrant purple-pink and white flowers. Dislikes full sun
HEIGHT AND SPREAD: 3 × 3ft (0.9 × 0.9m)
BLOOMING PERIOD: Mid-winter to early spring
SOIL: Deep, fertile, humus-rich, tolerating moderate alkalinity.

7-9

5-8

4-8

LATIN NAME: *Erythronium revolutum* Johnsonii Group
COMMON NAME: Dog's tooth violet, trout lily
ALTERNATIVES: *E. revolutum*
DESCRIPTION: Tuberous perennial making low hummocks of green, lance-shaped leaves with distinctive brown mottling. The large, pink, nodding flowers on wiry stems have reflexed petals.
HEIGHT AND SPREAD: 8–12 × 6in (20–30 × 15cm)
BLOOMING PERIOD: Spring
SOIL: Humus-rich, moisture-retentive but well-drained.

LATIN NAME: *Epimedium grandiflorum* 'Rose Queen'
COMMON NAME: Barrenwort
ALTERNATIVES: *Epimedium × rubrum*
DESCRIPTION: Evergreen perennial forming low groundcover with attractive heart-shaped leaves which are green with coppery tinges. The unusual spurred flowers hang down in clusters on wiry stems.
HEIGHT AND SPREAD: 12 × 12in (30 × 30cm)
BLOOMING PERIOD: Spring
SOIL: Humus-rich, moisture-retentive.

BACK

LATIN NAME: *Rhododendron* hybrid cultivar
COMMON NAME: Deciduous azalea
ALTERNATIVES: Knaphill, Mollis and Exbury hybrids
DESCRIPTION: Deciduous shrub of open habit with green foliage often coloring well in autumn. Flower clusters in large heads, each bloom having prominent stigma and stamens. Light to strong fragrance.
HEIGHT AND SPREAD: 5–7 × 5–9ft (1.5–2.1 × 1.5–2.8m)
BLOOMING PERIOD: Mid to late spring
SOIL: Moisture-retentive, humus-rich, acidic.

5-7

4-9

LATIN NAME: *Magnolia* × *loebneri* 'Leonard Messel'
COMMON NAME: Star magnolia
ALTERNATIVES: None
DESCRIPTION: Upright shrub or small tree with fragrant, star-shaped blooms of pale lilac-pink opening before the foliage expands.
HEIGHT AND SPREAD: 20 × 13ft (6 × 4m)
BLOOMING PERIOD: Early spring
SOIL: Any fertile, well-drained preferably humus-rich. Tolerates alkalinity.

MIDDLE

2-10

LATIN NAME: *Paeonia suffruticosa* 'Duchess of Kent'
COMMON NAME: Peony
ALTERNATIVES: 'Sarah Bernhardt,' 'Madame Calot,' 'Mons. Jules Elie'
DESCRIPTION: Herbaceous perennial with large, dark green glossy leaves which are deeply divided. Bowl-shaped, semi-double blooms with serrated edges. New shoots deep red in spring. Support.
HEIGHT AND SPREAD: 28 × 28in (70 × 70cm)
BLOOMING PERIOD: Late spring to early summer
SOIL: Rich, well-drained but moisture-retentive.

LATIN NAME: *Paeonia officinalis* 'Rosea Plena'
COMMON NAME: Peony
ALTERNATIVES: 'Queen of Sheba,' 'Edulis Superba,' 'June Rose,' 'Gayborder June'
DESCRIPTION: Herbaceous perennial making a solid clump of dark green glossy leaves with rounded lobes. Fully double deep pink blooms. Dislikes disturbance. New growth may be damaged by late spring frosts.
HEIGHT AND SPREAD: 24 × 24in (61 × 61cm)
BLOOMING PERIOD: Late spring
SOIL: Rich, well-drained but moisture-retentive.

2-10

FRONT

4-8

LATIN NAME: *Daphne* × *burkwoodii*
COMMON NAME: Burkwood daphne
ALTERNATIVES: 'Somerset'
DESCRIPTION: Shrub with upright branches clothed in narrow gray-green leaves. Rounded clusters of highly fragrant flowers at branch tips. After hot summers, may produce spherical, orange-red berries.
HEIGHT AND SPREAD: 2½ × 2½ft (75 × 75cm)
BLOOMING PERIOD: Spring to early summer
SOIL: Neutral to acid. Well-cultivated, humus-rich.

3-10

LATIN NAME: *Dicentra* 'Spring Morning'
COMMON NAME: Fringed bleeding heart
ALTERNATIVES: 'Stuart Boothman' syn. 'Boothman's Variety'
DESCRIPTION: Herbaceous perennial with ferny gray-green foliage making spreading hummocks. Arching flower stems bear rows of pendulous, heart-shaped blooms. Excellent groundcover.
HEIGHT AND SPREAD: 12 × 12in (30 × 30cm)
BLOOMING PERIOD: Late spring to mid-summer
SOIL: Moisture-retentive, humus-rich.

BACK

LATIN NAME: *Clematis montana var. rubens*
COMMON NAME: Pink anemone clematis
ALTERNATIVES: 'Elizabeth,' 'Picton's,' 'Tetrarose'
DESCRIPTION: Rapidly climbs to the top of a fence where it spreads sideways and smothers it with a mass of delicate bronzy-purple foliage. In late spring the fragrant, pale mauve-pink four-petalled flowers are stunning.
HEIGHT AND SPREAD: 25ft (7.6m) × indefinite spread
BLOOMING PERIOD: Late spring to early summer
SOIL: Any well-drained fertile but moisture retentive.

5-9

4-9

LATIN NAME: *Kalmia latifolia* 'Ostbo Red'
COMMON NAME: Calico bush, mountain laurel
ALTERNATIVES: 'Nancy,' 'Nathan Hale,' 'Pink Charm'
DESCRIPTION: Evergreen shrub producing large clusters of deep pink waxy blooms. The deep red contrasting flower buds are distinctively ridged. May take several years to begin flowering freely.
HEIGHT AND SPREAD: 10 × 10ft (3 × 3m)
BLOOMING PERIOD: Late spring to early summer
SOIL: Requires acid conditions. Deep soil with organic matter.

2-10

LATIN NAME: *Paeonia* (garden hybrid)
COMMON NAME: Herbaceous peony
ALTERNATIVES: 'Gleam of Light,' 'Pink Delight,' 'Dinner Plate'
DESCRIPTION: Perennial making a bushy plant with handsome, deeply divided leaves and large, bowl-shaped blooms with tissue-paper petals and a central boss of stamens. Spring shoots rich purple-red.
HEIGHT AND SPREAD: 2½–3½ × 3ft (75–120 × 90cm)
BLOOMING PERIOD: Late spring to mid-summer depending on variety
SOIL: Rich, well-cultivated, moisture-retentive but not waterlogged.

MIDDLE

6-10

LATIN NAME: *Rhododendron* 'Betty'
COMMON NAME: Evergreen azalea
ALTERNATIVES: 'Blaauw's Pink,' 'Hino-mayo'
DESCRIPTION: Evergreen shrub making a low dome of dense branches. Small, dark, glossy leaves obscured by flowers. In severe winters die-back may occur, but plants cut back hard may recover.
HEIGHT AND SPREAD: 2½ × 3ft (75 × 90cm)
BLOOMING PERIOD: Mid to late spring
SOIL: Acid, moisture-retentive, humus-rich.

LATIN NAME: *Heuchera sanguinea*
COMMON NAME: Coral bells, Alum root
ALTERNATIVES: 'Rosemary Bloom,' × *Heucherella* 'Bridget Bloom'
DESCRIPTION: Evergreen perennial making low mounds of jagged-edged leaves, ideal for edging, and many wiry stems carrying tiny bell flowers. Plant deeply and divide every 3–4 years.
HEIGHT AND SPREAD: 12 × 12in (30 × 30cm)
BLOOMING PERIOD: Late spring to mid-summer
SOIL: Fertile, well-drained.

3-10

FRONT

5-10

LATIN NAME: *Houttuynia cordata* 'Chameleon'
COMMON NAME: Known by Latin name
ALTERNATIVES: None
DESCRIPTION: Perennial with fleshy, boldly-variegated, heart-shaped leaves. Small white flowers in summer. Foliage smells of Seville oranges when crushed. May be highly invasive.
HEIGHT AND SPREAD: 18in (45cm) × indefinite
BLOOMING PERIOD: Summer
SOIL: Moisture-retentive to wet.

BACK

LATIN NAME: *Clematis* 'Nelly Moser'
COMMON NAME: Large-flowered clematis
ALTERNATIVES: 'Bees Jubilee'
DESCRIPTION: Climber with large, striped blooms – deeper pink on pale mauve-pink. Prune immediately after flowering. A lesser flowering in early autumn may occur. Needs support.
HEIGHT AND SPREAD: 11 × 3ft (3.5 × 0.9m)
BLOOMING PERIOD: Early summer (possible repeat early autumn)
SOIL: Moisture-retentive. Plant several inches deep in case of wilt.

5-9

LATIN NAME: *Tamarix tetrandra*
COMMON NAME: None
ALTERNATIVES: None
DESCRIPTION: Shrub with wiry stems and fluffy flower plumes on bare wood before the scale-like leaves appear. Excellent wind-resistant seaside plant. Prune hard immediately after flowering to keep in good shape and health.
HEIGHT AND SPREAD: 8 × 8ft (2.5 × 2.5m)
BLOOMING PERIOD: Late spring to early summer
SOIL: Well-drained sand or loam. Drought tolerant.

6-9

MIDDLE

LATIN NAME: *Rhododendron* cultivar
COMMON NAME: Evergreen azalea
ALTERNATIVES: 'Azuma Kagami'
DESCRIPTION: Evergreen shrub with small, leathery, glossy leaves and a rounded habit. Single or double blooms, often attractively streaked and spotted inside are produced in abundance.
HEIGHT AND SPREAD: 4 × 4ft (1.2 × 1.2m)
BLOOMING PERIOD: Late spring
SOIL: Humus-rich, moisture-retentive and acid (no alkalinity).

6-7

LATIN NAME: *Persicaria bistorta* 'Superba' syn. *Polygonum b.* 'Superbum'
COMMON NAME: Bistort, snakeweed
ALTERNATIVES: None
DESCRIPTION: Perennial forming spreading clumps of coarse, lance-shaped leaves and upright fluffy "pokers" of soft pink. Lovely in the damp garden with lush waterside plants or, given moisture, in the shade of trees.
HEIGHT AND SPREAD: 2½ × 2ft (75 × 60cm)
BLOOMING PERIOD: Late spring to late summer depending on soil moisture
SOIL: Moisture-retentive to damp.

4-9

FRONT

LATIN NAME: *Paeonia veitchii*
COMMON NAME: Herbaceous peony
ALTERNATIVES: *P. v. woodwardii*
DESCRIPTION: Perennial making a bushy plant with light green, elegant, fingered leaves and crimson-pink bowl-shaped blooms. May seed itself. Attractive bluish seeds visible when pods burst open.
HEIGHT AND SPREAD: 1 × 1ft (30 × 30cm)
BLOOMING PERIOD: Late spring to early summer
SOIL: Rich, well-cultivated, moisture-retentive but not waterlogged.

5-8

LATIN NAME: *Erigeron* 'Charity'
COMMON NAME: Fleabane
ALTERNATIVES: 'Quakeress,' 'Foerster's Liebeling,' 'Dimity'
DESCRIPTION: Perennial forming low clumps of lance-shaped foliage and masses of daisy flowers with yellow centers. Flowers over a long period. Useful for seaside gardens.
HEIGHT AND SPREAD: 2 × 2ft (60 × 60cm)
BLOOMING PERIOD: Early summer to late summer
SOIL: Reasonably fertile, well-drained.

5-10

6-7

LATIN NAME: *Syringa × josiflexa* 'Bellicent'
COMMON NAME: Lilac
ALTERNATIVES: None
DESCRIPTION: Shrub, upright at first, then the branches arch over gracefully. Open flower panicles of pale pink tubular flowers hang down. Fragrant. Worth the space in larger gardens.
HEIGHT AND SPREAD: 12 × 15ft (4 × 5m)
BLOOMING PERIOD: Late spring to early summer
SOIL: Any, well-drained.

5-9

LATIN NAME: *Wisteria floribunda* 'Rosea' syn. 'Honko'
COMMON NAME: Japanese wisteria
ALTERNATIVES: None
DESCRIPTION: Climber. Vigorous woody-stemmed growth. Large, pinnate leaves and long flower racemes best when allowed to hang. Requires careful pruning to encourage flowering and control growth.
HEIGHT AND SPREAD: 28ft (9m)
BLOOMING PERIOD: Early summer (early spring in Australia and New Zealand)
SOIL: Fertile, well-drained, moisture retentive.

3-10

LATIN NAME: *Aquilegia vulgaris* seedling
COMMON NAME: Granny's bonnets, columbine
ALTERNATIVES: *A. × hybrida* Music Series, *A. × hybrida* 'Dragonfly'
DESCRIPTION: Perennial which seeds itself freely and often crosses with other kinds. Foliage like gray-green maidenhair fern and upright wiry stems topped with nodding bell flowers.
HEIGHT AND SPREAD: 3 × 1½ft (90 × 45cm)
BLOOMING PERIOD: Early summer
SOIL: Average well-drained but not dry soil.

3-9

LATIN NAME: *Lupinus* hybrid
COMMON NAME: Lupin
ALTERNATIVES: Gallery hybrids, Russell hybrids
DESCRIPTION: Perennial producing a mound of palmate leaves topped with compact spires of pea-like flowers. Deadhead to prevent self-seeding and promote production of further blooms.
HEIGHT AND SPREAD: 4 × 1½ft (1.2 × 0.45m)
BLOOMING PERIOD: Early summer
SOIL: Well-drained, slightly alkaline.

LATIN NAME: *Acroclinium roseum* syn. *Helipterum roseum* variety
COMMON NAME: Everlasting flower
ALTERNATIVES: 'Bonny,' *A. r. grandiflorum* 'Goliath,' 'Double Rose-Pink'
DESCRIPTION: Wiry stems with papery flower heads, usually with distinct yellow centers. Similar in appearance to the straw flower, *Helichrysum monstrosum*. Excellent for drying and keeps color well.
HEIGHT AND SPREAD: 12 × 12in (30 × 30cm)
BLOOMING PERIOD: Mid-summer to early autumn (spring in Australia)
SOIL: Does well on dry, poor soils but will adapt to most conditions.

LATIN NAME: *Centranthus macrosiphon*
COMMON NAME: Spur valerian, centranthus
ALTERNATIVES: None
DESCRIPTION: Hardy annual version of the perennial *Centranthus ruber* with dense, dome-shaped heads of tiny bright rose-pink blooms.
HEIGHT AND SPREAD: 18 × 18in (45 × 45cm)
BLOOMING PERIOD: Summer
SOIL: Any well-drained, including poor, stony.

BACK

6-9

LATIN NAME: *Cornus florida* 'Apple Blossom'
COMMON NAME: Flowering dogwood
ALTERNATIVES: 'Spring Song,' 'Stokes' Pink,' *C. f.* var. *rubra*
DESCRIPTION: Small tree or large shrub with spreading habit. Deeply veined leaves. Insignificant central flowers are surrounded by four showy petal-like bracts.
HEIGHT AND SPREAD: 20 × 25ft (6 × 8m)
BLOOMING PERIOD: Spring to early summer
SOIL: Fertile, well-drained, moisture-retentive and lime free.

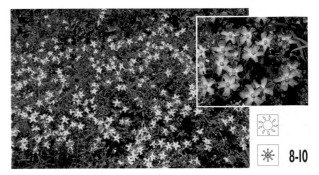

7-9

LATIN NAME: *Indigofera kirilowii*
COMMON NAME: Kirilow indigo
ALTERNATIVES: *I. heterantha*, *I. australis*
DESCRIPTION: Shrub with suckering habit ideal for groundcover. Light green pinnate leaves produce a ferny effect and it has clusters of rose-colored pea-like flowers. Prune to ground in spring.
HEIGHT AND SPREAD: 5 × 5ft (1.5 × 1.5m+)
BLOOMING PERIOD: Summer
SOIL: Any, well-drained.

MIDDLE

4-9

LATIN NAME: *Lupinus* hybrid
COMMON NAME: Lupin, Lupine
ALTERNATIVES: 'La Chatelaine,' 'Blushing Bride,' 'Lady Fayre,' Russell Hybrids
DESCRIPTION: Perennial producing a mound of palmate leaves topped with compact spires of pea-like flowers. Deadhead to prevent self-seeding and promote production of further blooms. Aphids may be a problem.
HEIGHT AND SPREAD: 4 × 1½ft (1.2 × 0.45m)
BLOOMING PERIOD: Early summer
SOIL: Well-drained, slightly alkaline.

8-10

LATIN NAME: *Cistus* 'Grayswood Pink'
COMMON NAME: Rock-rose
ALTERNATIVES: *C. × hybridus*, *C. × 'Sunset'*
DESCRIPTION: Evergreen shrub with small gray-green leaves and a profusion of circular blooms. Low-growing with a wide spreading habit. One of the hardiest. Erroneously sold as *C.* 'Silver Pink'.
HEIGHT AND SPREAD: 2–2½ × 8ft (0.60–0.75 × 2.4m)
BLOOMING PERIOD: Late spring to mid-summer
SOIL: Well-drained, good for poor, sandy soils.

FRONT

3-9

LATIN NAME: *Centaurea hypoleuca* 'John Coutts'
COMMON NAME: Knapweed
ALTERNATIVES: *C. dealbata* 'Steenbergii'
DESCRIPTION: Perennial with flowers having thistle-like centers surrounded by rings of showy ray florets. Leaves soft gray-green with gray-white downy undersides, deeply lobed. Silvery seed heads.
HEIGHT AND SPREAD: 2 × 1½ft (60 × 45cm)
BLOOMING PERIOD: Early summer to early autumn
SOIL: Free-draining, does well on poor soils including limey.

LATIN NAME: *Lobularia maritima* 'Wonderland'
COMMON NAME: Sweet alyssum
ALTERNATIVES: 'Rosie O'Day'
DESCRIPTION: Hardy annual forming low spreading hummocks smothered in flowers of deep pinkish red. Avoid rich soils as this reduces flowering. Drought will also curtail flowering.
HEIGHT AND SPREAD: 3–6 × 9in (7–15 × 22cm)
BLOOMING PERIOD: Early summer to early autumn
SOIL: Well-drained but not dry. Reasonably fertile but not too rich.

4-9

LATIN NAME: *Weigela florida* 'Variegata'
COMMON NAME: Known by Latin name
ALTERNATIVES: *Weigela* 'Praecox Variegata'
DESCRIPTION: Shrub with white-variegated foliage and clusters of deep-rose open-mouthed flowers mainly in early summer. Flowers on second year wood. Prune a third of old wood after flowering.
HEIGHT AND SPREAD: 6–7 × 6–7ft (1.8–2.2 × 1.8–2.2m)
BLOOMING PERIOD: Mainly late spring to early summer
SOIL: Any reasonably fertile soil.

LATIN NAME: *Pandorea jasminoides* syn. *Tecoma jasminoides*
COMMON NAME: Bower vine
ALTERNATIVES: 'Rosea Superba'
DESCRIPTION: Evergreen twining climber with leaves divided into leaflets. Showy, funnel shaped flowers, white flushed pink, darkening in the throat. The form 'Charisma' has bright, yellow-variegated leaves.
HEIGHT AND SPREAD: To 19ft (6m)
BLOOMING PERIOD: Summer to autumn
SOIL: Fertile, well-drained.

9-10

5-9

4-10

LATIN NAME: *Monarda didyma* 'Croftway Pink'
COMMON NAME: Bee balm, Oswego tea, bergamot
ALTERNATIVES: 'Beauty of Cobham'
DESCRIPTION: Herbaceous perennial with aromatic leaves forming a basal clump. Many upright stems carry whorls of hooded flowers with prominent bracts. Attractive to bees. Dry flowers for potpourri.
HEIGHT AND SPREAD: 3 × 1½ft (90 × 45cm)
BLOOMING PERIOD: Summer
SOIL: Moisture-retentive to damp.

LATIN NAME: *Rosa gallica* 'Versicolor' syn. *R. mundi*
COMMON NAME: Variegated apothecary's rose
ALTERNATIVES: 'Tricolore de Flandre,' 'George Vibert'
DESCRIPTION: Shrub rose with stems which sometimes bow under the weight of the crimson and pale-pink striped flowers. Prune in spring. May revert to plain crimson form. Slightly fragrant.
HEIGHT AND SPREAD: 2½ × 3ft (75 × 90cm)
BLOOMING PERIOD: Summer
SOIL: Fertile, moisture-retentive, humus-rich. Avoid strong alkaline.

6-10

LATIN NAME: *Matthiola incana*
COMMON NAME: Stock
ALTERNATIVES: Ten-week stocks e.g. 'Appleblossom'
DESCRIPTION: Biennial with broad, fleshy gray-green leaves and spikes of fragrant double flowers. Sow outdoors in early summer, prick out into pots to overwinter in a coldframe and plant out in spring.
HEIGHT AND SPREAD: 1½ × 1ft (45 × 30cm)
BLOOMING PERIOD: Early summer
SOIL: Any well-drained. Good on limey soils.

LATIN NAME: *Dianthus* 'Strawberry Parfait'
COMMON NAME: Annual pink
ALTERNATIVES: 'Raspberry Parfait,' 'Colour Magician,' 'Snowfire'
DESCRIPTION: Annual producing low hummocks smothered in flowers with serrated petals and dark central blotch. Narrow dark green leaves. There are several similar seed strains of *Dianthus chinensis*.
HEIGHT AND SPREAD: 6–8 × 9in (15–20 × 22cm)
BLOOMING PERIOD: Late spring to mid-autumn
SOIL: Well-drained neutral to alkaline.

PINK

BACK

7-9

LATIN NAME: *Indigofera heterantha* syn. I. *gerardiana*
COMMON NAME: Indigo bush
ALTERNATIVES: None
DESCRIPTION: Shrub with wide spreading branches covered in pinnate leaves giving a ferny appearance. The lilac-pink blooms are produced over a long period. May be cut to ground in hard winters.
HEIGHT AND SPREAD: 5½ × 8ft (1.6 × 2.4m)
BLOOMING PERIOD: Early summer to early autumn
SOIL: Any reasonably fertile, well-drained.

LATIN NAME: *Dipelta floribunda*
COMMON NAME: Known by Latin name
ALTERNATIVES: None
DESCRIPTION: Shrub flowering on previous year's wood. Produces many tubular blooms with a wide-flaring mouth and yellow throat. Scented. Attractive peeling bark on mature specimens. Becomes tree-like.
HEIGHT AND SPREAD: 13 × 6ft (4 × 2m)
BLOOMING PERIOD: Late spring to early summer
SOIL: Any fertile soil including chalk.

6-9

MIDDLE

8-10

LATIN NAME: *Cistus* × *purpureus*
COMMON NAME: Rock-rose
ALTERNATIVES: 'Peggy Sammons,' 'Brilliancy,' C. xp. 'Betty Taudevin'
DESCRIPTION: Evergreen shrub with upright stems clothed in narrow, gray-green leaves. Large flowers with petals looking like tissue-paper, deep pink with a purple-brown blotch at the base.
HEIGHT AND SPREAD: 5 × 3ft (1.5 × 0.9m)
BLOOMING PERIOD: Early to late summer
SOIL: Well-drained, tolerating poor, sandy conditions.

LATIN NAME: *Rodgersia pinnata*
COMMON NAME: Known by Latin name
ALTERNATIVES: 'Superba'
DESCRIPTION: Perennial with very large pinnate leaves divided into 5–9 leaflets. Fluffy flower plumes of pale pink producing attractive bronzy colored persistent seed heads. 'Superba' is a richer pink.
HEIGHT AND SPREAD: 3 × 2ft (90 × 60cm)
BLOOMING PERIOD: Summer
SOIL: Moisture-retentive to boggy.

4-9

FRONT

4-9

LATIN NAME: *Geranium endressii*
COMMON NAME: Cranesbill
ALTERNATIVES: G. × oxonianum 'A.T. Johnson,' G.o. 'Wargrave Pink'
DESCRIPTION: Semi-evergreen perennial groundcover with prettily divided light green leaves and bright pink flowers produced over a long period. Weed-suppressing and excellent for beds under trees.
HEIGHT AND SPREAD: 18 × 24in (45 × 60cm)
BLOOMING PERIOD: Summer to autumn
SOIL: Any, avoiding boggy conditions.

6-10

LATIN NAME: *Phuopsis stylosa*
COMMON NAME: Known by Latin name
ALTERNATIVES: None
DESCRIPTION: Perennial with lax stems clothed in narrow leaves in whorls giving the plant a delicate, starry look when not in flower. Spherical heads of tiny flowers produced over a long period.
HEIGHT AND SPREAD: 12 × 24in+ (30 × 60cm+)
BLOOMING PERIOD: Summer
SOIL: Any, well-drained, fertile.

LATIN NAME: *Filipendula rubra* 'Venusta'

COMMON NAME: Queen of the Prairies

ALTERNATIVES: *F. rubra, F. palmata,* and cultivars, *F. purpurea*

DESCRIPTION: Perennial of vigorous spreading habit producing very tall, stout flower stems with great feathery heads and large, jagged leaves. For a more restricted area choose *F. palmata* or *F. purpurea*.

HEIGHT AND SPREAD: 6–8 × 4ft (1.8–2.4 × 1.2m)

BLOOMING PERIOD: Mid-summer

SOIL: Moisture-retentive to boggy.

3-9

LATIN NAME: *Rosa* 'Kew Rambler'

COMMON NAME: Rambler rose

ALTERNATIVES: 'Blush Rambler'

DESCRIPTION: Climber of vigorous growth, unlike many modern climbing roses produces only one flush of flowers. Blooms single like a wild rose with central boss of stamens accentuated by white eye.

HEIGHT AND SPREAD: 16–19 × 16–19ft (5–6 × 5–6m)

BLOOMING PERIOD: Summer

SOIL: Fertile, moisture-retentive.

5-9

LATIN NAME: *Rosa* 'Romance' syn. 'Tanezamor'

COMMON NAME: Cluster-flowered (floribunda) bush rose

ALTERNATIVES: 'Heidi Jayne,' 'Keepsake' ('Esmeralda'), 'Escapade'

DESCRIPTION: Shrub with dark green foliage and branching stems bearing good-sized, double, rich-pink blooms with some scent. Feed regularly and mulch with manure or other organic matter.

HEIGHT AND SPREAD: 40 × 28in (1 × 0.7m)

BLOOMING PERIOD: Late spring to mid-autumn

SOIL: Rich, moisture-retentive to heavy. Dislikes extreme alkalinity.

5-9

LATIN NAME: *Rosa* 'Brother Cadfael'

COMMON NAME: English rose

ALTERNATIVES: 'Mary Rose,' 'Bibi Maizoon' syn. 'Ausdimindo'

DESCRIPTION: Shrub with bushy habit and very large, globular flower heads looking like double peonies. They have a good scent and are held on stout stems. Some repeat flowering into autumn.

HEIGHT AND SPREAD: 3½ × 2½ft (1.06 × 0.75m)

BLOOMING PERIOD: Early summer to early autumn

SOIL: Rich, moisture-retentive even heavy. Dislikes extreme alkalinity.

5-9

LATIN NAME: *Astilbe* 'Hyacinth'

COMMON NAME: Known by Latin name

ALTERNATIVES: 'Europa,' 'Rhineland,' 'Cattleya,' 'Erica'

DESCRIPTION: Perennial with fern-like foliage and fluffy, tapering, branched flower plumes. Attractive brown seed heads in autumn/winter. On drier soils, plant in a lightly shaded spot and mulch.

HEIGHT AND SPREAD: 2½ × 2ft (75 × 60cm)

BLOOMING PERIOD: Summer

SOIL: Humus-rich, moist to boggy.

4-8

LATIN NAME: *Oenothera speciosa* 'Rosea'

COMMON NAME: Showy evening primrose

ALTERNATIVES: 'Ballerina,' 'Pink Petticoats'

DESCRIPTION: Perennial, short-lived, spreading via underground rhizomes. Narrow leaves and circular blooms which, despite the common name, open in daytime. Invasive.

HEIGHT AND SPREAD: 18 × 12in (45 × 30cm)

BLOOMING PERIOD: Late spring to late summer

SOIL: Well-drained, not too rich. Dislikes winter wet.

5-10

BACK

LATIN NAME: *Lavatera 'Rosea'*
COMMON NAME: Tree mallow
ALTERNATIVES: 'Kew Rose'
DESCRIPTION: Semi-evergreen shrub. Upright, branching habit. Large, lobed, gray-green leaves. Vigorous. Will continue flowering until frost. Cut hard back in spring to control size and improve habit.
HEIGHT AND SPREAD: 10 × 10ft (3 × 3m)
BLOOMING PERIOD: Early summer to mid-autumn
SOIL: Well-drained, even dry but not poor.

❄ 8-10

5-9

LATIN NAME: *Rosa 'Cornelia'*
COMMON NAME: Shrub rose
ALTERNATIVES: 'Sarah van Fleet,' 'Mary Rose'
DESCRIPTION: Shrub rose (hybrid musk) with vigorous growth and spreading habit bearing large clusters of fragrant double blooms, pale pink becoming deeper toward autumn. Neat, dark leaves.
HEIGHT AND SPREAD: 5 × 5ft (1.5 × 1.5m)
BLOOMING PERIOD: Mid-summer to mid-autumn
SOIL: Rich, heavy, moisture-retentive.

MIDDLE

LATIN NAME: *Cosmos bipinnatus* Sensation series
COMMON NAME: Known by Latin name
ALTERNATIVES: 'Seashells Mixed,' 'Picotee,' 'Daydream'
DESCRIPTION: Half-hardy annual with ferny foliage and large, dish-shaped blooms on straight stems. For earlier bloom, start indoors in early to mid-spring and plant out once risk of frost has passed.
HEIGHT AND SPREAD: 3 × 2ft (90 × 60cm)
BLOOMING PERIOD: Early summer to early autumn
SOIL: Moisture-retentive but well-drained.

❄ 4-9

LATIN NAME: *Lupinus polyphyllus* hybrids
COMMON NAME: Lupin
ALTERNATIVES: Russell Hybrids, 'Loveliness'
DESCRIPTION: Perennial producing a mound of palmate leaves topped with compact spires of pea-like flowers. Deadhead to prevent self-seeding and promote production of further blooms.
HEIGHT AND SPREAD: 4 × 2ft (1.2 × 0.6m)
BLOOMING PERIOD: Early summer
SOIL: Fertile, well-drained, preferably limey.

FRONT

LATIN NAME: *Callistephus chinensis*
COMMON NAME: Chinese aster
ALTERNATIVES: Pompon Series, Milady Series
DESCRIPTION: Produces a mass of single, double, or pompon-shaped blooms mainly in pastel shades. Deadhead regularly to prolong flowering.
HEIGHT AND SPREAD: 12–24 × 12–18in (30–60 × 30–45cm)
BLOOMING PERIOD: Mid-summer to frosts
SOIL: Moisture-retentive. Add lime if acid.

LATIN NAME: *Verbena × hybrida 'Aveyron'*
COMMON NAME: Known by Latin name
ALTERNATIVES: 'Sissinghurst,' 'Silver Anne' (both mildew resistant)
DESCRIPTION: Annual or tender perennial. Well-branched, small, serrated edged leaves. Flowers in dome-shaped clusters. Provides dense, flower covered groundcover. Susceptible to mildew.
HEIGHT AND SPREAD: 6–8 × 18in (15–20 × 45cm)
BLOOMING PERIOD: Early summer to frosts
SOIL: Moisture-retentive but free-draining.

LATIN NAME: *Lathyrus odoratus*
COMMON NAME: Sweet pea
ALTERNATIVES: Large selection in seed catalogs.
DESCRIPTION: Annual climber with fragrant pea-like winged flowers climbing with tendrils. Excellent for cutting. Oval-shaped leaves in pairs. Provide support in the form of twiggy sticks or fine mesh pea and bean netting.
HEIGHT AND SPREAD: 9 × 3ft (2.7 × 0.9m)
BLOOMING PERIOD: Mid-summer to early autumn (begins in spring in Australia)
SOIL: Deep, rich, moisture retentive.

LATIN NAME: *Alcea rosea*
COMMON NAME: Hollyhock
ALTERNATIVES: Various singles and doubles, e.g. 'Chater's Double'
DESCRIPTION: Biennial. Flowers on tall, upright stems above basal clump of lobed leaves. Sow new plants annually to avoid the disease rust which forms orange pustules on the backs of the leaves and weakens growth.
HEIGHT AND SPREAD: 6–9 × 2ft (1.8–2.7 × 0.6m)
BLOOMING PERIOD: Summer to early autumn
SOIL: Prefers heavy, rich soil, moist in summer.

2-10

4-9

LATIN NAME: *Lilium* 'Acapulco'
COMMON NAME: Lily
ALTERNATIVES: 'Journey's End,' 'Stargazer'
DESCRIPTION: Bulb producing upright stems clothed in narrow pointed leaves. Large, trumpet shaped flowers. Scented. Plant in pockets between other lower growing plants.
HEIGHT AND SPREAD: 3ft (90cm)
BLOOMING PERIOD: Mid-summer
SOIL: Well-drained, but moisture-retentive.

3-10

LATIN NAME: *Echinacea purpurea* 'Robert Bloom'
COMMON NAME: Purple coneflower
ALTERNATIVES: 'Magnus'
DESCRIPTION: Perennial with stiff, upright stems topped with large daisy-like flowers each with a glowing gingery-brown dome-shaped center. Attractive to bees and butterflies.
HEIGHT AND SPREAD: 3–4 × 1½ft (90–120 × 45cm)
BLOOMING PERIOD: Summer
SOIL: Well-drained but moist in summer.

LATIN NAME: *Impatiens* 'Accent Series' F1
COMMON NAME: Busy Lizzie
ALTERNATIVES: Super Elfin F1, Novette F1
DESCRIPTION: Annual with fleshy stems and oval, pointed leaves. Masses of rounded blooms continually produced. May be tricky to raise from seed. Useful in shady borders.
HEIGHT AND SPREAD: 8–10 × 10in (20–25 × 25cm)
BLOOMING PERIOD: Late spring till the frosts (year round in Australia)
SOIL: Humus-rich, moisture-retentive.

9-10

LATIN NAME: *Argyranthemum* 'Gill's Pink'
COMMON NAME: Marguerite daisy
ALTERNATIVES: 'Petite Pink,' 'Champagne Daisy'
DESCRIPTION: Tender evergreen perennial with woody stem bases. Bushy plants with finely divided foliage and daisy-like flowers continually produced. Overwinter plants under glass or take cuttings.
HEIGHT AND SPREAD: 18–24 × 18in (45–60 × 45cm)
BLOOMING PERIOD: Mid-summer to mid-autumn
SOIL: Well-drained. Lime and drought-tolerant.

PINK

BACK

5-9

LATIN NAME: *Rosa* 'New Dawn'
COMMON NAME: Climbing rose
ALTERNATIVES: 'Albertine,' 'Dr. W. van Fleet'
DESCRIPTION: Climber. Vigorous, repeat-flowering, with neat, glossy leaves. Well-formed flowers, the deeper pink buds making a lovely contrast with the open blooms. Some scent. Ideal for a pergola.
HEIGHT AND SPREAD: 15 × 15ft (4.6 × 4.6m)
BLOOMING PERIOD: Early summer to mid-autumn
SOIL: Prefers rich, heavy, moisture-retentive.

8-10

LATIN NAME: *Ceanothus × pallidus* 'Marie Simon'
COMMON NAME: California lilac
ALTERNATIVES: 'Perle Rose'
DESCRIPTION: Deciduous shrub with small rounded leaves and fluffy, flesh-pink blooms. Very long-blooming. Makes a superb background shrub in the mixed border. Cut hard back in spring.
HEIGHT AND SPREAD: 5 × 5ft (1.5 × 1.5m)
BLOOMING PERIOD: Summer to early autumn
SOIL: Well-drained. Avoid extreme alkaline.

MIDDLE

4-9

LATIN NAME: *Astrantia major* 'Buckland'
COMMON NAME: Masterwort
ALTERNATIVES: *A. m. rosea, A. m. rubra*
DESCRIPTION: Perennial forming a basal clump of lobed leaves and upright branching stems with flower heads which bear close scrutiny. The clusters of tiny blooms are surrounded by papery bracts.
HEIGHT AND SPREAD: 24+ × 18in (60+ × 45cm)
BLOOMING PERIOD: Early summer to early autumn
SOIL: Well-drained but moisture-retentive.

5-9

LATIN NAME: *Rosa* 'Ballerina'
COMMON NAME: Shrub rose
ALTERNATIVES: 'Yesterday,' 'Frau Dagmar Hastrup'
DESCRIPTION: Modern shrub rose forming a mound of stems smothered along their length with large clusters of pale pink, white-centered blooms. May succumb to mildew later in the season.
HEIGHT AND SPREAD: 40 × 48in (1 × 1.2m)
BLOOMING PERIOD: Early summer to mid-autumn
SOIL: Prefers rich, heavy, moisture-retentive.

FRONT

6-9

LATIN NAME: *Lavandula angustifolia* 'Hidcote Pink'
COMMON NAME: Old English lavender
ALTERNATIVES: 'Loddon Pink,' 'Rosea'
DESCRIPTION: Shrub with low, rounded habit and narrow gray-green aromatic leaves. Important source of nectar for bees and butterflies. Cut back after flowering to keep compact. Do not cut into old wood.
HEIGHT AND SPREAD: 18–24 × 18–24in (45–60 × 45–60cm)
BLOOMING PERIOD: Mid-summer
SOIL: Well-drained, enjoys limey soils.

LATIN NAME: *Crepis rubra*
COMMON NAME: Known by Latin name
ALTERNATIVES: 'Rosea'
DESCRIPTION: Hardy annual. Basal rosette of lance-shaped leaves with upright stems topped with flowers like pink dandelions. Deadhead to prevent seeding.
HEIGHT AND SPREAD: 12–18 × 6in (30–45 × 15cm)
BLOOMING PERIOD: Mid to late summer
SOIL: Well-drained, not over-manured.

4-9

LATIN NAME: *Actinidia kolomikta*
COMMON NAME: Known by Latin name
ALTERNATIVES: 'Arctic Beauty'
DESCRIPTION: Climber with large pink and white splashed leaves. Prefers warm, sheltered aspect and moisture in summer. Vigorous and best displayed when allowed plenty of room to develop. Support.
HEIGHT AND SPREAD: 13 × 13ft (4 × 4m)
BLOOMING PERIOD: Flowers insignificant
SOIL: Neutral to acid, rich, well-drained.

8-10

LATIN NAME: *Lavatera* 'Barnsley'
COMMON NAME: Tree mallow
ALTERNATIVES: 'Candy Floss'
DESCRIPTION: Semi-evergreen shrub with a bushy, upright habit and large, lobed, gray-green leaves. Prolific flowerer. Cut hard back in spring. May revert to all-pink.
HEIGHT AND SPREAD: 10 × 10ft (3 × 3m)
BLOOMING PERIOD: Early summer to mid-autumn
SOIL: Well-drained, even dry but not poor.

3-10

LATIN NAME: *Achillea* 'Appleblossom' syn. 'Apfelblüte'
COMMON NAME: Yarrow
ALTERNATIVES: Galaxy Hybrids, 'Summer Pastels'
DESCRIPTION: Perennial with feathery foliage and branched stems topped with flat flower heads. May need staking. The horizontal line created by the flowers contrasts well with strongly upright stems.
HEIGHT AND SPREAD: 36 × 24in (90 × 60cm)
BLOOMING PERIOD: Early summer to early autumn
SOIL: Any well-drained but moisture-retentive.

5-10

LATIN NAME: *Sidalcea* 'Elsie Heugh'
COMMON NAME: Known by Latin name
ALTERNATIVES: 'Sussex Beauty,' 'Loveliness'
DESCRIPTION: Perennial with hollyhock-like flower spires rising from a large basal clump of leaves. The silky flowers have fringed petals. May need staking, particularly in exposed gardens.
HEIGHT AND SPREAD: 4 × 1½ft (1.2 × 0.45m)
BLOOMING PERIOD: Summer
SOIL: Any well-drained.

3-10

LATIN NAME: *Gypsophila* 'Rosenschleir' ('Rosy Veil')
COMMON NAME: Baby's breath
ALTERNATIVES: 'Flamingo,' 'Pink Beauty,' 'Pink Star'
DESCRIPTION: Perennial which produces a cloud of tiny ball-shaped flowers above a basal clump of foliage. An ideal plant to act as a foil for more substantial blooms. Dislikes disturbance.
HEIGHT AND SPREAD: 12 × 18in (30 × 45cm)
BLOOMING PERIOD: Summer
SOIL: Enjoys deep, limey, well-drained soil.

6-10

LATIN NAME: *Penstemon* 'Thorn' (syn. 'Apple Blossom')
COMMON NAME: Known by Latin name
ALTERNATIVES: 'Evelyn,' 'Pink Endurance,' 'Pink Beauty'
DESCRIPTION: Semi-evergreen, bushy perennial with upright stems clothed in narrow leaves. Tubular flowers. Plants quite hardy - winter wet and dead leaves or mulch covering the crown kills them rather than the cold.
HEIGHT AND SPREAD: 18 × 18in (45 × 45cm)
BLOOMING PERIOD: Early summer to mid-autumn
SOIL: Fertile, well-drained.

BACK

LATIN NAME: *Escallonia* 'Donard Beauty'
COMMON NAME: Known by Latin name
ALTERNATIVES: None
DESCRIPTION: Evergreen shrub, sturdy but with a somewhat arching habit. Small, leathery dark green leaves and small, deep pink flowers, tubular with a flared mouth, produced along the length of the stem.
HEIGHT AND SPREAD: 10 × 13ft (3 × 4m)
BLOOMING PERIOD: Early summer
SOIL: Tolerates a wide range of conditions but dislikes extreme alkalinity.

8-10

LATIN NAME: *Bougainvillea* 'Dauphine'
COMMON NAME: Known by Latin name
ALTERNATIVES: 'Double Pink,' 'Flamingo Pink,' 'Pink Champagne' (syn. 'Mahara Pink')
DESCRIPTION: Semi-evergreen climber with woody stems requiring support. Bold, creamy-white variegation on leaves. Inconspicuous flowers surrounded by large showy papery bracts. Susceptible to mealy bug and whitefly.
HEIGHT AND SPREAD: 15ft (5m)
BLOOMING PERIOD: Summer
SOIL: Well-drained, preferably fairly poor soil to avoid over-production of leaf.

9-10

MIDDLE

LATIN NAME: *Rosa* 'Blue Moon' syn. 'Mainzer Fastnacht,' 'Sissi'
COMMON NAME: Large-flowered (hybrid tea) bush rose
ALTERNATIVES: 'Paul Shirville,' 'Harry Edland'
DESCRIPTION: Shrub with upright growth and sparse leaf production with single, well-shaped blooms of unusual mauve-pink coloring. Lovely fragrance especially when cut.
HEIGHT AND SPREAD: 3 × 2ft (90 × 60cm)
BLOOMING PERIOD: Summer to autumn (spring in Australia)
SOIL: Prefers rich, moisture-retentive soils especially clay.

5-9

LATIN NAME: *Gladiolus* hybrid
COMMON NAME: Known by Latin name
ALTERNATIVES: 'Inca Queen,' 'Rose Supreme,' 'Gigi,' 'Pink Lady,' 'La France'
DESCRIPTION: Bulb with sword-shaped leaves and stout spikes of showy blooms, excellent for cutting. Plant every 10 days from late spring to mid-summer for a succession of blooms into autumn. Lift before frosts.
HEIGHT AND SPREAD: 36–48+ × 6–10in (0.9–1.2+ × 15–25cm)
BLOOMING PERIOD: Summer to autumn
SOIL: Well-drained, fertile, humus-rich.

9-10

FRONT

LATIN NAME: *Origanum laevigatum* 'Herrenhausen'
COMMON NAME: Ornamental marjoram
ALTERNATIVES: O. l. 'Hopleys'
DESCRIPTION: Herbaceous perennial carpeter for the front of a border forming rosettes of small leaves, topped by rounded clusters of pink flowers with purplish bracts. New spring growth tinged bronze.
HEIGHT AND SPREAD: 1½ × 1ft (45 × 30cm)
BLOOMING PERIOD: Mid-summer to early autumn
SOIL: Any well-drained, tolerating dry conditions.

5-10

LATIN NAME: *Rosa* 'The Fairy'
COMMON NAME: Shrub rose
ALTERNATIVES: 'Yesterday'
DESCRIPTION: Old-fashioned-looking groundcover rose with excellent foliage (small, glossy leaves) and clusters of small, double blooms like tiny rosettes. May also be trained into a weeping half standard.
HEIGHT AND SPREAD: 24 × 24+in (60 × 60+cm)
BLOOMING PERIOD: Mid to late summer (spring in Australia)
SOIL: Any fertile soil, preferring rich, somewhat heavy, moisture-retentive.

5-9

LATIN NAME: *Rosa* 'Pink Perpétué'

COMMON NAME: Climbing rose

ALTERNATIVES: 'Chaplin's Pink Climber,' 'Zephrine Drouhin,' 'Rosy Mantle'

DESCRIPTION: Climber with stiff, woody, branching stems which require tying in to supports. Fully double mid-pink flowers with a deep-pink reverse. Plentiful leathery, dark leaves. Little scent.

HEIGHT AND SPREAD: 9 × 8ft (2.8 × 2.5m)

BLOOMING PERIOD: Summer to autumn

SOIL: Prefers rich, moisture-retentive soils especially clay.

5-9

LATIN NAME: *Rosa* 'Albertine'

COMMON NAME: Climbing rose

ALTERNATIVES: 'New Dawn,' 'Aloha,' 'Compassion'

DESCRIPTION: Climber with woody stems needing support. Once-flowering with moderately large double blooms of pale salmon-pink deeper at the center. Good scent. Foliage susceptible to mildew in dry soils.

HEIGHT AND SPREAD: 15 × 12ft (5 × 4m)

BLOOMING PERIOD: Summer

SOIL: Prefers rich, moisture-retentive soils especially clay.

5-9

LATIN NAME: *Gladiolus communis* spp. *byzantinus*

COMMON NAME: Known by Latin name

ALTERNATIVES: 'Rose Charm'

DESCRIPTION: Herbaceous perennial spreading by underground stems or stolons. In light soils may be quite invasive. Spikes of magenta-pink tubular blooms and clumps of long, narrow leaves. Not for cold regions.

HEIGHT AND SPREAD: 3 × 1+ft (90 × 30+cm)

BLOOMING PERIOD: Early to mid-summer

SOIL: Any reasonably fertile. Spreads more slowly on heavy soils.

7-10

4-9

LATIN NAME: *Astrantia maxima*

COMMON NAME: Masterwort

ALTERNATIVES: *A. major rosea*

DESCRIPTION: Herbaceous perennial with flowers looking like old-fashioned posies – the central cluster surrounded by a collar of papery bracts. Three-lobed leaves.

HEIGHT AND SPREAD: 2–2½ × 1ft (60–75 × 30cm)

BLOOMING PERIOD: Mid to late summer

SOIL: Rich, well-drained but moisture-retentive.

8-9

LATIN NAME: *Geranium* × *riversleaianum* 'Russell Prichard'

COMMON NAME: Cranesbill

ALTERNATIVES: 'Mavis Simpson'

DESCRIPTION: Herbaceous perennial which each year sends out long prostrate branches covered in lobed, gray-green leaves and a mass of blooms. Slightly tender so plant in spring.

HEIGHT AND SPREAD: 9 × 36in (24 × 90cm)

BLOOMING PERIOD: Early summer to early autumn

SOIL: Any fertile, well-drained.

LATIN NAME: *Impatiens walleriana* 'Variegata'

COMMON NAME: Busy Lizzie

ALTERNATIVES: New Guinea Hybrid impatiens

DESCRIPTION: Tender perennial/annual with succulent stems, oval pointed leaves, boldly-variegated and carmine-pink circular blooms. Excellent for shade. Cut back and keep well-watered.

HEIGHT AND SPREAD: 6–12in (15–30cm)

BLOOMING PERIOD: Early summer to early autumn

SOIL: Any moisture-retentive.

BACK

5-9

LATIN NAME: *Lathyrus latifolius*
COMMON NAME: Everlasting pea, perennial pea
ALTERNATIVES: 'Rosa Perle' ('Pink Pearl'), *L. grandiflorus*, *L. tuberosus*
DESCRIPTION: Herbaceous climber, similar in appearance to the annual sweet pea but flattened stems and pinnate foliage of more substance. Fragrant, pea-like flowers.
HEIGHT AND SPREAD: 6+ × 6ft (1.8+ × 1.8m)
BLOOMING PERIOD: Summer to early autumn
SOIL: Any well-drained.

6-9

LATIN NAME: *Phytolacca polyandra* syn. *P. clavigera*
COMMON NAME: Poke weed, red ink plant
ALTERNATIVES: This species not commercially available in USA
DESCRIPTION: Herbaceous perennial of upright habit. Foliage has unpleasant smell. Pink flower spikes followed by glistening black berries (poisonous). Stems rich crimson in autumn with yellow foliage.
HEIGHT AND SPREAD: 4 × 2–4ft (1.2 × 0.6–1.2m)
BLOOMING PERIOD: Mid to late summer
SOIL: Fertile, moisture-retentive.

MIDDLE

LATIN NAME: *Lavatera* 'Silver Cup'
COMMON NAME: Annual mallow
ALTERNATIVES: 'Loveliness' syn. 'Sunset,' 'Pink Beauty'
DESCRIPTION: Bushy plant densely clothed with large, lobed gray-green leaves and producing a succession of showy, hibiscus-like blooms. Ideal as a gap filler in the mixed, shrub, or herbaceous border.
HEIGHT AND SPREAD: 30 × 24in (75 × 60cm)
BLOOMING PERIOD: Mid-summer to early autumn
SOIL: Any well-drained. Avoid very rich.

8-10

LATIN NAME: *Hebe* 'Great Orme'
COMMON NAME: Hebe, shrubby veronica
ALTERNATIVES: 'Simon Delaux,' 'Eveline,' 'Carnea'
DESCRIPTION: Evergreen shrub with narrow, glossy foliage and fluffy spikes of mid-pink aging to white giving a two-tone effect. Provide a sheltered site to prevent scorching from cold winds. Prune out damaged growth in spring.
HEIGHT AND SPREAD: 4 × 6ft (1.2 × 1.8m)
BLOOMING PERIOD: Summer
SOIL: Any well-drained, loose-textured. Avoid winter waterlogged soils.

FRONT

LATIN NAME: *Antirrhinum majus* variety
COMMON NAME: Snapdragon
ALTERNATIVES: Coronette Series F1, 'Butterfly Pink,' 'Potomac Pink,' 'Pan American Summer Pink'
DESCRIPTION: Produces branching spikes of densely-packed blooms. Small lanceolate leaves. Pinch out seedlings to encourage branching and remove main spike after flowering to encourage secondary spikes.
HEIGHT AND SPREAD: 1–2 × 1ft (30–60 × 30cm)
BLOOMING PERIOD: Summer to early autumn
SOIL: Any reasonably well-cultivated.

9-10

LATIN NAME: *Osteospermum jucundum* syn. *O. barberiae*
COMMON NAME: Known by Latin name
ALTERNATIVES: *O. j. compactum*, *O.* 'Stardust'
DESCRIPTION: Evergreen perennial/sub-shrub making dense mats of foliage topped with daisy-like flowers which remain closed on dull days. Ideal groundcover for dry banks and the front of sunny borders.
HEIGHT AND SPREAD: 1 × 1ft (30 × 30cm)
BLOOMING PERIOD: Summer to autumn
SOIL: Any well-drained, tolerating drought.

LATIN NAME: *Galega officinalis* 'Duchess of Bedford'
COMMON NAME: Goat's rue
ALTERNATIVES: 'His Majesty,' 'Lady Wilson'
DESCRIPTION: Herbaceous perennial of statuesque proportions with pinnate leaves and a long succession of pea-like flowers in branched spikes. Once commonly planted as a back of the border plant. Needs support.
HEIGHT AND SPREAD: 5 × 3ft (1.5 × 0.9m)
BLOOMING PERIOD: Summer
SOIL: Any well-drained.

3-9

LATIN NAME: *Lavatera* 'Candy Floss'
COMMON NAME: Tree mallow, lavatera
ALTERNATIVES: 'Bredon Springs,' 'Barnsley,' 'Rosea'
DESCRIPTION: Semi-evergreen shrub with large, gray-green lobed leaves and a succession of large, hibiscus-shaped flowers produced in the leaf axils. As the branches grow, so more flowers are produced. Prune hard in spring.
HEIGHT AND SPREAD: 6 × 4ft (1.75 × 1.25m)
BLOOMING PERIOD: Summer to autumn
SOIL: Any well-drained avoiding very rich.

8-10

BACK

LATIN NAME: *Lavatera* 'Pink Beauty'
COMMON NAME: Annual mallow
ALTERNATIVES: 'Loveliness' syn. 'Sunset,' 'Silver Cup'
DESCRIPTION: Bushy plant densely clothed with large, lobed gray-green leaves and producing a succession of showy, hibiscus-like blooms. Ideal as a gap filler. Lighter shade than 'Silver Cup' with dark veins.
HEIGHT AND SPREAD: 30 × 24in (75 × 60cm)
BLOOMING PERIOD: Mid-summer to early autumn
SOIL: Any well-drained. Avoid very rich.

LATIN NAME: *Consolida* 'Sublime'
COMMON NAME: Larkspur, annual delphinium
ALTERNATIVES: 'Giant Imperial Series' e.g. 'Pink Perfection,' 'Rosalie'
DESCRIPTION: Annual with tall spikes of double flowers which are excellent for cutting. Avoid a windy site and provide support to prevent damage. Good filler to give height in newly-planted borders.
HEIGHT AND SPREAD: 3–4 × 2ft (0.9–1.2 × 0.6m)
BLOOMING PERIOD: Summer
SOIL: Well-drained, not overly rich.

MIDDLE

LATIN NAME: *Osteospermum ecklonis caulescens*
COMMON NAME: Known by Latin name
ALTERNATIVES: 'Lady Leitrim'
DESCRIPTION: Evergreen perennial/sub-shrub making dense mats of strap-shaped aromatic foliage topped with deep blue centered flowers with a blue-gray reverse. Flowers age to pale pink.
HEIGHT AND SPREAD: 1 × 1ft (30 × 30cm)
BLOOMING PERIOD: Summer to autumn
SOIL: Any well-drained, tolerating drought.

8-10

LATIN NAME: *Persicaria capitata* 'Pink Bubbles'
COMMON NAME: Pinkhead knotweed
ALTERNATIVES: 'Magic Carpet'
DESCRIPTION: Tender perennial groundcover or trailer with pointed green leaves banded with a bronze "v." Spherical pink flower heads in abundance. Will self-seed in some areas.
HEIGHT AND SPREAD: 4–6 × 9in (10–15 × 22cm)
BLOOMING PERIOD: Summer
SOIL: Any well-drained.

FRONT

8-10

BACK

❄ 4-9

LATIN NAME: Sanguisorba obtusa
COMMON NAME: Japanese burnet
ALTERNATIVES: None
DESCRIPTION: Herbaceous perennial with attractive blue-green leaves above which are held branching flower stems bearing fluffy bottle-brushes of rose-pink. Best when provided with support.
HEIGHT AND SPREAD: 4 × 2ft (1.2 × 0.6m)
BLOOMING PERIOD: Mid- to late summer
SOIL: Moisture-retentive to damp.

9-10

LATIN NAME: Bougainvillea cultivar
COMMON NAME: Known by Latin name
ALTERNATIVES: 'Pink Champagne' syn. 'Mahara Pink,' 'Flamingo Pink'
DESCRIPTION: Tender evergreen climber with twiggy growth and broad, light green leaves, covered at flowering time with tiny white flowers surrounded by large, papery, colored bracts. Prune lightly after flowering.
HEIGHT AND SPREAD: 12–24+ × 12–24ft (3.7–7.3+ × 3.7–7.3m)
BLOOMING PERIOD: Summer to early autumn
SOIL: Any well-drained.

MIDDLE

LATIN NAME: Celosia spicata 'Flamingo Feather'
COMMON NAME: Prince of Wales' Feather, Celosia
ALTERNATIVES: None
DESCRIPTION: Annual with wiry stems topped with feathery tapering plumes bicolored pale and deep pink. Needs a warm, sheltered site. May be cut for drying to make indoor arrangements.
HEIGHT AND SPREAD: 24–30 × 18in (30–75 × 45cm)
BLOOMING PERIOD: Summer to early autumn
SOIL: Any well-drained. Dislikes heavy ground.

❄ 7-10

LATIN NAME: Crinum × powellii
COMMON NAME: Known by Latin name
ALTERNATIVES: 'Haarklemense,' 'Krelagei,' 'Ellen Bosanquet'
DESCRIPTION: Bulb with limp, strap-like leaves and a stout stem bearing large sweetly-scented, trumpet-shaped blooms. Plant with neck of bulb above soil level. Mulch heavily or plant against a warm wall in cold areas.
HEIGHT AND SPREAD: 4 × 3ft (1.2 × 0.9m)
BLOOMING PERIOD: Late summer
SOIL: Deeply-cultivated, rich, moisture-retentive.

FRONT

9-10

LATIN NAME: Argyranthemum 'Vancouver'
COMMON NAME: Marguerite daisy, Paris daisy
ALTERNATIVES: 'Mary Wooton,' 'Gill's Pink'
DESCRIPTION: Tender perennial with highly dissected foliage and branched flower stems bearing large daisy-like blooms with a flattened central disk. Best in part shade to prevent bleaching.
HEIGHT AND SPREAD: 2 × 1½ft (60 × 45cm)
BLOOMING PERIOD: Early summer to mid-autumn
SOIL: Any well-drained.

LATIN NAME: Salvia viridis
COMMON NAME: Ornamental sage
ALTERNATIVES: 'Claryssa Pink,' 'Pink Lady'
DESCRIPTION: Hardy annual with brightly colored flower bracts looking like leaves. Excellent for drying to use in indoor arrangements. Mixtures or single colors available.
HEIGHT AND SPREAD: 18 × 12in (45 × 30cm)
BLOOMING PERIOD: Summer to early autumn
SOIL: Any well-drained.

Latin name: *Lythrum salicaria* 'Firecandle' syn. 'Feuerkerze'
Common name: Purple loosestrife
Alternatives: 'Happy,' 'Robert,' 'Morden Pink,' 'The Beacon'
Description: Herbaceous perennial for the moist border producing spikes of rich pink flowers on wiry stems. May give good autumn color.
Height and spread: 4 × 1½ft (1.2 × 0.45m)
Blooming period: Late summer
Soil: Moist to boggy.

4-10

Latin name: *Rosa* 'Felicia'
Common name: Shrub rose
Alternatives: 'Aloha,' 'Cornelia,' 'Constance Spry,' 'Shropshire Lass'
Description: Modern shrub rose with fragrant light pink and pale yellow blooms produced in large clusters over a long period. Foliage dark and glossy.
Height and spread: 5 × 7ft (1.5 × 2.2m)
Blooming period: Summer to early autumn (spring in Australia)
Soil: Prefers rich, moisture-retentive. Happy on heavy soils.

5-9

Latin name: *Cleome spinosa*
Common name: Spider flower
Alternatives: 'Colour Fountains Mxd,' 'Rose Queen,' 'Cherry Queen'
Description: Half-hardy annual. Tropical appearance with tall stems topped by large heads of lightly fragrant flowers with long protruding stamens. Handsome palmate leaves. Self-sows.
Height and spread: 2–4 × 1½ft (0.6–1.2 × 0.45cm)
Blooming period: Mid-summer to early autumn
Soil: Any well-drained.

Latin name: *Centranthus* syn. *Kentranthus*
Common name: Red valerian, Jupiter's beard, Keys-of-heaven
Alternatives: When naturalized, produces shades from white through deep pink
Description: Herbaceous perennial with broad fleshy gray-green leaves and compact cone-shaped heads of tiny tubular flowers which are attractive to bees. Self-seeds. Good seaside plant.
Height and spread: 2½–3 × 1½ft (75–90 × 45cm)
Blooming period: Summer
Soil: Thrives on poor, stony soils including lime-rich.

4-10

Latin name: *Nicotiana alata*
Common name: Flowering tobacco
Alternatives: Domino F1 Series e.g. 'Salmon Pink'
Description: Half-hardy annual or perennial with broad, hairy leaves making a basal rosette from which the upright stems, bearing outward facing flowers, appear. Fragrant in early evening. May self-sow.
Height and spread: 12–14 × 12in (30–35 × 30cm)
Blooming period: Summer to early autumn
Soil: Any reasonably fertile, moisture-retentive.

Latin name: *Physostegia virginiana* 'Vivid'
Common name: Obedient plant, false dragonhead
Alternatives: 'Rosy Spire'
Description: Herbaceous perennial producing spikes of curious "hinged" flowers which stay in position when moved hence the common name. Spreading root system produces a dense mat of foliage.
Height and spread: 12–15 × 12in (30–38 × 30cm)
Blooming period: Early autumn
Soil: Any fertile, moisture-retentive. Avoid dry, poor soils.

3-10

PINK

BACK

LATIN NAME: *Lespedeza thunbergii*
COMMON NAME: Thunberg lespedeza, *bush clover*
ALTERNATIVES: *L. bicolor*
DESCRIPTION: Shrub with arching stems covered in trifoliate leaves and terminating in many rose-purple, pea-like flowers. Seen to best advantage growing on a bank. Usually cut to ground in winter but flowers on new wood.
HEIGHT AND SPREAD: 6 × 6ft (1.8 × 1.8m)
BLOOMING PERIOD: Early autumn
SOIL: Well-drained.

5-8

LATIN NAME: *Colletia hystrix* 'Rosea' syn. *C. armata* 'Rosea'
COMMON NAME: Known by Latin name
ALTERNATIVES: None
DESCRIPTION: Shrub which has stout thorns in place of leaves. The whole plant is gray-green in color with paler young growth. Small tubular flowers, vanilla scented, smother the plant in late season.
HEIGHT AND SPREAD: 8 × 12ft (2.5 × 3.5m)
BLOOMING PERIOD: Late summer to autumn
SOIL: Well-drained.

8-10

MIDDLE

3-9

LATIN NAME: *Phlox paniculata* cultivar
COMMON NAME: Border phlox
ALTERNATIVES: 'Mother of Pearl,' 'Europe,' Elizabeth Arden'
DESCRIPTION: Herbaceous perennial producing many upright stems from the rootstock covered in willow-like leaves. Domed clusters of richly-scented rounded flowers in late summer.
HEIGHT AND SPREAD: 2½–3ft (75–90cm)
BLOOMING PERIOD: Mid- to late summer
SOIL: Fertile, moisture-retentive, humus-rich. Avoid heavy clay.

LATIN NAME: *Zinnia elegans*
COMMON NAME: Common zinnia
ALTERNATIVES: 'Dahlia-flowered Mixed,' 'State Fair Mixed' (dwarf)
DESCRIPTION: Annual with stiff, upright stems carrying hairy leaves and topped with solid-petalled dahlia-like blooms. Many varieties available in various colors and flower shapes. Dislikes cold, wet summers.
HEIGHT AND SPREAD: 2½–3ft (75–90cm)
BLOOMING PERIOD: Mid-summer to mid-autumn
SOIL: Well-drained, humus enriched.

FRONT

6-8

LATIN NAME: *Sorbus reducta*
COMMON NAME: Creeping mountain ash
ALTERNATIVES: None
DESCRIPTION: Shrub making a low, spreading thicket of stems with gray-green pinnate leaves. Heads of white flowers in summer develop into clusters of pink berries. Good bronzy-red autumn color.
HEIGHT AND SPREAD: 12 × 36+in (30 × 90+cm)
BLOOMING PERIOD: Summer
SOIL: Any reasonably cultivated.

10

LATIN NAME: *Verbena hybrida* cultivar
COMMON NAME: Known by Latin name
ALTERNATIVES: 'Tapien Pink' syn. 'Sunver,' 'Silver Anne,' 'Sissinghurst'
DESCRIPTION: Tender perennial of stiff, branched habit, sometimes trailing, with small toothed-edged leaves and domed flower clusters. Susceptible to mildew in dry conditions.
HEIGHT AND SPREAD: 6–18 × 12–18in (15–45 × 30–45cm)
BLOOMING PERIOD: Early summer to mid-autumn
SOIL: Well-drained but moisture-retentive.

BACK

LATIN NAME: *Passiflora* cultivar
COMMON NAME: Passion flower
ALTERNATIVES: *P. sanguinolenta, P. mollissima, P. × violacea, P. × alato-caerulea*
DESCRIPTION: Semi-evergreen climber of vigorous habit with lobed leaves and climbing tendrils. Requires support. Large, showy blooms sometimes followed by attractive fruits. May be cut back hard in spring to control size.
HEIGHT AND SPREAD: 10–16+ft (3–5+m)
BLOOMING PERIOD: Spring to autumn
SOIL: Well-drained.

9-10

LATIN NAME: *Hydrangea paniculata* 'Unique'
COMMON NAME: Panicle hydrangea
ALTERNATIVES: 'Floribunda,' 'Grandiflora,' 'Praecox'
DESCRIPTION: Shrub with upright branches terminating in large, cone-shaped flowers consisting of tiny fertile florets and many showy sterile bracts. Unique's impressive blooms gradually turn a deep purple-pink.
HEIGHT AND SPREAD: 10 × 10ft (3 × 3m)
BLOOMING PERIOD: Mid-summer to autumn
SOIL: Fertile, moisture-retentive. Avoid markedly alkaline soils.

3-9

LATIN NAME: *Salvia involucrata* 'Bethellii'
COMMON NAME: Ornamental sage
ALTERNATIVES: 'Deschampsia'
DESCRIPTION: Sub-shrub with a woody base and bushy habit with long, pointed leaves and spikes of pink buds opening to bright cerise-pink flowers. Needs the protection of a warm wall in colder areas.
HEIGHT AND SPREAD: 4 × 3ft (1.2 × 0.9m)
BLOOMING PERIOD: Late summer to autumn
SOIL: Well-drained.

9-10

MIDDLE

LATIN NAME: *Rosa* 'Gertrude Jekyll'
COMMON NAME: English rose
ALTERNATIVES: 'Mary Rose,' 'Brother Cadfael'
DESCRIPTION: Shrub rose with medium-sized double deep-pink blooms of old rose character. Well-developed fragrance. Vigorous but with rather lanky growth which may need support in more exposed gardens.
HEIGHT AND SPREAD: 4 × 3½ft (1.2 × 1.06m)
BLOOMING PERIOD: Spring to mid-autumn
SOIL: Fertile, moisture-retentive, humus-rich. Good on clay.

5-10

LATIN NAME: *Diascia* 'Ruby Field'
COMMON NAME: Known by Latin name
ALTERNATIVES: *D. cordata, D. rigescens, D. vigilis.* Also many new cultivars
DESCRIPTION: Semi-evergreen tender perennial with fine trailing stems covered in very small leaves and producing upright spikes of pink, shell-shaped flowers.
HEIGHT AND SPREAD: 3 × 6in (8 × 15cm)
BLOOMING PERIOD: Summer to mid-autumn
SOIL: Well-drained but not dry in summer.

8-10

FRONT

10

LATIN NAME: *Pelargonium* cultivar
COMMON NAME: Ivy-leaved geranium
ALTERNATIVES: 'Hederinum' syn. 'Balcon Rose,' 'Cascade Pink'
DESCRIPTION: Tender perennial with stiff, trailing stems clothed in succulent, ivy-shaped leaves. Open clusters of starry flowers. Balcony or Continental types produce long trailing stems.
HEIGHT AND SPREAD: 6–12 × 12–24in (15–30 × 30–60cm)
BLOOMING PERIOD: Spring to autumn
SOIL: Well drained. Tolerates poor soils.

BACK

❄ **4-9**

❄ **5-10**

LATIN NAME: *Lonicera periclymenum* 'Serotina'
COMMON NAME: Late Dutch honeysuckle, woodbine
ALTERNATIVES: 'Belgica,' *L. japonica repens*
DESCRIPTION: Climber with twining habit and oval leaves in pairs along the stem. Tubular flowers in clusters towards the top of the plant, especially fragrant in the evening.
HEIGHT AND SPREAD: 12–20 × 12–20ft (3.7–6 × 3.7–6m)
BLOOMING PERIOD: Mid-summer to mid-autumn
SOIL: Deeply cultivated, fertile, moisture-retentive.

LATIN NAME: *Rosa* 'Zéphirine Drouhin'
COMMON NAME: Thornless climbing rose
ALTERNATIVES: 'Kathleen Harrop,' 'Parade,' 'Galway Bay'
DESCRIPTION: Climbing Bourbon rose with almost spineless stems and semi-evergreen foliage. Large, double, crimson-pink blooms. Very well scented. Suffers from blackspot and mildew in bad years.
HEIGHT AND SPREAD: 10 × 6ft (3 × 1.8m)
BLOOMING PERIOD: Spring to autumn
SOIL: Rich, moisture-retentive, humus-rich. Good on fertile clay loam.

MIDDLE

❄ **5-9**

LATIN NAME: *Helichrysum bracteatum*
COMMON NAME: Strawflower, everlasting flower
ALTERNATIVES: 'Monstrosum Series'
DESCRIPTION: Half-hardy annual with stiff upright, sparsely-branched stems and large, rounded flower heads consisting of papery bracts. May be cut for drying for use in indoor arrangements.
HEIGHT AND SPREAD: 3 × 1ft (90 × 30cm)
BLOOMING PERIOD: Mid-summer to mid-autumn
SOIL: Well-drained.

LATIN NAME: *Rosa* 'Ferdinand Pichard'
COMMON NAME: Shrub rose
ALTERNATIVES: *R. gallica* 'Versicolor,' 'Tricolore de Flandre'
DESCRIPTION: Hybrid Perpetual shrub rose with tight clusters of fragrant double blooms, palest pink streaked crimson and red. Bushy habit.
HEIGHT AND SPREAD: 4+ × 3ft (1.2+ × 0.9m)
BLOOMING PERIOD: Spring to autumn
SOIL: Rich, moisture-retentive, humus-rich. Good on well-cultivated clay soils.

FRONT

💧 **10**

💧 **10**

LATIN NAME: *Pelargonium* 'Mrs. Parker'
COMMON NAME: Zonal geranium
ALTERNATIVES: None
DESCRIPTION: Tender perennial with rounded, scalloped-edged aromatic leaves with a broad creamy-white margin and rounded heads of deep pink flowers. Roots easily from cuttings.
HEIGHT AND SPREAD: 12 × 9in (30 × 23cm)
BLOOMING PERIOD: Spring to mid-autumn
SOIL: Any well-drained.

LATIN NAME: *Pelargonium* cultivar
COMMON NAME: Zonal geranium
ALTERNATIVES: Century F1 and Video Series, Multibloom types
DESCRIPTION: Tender perennial with rounded, scalloped-edged aromatic leaves usually with a darker banding or zone. Bold, rounded heads of flowers with rounded petals.
HEIGHT AND SPREAD: 12–18 × 12in (30–45 × 30cm)
BLOOMING PERIOD: Spring to mid-autumn
SOIL: Any well-drained.

LATIN NAME: *Lagerstroemia indica*
COMMON NAME: Crepe myrtle
ALTERNATIVES: 'Biloxi,' 'Comanche,' 'Hopi,' 'Neat East'
DESCRIPTION: Shrub or small tree with oval leaves and cone-shaped clusters of ruffled flowers at stem tips. Severe winter cold may kill stems to ground level, but they regrow quickly.
HEIGHT AND SPREAD: 22 × 16ft (7 × 5m)
BLOOMING PERIOD: Summer
SOIL: Well-drained.

7-9

LATIN NAME: *Mandevilla splendens* syn. *Dipladenia splendens*
COMMON NAME: Mandevilla
ALTERNATIVES: *M.* × *amoena* 'Alice du Pont'
DESCRIPTION: Twining climber of loose, open habit with glossy evergreen, heavily-veined leaves and trumpet-shaped blooms, widely flared at the mouth. Fragrant.
HEIGHT AND SPREAD: 10–20 × 10–20ft (3–6 × 3–6m)
BLOOMING PERIOD: Late spring to early autumn
SOIL: Well-drained but moisture-retentive. Dislikes extreme alkalinity.

10

6-10

LATIN NAME: *Anemone hupehensis* 'Splendens'
COMMON NAME: Japanese anemone
ALTERNATIVES: 'Hadspen Abundance,' 'September Charm'
DESCRIPTION: Herbaceous perennial with three-lobed jagged edged leaves and wiry flower stems with spherical buds opening to darker and lighter pink petalled blooms. Dislikes disturbance.
HEIGHT AND SPREAD: 2½ × 1½ft (75 × 45cm)
BLOOMING PERIOD: Late summer to early autumn
SOIL: Moisture-retentive, well-drained to heavy soil. Tolerates lime.

6-10

LATIN NAME: *Anemone hupehensis* var. *japonica* 'Prinz Heinrich'
COMMON NAME: Japanese anemone
ALTERNATIVES: 'Hadspen Abundance,' 'September Charm'
DESCRIPTION: Herbaceous perennial with three-lobed jagged edged leaves and wiry flower stems with spherical buds opening to deep purple-pink. Dislikes disturbance.
HEIGHT AND SPREAD: 2½ × 1½ft (75 × 45cm)
BLOOMING PERIOD: Late summer to early autumn
SOIL: Moisture-retentive, well-drained to heavy soil. Tolerates lime.

4-10

LATIN NAME: *Bergenia* 'Morgenröte'
COMMON NAME: Bergenia, Elephant's ears
ALTERNATIVES: 'Abendglöcken,' 'Wintermarchen'
DESCRIPTION: Evergreen perennial producing clumps of large rounded leaves of leathery texture. Deep pink heads of fleshy flowers appear above the leaves in spring and also often later in summer.
HEIGHT AND SPREAD: 18 × 12in (45 × 30cm)
BLOOMING PERIOD: Spring and again in summer
SOIL: Any soil, but best on reasonably fertile, moisture-retentive loam.

LATIN NAME: *Begonia semperflorens* 'Pink Devil F1'
COMMON NAME: Fibrous-rooted or bedding begonia
ALTERNATIVES: F1 hybrids like Devil, Excel and Olympia
DESCRIPTION: Half-hardy annual making low clumps of rounded fleshy leaves and producing a constant show of small, four-petalled blooms. Varieties with bronze or green leaves.
HEIGHT AND SPREAD: 4–6 × 6in (10–15 × 15cm)
BLOOMING PERIOD: Summer to mid-autumn
SOIL: Humus-rich, moisture-retentive but some drought tolerance.

37

BACK

LATIN NAME: *Dierama pendulum*
COMMON NAME: Wand flower, angel's fishing rod, Venus' fishing rod
ALTERNATIVES: *D. pulcherimum* and forms
DESCRIPTION: Bulbous perennial making a basal clump of narrow, grassy foliage from which the long arching flower stems arise. The pendulous blooms are bell-shaped and purple-pink. Self-seeds.
HEIGHT AND SPREAD: 60 × 6–8in (150 × 15–20cm)
BLOOMING PERIOD: Late summer
SOIL: Moisture-retentive to damp.

7-10

LATIN NAME: *Hibiscus rosa-sinensis* 'The President'
COMMON NAME: Rose of China, Chinese hibiscus
ALTERNATIVES: 'Flower Girl,' 'Mrs. George Davis'
DESCRIPTION: Evergreen shrub of bushy habit with broad, tapering glossy-green leaves which have a toothed edge. Large funnel-shaped blooms of mid-pink with a prominent column of stigma and stamens.
HEIGHT AND SPREAD: 5–10 × 5–10ft (1.5–3 × 1.5–3m)
BLOOMING PERIOD: Spring to autumn
SOIL: Fertile, well-drained.

9-10

MIDDLE

LATIN NAME: *Fuchsia* 'Molesworth'
COMMON NAME: Bush fuchsia
ALTERNATIVES: 'Garden News,' 'Display,' and many others
DESCRIPTION: Tender shrub of bushy habit with small lance-shaped to oval leaves and double blooms consisting of cerise-pink sepals and a white "skirt" of petals. Remove faded blooms. Overwinter frost-free.
HEIGHT AND SPREAD: 3 × 2½ft (0.9 × 0.75m)
BLOOMING PERIOD: Summer to mid-autumn
SOIL: Fertile, humus-rich, moisture-retentive. Feed well in summer.

9-10

LATIN NAME: *Phlox paniculata* 'Eva Cullum'
COMMON NAME: Border phlox, garden phlox
ALTERNATIVES: 'Europa,' 'Elizabeth Arden'
DESCRIPTION: Clump-forming herbaceous perennial with upright stems clothed in slender, lance-shaped leaves and topped with clusters of rounded blooms, pink with a darker eye. Fragrant.
HEIGHT AND SPREAD: 3 × 1½ft (0.9 × 0.45m)
BLOOMING PERIOD: Mid- to late summer
SOIL: Fertile, moisture-retentive but well-drained.

3-9

FRONT

LATIN NAME: *Lychnis coronaria*
COMMON NAME: Dusty miller, rose campion
ALTERNATIVES: 'Angel's Blush'
DESCRIPTION: Herbaceous perennial with silver-gray felted leaves making a basal rosette from which silvery white branched flower stems arise carrying cerise-pink rounded blooms. Self-seeds readily.
HEIGHT AND SPREAD: 36 × 18in (90 × 45cm)
BLOOMING PERIOD: Summer
SOIL: Well-drained to dry.

3-10

LATIN NAME: *Persicaria affinis* cv. (syn. *Polygonum affine* cv.)
COMMON NAME: Knotweed
ALTERNATIVES: 'Donald Lowndes,' 'Darjeeling Red,' 'Superba' ('Dimity')
DESCRIPTION: Semi-evergreen mat-like groundcover with glossy, lance-shaped leaves turning bronze in winter and bearing fluffy, upright spikes of red buds opening to pink giving a two-tone effect.
HEIGHT AND SPREAD: 9 × 12in (23 × 30cm)
BLOOMING PERIOD: Summer to autumn
SOIL: Any well-drained but moisture-retentive to moist.

3-9

LATIN NAME: *Nerium oleander*
COMMON NAME: Oleander (Warning – highly poisonous)
ALTERNATIVES: 'Punctatum' ('Monsieur Belaguier'), 'Splendens'
DESCRIPTION: Evergreen shrub of upright, bushy habit with slender, oblong leaves of leathery texture. Flowers shaped like cartwheels and available in many shades of pink as well as red, white, yellow, and apricot. Good for coastal areas.
HEIGHT AND SPREAD: 11 × 9ft (3.3 × 2.7m)
BLOOMING PERIOD: Spring to autumn
SOIL: Well-drained.

8-10

LATIN NAME: *Rosa* 'Constance Spry'
COMMON NAME: English rose, large-flowered shrub/climbing rose
ALTERNATIVES: 'Mary Rose,' 'Aloha'
DESCRIPTION: Shrub rose which may also be trained as a climber to cover a larger area than stated. Grayish green foliage and large, fully double, old-fashioned blooms with a myrrh fragrance.
HEIGHT AND SPREAD: 6 × 5ft (1.8 × 1.5m)
BLOOMING PERIOD: Summer
SOIL: Fertile, well-drained but moisture-retentive and humus-rich.

5-9

BACK

LATIN NAME: *Erica terminalis* syn. *E. stricta*
COMMON NAME: Corsican heath
ALTERNATIVES: None
DESCRIPTION: Evergreen shrub of strongly upright habit with needle-like foliage in mid- to light green and terminal clusters of tiny bell-shaped pink blooms. These fade to gingery brown remaining attractive through winter.
HEIGHT AND SPREAD: 3+ × 2½ft (0.9+ × 0.75m)
BLOOMING PERIOD: Early summer to early autumn
SOIL: Well-drained. Tolerates lime.

6-10

3-9

MIDDLE

LATIN NAME: *Chelone obliqua*
COMMON NAME: Turtlehead
ALTERNATIVES: None
DESCRIPTION: Herbaceous perennial forming a clump with stiff, upright stems well clothed in dark green, lance-shaped leaves with a toothed margin. Terminal flower spikes with hooded lilac-pink blooms.
HEIGHT AND SPREAD: 3 × 1½ft (0.9 × 0.45m)
BLOOMING PERIOD: Late summer to mid-autumn
SOIL: Moisture-retentive to damp.

8-10

4-10

FRONT

LATIN NAME: *Penstemon* 'Hewell Pink Bedder'
COMMON NAME: Known by Latin name
ALTERNATIVES: 'Appleblossom,' 'Thorn,' 'Pink Beauty,' 'Pink Endurance'
DESCRIPTION: Evergreen perennial of bushy, upright habit with stems well-clothed in lance-shaped, glossy, mid-green leaves. Tubular flowers of rich shell-pink with a white throat. Root from cuttings.
HEIGHT AND SPREAD: 18 × 18in (45 × 45cm)
BLOOMING PERIOD: Summer
SOIL: Well-drained.

LATIN NAME: *Sedum spectabile*
COMMON NAME: Showy stonecrop
ALTERNATIVES: 'Brilliant,' 'Meteor,' 'September Glut,' 'Autumn Joy'
DESCRIPTION: Perennial with succulent leaves and stems. Foliage rounded and gray-green. The light apple-green buds are attractive through summer and open blooms are beloved by butterflies.
HEIGHT AND SPREAD: 18 × 18in (45 × 45cm)
BLOOMING PERIOD: Late summer to early autumn
SOIL: Well-drained to dry.

BACK

8-10

LATIN NAME: *Phormium* 'Pink Panther'
COMMON NAME: New Zealand flax or fiber-lily
ALTERNATIVES: 'Sundowner,' 'Maori Sunrise,' 'Pinkie'
DESCRIPTION: Evergreen perennial with sword-shaped leaves from ground level. Foliage is variegated with a broad, deep pink stripe down center of each leaf. Tall flower stems on mature plants.
HEIGHT AND SPREAD: 5 × 7ft (1.5 × 2.1m)
BLOOMING PERIOD: Mid-summer
SOIL: Well-drained.

LATIN NAME: *Lilium* 'Journey's End'
COMMON NAME: Hybrid lily
ALTERNATIVES: 'Star Gazer,' 'Pink Beauty,' 'Pink Perfection Strain'
DESCRIPTION: Bulb producing long flowering stems covered with slender, willow-like leaves and topped with large, trumpet to star-shaped blooms with slightly reflexed petals – deep pink edged white wth darker speckles.
HEIGHT AND SPREAD: 5ft (1.5m)
BLOOMING PERIOD: Mid-summer
SOIL: Well-drained, humus-rich.

5-8

MIDDLE

8-10

LATIN NAME: *Clerodendrum bungei*
COMMON NAME: Glory flower, clerodendrum
ALTERNATIVES: None
DESCRIPTION: Sub-shrub spreading by underground suckers, invasive unless restricted by walls and paving. Stems covered in heart-shaped leaves. Flowers magenta-pink in dome-shaped clusters.
HEIGHT AND SPREAD: 3 × 8ft (0.9 × 2.4m)
BLOOMING PERIOD: Late summer to autumn
SOIL: Any well-drained soil.

9-10

LATIN NAME: *Fuchsia* 'Garden News'
COMMON NAME: Known by Latin name
ALTERNATIVES: Half-hardy hybrid fuchsias/bedding fuchsias
DESCRIPTION: Half-hardy bush fuchsia of tall, upright habit carrying many large double blooms with soft pink sepals, and a frilly "skirt" of cerise-red. Protect against frost.
HEIGHT AND SPREAD: 4+ × 2½ft (1.2+ × 0.75m)
BLOOMING PERIOD: Late spring to mid-autumn
SOIL: Fertile, humus-rich, moisture-retentive but well-drained.

FRONT

LATIN NAME: *Astilbe chinensis* 'Pumila'
COMMON NAME: Known by Latin name
ALTERNATIVES: 'Serenade,' A. 'Sprite,' A. 'Bronze Elegans,' A. 'Denkellachs'
DESCRIPTION: Herbaceous perennial with creeping roots making low groundcover for retentive soils. Dense coverage of stiff, fern-like foliage and mauve-pink flower spikes late in the season.
HEIGHT AND SPREAD: 18 × 12in (45 × 30cm)
BLOOMING PERIOD: Late summer to early autumn
SOIL: Cool, moisture-retentive to damp.

4-8

7-9

LATIN NAME: *Cyclamen cilicium*
COMMON NAME: Known by Latin name
ALTERNATIVES: C. *hederifolium* syn. C. *neapolitanum*
DESCRIPTION: Tuberous perennial with heart-shaped leaves marked with silver. The pale pink blooms have elegantly twisted petals and a dark stain at the mouth. Flowers just before or with leaves.
HEIGHT AND SPREAD: 4 × 2–4in (10 × 5–10cm)
BLOOMING PERIOD: Early to late autumn
SOIL: Well-drained, humus-rich.

LATIN NAME: *Fuchsia* 'Mrs. Popple'
COMMON NAME: Known by Latin name
ALTERNATIVES: 'Chillerton Beauty,' 'Madame Cornelissen'
DESCRIPTION: Shrub with small dark green leaves tinged purple. Many large single blooms with cerise-pink sepals and a "skirt" of plum-purple petals. May die back to ground level but regrows from base.
HEIGHT AND SPREAD: 4 × 5ft (1.2 × 1.5m)
BLOOMING PERIOD: Late spring to mid-autumn
SOIL: Fertile, well-drained, moisture-retentive and humus-rich.

8-10

3-10

LATIN NAME: *Eupatorium purpureum*
COMMON NAME: Joe Pye weed
ALTERNATIVES: *E. purpureum* subsp. *maculatum* 'Atropurpureum'
DESCRIPTION: Herbaceous perennial with unbranched, deep purple-flushed stems. Lanceolate leaves in whorls. Dome-shaped heads made up of tiny pinkish purple flowers. Attractive to butterflies.
HEIGHT AND SPREAD: 6–8 × 3ft (1.8–2.4 × 0.9m)
BLOOMING PERIOD: Late summer to mid-autumn
SOIL: Rich, moisture-retentive to damp.

8-9

LATIN NAME: *Dendranthema* 'Grandchild'
COMMON NAME: Autumn-flowering chrysanthemum
ALTERNATIVES: 'Pink Lady,' 'Pink Sheffield,' 'Pink Champagne,' 'Venice'
DESCRIPTION: Herbaceous perennial with branched stems and lobed leaves. Sprays of double soft pink blooms toning deeper pink at center. Petals reflexed. Renew from cuttings taken from rootstock in spring.
HEIGHT AND SPREAD: 4 × 2–2½ft (1.2 × 0.6–0.75m)
BLOOMING PERIOD: Late summer to mid-autumn
SOIL: Fertile, well-drained.

8-9

LATIN NAME: *Dendranthema* syn. *Chrysanthemum* cultivar
COMMON NAME: Autumn-flowering chrysanthemum
ALTERNATIVES: 'Grandchild,' 'Pink Lady,' 'Pink Sheffield,' 'Venice'
DESCRIPTION: Herbaceous perennial with upright branched stems and lobed leaves. Sprays of single, semi-double or double flowers. Renew from cuttings taken in spring.
HEIGHT AND SPREAD: 4 × 2–2½ft (1.2 × 0.6–0.75m)
BLOOMING PERIOD: Late summer to mid-autumn
SOIL: Fertile, well-drained.

4-10

LATIN NAME: *Aster amellus* 'Jacqueline Genebrier'
COMMON NAME: Michaelmas daisy, Fall aster, Italian aster
ALTERNATIVES: 'Sonia,' 'Lady Hindlip,' 'Nocturn,' 'Pink Zenith'
DESCRIPTION: Herbaceous perennial with small, lanceolate leaves and a profusion of deep mauve-pink daisies with yellow centers. Support to prevent plants flopping under the weight of flowers.
HEIGHT AND SPREAD: 12 × 18in (30 × 45cm)
BLOOMING PERIOD: Late summer to early autumn
SOIL: Any reasonably fertile, drained soil.

4-9

LATIN NAME: *Aster novi-belgii* 'Jenny'
COMMON NAME: Michaelmas daisy, Fall aster, New York aster
ALTERNATIVES: 'Little Pink Beauty,' 'Chatterbox,' 'Pink Lace'
DESCRIPTION: Herbaceous perennial. A dwarf cultivar with cerise-pink double blooms highlighted by a yellow "eye." Compact habit so does not need staking. Lift and divide every two to three years.
HEIGHT AND SPREAD: 12 × 12–18in (30 × 30–45cm)
BLOOMING PERIOD: Late summer to early autumn
SOIL: Any reasonably fertile, drained soil.

BACK

6-9

LATIN NAME: *Hydrangea macrophylla* 'Lilacina'
COMMON NAME: Lacecap hydrangea
ALTERNATIVES: 'Teller Rosa,' 'Beauté Vendômoise'
DESCRIPTION: Shrub with large, oval leaves coming to a sharp point and heads composed of tiny inner fertile flowers (blue-purple) surrounded by showy sterile flowers (mauve-pink on alkaline soils).
HEIGHT AND SPREAD: 6 × 8–10ft (1.8–2.4 × 3m)
BLOOMING PERIOD: Summer to early autumn
SOIL: Fertile, humus-rich and moist. Acid makes flowers mauve-blue.

6-9

LATIN NAME: *Hydrangea macrophylla* cultivar
COMMON NAME: Mop head hydrangea, hortensia, big leaf hydrangea
ALTERNATIVES: 'Blauer Prinz,' 'Holstein,' 'King George,' 'Niedersachsen'
DESCRIPTION: Shrub with broad leaves tapering to a point and rounded heads mainly of large sterile florets in pale pink. Color changes from pink on alkaline to blue or purple on acid soils.
HEIGHT AND SPREAD: 6–10 × 6–10ft (1.8 × 3m)
BLOOMING PERIOD: Mid-summer to late autumn
SOIL: Alkaline, fertile, humus-rich, moisture-retentive.

MIDDLE

8-9

LATIN NAME: *Dendranthema* 'Yvonne Arnaud'
COMMON NAME: Autumn flowering or florists' chrysanthemum
ALTERNATIVES: 'Pink Lady,' 'Pink Sheffield,' 'Pink Champagne,' 'Venice'
DESCRIPTION: Herbaceous perennial with branching flower stems clothed in lobed leaves, bearing large double blooms in deep mauve-pink. Renew from cutting from lifted rootstock in spring.
HEIGHT AND SPREAD: 4 × 2½ft (1.2 × 0.75m)
BLOOMING PERIOD: Early autumn
SOIL: Any fertile, drained.

8-9

LATIN NAME: *Dendranthema* 'Pennine Oriel'
COMMON NAME: Autumn flowering or florists' spray chrysanthemum
ALTERNATIVES: Anemone-centered chrysanthemum cultivars
DESCRIPTION: Herbaceous perennial with branching stems clothed in lobed leaves and bearing sprays of anemone-centered flowers with a ring of very pale pink petals and a raised central dome of yellow.
HEIGHT AND SPREAD: 4 × 2–2½ft (1.2 × 0.6–0.75m)
BLOOMING PERIOD: Early autumn
SOIL: Any fertile, drained.

FRONT

8-10

LATIN NAME: *Amaryllis belladonna*
COMMON NAME: Belladonna lily, Jersey lily
ALTERNATIVES: 'Johannesburg'
DESCRIPTION: Bulb with purple-tinged stems topped with clusters of trumpet-shaped blooms. Needs plenty of moisture in early summer. Strap-shaped leaves appear after flowers. Needs a sheltered spot.
HEIGHT AND SPREAD: 24 × 12in (60 × 30cm)
BLOOMING PERIOD: Late summer to early autumn
SOIL: Deep, fertile, humus-rich.

6-10

LATIN NAME: *Schizostylis coccinea* 'Sunrise'
COMMON NAME: Crimson-flag, kaffir lily
ALTERNATIVES: 'Fenland Daybreak'
DESCRIPTION: Herbaceous perennial with a mat of fleshy rhizomes. Grassy foliage and slender spikes of salmon-pink, cup-shaped blooms. Requires plenty of moisture in summer. Mulch for winter protection.
HEIGHT AND SPREAD: 24 × 9–12in (60 × 23–30cm)
BLOOMING PERIOD: Mid-autumn to early winter
SOIL: Fertile, humus-rich, moisture-retentive.

6-9

LATIN NAME: *Hydrangea macrophylla* cultivar
COMMON NAME: Mop head hydrangea, hortensia, big leaf hydrangea
ALTERNATIVES: 'Hamburg,' 'Europa,' 'Heinrich Seidel'
DESCRIPTION: Shrub with broad oval leaves tapering to a fine point. Good red-purple or bronze autumn tints. Rounded heads of deep pink sterile florets fading to biscuit in autumn and winter.
HEIGHT AND SPREAD: 6–10 × 6–10ft (1.8–3 × 1.8–3m)
BLOOMING PERIOD: Mid-summer to late autumn
SOIL: Alkaline, fertile, humus-rich, moisture-retentive.

6-9

LATIN NAME: *Hydrangea serrata* 'Grayswood'
COMMON NAME: Known by Latin name
ALTERNATIVES: *H. macrophylla* 'Teller Rosa,' *H. m.* 'Lilacina'
DESCRIPTION: Shrub with lanceolate leaves, with a serrated edge and purple-red tinted in autumn. Lace-cap blooms with blue central flowers with pale pink bracts deepening to crimson by autumn.
HEIGHT AND SPREAD: 4–5 × 6ft (1.2–1.5 × 1.8m)
BLOOMING PERIOD: Early summer to mid-autumn
SOIL: Acid, fertile, humus-rich, moisture-retentive.

LATIN NAME: *Aster ericoides* 'Esther'
COMMON NAME: Heath aster
ALTERNATIVES: 'Pink Cloud,' 'Pink Star'
DESCRIPTION: Herbaceous perennial with fine, wiry stems covered with dark green scale-like leaves. Masses of tiny pale pink daisy flowers on much-branched stems remain starry and attractive when faded.
HEIGHT AND SPREAD: 30 × 20in (75 × 50cm)
BLOOMING PERIOD: Autumn
SOIL: Any fertile, well-drained.

3-10

5-9

LATIN NAME: *Dendranthema* 'Princess'
COMMON NAME: Korean chrysanthemum
ALTERNATIVES: 'Anne,' 'Columbine' and other pink-flowered cultivars
DESCRIPTION: Herbaceous perennial with double dome-shaped blooms of salmon-pink and lobed leaves. Korean types are hardier than florists' or spray chrysanthemums and may be mulched over winter.
HEIGHT AND SPREAD: 2 × 1½ft (0.6 × 0.45m)
BLOOMING PERIOD: Early autumn
SOIL: Fertile, well-drained.

LATIN NAME: *Schizostylis coccinea* 'Hilary Gould'
COMMON NAME: Crimson-flag, kaffir lily
ALTERNATIVES: 'Professor Barnard'
DESCRIPTION: Herbaceous perennial with a mat of fleshy rhizomes. Grassy foliage and slender spikes of rich pink, cup-shaped blooms. Requires plenty of moisture in summer. Mulch for winter protection in cooler regions.
HEIGHT AND SPREAD: 24 × 9–12in (60 × 23–30cm)
BLOOMING PERIOD: Early autumn to mid-autumn
SOIL: Fertile, humus-rich, moisture-retentive to moist.

6-10

LATIN NAME: *Schizostylis coccinea* 'Mrs. Hegarty'
COMMON NAME: Crimson-flag, kaffir lily
ALTERNATIVES: 'Jennifer,' 'Viscountess Byng'
DESCRIPTION: Herbaceous perennial with a mat of fleshy rhizomes. Grassy foliage and slender spikes of pale pink, cup-shaped blooms. Requires plenty of moisture in summer. Mulch for winter protection in cooler regions.
HEIGHT AND SPREAD: 24 × 9–12in (60 × 23–30cm)
BLOOMING PERIOD: Early autumn to mid-autumn
SOIL: Fertile, humus-rich, moisture-retentive to moist.

6-10

BACK

LATIN NAME: *Viburnum × bodnantense* 'Dawn'
COMMON NAME: Known by Latin name
ALTERNATIVES: 'Deben,' 'Charles Lamont'
DESCRIPTION: Shrub of strongly upright habit with oval, pointed leaves in dark green with red stalks and heavy venation, smelling of sweet peppers when crushed. Ball-shaped clusters of honey-scented blooms.
HEIGHT AND SPREAD: 12 × 13ft (3.5 × 4m)
BLOOMING PERIOD: Autumn to early spring
SOIL: Well-drained.

5-8

LATIN NAME: *Rosa* 'Compassion'
COMMON NAME: Climbing rose
ALTERNATIVES: 'New Dawn,' 'Aloha,' 'Pink Perpétué'
DESCRIPTION: Climber of stiff, upright growth with large, dark green leaves. Plenty of foliage on the lower stems. Large, double pink blooms tinged apricot. Scented.
HEIGHT AND SPREAD: 10 × 8ft (3 × 2.5m)
BLOOMING PERIOD: Summer to early autumn (from spring in mild areas)
SOIL: Fertile, well-drained but moisture-retentive. Good on clay.

5-9

MIDDLE

LATIN NAME: *Dahlia* 'Roberta'
COMMON NAME: Known by Latin name
ALTERNATIVES: 'Pink Lady,' 'Pink Ball,' 'Noreen'
DESCRIPTION: Tender perennial with tuberous roots that in colder regions must be overwintered in frost-free conditions indoors. Large pinnate leaves and upright, branched stems bearing large, pink, ball-shaped blooms.
HEIGHT AND SPREAD: 3–4 × 3–4ft (0.9–1.2 × 0.9–1.2m)
BLOOMING PERIOD: Summer to autumn
SOIL: Fertile, well-drained, moisture-retentive, and humus-rich.

9-10

LATIN NAME: *Dahlia* 'Amour Pink'
COMMON NAME: Known by Latin name
ALTERNATIVES: 'Gilt Edge,' 'Gay Princess,' 'Jocondo'
DESCRIPTION: Tender perennial with tuberous roots that in colder regions must be overwintered in frost-free conditions indoors. Large pinnate leaves and upright, branched stems bearing compact, rounded blooms.
HEIGHT AND SPREAD: 3–4 × 3–4ft (0.9–1.2 × 0.9–1.2m)
BLOOMING PERIOD: Summer to autumn
SOIL: Fertile, well-drained, moisture-retentive, and humus-rich.

9-10

FRONT

LATIN NAME: *Calluna vulgaris* 'Silver Rose'
COMMON NAME: Scotch heather, ling
ALTERNATIVES: 'H. E. Beale,' 'Peter Sparkes,' 'Elsie Purnell'
DESCRIPTION: Evergreen shrublet with scale-like leaves and a profusion of slender, upright stems forming a dense carpet. Tiny bell-shaped blooms of mid-pink.
HEIGHT AND SPREAD: 15 × 36in (40 × 90cm)
BLOOMING PERIOD: Mid-summer to early autumn
SOIL: Acid, humus-rich, well-drained.

4-7

LATIN NAME: *Cyclamen hederifolium* syn. *C. neapolitanum*
COMMON NAME: Autumn-flowering cyclamen, hardy cyclamen
ALTERNATIVES: *C. cilicium, C. mirabile*
DESCRIPTION: Tuberous-rooted perennial which flowers just before or as the foliage is developing. The perfumed flowers are nodding, with reflexed petals, and the leaves are heart-shaped and patterned.
HEIGHT AND SPREAD: 4 × 4–6in (10 × 10–15cm)
BLOOMING PERIOD: Autumn
SOIL: Well-drained, humus-rich.

5-7

LATIN NAME: *Rosa* 'Queen Elizabeth'
COMMON NAME: Bush, cluster-flowered or floribunda rose
ALTERNATIVES: 'Congratulations,' 'Mary Rose,' 'Queen of Denmark'
DESCRIPTION: Shrub of strongly upright, vigorous growth with large, dark green leaves and clusters of large, well-shaped blooms in soft pink.
HEIGHT AND SPREAD: 10 × 2½ft (3 × 0.8m)
BLOOMING PERIOD: Summer to early autumn (from spring in mild areas)
SOIL: Fertile, well-drained but moisture-retentive, good on clay.

5-9

5-9

LATIN NAME: *Rosa* 'Handel'
COMMON NAME: Climbing rose
ALTERNATIVES: 'Pink Perpetué,' 'Coral Dawn,' 'Compassion'
DESCRIPTION: Climber of upright habit with dark leaves and large double blooms which are crimson in bud opening to petals of creamy-white edged raspberry-pink.
HEIGHT AND SPREAD: 10 × 7ft (3 × 2.2m)
BLOOMING PERIOD: Summer to early autumn (from spring in mild areas)
SOIL: Fertile, well-drained but moisture-retentive. Good on clay soils.

9-10

LATIN NAME: *Dahlia* 'Hamari Rose'
COMMON NAME: Known by Latin name
ALTERNATIVES: 'Noreen,' 'Hallmark'
DESCRIPTION: Tender perennial with tuberous roots that in colder regions must be overwintered in frost-free conditions indoors. Large pinnate leaves and upright stems bearing pompon-shaped blooms.
HEIGHT AND SPREAD: 3–4 × 3–4ft (0.9–1.2 × 0.9–1.2m)
BLOOMING PERIOD: Summer to autumn
SOIL: Fertile, well-drained, moisture-retentive, and humus-rich.

6-9

LATIN NAME: *Gaultheria mucronata* 'Lilacina' syn. *Pernettya m.* 'Lilacina'
COMMON NAME: Known by Latin name
ALTERNATIVES: 'Bell's Seedling,' 'Pink Pearl,' 'Sea Shell'
DESCRIPTION: Evergreen shrub of bushy, spreading habit with upright stems covered in small, dark green, glossy leaves. On female plants, the insignificant white flowers are followed by deep pink berries.
HEIGHT AND SPREAD: 2½ × 4ft (0.75 × 1.2m)
BLOOMING PERIOD: Early summer
SOIL: Acid, moisture-retentive, and humus-rich.

4-7

LATIN NAME: *Colchicum autumnale*
COMMON NAME: Autumn crocus, meadow saffron (poisonous)
ALTERNATIVES: *C. a.* 'Pleniflorum,' *C. speciosum*, 'Pink Goblet'
DESCRIPTION: Corm which flowers before the foliage, the long stems bearing pale pink blooms shaped like wine flutes. Bold, oblong leaves in spring. Excellent planted in clumps between deciduous shrubs.
HEIGHT AND SPREAD: 4–6 × 4–6in (10–15 × 10–15cm)
BLOOMING PERIOD: Autumn
SOIL: Well-cultivated, humus-rich and moisture-retentive.

5-7

LATIN NAME: *Colchicum speciosum* 'Atrorubens'
COMMON NAME: Showy colchicum (poisonous)
ALTERNATIVES: *C. autumnale*
DESCRIPTION: Corm producing stout-stemmed, cup-shaped blooms of rich pink which are relatively weather-resistant. The large basal leaves are produced in late winter or early spring.
HEIGHT AND SPREAD: 6–8 × 6–8in (15–20 × 15–20cm)
BLOOMING PERIOD: Autumn
SOIL: Well-cultivated, humus-rich and moisture-retentive.

ORANGE

RANGING FROM PALE BUFF SHADES TO RUSTY BROWNS, THE COLOR ORANGE TAKES IN SUBTLE HUES LIKE PEACH, APRICOT, AND AMBER, AS WELL AS PURE TANGERINE AND INTENSE, SOME WOULD SAY GARISH, ORANGES EPITOMIZED BY MARIGOLDS. IN THE GENTLE LIGHT OF AUTUMN, ALL SHADES OF ORANGE, WHETHER LEAF, BERRY, OR BLOOM, SEEM TO GLOW. AT THIS TIME BLUE AND PURPLE FLOWERS ADD A RICHNESS THAT IS IMPOSSIBLE TO APPRECIATE IN SUMMER LIGHT.

GREEN IS A NATURAL FOIL FOR ORANGE. IF YOU WANT TO AVOID DAZZLING YOURSELF IN SUMMER, IT'S WISE TO HAVE QUITE A HIGH PROPORTION OF LEAFY LUXURIANCE TO COOL EVERYTHING DOWN. SKY-BLUE AND LIME-GREEN WILL ALSO DO THE TRICK. BRONZE AND PURPLE-GREEN FOLIAGE COMPLEMENT TRUE ORANGE WELL. PURPLE-BLACK LEAVES CAN BE TOO HARSH A CONTRAST, AND,

THOUGH POPULAR, BRIGHT SILVER CAN ALSO BE A MISTAKE. BLUE-GRAY OR BLUE-GREEN LEAVES TEND TO MAKE A GOOD PARTNERSHIP.

PREDOMINANTLY ORANGE COLOR SCHEMES, PERHAPS WITH TOUCHES OF SCARLET AND GOLD, CONVEY DRY, DUSTY HEAT. TERRACOTTA WORKS WELL IN SUCH A PLANTING IN THE FORM OF ORNAMENTS, CONTAINERS, OR SCULPTURE AND RED BRICK MAKES A VERY SUITABLE BACKDROP. FOR A REALLY RICH, MODERN SCHEME, TRY VIVID LIGHT AND DARK ORANGE SHADES WITH PURPLE-BLUE AND BLUE-GRAY FOLIAGE, ACCENTED WITH DEEP VELVET-PURPLE AND ROYAL BLUE BLOOMS. THERE ARE MANY QUICK AND EASY ORANGE ANNUALS TO CHOOSE FROM, SO WHY NOT HAVE FUN AND EXPERIMENT WITH ORANGE AS A COLOR BEFORE COMMITTING YOURSELF TO MORE LONG-TERM PLANTINGS.

LEFT: *Orange French marigolds and rudbeckias make a sunny arrangement.*

BACK

10

LATIN NAME: *Thunbergia gregorii* syn. *T. gibsonii*
COMMON NAME: Known by Latin name
ALTERNATIVES: *T. alata*
DESCRIPTION: Tender, woody-stemmed climber grown from seed each year and requiring support for its twining stems. Evergreen foliage, triangular in outline with winged stems and orange blooms.
HEIGHT AND SPREAD: 10ft (3m)
BLOOMING PERIOD: Summer
SOIL: Fertile, well-drained.

LATIN NAME: *Thunbergia alata*
COMMON NAME: Black-eyed Susan
ALTERNATIVES: *T. gregorii*
DESCRIPTION: Climber with twining stems requiring support. Eye-catching orange blooms with dark brown centers which appear black, hence common name. Grow from seed sown in spring.
HEIGHT AND SPREAD: 10ft (3m)
BLOOMING PERIOD: Early summer to early autumn
SOIL: Fertile, well-drained.

MIDDLE

5-8

LATIN NAME: *Fritillaria imperialis*
COMMON NAME: Crown imperial
ALTERNATIVES: 'Orange Brilliant'
DESCRIPTION: Bulb producing stems clothed in whorls of glossy, light green lanceolate leaves and terminating in a cluster of large, hanging bells with protruding stamens crowned by a tuft of leaves.
HEIGHT AND SPREAD: 3–5 × 1½ft (0.9–1.5 × 0.45m)
BLOOMING PERIOD: Spring
SOIL: Fertile, humus-rich, well-drained.

5-9

LATIN NAME: *Lilium* 'Rosefire'
COMMON NAME: Hybrid lily
ALTERNATIVES: 'Enchantment'
DESCRIPTION: Bulb with stems clothed in lanceolate leaves. Toward the stem tips are upward facing, star-shaped blooms which are orange-red with yellow throats. As many as 20 blooms per stem.
HEIGHT AND SPREAD: 3ft (0.9m)
BLOOMING PERIOD: Early summer
SOIL: Fertile, well-drained, humus-rich.

FRONT

LATIN NAME: *Hippeastrum* 'Pamela' syn. *Amaryllis* 'Pamella'
COMMON NAME: Amaryllis
ALTERNATIVES: 'Orange Sovereign'
DESCRIPTION: Bulb with stout stems carrying several very large, outward-facing trumpet blooms of deep orange-red at the top. Strap-like foliage. Lift bulbs to dry off when leaves die down and re-plant in autumn.
HEIGHT AND SPREAD: 12–20 × 12in (30–50 × 30cm)
BLOOMING PERIOD: Late winter to spring
SOIL: Well-drained.

9-10

LATIN NAME: *Dimorphotheca aurantiaca* syn. *D. sinuata*
COMMON NAME: Star of the Veldt
ALTERNATIVES: 'Hybrid Mixture,' 'Salmon Queen,' 'Giant Orange'
DESCRIPTION: Hardy annual producing a mass of large, daisy blooms in shades of cream through pale peach to vibrant orange highlighted by a black ring round the center. Flowers close in cloudy weather.
HEIGHT AND SPREAD: 6–15 × 12in (15–38 × 30cm)
BLOOMING PERIOD: Early summer to early autumn
SOIL: Any well-drained. Tolerates thin, poor soils.

LATIN NAME: *Abutilon pictum* 'Thompsonii,' syn. *A. striatum*
COMMON NAME: Known by Latin name
ALTERNATIVES: A. 'Kentish Belle' Giant Hybrids
DESCRIPTION: Evergreen shrub of upright habit with large, 3–5 lobed leaves heavily mottled yellow. Pendant, bell-shaped blooms in rich orange, veined red. Makes a striking "dot" plant and gives a sub-tropical feel to borders.
HEIGHT AND SPREAD: 7 × 6ft (2.2 × 1.8m)
BLOOMING PERIOD: Summer to autumn
SOIL: Fertile, well-drained.

9-10

5-7

LATIN NAME: *Lonicera × tellmanniana*
COMMON NAME: Tellman honeysuckle
ALTERNATIVES: L. × brownii cultivars, L. × heckrotii 'Goldflame'
DESCRIPTION: Climber with twining stems clothed in gray-green leaves. The clusters of coppery-yellow tubular flowers with protruding stamens open from red-tinged buds. Susceptible to mildew.
HEIGHT AND SPREAD: 15 × 15ft (4.6 × 4.6m)
BLOOMING PERIOD: Early to mid-summer
SOIL: Fertile, humus-rich, moisture-retentive. Mulch to keep roots cool.

5-9

LATIN NAME: *Euphororbia griffithii*
COMMON NAME: Spurge, milkweed
ALTERNATIVES: 'Fireglow', 'Dixter'
DESCRIPTION: Herbaceous perennial with upright stems clothed in lanceolate leaves with a red midrib. In some cultivars foliage is red-tinted. Clusters of tiny flowers with orange-red bracts. Irritant sap.
HEIGHT AND SPREAD: 36 × 20in (90 × 50cm)
BLOOMING PERIOD: Early summer
SOIL: Fertile, moisture-retentive.

3-10

LATIN NAME: *Trollius × cultorum* 'Orange Princess'
COMMON NAME: Globeflower
ALTERNATIVES: 'Prichard's Giant,' T. chinensis, T. c. 'Imperial Orange'
DESCRIPTION: Herbaceous perennial with deeply divided leaves and slender, branched stems carrying the globe-shaped, semi-double blooms. Best on retentive to damp soil.
HEIGHT AND SPREAD: 36 × 18in (90 × 45cm)
BLOOMING PERIOD: Spring
SOIL: Moisture-retentive to damp.

5-10

LATIN NAME: *Helianthemum nummularium* cultivar
COMMON NAME: Rock rose, sun rose
ALTERNATIVES: 'Fire Dragon,' 'Ben Nevis,' 'Ben More'
DESCRIPTION: Evergreen shrub with low, dome-shaped to spreading habit with gray-green leaves and clusters of buds opening to blooms of deep orange-red. Trim lightly when flowering finishes.
HEIGHT AND SPREAD: 9–12 × 18in (23–30 × 45cm)
BLOOMING PERIOD: Late spring to mid-summer
SOIL: Well-drained.

LATIN NAME: *Calendula officinalis* 'Touch of Red'
COMMON NAME: Calendula, pot marigold
ALTERNATIVES: 'Gypsy Festival,' 'Art Shades,' 'Fiesta Gitana,' 'Radio'
DESCRIPTION: Hardy annual with oblong to oval leaves and stiff flower stems topped with semi-double daisy flowers in orange, lemon and cream with red and dark chocolate center. Deadhead regularly.
HEIGHT AND SPREAD: 16 × 12in (40 × 30cm)
BLOOMING PERIOD: Early summer to early autumn (may be longer)
SOIL: Well-drained. Very hot, dry conditions may promote mildew.

BACK

LATIN NAME: *Buddleja globosa* syn. Buddleia globosa

COMMON NAME: Globe butterfly bush, Orange butterfly bush

ALTERNATIVES: *B. × weyeriana*, *B. × w.* 'Sungold' and 'Golden Glow'

DESCRIPTION: Semi-evergreen shrub of large proportion with deep-green pointed leaves and unusual spherical heads in clusters. Fragrant. Benefits from pruning after flowering or for *B. × weyeriana*, in spring.

HEIGHT AND SPREAD: 10 × 10ft (3 × 3m)

BLOOMING PERIOD: Early summer

SOIL: Any well-drained soil.

7-9

LATIN NAME: *Lonicera × brownii*

COMMON NAME: Scarlet trumpet honeysuckle, Brown's honeysuckle

ALTERNATIVES: 'Fuchsioides'

DESCRIPTION: Twining climber with oval leaves in pairs and clusters of tubular orange-red flowers. Little fragrance. Like most honeysuckles, tends to flower at the top of its support. May suffer from aphids or mildew.

HEIGHT AND SPREAD: 14 × 14ft (4.3 × 4.3m)

BLOOMING PERIOD: Early summer to early autumn

SOIL: Any well-drained soil.

5-10

MIDDLE

5-10

LATIN NAME: *Geum* 'Fire Opal'

COMMON NAME: Known by Latin name

ALTERNATIVES: 'Princess Juliana,' 'Dolly North'

DESCRIPTION: Herbaceous perennial making mounds of lobed leaves with long branched flower stems carrying clusters of double blooms. Regular division keeps plants young and enhances flowering.

HEIGHT AND SPREAD: 32 × 18in (80 × 45cm)

BLOOMING PERIOD: Early summer (to autumn in good conditions)

SOIL: Rich, moisture-retentive but well-drained.

LATIN NAME: *Coreopsis tinctoria*

COMMON NAME: Tickseed, Plains coreopsis

ALTERNATIVES: None

DESCRIPTION: Hardy annual with narrow, pointed leaves and finely-branched flower stems carrying a profusion of disk-shaped single flowers with a prominent central zone. Dwarf forms available.

HEIGHT AND SPREAD: 24–36 × 18in (60–90 × 45cm)

BLOOMING PERIOD: Late spring to early autumn

SOIL: Any well-drained, avoiding heavy clay.

FRONT

9-10

LATIN NAME: *Verbena hybrida* 'Peaches and Cream'

COMMON NAME: Known by Latin name

ALTERNATIVES: None

DESCRIPTION: Tender perennial, usually raised from seed with small, toothed leaves and domed heads of small flowers shaded pale pinky-orange and cream. Verbenas can suffer from mildew.

HEIGHT AND SPREAD: 8 × 12in (20 × 30cm)

BLOOMING PERIOD: Early summer to mid-autumn

SOIL: Fertile, moisture-retentive.

10

LATIN NAME: *Begonia* Tuberhybrida

COMMON NAME: Tuberous-rooted begonia

ALTERNATIVES: Non-stop F1

DESCRIPTION: Tender perennial with succulent, brittle stems and broad, tapering leaves with serrated edges. Male flowers large, double with delicate petals, flanking female buds best removed.

HEIGHT AND SPREAD: 9–18 × 12in (22–45 × 30cm)

BLOOMING PERIOD: Early summer to early autumn

SOIL: Rich, moisture-retentive.

LATIN NAME: *Eremurus stenophyllus*
COMMON NAME: Foxtail lily
ALTERNATIVES: *E. stenophyllus* subsp. *stenophyllus*, 'Shelford Hybrids'
DESCRIPTION: Bulbous plant, spectacular in bloom, producing solid, tapering spires of tiny yellow flowers tinged orange. Color changes to burnt orange as the flower matures. Basal rosette of leaves dies away before flowering.
HEIGHT AND SPREAD: 5 × 2ft (1.5 × 0.6m)
BLOOMING PERIOD: Summer
SOIL: Well-drained, especially over winter to increase chances of survival.

6-9

7-10

LATIN NAME: *Campsis grandiflora*
COMMON NAME: Trumpet creeper
ALTERNATIVES: *C. radicans, C. × tagliabuana* 'Madame Galen'
DESCRIPTION: Twining climber with divided leaves and orange-red, trumpet-shaped blooms in clusters. In cool climates will only flower well if grown against a sun-baked wall.
HEIGHT AND SPREAD: 16–30 × 16–30ft (4.8–9.1 × 4.8–9.1m)
BLOOMING PERIOD: Late summer to early autumn
SOIL: Rich, deep, well-cultivated loam.

5-9

LATIN NAME: *Rosa* 'Southampton'
COMMON NAME: Cluster-flowered (floribunda) bush rose
ALTERNATIVES: 'Glenfiddich,' 'Elizabeth of Glamis,' 'Fragrant Delight'
DESCRIPTION: Bush rose with apricot petals which are flushed red. Good scent. Glossy leaves. As with all repeat-flowering roses, deadhead regularly to encourage further flowering.
HEIGHT AND SPREAD: 40 × 30in (100 × 75cm)
BLOOMING PERIOD: Spring to mid-autumn
SOIL: Rich, moisture-retentive. Use organic mulch on light soils.

5-9

LATIN NAME: *Rosa* 'L'Oreal Trophy'
COMMON NAME: Large-flowered (hybrid tea) bush rose
ALTERNATIVES: 'Just Joey,' 'Alpine Sunset'
DESCRIPTION: Bush rose of upright habit with large, well-shaped double blooms which have some scent. Glossy foliage. Deadhead regularly to encourage further flowering.
HEIGHT AND SPREAD: 48 × 30in (120 × 75cm)
BLOOMING PERIOD: Spring to mid-autumn
SOIL: Rich, moisture-retentive. Use organic mulch on light soils.

LATIN NAME: *Tagetes erecta* variety
COMMON NAME: African marigold
ALTERNATIVES: F1 hybrid series e.g. Marvel, Perfection, Inca, Zenith
DESCRIPTION: Half-hardy annual of stiffly erect habit with large, deeply divided, dark green leaves and globular flower heads. Even with the sterile Afro-French marigolds it is best to deadhead.
HEIGHT AND SPREAD: 18–36 × 18in (45–91 × 45cm)
BLOOMING PERIOD: Summer
SOIL: Any well-drained.

LATIN NAME: *Tropaeolum majus* 'Alaska Mixed'
COMMON NAME: Variegated nasturtium
ALTERNATIVES: None
DESCRIPTION: Hardy annual with spreading habit. Almost circular, white-marbled leaves and large, trumpet-shaped, spurred blooms in various shades of orange and yellow. Susceptible to caterpillar attack.
HEIGHT AND SPREAD: 12 × 12in (30 × 30cm)
BLOOMING PERIOD: Summer to early autumn
SOIL: Well-drained, not too rich otherwise flowering is very poor.

51

BACK

LATIN NAME: *Tecoma capensis* syn. *Tecomaria capensis, Bignonia capensis*
COMMON NAME: Cape honeysuckle
ALTERNATIVES: *Bignonia capreolata*
DESCRIPTION: Tender climber of scrambling habit, evergreen, with dark green, rounded leaflets with serrated edges. Showy orange-red tubular flowers with flared mouths.
HEIGHT AND SPREAD: 6–10ft (1.8–3m)
BLOOMING PERIOD: Spring to summer
SOIL: Fertile, well-drained.

9-10

5-7

LATIN NAME: *Colutea × media*
COMMON NAME: Bladder senna
ALTERNATIVES: 'Copper Beauty'
DESCRIPTION: Shrub of open habit with pinnate leaves and pea-like flowers of yellow, tinged coppery-orange. Attractive, red-tinged, bladder-like seed pods of papery texture appear after flowers.
HEIGHT AND SPREAD: 10 × 10ft (3 × 3m)
BLOOMING PERIOD: Summer
SOIL: Well-drained.

MIDDLE

5-9

LATIN NAME: *Lilium* 'Melon Time'
COMMON NAME: Hybrid lily
ALTERNATIVES: Hybrid lilies e.g. Mid-century hybrids, Bellingham hybrids
DESCRIPTION: Bulb with tall, unbranched stems covered in lanceolate leaves and bearing soft, tangerine-orange, star-shaped blooms. Mulch in autumn to provide winter protection in colder areas.
HEIGHT AND SPREAD: 4 × 1ft (1.2 × 0.3m)
BLOOMING PERIOD: Summer
SOIL: Fertile, humus-rich, well-drained.

5-9

LATIN NAME: *Lilium* 'Staccato'
COMMON NAME: Hybrid lily
ALTERNATIVES: 'Enchantment'
DESCRIPTION: Bulb, early flowering with upright-pointing flowers produced singly or in clusters, deep orange, star-shaped. Stems clothed in lanceolate green leaves.
HEIGHT AND SPREAD: 3–4 × 1ft (0.9–1.2 × 0.3m)
BLOOMING PERIOD: Summer
SOIL: Fertile, humus-rich, well-drained.

FRONT

LATIN NAME: *Dorotheanthus bellidiformis* syn. *Mesembryanthemum*
COMMON NAME: Ice plant, Livingstone daisy
ALTERNATIVES: Single-color varieties, Magic Carpet Hybrids
DESCRIPTION: Half-hardy annual making low, carpeting growth of succulent stems and fleshy leaves. In a hot, dry site plants become smothered in large, fine-petalled daisy flowers.
HEIGHT AND SPREAD: 4–6 × 8in (10–15 × 20cm)
BLOOMING PERIOD: Early summer to early autumn
SOIL: Light, well-drained, not too rich.

8-10

LATIN NAME: *Gerbera jamesonii* hybrids
COMMON NAME: Gerbera, African daisy, Transvaal daisy
ALTERNATIVES: Duplex Hybrids, Festival Hybrids
DESCRIPTION: Half-hardy perennial with a rosette of jagged-edged leaves and very large, solid daisy flowers on long, single stems. Propagate from cuttings from side shoots in summer or division.
HEIGHT AND SPREAD: 24 × 24in (60 × 60cm)
BLOOMING PERIOD: Spring to summer
SOIL: Light, well-drained.

LATIN NAME: *Eccremocarpus scaber* 'Tresco Hybrids'
COMMON NAME: Chilean glory flower
ALTERNATIVES: *E. scaber*
DESCRIPTION: Tender semi-evergreen climber, grown as an annual in colder regions with pinnate leaves and clusters of tubular, orange-red flowers. Climbs by tendrils. May be allowed to scramble over large shrubs.
HEIGHT AND SPREAD: 6–10 × 6–10ft (1.8–3 × 1.8–3m)
BLOOMING PERIOD: Summer to early autumn
SOIL: Fertile, well-drained, humus-rich.

9-10

8-10

LATIN NAME: *Ipomoea lobata* syn. *I. versicolor*, syn. *Mina lobata*
COMMON NAME: Cypress vine
ALTERNATIVES: None
DESCRIPTION: Evergreen twining climber usually grown as an annual, with large, three-lobed leaves and unusual blooms composed of one-sided spikes which turn from red through cream as they age.
HEIGHT AND SPREAD: 15ft (4.5m)
BLOOMING PERIOD: Summer
SOIL: Fertile, humus-rich and moisture-retentive.

5-9

LATIN NAME: *Lilium* cultivar
COMMON NAME: Hybrid lily
ALTERNATIVES: Hybrid lilies e.g. Mid-century hybrids, Bellingham hybrids
DESCRIPTION: Bulb with upward-facing star-shaped blooms of palest creamy-orange with dark speckles. Stems clothed in lanceolate green leaves.
HEIGHT AND SPREAD: 3–4 × 1ft (0.9–1.2 × 0.3m)
BLOOMING PERIOD: Summer
SOIL: Fertile, humus-rich, well-drained.

5-9

LATIN NAME: *Lilium* 'Enchantment'
COMMON NAME: Hybrid lily
ALTERNATIVES: Hybrid lilies e.g. Mid-century hybrids, Bellingham hybrids
DESCRIPTION: Bulb with upward stems well-clothed in lanceolate leaves and topped by large, clear orange, star-shaped blooms with reflexed petals. Darker speckling and dark, contrasting anthers.
HEIGHT AND SPREAD: 2–3 × 1ft (0.6–0.9 × 0.3m)
BLOOMING PERIOD: Summer
SOIL: Fertile, humus-rich, well-drained.

10

LATIN NAME: *Clivia miniata*
COMMON NAME: Known by Latin name
ALTERNATIVES: 'Flame,' 'French Hybrid'
DESCRIPTION: Tender rhizomatous perennial forming evergreen, strap-shaped leaves and stout stems topped by 10–20 trumpet-shaped blooms. Water well summer and autumn, less at other times.
HEIGHT AND SPREAD: 16 × 12–24in (40 × 30–60cm)
BLOOMING PERIOD: Spring to summer
SOIL: Well-drained.

LATIN NAME: *Mimulus × hybridus* 'Malibu Orange'
COMMON NAME: Monkey flower, monkey musk
ALTERNATIVES: F1 hybrids, Calypso Hybrids, 'Mandarin'
DESCRIPTION: Half-hardy annual with paired leaves with serrated edges. Flowers velvety-orange with deeper speckling in the throat.
HEIGHT AND SPREAD: 6–12 × 9in (15–30 × 23cm)
BLOOMING PERIOD: Early summer to mid-autumn
SOIL: Fertile, humus-rich, moisture-retentive.

ORANGE

BACK

7-10

LATIN NAME: *Stipa gigantea*
COMMON NAME: Golden oats. Avoid in fire-prone areas.
ALTERNATIVES: *Deschampsia caespitosa* 'Golden Veil'
DESCRIPTION: Evergreen ornamental grass which makes a solid clump of narrow, arching, grayish green leaves overtopped by long elegant flower stems bearing arching sprays of oat-like flowers.
HEIGHT AND SPREAD: 6 × 3ft (1.8 × 0.9m)
BLOOMING PERIOD: Summer
SOIL: Well-drained.

9-10

LATIN NAME: *Hibiscus rosa-sinensis* 'Loe Orange'
COMMON NAME: Rose of China, Chinese hibiscus
ALTERNATIVES: 'Celia,' Orange Pride'
DESCRIPTION: Evergreen shrub or small tree with glossy, deep green, oval leaves with a toothed edge and showy funnel-shaped blooms of pure tangerine-orange.
HEIGHT AND SPREAD: 5–10 × 5–10ft (1.5–3 × 1.5–3m)
BLOOMING PERIOD: Spring to autumn
SOIL: Fertile, well-drained.

MIDDLE

LATIN NAME: *Rosa* 'Whisky Mac' syn. *Rosa* 'Whisky'
COMMON NAME: Large-flowered or hybrid tea bush rose
ALTERNATIVES: 'Just Joey,' 'Fragrant Delight'
DESCRIPTION: Bush rose with large double amber-yellow blooms. Scented. The flowers are set off well by the new leaf and shoot growth, which is deep red-tinged.
HEIGHT AND SPREAD: 30 × 24in (0.9 × 0.6m)
BLOOMING PERIOD: Summer to autumn (from spring in mild areas)
SOIL: Fertile, well-drained, humus-rich, moisture-retentive.

5-9

LATIN NAME: *Rosa* 'Julia's Rose'
COMMON NAME: Large-flowered or hybrid tea bush rose
ALTERNATIVES: 'Buff Beauty'
DESCRIPTION: Bush rose with large double blooms of an unusual tan overlaid pink. Some fragrance. The growth is not especially robust, and the shrub is open and sparsely-branched.
HEIGHT AND SPREAD: 30 × 24in (75 × 60cm)
BLOOMING PERIOD: Summer to autumn (from spring in mild areas)
SOIL: Fertile, well-drained, humus-rich, moisture-retentive, good on clay.

5-9

FRONT

5-9

LATIN NAME: *Rosa* 'Shine On'
COMMON NAME: Patio rose
ALTERNATIVES: 'Rainbow's End,' 'Orange Honey,' 'Darling Flame'
DESCRIPTION: Very low-growing rose with small, double blooms of rich orange. Suitable for planting at the front of a border, as a single planting for a low bed, or in containers.
HEIGHT AND SPREAD: 12 × 12in (30 × 30cm)
BLOOMING PERIOD: Summer to autumn (from spring in mild areas)
SOIL: Fertile, well-drained, humus-rich, moisture-retentive.

3-10

LATIN NAME: *Gaillardia* 'Goblin' syn. 'Kobold'
COMMON NAME: Blanket flower, gaillardia
ALTERNATIVES: 'Mandarin,' 'Dazzler'
DESCRIPTION: Short-lived perennial with bold circular blooms of deep orange-red edged yellow. Gray-green, lance-shaped leaves. Needs dividing every three years.
HEIGHT AND SPREAD: 9 × 12in (23 × 30cm)
BLOOMING PERIOD: Spring to mid-autumn
SOIL: Light, well-drained.

LATIN NAME: *Rosa* 'Schoolgirl'
COMMON NAME: Climbing rose
ALTERNATIVES: 'Breath of Llfe,' 'Compassion,' 'Joseph's Coat'
DESCRIPTION: Climber with stiff, upright branches and large, sparse leaves. The large, double blooms are a lovely apricot shade and fragrant. Deadhead and tie stems into supports as they grow.
HEIGHT AND SPREAD: 10 × 8ft (3 × 2.5m)
BLOOMING PERIOD: Summer to autumn (from spring in mild areas)
SOIL: Fertile, well-drained, humus-rich, and moisture-retentive.

LATIN NAME: *Rosa* 'Golden Celebration'
COMMON NAME: English rose, shrub rose
ALTERNATIVES: 'Graham Thomas'
DESCRIPTION: Rose of bushy habit bearing large, old-fashioned-looking double blooms of amber-yellow. Lovely for planting en masse with soft blue and lilac herbaceous perennials and annuals.
HEIGHT AND SPREAD: 6 × 4ft (2 × 1.2m)
BLOOMING PERIOD: Summer (from spring in mild areas)
SOIL: Fertile, well-drained, humus-rich, moisture-retentive.

LATIN NAME: *Rosa* 'Just Joey'
COMMON NAME: Large-flowered or hybrid tea bush rose
ALTERNATIVES: 'Fragrant Delight'
DESCRIPTION: Bush rose of vigorous upright habit with beautifully shaped, large double blooms in soft orange blended with pink. Fragrant. Good glossy, dark green leaves. Sparse habit.
HEIGHT AND SPREAD: 30 × 24in (75 × 60cm)
BLOOMING PERIOD: Summer to autumn (from spring in mild areas)
SOIL: Fertile, well-drained, humus-rich, moisture-retentive.

LATIN NAME: *Digitalis ferruginea*
COMMON NAME: Rusty foxglove
ALTERNATIVES: *D. purpurea* 'Foxy,' *D. × mertonensis, D. parviflora*
DESCRIPTION: Short-lived perennial usually grown as a biennial with upright spikes of soft orangey-brown and yellow tubular blooms. Coarse, oval leaves form a basal rosette.
HEIGHT AND SPREAD: 3–4 × 1ft (0.9–1.2 × 0.3m)
BLOOMING PERIOD: Mid-summer
SOIL: Well-drained but humus-rich and moist.

LATIN NAME: *Rudbeckia* 'Marmalade'
COMMON NAME: Coneflower
ALTERNATIVES: 'Rustic Dwarfs,' 'Goldilocks,' 'Becky,' 'Toto'
DESCRIPTION: Half-hardy annual useful for late summer color and as a gap filler in newly planted borders. Plentiful lance-shaped leaves and wiry, upright stems bearing orange daisies with a central black cone.
HEIGHT AND SPREAD: 14–18 × 24in (35–45 × 60cm)
BLOOMING PERIOD: Summer to mid-autumn
SOIL: Well-drained but moisture-retentive.

LATIN NAME: *Zinnia* 'Peter Pan Series'
COMMON NAME: Known by Latin name
ALTERNATIVES: 'Star' series, 'Hobgoblin'
DESCRIPTION: Dwarf-growing zinnia with richly colored, fully double blooms on stiff, upright stems. Oval to lance-shaped leaves. Susceptible to mildew.
HEIGHT AND SPREAD: 10 × 6in (25 × 15cm)
BLOOMING PERIOD: Mid-summer to mid-autumn
SOIL: Well-drained but humus-rich.

ORANGE

BACK

6-10

LATIN NAME: *Phygelius capensis* 'Coccineus'
COMMON NAME: Cape figwort
ALTERNATIVES: *P. capensis*, 'Winchester Fanfare'
DESCRIPTION: Evergreen or semi-evergreen perennial with dark green triangular-shaped leaves and long flower stems bearing tubular, orange-red blooms with a yellow throat. Taller grown against a wall.
HEIGHT AND SPREAD: 4–5 × 6ft (1.2–1.5 × 1.8m)
BLOOMING PERIOD: Mid-summer to early autumn
SOIL: Any well-drained.

LATIN NAME: *Anigozanthos flavidus*
COMMON NAME: Kangaroo paw
ALTERNATIVES: *Anigozanthos* hybrids
DESCRIPTION: Herbaceous perennial with a basal clump of long, narrow leaves and tall, branched flower stems bearing many furry tubular blooms attractive to birds in their native country. Cut back spent blooms for reflowering.
HEIGHT AND SPREAD: 4 × 1½ft (1.2 × 0.45m)
BLOOMING PERIOD: Spring and summer
SOIL: Well-drained but moisture-retentive.

9-10

MIDDLE

5-9

LATIN NAME: *Rosa* 'Troika' syn. 'Royal Dane'
COMMON NAME: Large-flowered (hybrid tea) bush rose
ALTERNATIVES: 'Alpine Sunset,' 'Apricot Silk,' 'Sheila's Perfume'
DESCRIPTION: Bush rose with a strong, bushy habit and glossy foliage. The single blooms are large, fully double, mainly orange-red with pink and yellow shading, becoming paler with age. Good scent.
HEIGHT AND SPREAD: 36 × 30in (90 × 76cm) to 4ft (1.2m) in Australia
BLOOMING PERIOD: Late spring to mid-autumn
SOIL: Fertile, moisture-retentive and humus-rich. Does well on clay.

7-10

LATIN NAME: *Alstroemeria aurea* syn. *A. aurantiaca*
COMMON NAME: Peruvian lily
ALTERNATIVES: 'Dover Orange,' 'Orange King,' Princess hybrid series
DESCRIPTION: Herbaceous perennial with wiry stems and narrow leaves. Lily-like blooms of strong orange, speckled at the throat. Rootstock can be invasive. Excellent hybrids in a wide range of shades.
HEIGHT AND SPREAD: 3 × 1ft (0.9 × 0.3m)
BLOOMING PERIOD: Summer
SOIL: Well-drained.

FRONT

9-10

LATIN NAME: *Arctotis* × *hybrida* 'Apricot'
COMMON NAME: African daisy, aurora daisy
ALTERNATIVES: 'Harlequin Mixed,' 'Large-flowered Hybrids'
DESCRIPTION: Tender perennial making rosettes of silvery-green, cut foliage. Stems bear daisy flowers in apricot with a darker orange center and black ring which close in shade. Grow from cuttings.
HEIGHT AND SPREAD: 12–18 × 9–18in (30–45 × 23–45cm)
BLOOMING PERIOD: Summer
SOIL: Well-drained.

9-10

LATIN NAME: *Arctotis* × *hybrida* 'Flame'
COMMON NAME: African daisy, aurora daisy
ALTERNATIVES: 'Harlequin Mixed,' 'Large-flowered Hybrids'
DESCRIPTION: Tender perennial making rosettes of silvery-green, cut foliage. Single stems bear large daisy flowers in tangerine with a contrasting gray center which close in shade. Grow from cuttings.
HEIGHT AND SPREAD: 12–18 × 9–18in (30–45 × 23–45cm)
BLOOMING PERIOD: Summer
SOIL: Well-drained.

BACK

LATIN NAME: *Macleaya microcarpa*
COMMON NAME: Plume poppy, bocconia
ALTERNATIVES: Kelway's 'Coral Plume' (syn. 'Coral Plume')
DESCRIPTION: Herbaceous perennial with invasive spreading roots. Large, rounded leaves with a beautifully cut edge in gray-green with a gray-white underside. Tall plumes of tiny buff or orangy-pink flowers.
HEIGHT AND SPREAD: 7 × 3ft (2.1 × 0.9m)
BLOOMING PERIOD: Summer
SOIL: Well-drained.

❄ 4-10

LATIN NAME: *Desfontainia spinosa* 'Harold Comber'
COMMON NAME: Known by Latin name
ALTERNATIVES: *D. spinosa*
DESCRIPTION: Evergreen shrub of upright habit with dark green, holly-like leaves and small, tubular blooms of scarlet-red to orange tipped yellow. Has slow growth rate and takes years to reach height given.
HEIGHT AND SPREAD: 5½ × 4ft (1.6 × 1.2m)
BLOOMING PERIOD: Mid-summer
SOIL: Acid, well-drained, humus-rich.

💧 8-10

MIDDLE

❄ 5-8

LATIN NAME: *Lilium* 'Gran Paradiso'
COMMON NAME: Lily hybrid
ALTERNATIVES: Hybrid cultivars e.g. Bellingham hybrids
DESCRIPTION: Bulb with upright stems clothed in green, lanceolate leaves. Large, star-shaped blooms of deep orange-red borne singly or in umbels at the top of the stems.
HEIGHT AND SPREAD: 3 × 1ft (0.9 × 0.3m)
BLOOMING PERIOD: Summer
SOIL: Fertile, well-drained, humus-rich.

❄ 3-10

LATIN NAME: *Hemerocallis* 'Penelope Vestey'
COMMON NAME: Daylily
ALTERNATIVES: 'Stoke Poges,' 'Varsity,' 'Luxury Lace,' 'Doll House'
DESCRIPTION: Herbaceous perennial making a clump of long, arching leaves and tall branched, wiry stems bearing trumpet-shaped blooms of very pale peach with broad, ruffled petals. Excellent spring foliage.
HEIGHT AND SPREAD: 36 × 24in (90 ×60cm)
BLOOMING PERIOD: Mid- to late summer
SOIL: Fertile, moisture-retentive to moist.

FRONT

💧 9-10

LATIN NAME: *Calceolaria* 'Kentish Hero'
COMMON NAME: Slipper flower, calceolaria
ALTERNATIVES: 'Camden Hero,' 'John Innes'
DESCRIPTION: Tender perennial with wiry stems bearing small, "pouched" flowers in bright orange darkening with age. Basal clump of leaves broadly oval in shape and evergreen.
HEIGHT AND SPREAD: 6–8 × 10–12in (15–20 × 25–30cm)
BLOOMING PERIOD: Summer (from spring in Australia)
SOIL: Well-drained, humus-rich.

LATIN NAME: *Eschscholzia californica*
COMMON NAME: California poppy
ALTERNATIVES: 'Dali,' 'Apricot Blush,' 'Apricot Chiffon,' 'Mikado'
DESCRIPTION: Hardy annual with ferny gray-green foliage in tufted clumps and slender stems bearing cup-shaped four-petalled blooms. Self-seeds. Dislikes root disturbance. Deadhead to prolong flowering.
HEIGHT AND SPREAD: 6–12 × 6in (15–30 × 15cm)
BLOOMING PERIOD: Early summer to early autumn
SOIL: Well-drained. Flowers best on relatively poor soil.

BACK

LATIN NAME: *Lilium lancifolium* var. Splendens syn. *L. tigrinum* 'Splendens'
COMMON NAME: Tiger lily
ALTERNATIVES: *L. lancifolium, L. superbum*
DESCRIPTION: Bulb with tall, unbranched stems and slender foliage. Many blooms per stem. The petals are spotted and strongly reflexed.
HEIGHT AND SPREAD: 2–5+ft (60–150cm)
BLOOMING PERIOD: Late summer to early autumn
SOIL: Any fertile soil, preferably acid but will tolerate lime.

LATIN NAME: *Helianthus annus* 'Velvet Queen'
COMMON NAME: Sunflower
ALTERNATIVES: 'Autumn Beauty'
DESCRIPTION: Half-hardy annual with tall, stout stems clothed in broad, somewhat coarse foliage and topped with very large daisy flowers. Makes an interesting change from the usual yellow varieties.
HEIGHT AND SPREAD: 5 × 1½–2ft (150 × 45–60cm)
BLOOMING PERIOD: Summer to early autumn
SOIL: Any well-drained.

MIDDLE

LATIN NAME: *Hemerocallis* 'Stoke Poges'
COMMON NAME: Day Lily
ALTERNATIVES: 'May Colven,' 'Orange Bright,' 'Orange Tex'
DESCRIPTION: Herbaceous perennial making spreading clumps of long, narrow arching leaves. Slender flower stems bear loose clusters of flared, trumpet-shaped blooms which each last only a day.
HEIGHT AND SPREAD: 2½ × 2ft (75 × 60cm)
BLOOMING PERIOD: Summer
SOIL: Fertile, moisture-retentive.

LATIN NAME: *Hemerocallis* cultivar
COMMON NAME: Day Lily
ALTERNATIVES: 'May Colven', 'Penelope Vesty,' 'Orange Velvet'
DESCRIPTION: Herbaceous perennial making spreading clumps of long, narrow arching leaves, especially attractive in spring. Flower clusters open over time with each bloom lasting a day.
HEIGHT AND SPREAD: 3–5 × 2–3ft (90–150 × 60–90cm)
BLOOMING PERIOD: Summer
SOIL: Fertile, moisture-retentive.

FRONT

LATIN NAME: *Eschscholzia californica* 'Red Chief'
COMMON NAME: California poppy
ALTERNATIVES: 'Dalli,' 'Mikado,' 'Apricot Chiffon,' 'Orange King'
DESCRIPTION: Hardy annual producing loose hummocks of fine, ferny gray-green foliage and many poppy-like flowers. Will self-seed and establish in cracks in paving and gravel.
HEIGHT AND SPREAD: 6–12 ×12in (15–30 × 30cm)
BLOOMING PERIOD: Early summer to early autumn
SOIL: Well-drained to dry. Avoid rich soils.

LATIN NAME: *Zinnia angustifolia* 'Star Orange'
COMMON NAME: Known by Latin name
ALTERNATIVES: Star Series
DESCRIPTION: Half-hardy annual differing from the usual large-flowered types in making spreading domes suitable for groundcover. Prick out carefully as zinnias dislike root disturbance.
HEIGHT AND SPREAD: 13–15 ×12in (33–38 × 30cm)
BLOOMING PERIOD: Mid-summer to mid-autumn
SOIL: Any reasonable, well-drained soil.

LATIN NAME: *Helenium autumnale* cultivar
COMMON NAME: Common sneezeweed
ALTERNATIVES: 'Septemberfuchs,' 'Zimbelstern,' 'Moerheim Beauty'
DESCRIPTION: Herbaceous perennial with tall stems which are best supported. Many daisy-like heads produced, the flower characterized by a raised, dark brown knob. Needs frequent division.
HEIGHT AND SPREAD: 3–5 × 1½ft (90–150 × 45cm)
BLOOMING PERIOD: Late summer to early autumn
SOIL: Any reasonably fertile, avoiding waterlogged.

3-10

LATIN NAME: *Tithonia rotundifolia*
COMMON NAME: Annual tithonia, Mexican sunflower
ALTERNATIVES: 'Torch,' 'Goldfinger'
DESCRIPTION: Half-hardy annual making sturdy "dot" plants among low-growing bedding. Large oval-shaped leaves and dahlia-like flowers which are slightly scented. Stake taller plants.
HEIGHT AND SPREAD: 2½–5 × 1½–3ft (75–150 × 45–90cm)
BLOOMING PERIOD: Mid-summer to mid-autumn
SOIL: Well-drained.

LATIN NAME: *Crocosmia* hybrids
COMMON NAME: Montbretia
ALTERNATIVES: 'Severn Sunrise,' 'Emily McKenzie,' 'Jackanapes'
DESCRIPTION: Bulbous plant spreading beneath soil surface to form large clumps. Broad grassy leaves and arching spikes of tubular flowers widely flared at the mouth. Needs frequent division.
HEIGHT AND SPREAD: 24 × 9+in (60 × 23+cm)
BLOOMING PERIOD: Summer to late-autumn depending on cultivar
SOIL: Any moisture-retentive. Dislikes very heavy clay.

6-10

LATIN NAME: *Pyracantha* 'Orange Charmer'
COMMON NAME: Firethorn
ALTERNATIVES: 'Golden Charmer,' 'Orange Glow'
DESCRIPTION: Evergreen shrub with small, neat glossy leaves and very thorny stems. Creamy-white flowers in early summer with clusters of small, brightly colored berries ripening by early autumn. Suitable for wall-training.
HEIGHT AND SPREAD: 12 × 6ft (3.5 × 2m)
BLOOMING PERIOD: Early summer. Berries from early autumn
SOIL: Tolerates a wide range but best on moisture-retentive soil and does well on clay.

BACK

4-9

LATIN NAME: *Helichrysum bracteatum*
COMMON NAME: Strawflower, everlasting flower
ALTERNATIVES: Monstrosum series
DESCRIPTION: Hardy annual with stiff, barely-branched stems and many papery flower heads with blooms made up of colorful dry bracts. Excellent for cutting and drying for winter arrangements.
HEIGHT AND SPREAD: 1–3 ×1ft (30–90 × 30cm)
BLOOMING PERIOD: Spring to autumn
SOIL: Any well-drained.

MIDDLE

LATIN NAME: *Cuphea cyanaea*
COMMON NAME: Cigar flower
ALTERNATIVES: *Cuphea ignea, C. caeciliae*
DESCRIPTION: Tender, evergreen sub-shrub making a rounded bush with small leaves and masses of tubular blooms which are orange-red tipped yellow. Makes a long-flowering bedding plant.
HEIGHT AND SPREAD: 2 × 2ft (60 × 60cm)
BLOOMING PERIOD: Summer to mid-autumn
SOIL: Fertile, well-drained.

FRONT

9-10

59

BACK

❄ 3-10

LATIN NAME: *Helenium* 'Waldtraut'
COMMON NAME: Sneezeweed
ALTERNATIVES: 'Zimbelstern' ('Cymbal Star), 'Chipperfield Orange'
DESCRIPTION: Herbaceous perennial, clump-forming, bearing tall stems topped by sprays of daisy-like flowers, golden-yellow overlaid with brown and a brown central knob. Needs frequent division.
HEIGHT AND SPREAD: 3–4 × 1½ft (0.9–1.2 × 0.45–0.6m)
BLOOMING PERIOD: Mid-summer to late summer
SOIL: Any well-drained. Avoid winter waterlogging.

LATIN NAME: *Canna* hybrid
COMMON NAME: Indian shot
ALTERNATIVES: 'General Eisenhower,' 'La Gloire,' 'Semaphore,' 'Wyoming'
DESCRIPTION: Tender perennial making single stems clothed in large, banana-like leaves of green overlaid with purple-bronze. Exotic-looking, deep orange blooms produced late in the season. In cold-winter areas, lift rhizomes and store.
HEIGHT AND SPREAD: 3–4 × 1½ft (0.9–1.2 × 0.45–0.6m)
BLOOMING PERIOD: Mid-summer to autumn
SOIL: Fertile, humus-rich and moisture-retentive.

💧 8-10

MIDDLE

💧 9-10

LATIN NAME: *Dahlia* 'Bednall Beauty'
COMMON NAME: Dwarf bedding dahlia
ALTERNATIVES: 'Hamari Sunset'
DESCRIPTION: Tender tuberous perennial with stems clothed in bronze-purple leaves divided into oval leaflets. Very pale orange, rounded blooms. Deadhead regularly. In cold regions, lift after frost.
HEIGHT AND SPREAD: 2–3 × 1½–2ft (0.6–0.9 × 0.45–0.6m)
BLOOMING PERIOD: Mid-summer to autumn
SOIL: Fertile, well drained, humus-rich and moisture-retentive.

💧 9-10

LATIN NAME: *Dahlia* cultivar
COMMON NAME: Collerette dahlia
ALTERNATIVES: 'Chimborazo,' 'Dandy Mixed'
DESCRIPTION: Tender, tuberous perennial with leaves divided into oval leaflets. Flowers with outer ring of dark, reddish orange broad petals and inner circle of tufted petals in yellow around central disk.
HEIGHT AND SPREAD: 2–3 × 2ft (0.6–0.9 × 0.6–0.9m)
BLOOMING PERIOD: Mid-summer to autumn
SOIL: Fertile, well drained, humus-rich and moisture-retentive.

FRONT

💧 9-10

LATIN NAME: *Dahlia* 'David Howard'
COMMON NAME: Decorative miniature dahlia
ALTERNATIVES: 'Redskin Mixed,' 'Diablo Mixed'
DESCRIPTION: Tuberous perennial with upright stems and divided, bronze-purple foliage. Orange circular blooms with rounded petals. In cooler regions, lift tubers after first frost and store over winter.
HEIGHT AND SPREAD: 30 × 30in (76 × 76cm)
BLOOMING PERIOD: Mid-summer to autumn
SOIL: Fertile, well-drained, humus-rich and moisture-retentive.

💧 9-10

LATIN NAME: *Dahlia* cultivar
COMMON NAME: Decorative miniature dahlia
ALTERNATIVES: 'Rigoletto Mixed,' 'Figaro Mixed'
DESCRIPTION: Tuberous perennial with upright stems and large, green leaves. Double, circular blooms with rounded petals in soft orange. Deadhead regularly. In cold regions, lift tubers after frost.
HEIGHT AND SPREAD: 30 × 30in (75 × 75cm)
BLOOMING PERIOD: Mid-summer to autumn
SOIL: Fertile, well-drained, humus-rich and moisture-retentive.

☀ ● 9-10

LATIN NAME: *Dahlia* cultivar
COMMON NAME: Cactus or semi-cactus dahlia
ALTERNATIVES: 'Biddenham Sunset,' 'Highgate Torch,' 'Melissa'
DESCRIPTION: Tender tuberous perennial with oval leaflets and tall, branched stems bearing double flowers with long, pointed petals. In cold regions, lift after first frost, cut down stems and store tubers.
HEIGHT AND SPREAD: 3–4 × 3–4ft (0.9–1.2 × 0.9–1.2m)
BLOOMING PERIOD: Mid-summer to autumn
SOIL: Fertile, well-drained, humus-rich and moisture-retentive.

LATIN NAME: *Dahlia* 'Sweet Content'
COMMON NAME: Decorative dahlia
ALTERNATIVES: 'Frank Hornsey,' 'East Anglian'
DESCRIPTION: Tender tuberous perennial with oval leaflets and tall stems bearing small, ball-shaped flowers of very pale orange with red tinting at the ends of the petals and middle of bloom. In cold regions, lift after first frost.
HEIGHT AND SPREAD: 3–4 × 3–4ft (0.9–1.2 × 0.9–1.2m)
BLOOMING PERIOD: Mid-summer to autumn
SOIL: Fertile, well-drained, humus-rich and moisture-retentive.

☀ ● 9-10

LATIN NAME: *Stipa calamagrostis* syn. *Achnatherum calamagrostis*
COMMON NAME: Silver spear grass, stipa
ALTERNATIVES: *Deschampsia caespitosa* 'Gold Pendant' ('Goldgehänge'), *D. c.* 'Bronze Veil' ('Bronzeschleier')
DESCRIPTION: Evergreen ornamental grass making a basal clump of bluish green, leaves topped by arching panicles of amber-brown. Best displayed at the front of a border.
HEIGHT AND SPREAD: 2½–3 × 4ft (0.75–0.9 × 1.2m)
BLOOMING PERIOD: Summer to autumn/winter
SOIL: Well-drained.

☀ ❄ 6-9

☀ ❄ 7-10

LATIN NAME: *Dendranthema* 'Chestnut Talbot Parade'
COMMON NAME: Autumn-flowering chrysanthemum
ALTERNATIVES: 'Bronze Fairy,' 'Salmon Fairy,' 'Tangerine'
DESCRIPTION: Herbaceous perennial with upright, branched stems clothed in lobed leaves and bearing many small, deep orange, domed blooms with strongly reflexed petals.
HEIGHT AND SPREAD: 3 × 2ft (0.9 × 0.6m)
BLOOMING PERIOD: Late summer to autumn
SOIL: Fertile, well drained.

☀ ❄ 6-10

☀ ❄ 6-10

LATIN NAME: *Dendranthema* 'Aline'
COMMON NAME: Korean chrysanthemum
ALTERNATIVES: 'Bronze Elite,' 'Copper Nob,' 'Debbie,' 'Louise,' 'Sheila'
DESCRIPTION: Herbaceous perennial, hardier than the outdoor florist's chrysanthemums, with branched stems carrying lobed leaves and topped by single blooms with spoon-shaped petals.
HEIGHT AND SPREAD: 24 × 24in (60 × 60cm)
BLOOMING PERIOD: Late summer to early autumn
SOIL: Fertile, well-drained.

LATIN NAME: *Dendranthema* 'Ruby Enbee Wedding'
COMMON NAME: Autumn flowering or indoor spray chrysanthemum
ALTERNATIVES: *Dendranthema rubellum* 'Apricot'
DESCRIPTION: Herbaceous perennial with upright, branching stems bearing lobed leaves and many semi-double blooms of dark burnt orange-red with greenish yellow centers.
HEIGHT AND SPREAD: 2–3 × 2ft (60–90 × 60cm)
BLOOMING PERIOD: Late summer to early autumn
SOIL: Fertile, well-drained.

ORANGE

BACK

9-10

LATIN NAME: *Dahlia* 'Parade'
COMMON NAME: Known by Latin name
ALTERNATIVES: 'Daleko Jupiter,' 'Breitner' (for Australia)
DESCRIPTION: Tender, tuberous-rooted perennial with tall, upright, branched stems and divided leaves with oval leaflets. The soft orange, semi-double flowers are rounded in outline.
HEIGHT AND SPREAD: 4 × 4ft (1.2 × 1.2m)
BLOOMING PERIOD: Mid-summer to autumn
SOIL: Fertile, humus-rich, well-drained but moisture-retentive.

LATIN NAME: *Dahlia* cultivar
COMMON NAME: Semi-cactus/decorative dahlia
ALTERNATIVES: 'Jaldec Jolly,' 'Gay Triumph'
DESCRIPTION: Tender, tuberous-rooted perennial with branched stems bearing divided leaves with oval leaflets. Orange blooms with tapering petals tipped white. In cold regions, lift tubers after frost and overwinter indoors.
HEIGHT AND SPREAD: 4 × 4ft (1.2 × 1.2m)
BLOOMING PERIOD: Late summer to autumn
SOIL: Fertile, humus-rich, well-drained, moisture-retentive.

9-10

MIDDLE

7-10

ATIN NAME: *Kniphofia caulescens*
COMMON NAME: Red hot poker, torch lily
ALTERNATIVES: 'Samuel's Sensation,' 'Prince Igor,' 'Royal Standard'
DESCRIPTION: Evergreen perennial making tussocks of stiff, narrow, blue-green leaves from which flower stems arise, bearing the poker-shaped blooms. Reddish orange buds open to yellow from the base.
HEIGHT AND SPREAD: 4 × 2ft (1.2 × 0.6m)
BLOOMING PERIOD: Late summer to early autumn
SOIL: Well-drained moisture-retentive for summer leaf growth.

8-10

LATIN NAME: *Kniphofia rooperi*
COMMON NAME: Red hot poker, torch lily
ALTERNATIVES: None
DESCRIPTION: Semi-evergreen perennial with arching, broadly grassy foliage and upright stems topped by oval shaped heads of orange-red which open yellow from the base upward. Mulch in cooler areas.
HEIGHT AND SPREAD: 4 × 2ft (1.2 × 0.6m)
BLOOMING PERIOD: Early to mid-autumn
SOIL: Well-drained moisture-retentive for summer leaf growth.

FRONT

LATIN NAME: *Iris foetidissima*
COMMON NAME: Gladwin iris or stinking iris
ALTERNATIVES: *I. f. var. citrina*
DESCRIPTION: Evergreen perennial making spreading clumps of glossy, dark green, narrow arching leaves. Stems carry small purple-brown, veined flowers followed by large pods which split to reveal bright orange berries.
HEIGHT AND SPREAD: 18 × 24in (45 × 60cm)
BLOOMING PERIOD: Early summer
SOIL: Excellent for colonizing difficult situations, dry or damp.

7-10

6-10

LATIN NAME: *Dendranthema* 'Starlet'
COMMON NAME: Korean chrysanthemum
ALTERNATIVES: 'Aline,' 'Louise,' 'Sheila'
DESCRIPTION: Herbaceous perennial with branched stems covered in lobed leaves and smothered in pale orange blooms with spoon-shaped petals and yellow centers. Hardier than florist's type.
HEIGHT AND SPREAD: 18 × 18in (45 × 45cm)
BLOOMING PERIOD: Early to mid-autumn
SOIL: Fertile, well-drained.

4-8

3-7

LATIN NAME: *Fothergilla major*
COMMON NAME: Large fothergilla
ALTERNATIVES: Monticola Group
DESCRIPTION: Shrub of slow-medium growth rate with broad, oval leaves, glaucous or gray-green in color which develop long-lasting, rich autumn tints. The fragrant spring flowers consist of white stamens.
HEIGHT AND SPREAD: 8–13 × 8–13ft (2.5–4 × 2.5–4m)
BLOOMING PERIOD: Early to mid-spring
SOIL: Acid, humus-rich, well-drained but moisture-retentive.

LATIN NAME: *Hippophae rhamnoides*
COMMON NAME: Sea buckthorn
ALTERNATIVES: None
DESCRIPTION: Shrub of upright to spreading habit forming underground suckers. May be invasive. Female plants bear clusters of orange-red berries. Plant in groups to ensure fruit.
HEIGHT AND SPREAD: 13 × 13ft (4 × 4m)
BLOOMING PERIOD: Insignificant
SOIL: Well-drained. Good on light, sandy soils and at seaside.

7-10

10

LATIN NAME: *Dendranthema* 'Fairway'
COMMON NAME: Autumn-flowering or florist's chrysanthemum
ALTERNATIVES: 'Oracle,' 'Bronze Yvonne Arnaud,' 'Flame Symbol'
DESCRIPTION: Herbaceous perennial with upright, branched stems clothed in lobed leaves and bearing large, globe-shaped heads of deep burnt-orange, shaded paler at tips and toward center.
HEIGHT AND SPREAD: 4 × 2–2½ft (1.2 × 0.6–0.75m)
BLOOMING PERIOD: Mid-autumn
SOIL: Fertile, well-drained.

LATIN NAME: *Strelitzia reginae*
COMMON NAME: Bird of paradise
ALTERNATIVES: None
DESCRIPTION: Tender evergreen perennial, with long-stalked, blue-green leaves with an oblong blade and exotic blooms like a bird's head with a "beak" of red-edged bracts and orange "feathers."
HEIGHT AND SPREAD: 3–4 × 2½ft (0.9–1.2 × 0.75m)
BLOOMING PERIOD: Spring and summer
SOIL: Fertile, well-drained; fertilize and water generously.

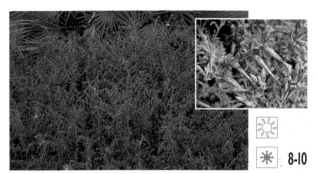

8-10

LATIN NAME: *Zauschneria californica*
COMMON NAME: California fuchsia
ALTERNATIVES: 'Dublin' syn. 'Glasnevin,' *Z. cana*
DESCRIPTION: Evergreen perennial of bushy habit with small leaves and stems bearing tubular flowers of brilliant orange-red. Needs sharp drainage and warm shelter to survive in colder areas.
HEIGHT AND SPREAD: 18 × 18in (45 × 45cm)
BLOOMING PERIOD: Late summer to early autumn
SOIL: Very well-drained.

LATIN NAME: *Calluna vulgaris* 'Wickwar Flame'
COMMON NAME: Ling, Scotch heather
ALTERNATIVES: 'Orange Queen,' 'Bonfire Brilliance,' 'Boskoop'
DESCRIPTION: Carpet-forming evergreen shrublet grown for its bright autumn and winter foliage coloring. Low stems covered in scale-like leaves of yellow, orange and pinky-red shading. Mauve-pink flower spikes.
HEIGHT AND SPREAD: 24 × 18in (60 × 45cm)
BLOOMING PERIOD: Late summer to autumn
SOIL: Acid, humus-rich, well-drained.

4-7

Green

When designing color schemes, we hardly give a second thought to green. It is the most common color in the garden, and, as such, the easiest to ignore. When you begin to look at foliage in its own right, you discover a wealth of shades. Rich greens make the perfect foil for most flower colors, especially those at the red end of the spectrum. Green leaves can be tinged orange, pink, red, or purple, and they can be distinctly glaucous or blue. Green mixed with yellow gives brilliant lime or acid shades. When a green leaf is covered with a white bloom, waxy coating, tiny hairs or wool, the overall color ranges from grays through silver to almost white. White- or yellow-variegated leaves introduce another huge selection of foliage variants. In fact, when you consider the tremendous range of foliage color and pattern, form and texture, you could easily plant a colorful and interesting border without using flowers. Look under the different colors for additional plants.

Green foliage is particularly important in shade where flowers tend not to perform so well. Here, lime-green, all-yellow, and yellow-variegated foliage of herbaceous plants and deciduous shrubs creates the effect of dappled light. Add some white flowers and create a scheme of cool elegance. With the exceptions of grasses and other wind-pollinated plants, green flowers are relatively rare, as they tend not to be seen by pollinating insects. However, they can look very stylish, providing an unusual complement for other blooms.

Left: *Hostas, among the most elegant of all shade plants, combine here to create cool, leafy luxuriance.*

BACK

6-8

LATIN NAME: *Buxus sempervirens* 'Elegantissima'
COMMON NAME: Variegated box
ALTERNATIVES: *Rhamnus alternus* 'Argenteovariegata'
DESCRIPTION: Evergreen shrub of densely branched habit with small, rounded leaves with creamy-white variegation. Forms a rounded shrub, which may be clipped to shape. Pungent leaves.
HEIGHT AND SPREAD: 4 × 3½ft (1.2 × 1.0m)
BLOOMING PERIOD: Insignificant
SOIL: Friable, well-drained but moisture retentive.

5-10

LATIN NAME: *Hedera helix* 'Eva'
COMMON NAME: Common ivy, English ivy
ALTERNATIVES: 'Anna Marie,' 'Adam,' 'Glacier'
DESCRIPTION: Evergreen climber, self-clinging via aerial roots but usually requiring initial support. Leaves grayish green in color with a broad, creamy-white margin. Leaves may appear scorched or die back in a very cold winter.
HEIGHT AND SPREAD: 4 × 3ft (1.2 × 0.9m)
BLOOMING PERIOD: Insignificant
SOIL: Any well-drained.

MIDDLE

7-10

LATIN NAME: *Pleioblastus variegatus*
COMMON NAME: Dwarf white-striped bamboo
ALTERNATIVES: *P. auricomus, Glyceria maxima* var. *variegata*
DESCRIPTION: Evergreen bamboo with a slow, creeping habit and narrow, oblong leaves boldly striped white. To promote fresh, brightly colored foliage, cut to ground level in early spring.
HEIGHT AND SPREAD: 30in (80cm) × indefinite
BLOOMING PERIOD: Not applicable
SOIL: Fertile, well-drained but moisture-retentive.

5-8

LATIN NAME: *Helictotrichon sempervirens*
COMMON NAME: Blue oat grass
ALTERNATIVES: *Festuca glauca* cultivars, *Leymus arenarius*
DESCRIPTION: Evergreen grass making tussocks of very narrow, blue-gray leaves. These are overtopped by arching flower spikes which look like blue oats and age to golden tan.
HEIGHT AND SPREAD: 2 × 2ft (0.9 × 0.6m)
BLOOMING PERIOD: Late summer
SOIL: Well-drained but not dry.

FRONT

4-8

LATIN NAME: *Chamaecyparis obtusa* 'Nana Lutea'
COMMON NAME: Hinoki or false cypress
ALTERNATIVES: None
DESCRIPTION: Dwarf conifer slowly making a broadly pyramidal bush of irregular outline. Scale-like leaves produced on flat, fanned branchlets. Golden yellow becoming more prominent with winter cold.
HEIGHT AND SPREAD: 18–24 × 12–18in (45–60 × 30–45cm)
BLOOMING PERIOD: None
SOIL: Any well-drained.

5-9

LATIN NAME: *Euonymus fortunei* 'Emerald 'n' Gold'
COMMON NAME: Known by Latin name
ALTERNATIVES: 'Blondy,' 'Sunspot,' 'Golden Prince,' 'Sunshine'
DESCRIPTION: Dwarf evergreen shrub making excellent groundcover. Grows taller if trained against a low wall. Glossy oval leaves broadly margined golden yellow. Pinkish red tints in winter cold.
HEIGHT AND SPREAD: 2 × 6ft (0.6 × 1.8m)
BLOOMING PERIOD: Insignificant
SOIL: Any well-drained.

LATIN NAME: *Viburnum rhytiodophyllum*
COMMON NAME: Leatherleaf viburnum
ALTERNATIVES: None
DESCRIPTION: Shrub of open habit with large, oblong leaves with deep venation. Flower buds overwinter and open creamy yellow. Red fruits. May be killed to the ground in winter but quickly regrows.
HEIGHT AND SPREAD: 12 × 12ft (3.5 × 3.5m)
BLOOMING PERIOD: Late spring to early summer
SOIL: Well-drained but moisture-retentive.

5-8

LATIN NAME: *Laurus nobilis*
COMMON NAME: Bay, sweet bay, bay laurel, poet's laurel
ALTERNATIVES: 'Aurea'
DESCRIPTION: Evergreen shrub with leathery, broadly lance-shaped, dark green leaves on a dense, conical bush. Leaves have a spicy, fruity aroma. May be damaged by exposure to cold winds and freezing temperatures.
HEIGHT AND SPREAD: 16 × 13ft (5 × 4m)
BLOOMING PERIOD: Spring
SOIL: Light, well-drained.

8-10

LATIN NAME: *Nephrolepis exaltata*
COMMON NAME: Sword fern, ladder fern
ALTERNATIVES: 'Bostoniensis' (below), 'Teddy Junior' (above)
DESCRIPTION: Evergreen fern with long, arching leaves divided into narrow leaflets giving the appearance of a ladder. There are several forms of this species, including the so-called Boston fern.
HEIGHT AND SPREAD: 3 × 3ft (0.9 × 0.9m)
BLOOMING PERIOD: Insignificant
SOIL: Moisture-retentive, humus-rich.

10

LATIN NAME: *Sansevieria trifasciata* 'Laurentii'
COMMON NAME: Mother-in-law's tongue, snake plant
ALTERNATIVES: *S. trifasciata*
DESCRIPTION: Rhizomatous perennial with succulent, evergreen leaves making a tight, vertical clump. Blades sword-shaped with pale and dark green horizontal banding and golden yellow margin. Greenish flowers appear erratically.
HEIGHT AND SPREAD: 18–48 × 4in (45–120 × 10cm)
BLOOMING PERIOD: Unpredictable
SOIL: Well-drained.

10

LATIN NAME: *Carex elata* 'Aurea' syn. *C. stricta* 'Bowles' Golden'
COMMON NAME: Bowles' golden sedge
ALTERNATIVES: *C. hachijoensis* 'Evergold'
DESCRIPTION: Evergreen perennial with very narrow arching leaves of green with yellow stripes. Yellow coloring most prominent in the summer. Does best in a moist or boggy site with full exposure.
HEIGHT AND SPREAD: 2 × 1½ft (0.6 × 0.45m)
BLOOMING PERIOD: Summer
SOIL: Moist to boggy.

5-8

LATIN NAME: *Festuca glauca*
COMMON NAME: Blue fescue
ALTERNATIVES: 'Blaufachs' ('Blue Fox'), 'Blauglut' ('Blue Glow')
DESCRIPTION: Evergreen tussock-forming grass with hair-like leaves of gray-blue. Varies in color; for brightest silvery blues, buy plants of named cultivars. Feathery flower spikes. Short-lived.
HEIGHT AND SPREAD: 9 × 12in (23 × 30cm)
BLOOMING PERIOD: Summer
SOIL: Well-drained.

5-8

GREEN

BACK

7-10

LATIN NAME: x *Fatshedera lizei*
COMMON NAME: Known by Latin name
ALTERNATIVES: 'Annemieke,' 'Variegata'
DESCRIPTION: Evergreen wall-shrub or groundcover. Thought to be a cross between *Hedera helix* and *Fatsia japonica*. Glossy, palmate leaves. Provide support, fan-training against a fence or wall.
HEIGHT AND SPREAD: 13 × 13ft (4 × 4m)
BLOOMING PERIOD: Year round on mature branches only
SOIL: Moisture-retentive but tolerant of a range of conditions.

7-9

LATIN NAME: *Skimmia × confusa* 'Kew Green'
COMMON NAME: Known by Latin name
ALTERNATIVES: None
DESCRIPTION: Evergreen shrub with oval leaves, dark green when grown in the correct conditions. A male variety with cone-shaped bud clusters of pale green opening to fragrant white flowers.
HEIGHT AND SPREAD: 4 × 4ft (1.2 × 1.2m)
BLOOMING PERIOD: Late spring
SOIL: Fertile, humus-rich and moisture-retentive. Neutral to acid.

MIDDLE

LATIN NAME: *Daphne laureola*
COMMON NAME: Spurge laurel
ALTERNATIVES: None
DESCRIPTION: Evergreen shrub, excellent for underplanting in shaded areas e.g. under trees. Foliage lanceolate, glossy, dark green making dense cover. Clusters of fragrant, creamy-yellow blooms in leaf axils.
HEIGHT AND SPREAD: 3 × 4ft (0.9 × 1.2m)
BLOOMING PERIOD: Late winter to early spring
SOIL: Typical woodland type—plenty of humus and leafmold. Fertile, moist.

7-8

·8-9

LATIN NAME: *Viburnum davidii*
COMMON NAME: David's viburnum
ALTERNATIVES: Male and female clones. Males necessary for fruit set
DESCRIPTION: Evergreen shrub of low, spreading habit. Dark, bluish green leaves with deep parallel veins and red stalks. White flowers in clusters with metallic-blue berries on female plants.
HEIGHT AND SPREAD: 3 × 5ft (0.9 × 1.5m)
BLOOMING PERIOD: Late spring to early summer (earlier in Australia)
SOIL: Any fertile, well-drained preferably humus-rich.

FRONT

LATIN NAME: *Helleborus foetidus*
COMMON NAME: Stinking hellebore
ALTERNATIVES: 'Wester Flisk,' *H. f.* Italian form, *H. lividus*, *H. argutifolius*
DESCRIPTION: Evergreen perennial with long-fingered dark green leaves in spreading mounds. Pendant clusters of bright, apple-green, cup-shaped flowers produced at shoot tips. Self-seeds readily.
HEIGHT AND SPREAD: 18 × 18in (45 × 45cm)
BLOOMING PERIOD: Winter to early spring
SOIL: Well-drained, humus-rich, moisture-retentive.

3-10

5-9

LATIN NAME: *Asplenium scolopendrium* syn. *Phyllitis scolopendrium*
COMMON NAME: Hart's tongue fern
ALTERNATIVES: Crispum Group, Cristatum Group
DESCRIPTION: Evergreen fern with long, undulating, strap-shaped leaves. Easily grown provided it has adequate moisture and shade, making an excellent contrast with cut-leaved ferns and other foliage plants.
HEIGHT AND SPREAD: 12 × 12in (30 × 30cm)
BLOOMING PERIOD: None
SOIL: Well-drained, humus-rich and moisture-retentive.

LATIN NAME: *Garrya elliptica*
COMMON NAME: Tassel bush, silk tassel tree
ALTERNATIVES: 'James Roof,' 'Pat Ballard'
DESCRIPTION: Evergreen shrub grown free-standing or against a wall. Leathery, dark green crinkled leaves and clusters of long, gray-green catkins on male clones. Catkins may become tangled in windy sites.
HEIGHT AND SPREAD: 12 × 12ft (3.6 × 3.6m)
BLOOMING PERIOD: Early winter to early spring
SOIL: Any reasonably fertile, drained soil.

8-9

LATIN NAME: *Euonymus japonicus*
COMMON NAME: Japanese euonymus
ALTERNATIVES: 'Grandifolia,' 'Microphyllus,' 'Latifolius Albo-marginatus'
DESCRIPTION: Evergreen shrub with glossy, oval, dark green foliage. Good for coastal gardens and useful for hedging. Greenish yellow insignificant blooms. Several variegated forms available.
HEIGHT AND SPREAD: 12 × 12ft (3.6 × 3.6m)
BLOOMING PERIOD: Late spring to early summer
SOIL: Any, even sandy coastal soils. Plants may scorch in cold winds.

7-9

LATIN NAME: *Thuja orientalis* 'Aurea Nana'
COMMON NAME: Known by Latin Name
ALTERNATIVES: None
DESCRIPTION: Dwarf evergreen conifer of broad, cone-shaped habit with dense, golden-yellow foliage in flat vertical plates. Slow-growing, but ultimately reaching a larger size than that given. Monitor for bagworm in US; hand-pick to control.
HEIGHT AND SPREAD: 2 × 2ft (0.6 × 0.6m)
BLOOMING PERIOD: Insignificant
SOIL: Any well-drained soil.

6-9

8-10

LATIN NAME: *Hebe ochracea* 'James Stirling'
COMMON NAME: Whipcord or cord-branched hebe
ALTERNATIVES: *H. ochracea, H. armstrongii*
DESCRIPTION: Evergreen shrub of spreading, dome-shaped habit with fine, branching stems covered in bright gold to olive green scale-like leaves. Scatterings of tiny white flowers sometimes produced.
HEIGHT AND SPREAD: 2 × 4ft (0.6 × 1.2m)
BLOOMING PERIOD: Summer
SOIL: Rich, deep, moisture-retentive but well-drained.

5-10

LATIN NAME: *Hedera helix* 'Little Diamond'
COMMON NAME: Variegated ivy
ALTERNATIVES: 'Glacier,' 'Luzei,' 'Adam'
DESCRIPTION: Evergreen trailer of bushy habit, particularly useful as dense groundcover with small, gray-green diamond-shaped leaves boldly variegated creamy-white.
HEIGHT AND SPREAD: 12 × 36in (30 × 90cm)
BLOOMING PERIOD: None
SOIL: Any well-drained.

4-8

LATIN NAME: *Chamaecyparis pisifera* 'Golden Mop'
COMMON NAME: Known by Latin name; also Japanese false cypress
ALTERNATIVES: *C. p.* 'Filifera Nana'
DESCRIPTION: Dwarf evergreen conifer of spreading, mound-like habit with thread-like pendulous stems covered in golden-green leaves. Seen to best advantage when allowed to cascade over an edge.
HEIGHT AND SPREAD: 2 × 3ft (0.6 × 0.9m)
BLOOMING PERIOD: None
SOIL: Well-drained.

BACK

LATIN NAME: *Hedera colchia* 'Dentata Variegata'
COMMON NAME: Persian ivy
ALTERNATIVES: *H. colchica* 'Sulphur Heart,' *H. canariensis* 'Glorie de Marengo'
DESCRIPTION: Evergreen self-clinging climber/groundcover plant with large leaves, green overlaid with cream and with irregular cream margins. Can take up to three years for vigorous growth to begin. Needs initial support.
HEIGHT AND SPREAD: 25 × 25ft (7.5 × 7.5m)
BLOOMING PERIOD: Autumn to winter
SOIL: Any well-drained.

6-10

LATIN NAME: *Pittosporum tenuifolium* 'Silver Queen' syn. 'Treseederi'
COMMON NAME: Kohuhu, pittosporum
ALTERNATIVES: 'Garnetti,' 'Deborah,' 'Irene Paterson'
DESCRIPTION: Evergreen shrub with small, densely packed, broadly oval leaves which are gray-green margined white. The maroon-black stems make an excellent contrast. Provide a sheltered site. Fragrant.
HEIGHT AND SPREAD: 13 × 8ft (4 × 2.5m)
BLOOMING PERIOD: Late spring
SOIL: Fertile, well-drained.

8-10

MIDDLE

LATIN NAME: *Miscanthus sinensis* 'Cascade'
COMMON NAME: Known by Latin name
ALTERNATIVES: 'Flamingo,' 'Silberfeder,' 'Rotsilber'
DESCRIPTION: Ornamental grass of slender, upright habit with very narrow, slightly curling leaves and arching sprays of silken, pinkish buff flower heads. Makes an excellent accent plant for the mixed border.
HEIGHT AND SPREAD: 4–5 × 1½–2ft (1.2–1.5 × 0.45–0.6m)
BLOOMING PERIOD: Autumn
SOIL: Moisture-retentive.

6-9

6-8

LATIN NAME: *Prunus laurocerasus* 'Zabeliana'
COMMON NAME: English laurel, cherry laurel
ALTERNATIVES: 'Otto Luyken'
DESCRIPTION: Evergreen shrub with large, oblong to oval pointed leaves of glossy deep green. Habit widely spreading with tiered branches responding well to pruning. Upright, fluffy flower spikes.
HEIGHT AND SPREAD: 3–6 × 13–16ft (1–2 × 4–5m)
BLOOMING PERIOD: Early summer
SOIL: Any reasonably well-drained.

FRONT

6-10

LATIN NAME: *Helleborus argutifolius* syn. *H. corsicus*
COMMON NAME: Corsican hellebore
ALTERNATIVES: *H. foetidus, H. lividus*
DESCRIPTION: Evergreen perennial making a rounded mass of large, deep gray-green, toothed leaves. Clusters of long-lasting, waxy, cup-shaped blooms in palest apple-green.
HEIGHT AND SPREAD: 2 × 3ft (0.6 × 0.9m)
BLOOMING PERIOD: Winter to spring
SOIL: Well-drained, humus-rich, moisture-retentive.

10

LATIN NAME: *Farfugium japonicum* 'Aureomaculata'
COMMON NAME: Leopard plant
ALTERNATIVES: None
DESCRIPTION: Clump-forming tender evergreen perennial with rounded, toothed leaves of deep green with yellow spots. May be planted out for summer as a foliage feature plant.
HEIGHT AND SPREAD: 2 × 2–3ft (0.6 × 0.6–0.9m)
BLOOMING PERIOD: Autumn
SOIL: Fertile, well-drained, moisture-retentive.

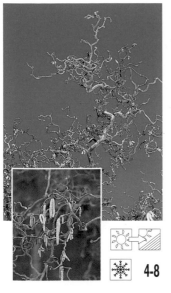

LATIN NAME: *Corylus avellana* 'Contorta'
COMMON NAME: Corkscrew hazel, contorted hazel, Harry Lauder's walking stick
ALTERNATIVES: *Corokia cotoneaster*
DESCRIPTION: Shrub with spiralling and twisted stems which make a fine feature in the winter garden; unfortunately, the broad green leaves are also contorted. Long yellow catkins in clusters before the leaves expand.
HEIGHT AND SPREAD: 10 × 13ft (3 × 4m)
BLOOMING PERIOD: Late winter to early spring
SOIL: Any.

4-8

8-10

LATIN NAME: *Fatsia japonica* syn. *Aralia sieboldii*
COMMON NAME: Japanese fatsia
ALTERNATIVES: 'Variegata'
DESCRIPTION: Evergreen shrub with very large, palmate leaves of glossy mid-green, making a rounded bush at first, becoming spreading. May be wall-trained. Drumstick flower heads.
HEIGHT AND SPREAD: 10 × 10ft (3 × 3m)
BLOOMING PERIOD: Year-round
SOIL: Fertile, humus-rich, moisture-retentive.

LATIN NAME: *Miscanthus sinensis* 'Flamingo'
COMMON NAME: Known by Latin name
ALTERNATIVES: 'Cascade,' 'Silberfeder,' 'Rotsilber'
DESCRIPTION: Ornamental grass of slender, upright habit with very narrow, slightly curling leaves, red stems and arching sprays of silken, pinkish buff flower heads. Good autumn color. Excellent accent plant.
HEIGHT AND SPREAD: 4 × 1½ft (1.2 × 0.45m)
BLOOMING PERIOD: Autumn
SOIL: Moisture-retentive.

6-9

8-10

LATIN NAME: *Ribes laurifolium*
COMMON NAME: Known by Latin name
ALTERNATIVES: *R. henryi, R. odoratum*
DESCRIPTION: Evergreen shrub of low, spreading habit with oval dull, dark green leaves which make an excellent foil for the pale yellowish green pendant flowers. Needs shelter to protect early blooms.
HEIGHT AND SPREAD: 3 × 5ft (0.9 × 1.5m)
BLOOMING PERIOD: Late winter to early spring
SOIL: Fertile, well-drained.

4-10

LATIN NAME: *Bergenia* (white-flowered cultivar)
COMMON NAME: Elephant's ears, bergenia
ALTERNATIVES: *B.* 'Bressingham White,' *B.* 'Silberlicht' (Silver Light)
DESCRIPTION: Evergreen perennial with large, rounded, leathery leaves of glossy green, sometimes developing purple-red tints in winter. Stout reddish flower stems bearing compact heads of bell-shaped blooms.
HEIGHT AND SPREAD: 12 × 20in (30 × 50cm)
BLOOMING PERIOD: Winter to spring
SOIL: Well-drained but preferably humus-rich and moisture-retentive.

7-9

LATIN NAME: *Carex buchananii*
COMMON NAME: Leatherleaf sedge
ALTERNATIVES: *C. comans* 'Bronze'
DESCRIPTION: Evergreen sedge of arching, dome-shaped habit with narrow leaves of unusual coppery hue. Insignificant brown flower spikes may be removed for a neater effect. Effective in groups.
HEIGHT AND SPREAD: 18 × 18in (45 × 45cm)
BLOOMING PERIOD: Summer
SOIL: Moisture-retentive.

BACK

LATIN NAME: *Physocarpus opulifolius* 'Luteus' syn. *P. ribesifolius* 'Aureus'
COMMON NAME: Ninebark, Eastern ninebark
ALTERNATIVES: 'Dart's Gold'
DESCRIPTION: Shrub of upright, bushy habit with golden-yellow lobed leaves. Clusters of small, off-white blooms. New stem growth mahogany-red. Foliage scorches in strong sunlight.
HEIGHT AND SPREAD: 8 × 8ft (2.5 × 2.5m)
BLOOMING PERIOD: Early to mid-summer (spring in Australia)
SOIL: Fertile, humus-rich, moisture-retentive. Dislikes extreme alkalinity.

2-7

4-9

LATIN NAME: *Weigela* 'Briant Rubidor' syn. *W.* 'Rubigold'
COMMON NAME: Known by Latin name
ALTERNATIVES: *Weigela japonica* 'Looymansii Aurea'
DESCRIPTION: Shrub of bushy, upright habit with golden-yellow lance-shaped leaves and deep, crimson-red, funnel-shaped blooms. On established plants, prune a third of oldest wood after flowering.
HEIGHT AND SPREAD: 4–5 × 4–5ft (1.2–2.5 × 1.2–2.5m)
BLOOMING PERIOD: Late spring to early summer (earlier in Australia)
SOIL: Any, fertile, well-drained but moisture-retentive soil.

MIDDLE

8-10

LATIN NAME: *Euphorbia characias*
COMMON NAME: Spurge, milkweed
ALTERNATIVES: *E. c.* subsp. *wulfenii* and forms
DESCRIPTION: Evergreen perennial. Bushy habit with upright stems clothed in narrow, curving, gray-green leaves. Greenish flower heads open from shepherd's-crook-like buds. Cut spent stems. Irritant.
HEIGHT AND SPREAD: 4 × 3ft (1.2 × 0.9m)
BLOOMING PERIOD: Early spring
SOIL: Well-drained.

8-10

LATIN NAME: *Euphorbia characias* subsp. *wulfenii* 'John Tomlinson'
COMMON NAME: Spurge, milkweed
ALTERNATIVES: 'Lambrook Gold'
DESCRIPTION: Evergreen perennial with upright stems covered in blue-green foliage giving them a bottle-brush appearance. Large yellow-green flower heads. Irritant sap. Care as for *E. characias*.
HEIGHT AND SPREAD: 4 × 3ft (1.2 × 0.9m)
BLOOMING PERIOD: Early spring
SOIL: Well-drained.

FRONT

8-10

LATIN NAME: *Euphorbia amygdaloides* var. *robbiae*
COMMON NAME: Wood spurge, milkweed
ALTERNATIVES: *E. a.* 'Purpurea,' 'Rubra'
DESCRIPTION: Evergreen perennial with creeping roots and stems carrying whorls of dark green foliage. Spires carry long-lasting, lime-green blooms. Good groundcover under trees. Irritant sap.
HEIGHT AND SPREAD: 2 × 2ft (0.6 × 0.6m)
BLOOMING PERIOD: Spring
SOIL: Any well-drained to dry. Moisture-retentive soil in full sun.

8-10

LATIN NAME: *Euphorbia myrsinites*
COMMON NAME: Spurge, milkweed
ALTERNATIVES: None
DESCRIPTION: Evergreen perennial. In its first year produces long trailing stems covered in fleshy, pointed gray-green leaves. The next year lime-green flowers appear. Irritant sap.
HEIGHT AND SPREAD: 3–6 × 8–12in (8–15 × 20–30cm)
BLOOMING PERIOD: Early summer
SOIL: Well-drained.

LATIN NAME: *Humulus lupulus* 'Aureus'
COMMON NAME: Golden hop
ALTERNATIVES: 'Taff's Variegated'
DESCRIPTION: Herbaceous climber with twining stems and large, lobed, golden-yellow leaves. Stems and foliage covered with bristle-like hairs. Golden "hop" flowers on male plants. Provide shelter from strong winds.
HEIGHT AND SPREAD: 20 × 20ft (6 × 6m)
BLOOMING PERIOD: Late summer to early autumn
SOIL: Fertile, humus-rich and moisture-retentive.

5-9

LATIN NAME: *Angelica archangelica*
COMMON NAME: Angelica
ALTERNATIVES: None
DESCRIPTION: Biennial or short-lived perennial herb with stout, upright stems and large, divided leaves. Greenish white, umbelliferous flower heads in second year from seed. Life-span extended if heads removed. Self-seeds.
HEIGHT AND SPREAD: 6 × 3ft (1.8 × 0.9m)
BLOOMING PERIOD: Late summer
SOIL: Well-drained.

4-9

LATIN NAME: *Matteuccia struthiopteris*
COMMON NAME: Shuttlecock or Ostrich fern
ALTERNATIVES: *Osmunda regalis*
DESCRIPTION: Deciduous fern with a narrow, shuttlecock-like habit, slowly making colonies via stolons. The delicate fronds are bright green in color when they unfurl in spring. Dark brown fertile fronds. Shelter from wind.
HEIGHT AND SPREAD: 3–4 × 2+ft (0.9–1.2 × 0.6+m)
BLOOMING PERIOD: Spring to autumn
SOIL: Humus-rich, moisture-retentive to boggy.

2-8

5-9

LATIN NAME: *Persicaria virginiana* 'Painter's Palette'
COMMON NAME: Painter's palette
ALTERNATIVES: None
DESCRIPTION: Herbaceous perennial with variegated leaves on upright stems. Foliage creamy-yellow with a central band of maroon. Shelter from wind.
HEIGHT AND SPREAD: 2–3 × 2ft (0.6–0.9 × 0.6m)
BLOOMING PERIOD: None
SOIL: Fertile, humus-rich, moisture-retentive.

LATIN NAME: *Adiantum raddianum*
COMMON NAME: Delta maidenhair fern
ALTERNATIVES: 'Fritz Luthi' and many others
DESCRIPTION: Semi-evergreen or evergreen fern with delicate, highly dissected fronds with very small, triangular leaflets. The stems are fine, wiry and purple-black in color. Requires shelter. Remove fading fronds.
HEIGHT AND SPREAD: 12 × 12in (30 × 30cm)
BLOOMING PERIOD: None
SOIL: Neutral to acid, humus-rich, moisture-retentive.

10

5-10

LATIN NAME: *Geranium phaeum* 'Samobor'
COMMON NAME: Mourning widow hardy geranium
ALTERNATIVES: G. 'Ann Folkard'
DESCRIPTION: Herbaceous perennial making a mound of shallowly-lobed leaves, roughly rounded in outline with maroon-purple zoning. Dark purple blooms with reflexed petals and protruding stamens.
HEIGHT AND SPREAD: 18 × 18in (45 × 45cm)
BLOOMING PERIOD: Late spring to early summer
SOIL: Any, other than boggy.

BACK

5-9

LATIN NAME: *Cotinus coggygria*
COMMON NAME: Smoketree, smoke bush
ALTERNATIVES: 'Flame,' 'Grace'
DESCRIPTION: Shrub of bushy habit with rounded to oval leaves, gray-green turning mid-green. Excellent autumn color. Cloud-like flower heads begin pale pinkish brown and age to gray.
HEIGHT AND SPREAD: 15 × 15ft (5 × 5m)
BLOOMING PERIOD: Mid-summer to autumn
SOIL: Any, but best on deep, rich soil.

5-9

LATIN NAME: *Miscanthus sinensis* 'Zebrinus'
COMMON NAME: Zebra grass or tiger grass
ALTERNATIVES: 'Tiger Tail' ('Pünktchen'), 'Strictus'
DESCRIPTION: Herbaceous grass forming a clump of upright stems with ribbon-like leaves arching over at the top. The foliage has distinct yellow bands across the blade. Silky flower heads in mid-autumn.
HEIGHT AND SPREAD: 4 × 1½ft (1.2 × 0.45m)
BLOOMING PERIOD: Mid-autumn
SOIL: Fertile, humus-rich, moisture-retentive.

MIDDLE

3-9

LATIN NAME: *Hosta sieboldiana* 'Francis Williams'
COMMON NAME: Hosta, plantain lily, funkia
ALTERNATIVES: 'Gold Standard,' 'Wide Brim'
DESCRIPTION: Herbaceous perennial with broad blue-green, pointed leaves of puckered and ribbed texture with irregular yellow margin. Whitish, bell-shaped blooms. Protect against slugs.
HEIGHT AND SPREAD: 2½ × 1½ft (75 × 45cm)
BLOOMING PERIOD: Early summer
SOIL: Fertile, humus-rich, moisture-retentive to moist.

3-9

LATIN NAME: *Hosta sieboldiana* 'Elegans'
COMMON NAME: Hosta, plantain lily, funkia
ALTERNATIVES: *H. sieboldiana*, 'Blue Angel,' 'Big Daddy'
DESCRIPTION: Herbaceous perennial of clump-forming habit with very broad leaves, up to 1ft (30cm) across, of blue-gray coloring. Ribbed, crinkled texture. Dense heads of lilac-white trumpet-shaped blooms.
HEIGHT AND SPREAD: 2½ × 3ft (75 × 90cm)
BLOOMING PERIOD: Summer
SOIL: Fertile, humus-rich, moisture-retentive to moist.

FRONT

3-9

LATIN NAME: *Alchemilla mollis*
COMMON NAME: Lady's mantle
ALTERNATIVES: *A. conjuncta, A. erythropoda, A. alpina*
DESCRIPTION: Herbaceous perennial with scalloped-edged leaves, covered in water-resistant hairs so after rain or heavy dew they are covered in droplets. Frothy greenish yellow blooms. Self-seeds.
HEIGHT AND SPREAD: 18 × 24in (45 × 60cm)
BLOOMING PERIOD: Early summer
SOIL: Any well-drained.

8-10

LATIN NAME: *Eryngium tricuspidatum*
COMMON NAME: Sea holly
ALTERNATIVES: *E. variifolium, E. bourgatii*
DESCRIPTION: Herbaceous perennial making a basal rosette of leaves with prominent white venation. The unusual silvery-green flower heads consist of a small central dome of tightly-packed blooms surmounted by very long spines.
HEIGHT AND SPREAD: 18 × 10in (45 × 25cm)
BLOOMING PERIOD: Late summer
SOIL: Any well-drained.

☀ **7-10**

LATIN NAME: *Gunnera manicata*
COMMON NAME: Known by Latin name
ALTERNATIVES: *G. tinctoria* syn. *G. chilensis*
DESCRIPTION: Herbaceous perennial from Brazil. Highly architectural with massive, jagged-edged leaves 5–6ft (1.5–1.8m) across. Stems and leaves covered with prickles. Cone-shaped flower heads.
HEIGHT AND SPREAD: 6 × 8ft (1.8 × 2.5m)
BLOOMING PERIOD: Early summer
SOIL: Rich, moist to boggy. Needs shelter from wind.

❄ **5-8**

LATIN NAME: *Acer palmatum* var. *dissectum*
COMMON NAME: Japanese maple
ALTERNATIVES: 'Crimson Queen,' Dissectum Viride Group
DESCRIPTION: Shrub of rounded, arching habit with finely cut palmate leaves. Foliage easily damaged by late spring frost, strong sun and dry winds. Excellent autumn color. Beautiful foliage plant.
HEIGHT AND SPREAD: 5 × 6ft (1.5 × 1.8m)
BLOOMING PERIOD: Early spring
SOIL: Best on neutral to acid, humus-rich and moisture-retentive.

LATIN NAME: *Hosta* (gold-leaved cultivar)
COMMON NAME: Hosta, plantain lily, funkia
ALTERNATIVES: 'Sum and Substance,' 'Sun Power,' 'Zounds,' 'Piedmont Gold,' 'Hydon Sunset'
DESCRIPTION: Herbaceous perennial with pointed leaves in butter-yellow to yellowish green, sometimes thick-textured and puckered. The trumpet-shaped flowers are whitish to lilac or mauve.
HEIGHT AND SPREAD: 2–2½ × 3ft (60–76 × 90cm)
BLOOMING PERIOD: Mid- to late summer
SOIL: Fertile, humus-rich, moisture-retentive to moist.

❄ **3-9**

LATIN NAME: *Amaranthus caudatus* 'Albiflorus'
COMMON NAME: White-flowered love-lies-bleeding
ALTERNATIVES: None
DESCRIPTION: Half-hardy annual of bushy habit with very large, broad, pointed green leaves and long tassels of greenish white blooms. Most often used as a centerpiece or "dot" plant in bedding displays giving a sub-tropical look.
HEIGHT AND SPREAD: 3–4 × 2½ft (0.9–1.2 × 0.75m)
BLOOMING PERIOD: Early summer to mid-autumn
SOIL: Any well-drained.

LATIN NAME: *Ballota* 'All Hallows Green'
COMMON NAME: Known by Latin name
ALTERNATIVES: *B. pseudodictamnus, B. acetabulosa*
DESCRIPTION: Evergreen sub-shrub with stems covered in woolly, lime-green rounded leaves with pale green bobble-shaped flower heads in the leaf axils. Tidy up winter-damaged foliage by cutting back to ground level in spring.
HEIGHT AND SPREAD: 12 × 18in (30 × 45cm)
BLOOMING PERIOD: Mid- to late summer
SOIL: Any well-drained.

❄ **8-10**

❄ **5-10**

LATIN NAME: *Salvia officinalis* 'Icterina'
COMMON NAME: Golden-variegated sage
ALTERNATIVES: None
DESCRIPTION: Evergreen or semi-evergreen perennial of domed habit with lance-shaped gray-green, aromatic leaves, splashed light green and gold. Small purple-blue blooms.
HEIGHT AND SPREAD: 2 × 3ft (0.6 × 0.9m)
BLOOMING PERIOD: Summer
SOIL: Any well-drained, preferably alkaline.

BACK

5-9

LATIN NAME: *Euonymus fortunei* 'Silver Queen'
COMMON NAME: Wintercreeper
ALTERNATIVES: *Rhamnus alaternus* 'Argenteovariegata'
DESCRIPTION: Evergreen shrub of bushy habit with small, oval-shaped leaves margined creamy-white. The new growth in spring is yellow-variegated. Insignificant flowers. Grows taller as a wall-trained shrub.
HEIGHT AND SPREAD: 7 × 5ft (2.1 × 1.5m)
BLOOMING PERIOD: Spring
SOIL: Fertile, well-drained.

9-10

LATIN NAME: *Cycas revoluta*
COMMON NAME: Cycad, Japanese sago palm
ALTERNATIVES: None
DESCRIPTION: Evergreen plant after many years producing one or several short woody trunks topped by a rosette of arching, palm-like leaves. Mature female plants may produce red fruits.
HEIGHT AND SPREAD: 10 × 10ft (3 × 3m)
BLOOMING PERIOD: Summer
SOIL: Well-drained, humus-rich and moisture-retentive.

MIDDLE

3-8

LATIN NAME: *Pinus strobus* 'Horsford'
COMMON NAME: Dwarf white pine
ALTERNATIVES: 'Minima,' 'Reinshaus'
DESCRIPTION: Evergreen shrub with dense clusters of short, yellowish green needle-like leaves producing a low, dome-shaped habit. Slow-growing, but will eventually reach stated height and spread.
HEIGHT AND SPREAD: 2½ × 4ft (0.75 × 1.2m)
BLOOMING PERIOD: Insignificant
SOIL: Any well-drained but moisture-retentive.

3-6

LATIN NAME: *Abies balsamea* f. *hudsonia*
COMMON NAME: Balsam fir
ALTERNATIVES: 'Nana'
DESCRIPTION: Evergreen shrub with densely-packed, mid-green, needle-like foliage on short branches. The plant grows into a round-topped dome and is slow-growing.
HEIGHT AND SPREAD: 3 × 4ft (0.9 × 1.2m)
BLOOMING PERIOD: Insignificant
SOIL: Well-drained, neutral to acid, moisture-retentive.

FRONT

9-10

LATIN NAME: *Astelia nervosa*
COMMON NAME: Kakaha
ALTERNATIVES: None
DESCRIPTION: Herbaceous perennial making spreading clumps of sword-like leaves in silver-green. In summer, pale brown scented flowers at the center of a rosette are followed by green berries.
HEIGHT AND SPREAD: 2 × 5ft (0.6 × 1.5m)
BLOOMING PERIOD: Summer
SOIL: Fertile, humus-rich and moisture-retentive.

3-10

LATIN NAME: *Plantago major* 'Rosularis'
COMMON NAME: Rose plantain
ALTERNATIVES: None
DESCRIPTION: Herbaceous perennial making low rosettes of broad, oval, dark green leaves above which are produced short stems bearing unusual flowers of greenish bracts which look like petals.
HEIGHT AND SPREAD: 6–12 × 8in (15–30 × 20cm)
BLOOMING PERIOD: Summer
SOIL: Any well-drained.

LATIN NAME: *Eryngium agavifolium* syn. *E. bromeliifolium*
COMMON NAME: Sea holly
ALTERNATIVES: *E. eburneum, E. yuccifolium*
DESCRIPTION: Evergreen perennial producing a basal rosette of succulent, saw-edged leaves and a tall, branching flower stem bearing the large, greenish thimble-shaped heads.
HEIGHT AND SPREAD: 5 × 2ft (1.5 × 0.6m)
BLOOMING PERIOD: Late summer
SOIL: Well-drained, even poor or limey. Tolerates drought once established.

6-10

7-9

LATIN NAME: *Griselinia littoralis* 'Variegata'
COMMON NAME: Variegated broadleaf
ALTERNATIVES: 'Bantry Bay,' 'Dixon's Cream,' 'Green Jewel'
DESCRIPTION: Evergreen shrub of bushy, upright habit with leathery, glossy oval leaves which are variegated bright green, gray-green and creamy-white. Very salt tolerant and suits milder coastal gardens.
HEIGHT AND SPREAD: 10 × 10ft (3 × 3m)
BLOOMING PERIOD: Early spring (insignificant)
SOIL: Any reasonable kind excluding excessively limy.

6-9

LATIN NAME: *Pennisetum villosum* syn. *P. longistylum*
COMMON NAME: Feather-top
ALTERNATIVES: *P. orientale, P. alopecuroides* and *P. o.* 'Woodside'
DESCRIPTION: Ornamental grass with undistinguished leaves but arching stems carrying beautiful pale, pinkish brown fluffy spikelets. These have long protruding bristles. May be an invasive self-seeder.
HEIGHT AND SPREAD: 36 × 20in (90 ×50cm)
BLOOMING PERIOD: Autumn
SOIL: Any well-drained.

LATIN NAME: *Veratrum viride*
COMMON NAME: False hellebore, Indian poke
ALTERNATIVES: None
DESCRIPTION: A group of herbaceous perennials grown mainly for their sculptural foliage. The large, broad, oval leaves have deep parallel veins and make a good clump at the base of the upright, flower stem.
HEIGHT AND SPREAD: 4 × 2ft (1.2 × 0.6m)
BLOOMING PERIOD: Summer
SOIL: Fertile, humus-rich and moisture-retentive to moist.

3-9

LATIN NAME: *Solenostemon* cultivar syn. *Coleus blumei* cultivar
COMMON NAME: Coleus, flame nettle
ALTERNATIVES: 'Wizard Mixed,' 'Sabre Mixed'
DESCRIPTION: Tender perennial often used as a house or conservatory plant or used as an annual in colder regions for container and bedding displays. Leaves come in a wide range of colors and patterns.
HEIGHT AND SPREAD: 6–18 × 6–12in (15–45 × 15–30cm)
BLOOMING PERIOD: Summer
SOIL: Any fertile, well-drained but retentive soil.

10

LATIN NAME: *Eucomis bicolor* 'Alba'
COMMON NAME: Pineapple Lily
ALTERNATIVES: *E. bicolor*
DESCRIPTION: Bulbous plant with a basal rosette of long, arching, strap-shaped leaves which produces a stout flower spike covered from tip to base with single white blooms. At the top is a pineapple-like tuft of short leaves.
HEIGHT AND SPREAD: 18 × 12in (45 × 30cm)
BLOOMING PERIOD: Late summer
SOIL: Fertile, well-drained.

8-10

BACK

9-10

LATIN NAME: *Chamaerops humilis*
COMMON NAME: Dwarf fan palm, European fan palm
ALTERNATIVES: *Trachycarpus fortunei*
DESCRIPTION: Evergreen, slow-growing palm with fan-shaped leaves up to 2ft (60cm) across. Trunk has a fibrous covering and leaf stems are spiny. Female plants have yellow flowers and brown fruits.
HEIGHT AND SPREAD: 16 × 13ft (4.8 × 4m)
BLOOMING PERIOD: Summer
SOIL: Well-drained.

5-9

LATIN NAME: *Miscanthus sinensis* 'Rotsilber' ('Silver-red')
COMMON NAME: Japanese silver grass
ALTERNATIVES: *M. s.* 'Gracillimus'
DESCRIPTION: Herbaceous grass forming a narrow column of long, very narrow green leaves with a silver stripe. The branched flower plumes are a rich red and carried well above the foliage.
HEIGHT AND SPREAD: 4 × 1½ft (1.2 × 0.45m)
BLOOMING PERIOD: Early autumn
SOIL: Fertile, well-drained but moisture-retentive.

MIDDLE

7-10

LATIN NAME: *Euphorbia longifolia*
COMMON NAME: Spurge, milkweed
ALTERNATIVES: *E. griffithii* and forms
DESCRIPTION: Herbaceous perennial making spreading clumps of upright stems clothed in narrowly lanceolate leaves with a conspicuous white midrib. The flowers are lime-green and appear in terminal clusters. Sap is a skin irritant.
HEIGHT AND SPREAD: 36 × 20in (90 × 50cm)
BLOOMING PERIOD: Early summer
SOIL: Fertile, moisture-retentive to moist.

7-9

LATIN NAME: *Silybum marianum*
COMMON NAME: Blessed Mary's thistle
ALTERNATIVES: None
DESCRIPTION: Biennial making a low mound of large, jagged, spiny leaves in dark green with white marbling. Purple thistle-like heads. Plant is like caviar for slugs and snails! Invasive in mild climates.
HEIGHT AND SPREAD: 4 × 2ft (1.2 × 0.6m)
BLOOMING PERIOD: Summer to early autumn
SOIL: Well-drained.

FRONT

7-10

LATIN NAME: *Galtonia viridiflora*
COMMON NAME: Spire lily, Cape hyacinth
ALTERNATIVES: *G. princeps*
DESCRIPTION: Bulbous plant making a low clump of handsome, gray-green, strap-shaped leaves above which the erect flower stems are borne. These carry up to 30 pale green hanging bell-shaped blooms.
HEIGHT AND SPREAD: 3 × 1ft (0.9 × 0.3m)
BLOOMING PERIOD: Late summer to early autumn
SOIL: Well-drained but moisture-retentive, especially during summer.

LATIN NAME: *Molucella laevis*
COMMON NAME: Bells of Ireland, shell flower
ALTERNATIVES: None
DESCRIPTION: Half-hardy annual often grown for fresh and dried flower arranging. Produces upright, dense spikes of tiny white flowers, each surrounded by a large, bright green, shell-shaped bract.
HEIGHT AND SPREAD: 24 × 8in (60 × 20cm)
BLOOMING PERIOD: Summer
SOIL: Fertile, very well-drained.

BACK

LATIN NAME: *Cortaderia selloana* 'Aureolineata' ('Gold-band')
COMMON NAME: Variegated pampas grass
ALTERNATIVES: None
DESCRIPTION: Evergreen tussock-forming grass with narrow, arching leaves margined golden-yellow. The foliage is very eye-catching and makes a useful contrast with broad-leaved plants. Upright white flower plumes. Invasive in mild climates.
HEIGHT AND SPREAD: 5–6 × 5ft (1.5–1.8 × 1.5m)
BLOOMING PERIOD: Early autumn
SOIL: Well-drained.

7-10

LATIN NAME: *Cortaderia selloana* 'Pumila'
COMMON NAME: Dwarf pampas grass
ALTERNATIVES: 'Silver Comet'
DESCRIPTION: Evergreen grass making a low tussock of narrow, arching gray-green leaves. In early autumn, tall flower stems emerge which carry silvery-white, fluffy flower plumes. An excellent compact variety for smaller gardens. Pampas grasses may become invasive.
HEIGHT AND SPREAD: 3–5 × 4–5ft (0.9–1.5 × 1.2–1.5m)
BLOOMING PERIOD: Early autumn
SOIL: Any well-drained.

7-10

MIDDLE

LATIN NAME: *Zantedeschia aethiopica* 'Green Goddess'
COMMON NAME: Arum lily, lily of the Nile
ALTERNATIVES: *Z. aethiopica,* 'Crowborough'
DESCRIPTION: Herbaceous perennial with deep green, broad, arrow-shaped leaves. Upright stems carry green spathes with a white throat which are lovely for flower arranging but need a contrasting backdrop.
HEIGHT AND SPREAD: 1½–3 × 1½–2ft (0.45–0.9 × 45–0.6m)
BLOOMING PERIOD: Summer
SOIL: Fertile, humus-rich and moisture-retentive to moist. Mulch heavily.

8-10

8-10

LATIN NAME: *Fuchsia* 'Genii'
COMMON NAME: Known by Latin name
ALTERNATIVES: 'Golden Treasure' and many others
DESCRIPTION: Shrub of bushy habit with slender stems clothed in small, lime-green leaves. Dropper-like cerise-red and purple flowers appear late in the season. Cut back hard in spring for best foliage.
HEIGHT AND SPREAD: 3–4 × 3ft (0.9–1.2 × 0.9m)
BLOOMING PERIOD: Mid-summer to early autumn
SOIL: Fertile, well-drained but moisture-retentive.

FRONT

LATIN NAME: *Pelargonium* 'Lady Plymouth'
COMMON NAME: Scented geranium
ALTERNATIVES: *P. crispum* 'Variegatum'
DESCRIPTION: Tender perennial with deeply lobed, gray-green and white variegated aromatic leaves. Small, purplish blooms in clusters but this is mainly a foliage variety.
HEIGHT AND SPREAD: 24 × 12in (60 × 30cm)
BLOOMING PERIOD: Summer to autumn
SOIL: Well-drained.

10

LATIN NAME: *Carlina àcaulis*
COMMON NAME: Carline or alpine thistle
ALTERNATIVES: None
DESCRIPTION: Herbaceous perennial making rosettes of spiny, deeply-toothed green leaves with a single, stemless, thistle-like head at the center. These are light brown surrounded by creamy-colored, papery bracts.
HEIGHT AND SPREAD: 3–4 × 6–9in (7.6–10 × 15–23cm)
BLOOMING PERIOD: Summer to autumn
SOIL: Well-drained.

5-9

79

Red

In nature, red is a warning sign and signifies danger. Bright red blooms are particularly attention-grabbing, especially when used sparingly against a green backdrop. Red is also the color which partially sighted people find easiest to discern.

We associate red with strong emotions - fiery passion, love, and anger - so this is not a color to use exclusively if you want to create a restful and calming scheme. When we think of the reds of romance and valentines, these tend to be the velvet reds, crimsons, and wine colors of roses and other blooms at the blue end of the scale. Bright clear reds coupled with rich greens suggest the Orient or tropical rainforest. In the Northern hemisphere, red winter berries along with white blooms and glossy green foliage bring to mind the festive season.

Blue-reds work well with other cool colors like deep blue, purple, silver, white, or pale lemon-yellow to give quite an old-fashioned look. In contrast, warm orange-reds combined with pure blues, golden yellows, clear oranges, white, and lime-green produce fresh, vibrant, and modern-looking schemes. Given a foil of deep-purple foliage and flower, you can successfully combine all shades of red - the bright reds adding a welcome vibrancy. The only combination likely to cause problems is orange-red with true pinks or blue-pinks. On the other hand, scarlet and cerise-pink make a strong display.

Left: *Red flowers like these tulips are among the most vivid and eyecatching in the garden.*

BACK

8-10

5-7

LATIN NAME: *Pieris formosa var. forrestii*
COMMON NAME: Lily of the valley shrub, andromeda
ALTERNATIVES: 'Wakehurst,' P. 'Forest Flame,' P. *japonica* 'Firecrest'
DESCRIPTION: Evergreen shrub with dark glossy foliage. New growth scarlet-red in spring. Vulnerable to late frost, provide a sheltered site. Tassels of buds through winter open to white, bell-shaped flowers.
HEIGHT AND SPREAD: 6 × 12ft (2 × 3.6m)
BLOOMING PERIOD: Spring
SOIL: Humus-rich, neutral to acid.

LATIN NAME: *Rhododendron* hybrid cultivar
COMMON NAME: Known by Latin name
ALTERNATIVES: 'Girard's Crimson,' 'Red Red,' 'Earl of Donoughmore'
DESCRIPTION: Evergreen shrub with broad, leathery leaves and cone-shaped flower buds opening to large trusses of showy, open-mouthed blooms. Best in part shade but will tolerate sun if sufficient moisture.
HEIGHT AND SPREAD: 10 × 13ft (3 × 4m)
BLOOMING PERIOD: Late spring to early summer
SOIL: Humus-rich, neutral to acid. Suffers if any lime is present.

MIDDLE

LATIN NAME: *Tropaeolum tricolorum*
COMMON NAME: Cornucopia nasturtium
ALTERNATIVES: None
DESCRIPTION: Herbaceous climber growing new fine stems from small underground tubers every year. Delicate leaves divided into about six lobes. Spurred flowers bright red, orange, and yellow with black markings.
HEIGHT AND SPREAD: 3–4 × 2ft (90–120 × 60cm)
BLOOMING PERIOD: Early spring to early summer
SOIL: Any well-drained.

8-10

4-9

LATIN NAME: *Papaver orientale* 'Lady Bird'
COMMON NAME: Oriental poppy
ALTERNATIVES: 'Allegro,' 'Marcus Perry'
DESCRIPTION: Herbaceous perennial with hairy, deeply-divided foliage. Stout stems bear bowl-shaped flowers with central knob which become the "pepper-pot" seed head. Foliage dies by mid-summer.
HEIGHT AND SPREAD: 2 × 1–3ft (60 × 30–90cm)
BLOOMING PERIOD: Early summer
SOIL: Any well-drained to dry and reasonably fertile.

FRONT

LATIN NAME: *Astilbe* 'Montgomery'
COMMON NAME: Known by Latin name
ALTERNATIVES: 'Fanal,' 'Red Sentinel,' 'Feuer' ('Fire'), 'Spartan'
DESCRIPTION: Herbaceous perennial with a spreading rootstock and attractive ferny foliage. Feathery, tapering plumes are held on wiry flower stems. The brown seed heads remain attractive through autumn and winter.
HEIGHT AND SPREAD: 2½ × 3ft (75 × 90cm)
BLOOMING PERIOD: Summer
SOIL: Moisture-retentive to boggy. Avoid dry soils.

4-8

3-9

LATIN NAME: *Tulipa* 'Cassini'
COMMON NAME: Tulip
ALTERNATIVES: 'Île de France,' 'Apeldoorn,' 'Red Shine'
DESCRIPTION: Bulb with broad, strap-like foliage and tall, straight stems carrying the cone-shaped buds which open wide on warm, bright days. Deadhead after flowering, leaving stems and leaves.
HEIGHT AND SPREAD: 15in (38cm)
BLOOMING PERIOD: Late spring
SOIL: Well-drained.

LATIN NAME: *Crinodendron hookerianum*
COMMON NAME: Lantern tree
ALTERNATIVES: None
DESCRIPTION: Evergreen shrub with a strongly upright habit and narrow, leathery dark green leaves. The crimson lantern-like flowers hang down from the underside of the branches. Needs shelter. Slow to establish.
HEIGHT AND SPREAD: 10 × 5ft (3 × 1.5m)
BLOOMING PERIOD: Late spring to early summer
SOIL: Humus-rich, neutral to acid.

9-10

LATIN NAME: *Clianthus puniceus*
COMMON NAME: Glory pea, parrot's bill, lobster claw
ALTERNATIVES: 'Cardinal' ('Red Cardinal')
DESCRIPTION: Evergreen lax-stemmed shrub with grayish-green pinnate leaves. Best tied onto a framework of wires. Spectacular claw-like flowers. Provide a warm, sheltered aspect in cooler regions.
HEIGHT AND SPREAD: 8–12 × 8–12ft (2.4–3.6 × 2.4–3.7m)
BLOOMING PERIOD: Early summer
SOIL: Well-drained.

8-10

4-9

LATIN NAME: *Pupaver orientale* var. *bracteatum*
COMMON NAME: Oriental poppy
ALTERNATIVES: 'Goliath Group'
DESCRIPTION: Herbaceous perennial with hairy, deeply-divided foliage. Stout stems bear bowl-shaped flowers with central knob which becomes the "pepper-pot" seed head. Foliage dies by mid-summer.
HEIGHT AND SPREAD: 3–4 × 1–3ft (90–120 × 30–90cm)
BLOOMING PERIOD: Late spring to early summer
SOIL: Any well-drained to dry and reasonably fertile.

6-9

LATIN NAME: *Rhododendron* 'Mother's Day'
COMMON NAME: Evergreen azalea
ALTERNATIVES: 'Addy Wery,' 'Scarlet Wonder,' 'Ima-shojo'
DESCRIPTION: Dwarf evergreen shrub making a mound of glossy, dark green leaves. New growth contrasting fresh green. Prolific buds open to smother the foliage. Prune out winter damage.
HEIGHT AND SPREAD: 3 × 4ft (90 × 120cm)
BLOOMING PERIOD: Mid-spring to late spring
SOIL: Humus-rich, neutral to acid. Suffers if any lime present.

4-8

LATIN NAME: *Astilbe* 'Fanal'
COMMON NAME: Known by Latin name
ALTERNATIVES: 'Montgomery,' 'Red Sentinel,' 'Feuer' ('Fire'), 'Spartan'
DESCRIPTION: Herbaceous perennial with a spreading rootstock and attractive bronze-tinged ferny foliage. New spring growth deep burgundy-red. Numerous feathery plumes held on wiry flower stems.
HEIGHT AND SPREAD: 2 × 3ft (60 × 90cm)
BLOOMING PERIOD: Summer
SOIL: Moisture-retentive to boggy. Avoid dry soils.

LATIN NAME: *Antirrhinum majus* variety
COMMON NAME: Snapdragon
ALTERNATIVES: 'Black Prince,' 'Dazzler,' 'Monarch Scarlet'
DESCRIPTION: Half-hardy annual with narrow, pointed leaves and branched stems holding dense, upright flower spikes. Pinch out seedlings to promote branching and remove fading spikes.
HEIGHT AND SPREAD: 1½ × 1ft (45 × 30cm)
BLOOMING PERIOD: Summer to autumn
SOIL: Fertile, well-drained.

BACK

LATIN NAME: *Rosa* 'Precious Platinum' (syn. 'Opa Potschke,' 'Red Star')
COMMON NAME: Large-flowered (hybrid tea) bush rose
ALTERNATIVES: 'Alec's Red,' 'Deep Secret,' 'My Love,' 'Royal William'
DESCRIPTION: Rose of bushy habit with good glossy leaves and very large, well-shaped double blooms in bright red. Very slight scent. Deadhead to prolong flowering and prune hard in spring.
HEIGHT AND SPREAD: 36 × 26in (90 × 65cm)
BLOOMING PERIOD: Summer to autumn
SOIL: Rich, moisture-retentive. Does well on clay.

5-9

LATIN NAME: *Rosa* 'Altissimo'
COMMON NAME: Climbing rose
ALTERNATIVES: 'Dublin Bay,' 'Danse de Feu,' 'Paul's Scarlet'
DESCRIPTION: Repeat-flowering climber with single deep red scented blooms and a large boss of golden-yellow stamens. Large deep green leathery leaflets. Moderately disease resistant.
HEIGHT AND SPREAD: 15 × 15ft (4.6 × 4.6m)
BLOOMING PERIOD: Summer to mid-autumn
SOIL: Humus-rich, moisture-retentive. Dislikes thin or limey soil.

5-9

MIDDLE

LATIN NAME: *Monarda* 'Cambridge Scarlet'
COMMON NAME: Bee balm, bergamot
ALTERNATIVES: 'Adam,' 'Capricorn,' 'Feuernschopf,' 'Mahogany'
DESCRIPTION: Herbaceous perennial making a mat of aromatic foliage from which arise many upright self-supporting stems with whorls of hooded flowers at the top half.
HEIGHT AND SPREAD: 36 × 18in (90 × 45cm)
BLOOMING PERIOD: Mid- to late summer
SOIL: Fertile, moisture-retentive.

4-10

LATIN NAME: *Potentilla fruticosa* 'Red Ace'
COMMON NAME: Shrubby cinquefoil
ALTERNATIVES: 'Red Robin'
DESCRIPTION: Low shrub of dense, twiggy habit covered with delicate pinnate leaves and small, flat circular blooms produced in flushes. 'Red Ace' does best in part shade to prevent bleaching of flowers.
HEIGHT AND SPREAD: 3 × 3ft (90 × 90cm)
BLOOMING PERIOD: Early summer to early autumn
SOIL: Any fertile, well-drained avoiding extreme alkalinity.

3-7

FRONT

LATIN NAME: *Nicotiana alata*
COMMON NAME: Flowering tobacco
ALTERNATIVES: 'Domino Crimson F1,' 'Domino Red F1'
DESCRIPTION: Half-hardy annual or perennial with broad, hairy leaves making a basal rosette from which the upright stems bearing outward facing flowers appear. Fragrant in early evening. May self-sow.
HEIGHT AND SPREAD: 12–14 × 12in (30–35 × 30cm)
BLOOMING PERIOD: Summer to early autumn
SOIL: Any reasonably fertile, moisture-retentive.

LATIN NAME: *Impatiens* variety
COMMON NAME: Busy Lizzie
ALTERNATIVES: 'Super Elfin Red Velvet F1,' 'Accent Red F1'
DESCRIPTION: Half-hardy annual/tender perennial with broad, tapering leaves. Circular blooms in abundance. Deep colors may bleach in full sun but perform well in moderate shade.
HEIGHT AND SPREAD: 6 × 9in (15 × 23cm)
BLOOMING PERIOD: Summer to early autumn (year-round in Australia)
SOIL: Fertile, moisture-retentive. Avoid hard, dry soils.

LATIN NAME: *Clematis 'Ville de Lyon'*
COMMON NAME: Known by Latin name
ALTERNATIVES: 'Madame Edouard Andre,' 'Niobe'
DESCRIPTION: Climber needing support. Pinnate leaves and large pointed buds opening almost flat reveal central boss of stamens. Often a second flush in autumn.
HEIGHT AND SPREAD: 12–15 × 12–15ft (3.6–4.6 × 3.6–4.6m)
BLOOMING PERIOD: Early summer to mid-autumn
SOIL: Cool, moisture-retentive, humus-rich. Roots should be shaded.

5-9

LATIN NAME: *Clematis 'Madame Julia Correvon'*
COMMON NAME: Known by Latin name
ALTERNATIVES: 'Kermesina'
DESCRIPTION: Climber with light crimson-red blooms, not as big as the large-flowered hybrids but very numerous and much less prone to clematis wilt. Cut down to 12in (30cm) in early spring. May be grown over a spring shrub.
HEIGHT AND SPREAD: 12 × 12ft (3.6 × 3.6m)
BLOOMING PERIOD: Early summer to early autumn
SOIL: Cool, moisture-retentive, humus rich. Roots should be shaded.

5-9

5-10

LATIN NAME: *Rosa 'Eye Paint'* syn. 'Maceye,' 'Tapis Persan'
COMMON NAME: Dwarf shrub rose
ALTERNATIVES: 'Phantom'
DESCRIPTION: Shrub of dense habit, well-covered in dark foliage. Striking single blooms (scarlet-red with a white 'eye'), in large clusters. Little scent.
HEIGHT AND SPREAD: 40 × 30in (100 × 75cm)
BLOOMING PERIOD: Summer to early autumn
SOIL: Rich, moisture-retentive. Does well on heavy soils e.g. clay.

LATIN NAME: *Lychnis chalcedonica*
COMMON NAME: Maltese cross, Jerusalem cross
ALTERNATIVES: 'Red Tiger'
DESCRIPTION: Herbaceous perennial with upright stems carrying cross shaped flowers of brilliant scarlet. Best given a spot sheltered from wind. The strong color needs careful placing.
HEIGHT AND SPREAD: 3–4 × 1ft (90–120 × 30cm)
BLOOMING PERIOD: Mid-summer
SOIL: Rich, moisture-retentive, but well-drained.

3-10

LATIN NAME: *Dianthus allwoodii* cultivar
COMMON NAME: Pink
ALTERNATIVES: 'Devon General,' 'Diane,' 'Becka Falls,' 'Ian'
DESCRIPTION: Evergreen perennial with narrow blue-green leaves making a dense low carpet. Branched flower stems carry the dense frilled flowers which often have a spicy clove scent. Short-lived but easy to take cuttings.
HEIGHT AND SPREAD: 12–18 × 12–18in (30–45 × 30–45cm)
BLOOMING PERIOD: Early summer to early autumn
SOIL: Light, well-drained. Avoid moist acid soils.

4-10

10

LATIN NAME: *Pelargonium* cultivar
COMMON NAME: Zonal geranium
ALTERNATIVES: 'Czar,' 'Classic Scarlet F1,' 'Sensation Cherry F1'
DESCRIPTION: Tender perennial or sub-shrub with succulent stems and scalloped-edged aromatic leaves. These may be flushed with red or pink or boldly zoned. Single or double blooms in rounded heads.
HEIGHT AND SPREAD: 12–15 × 12in (30–38 × 30cm)
BLOOMING PERIOD: Summer to mid-autumn
SOIL: Well-drained. Tolerates poor, stony ground.

BACK

7-10

LATIN NAME: *Callistemon rigidus*
COMMON NAME: Bottlebrush
ALTERNATIVES: *C. citrinus* 'Splendens,' *C. viminalis* 'Captain Cook'
DESCRIPTION: Evergreen shrub with stems arching over at tip, clothed in sharply pointed leaves. Red blooms with masses of long stamens resemble bottle-brushes. Needs shelter in cooler regions.
HEIGHT AND SPREAD: 7 × 7ft (2.1 × 2.1m)
BLOOMING PERIOD: Spring to early summer
SOIL: Fertile, well-drained.

LATIN NAME: *Hibiscus rosa-sinensis*
COMMON NAME: Rose of China
ALTERNATIVES: 'Island Empress,' 'Brilliant Red'
DESCRIPTION: Evergreen shrub of bushy habit with rigid, upright stems clothed with broad, oval, glossy leaves with serrated edges. Large, funnel-shaped blooms produced over a long period. May be cut hard back in spring.
HEIGHT AND SPREAD: 5–10 × 5–10ft (1.5–3 × 1.5–3m)
BLOOMING PERIOD: Summer to autumn/winter
SOIL: Fertile, well-drained but moisture-retentive.

9-10

MIDDLE

7-9

LATIN NAME: *Hibiscus moscheutos* 'Southern Belle'
COMMON NAME: Rose mallow
ALTERNATIVES: 'Disco Belle'
DESCRIPTION: Perennial which may be grown as an annual of bushy habit with broad, dull green leaves and spectacularly large, circular blooms up to 12in (30cm) across. Shelter from strong winds.
HEIGHT AND SPREAD: 3–4 × 3–4ft (0.9–1.2+ × 0.9–1.2m)
BLOOMING PERIOD: Late spring to summer
SOIL: Well-drained but moisture-retentive.

5-9

LATIN NAME: *Rosa* 'Beautiful Britain'
COMMON NAME: Cluster-flowered or floribunda rose
ALTERNATIVES: 'Captain Cook,' 'Evelyn Fison,' 'Trumpeter'
DESCRIPTION: Bush rose of medium size with a moderately open habit and rather sparse foliage. Small, well-shaped double flowers in clusters. Bright scarlet coloring. Some fragrance.
HEIGHT AND SPREAD: 3–4 × 3–4ft (0.9–1.2 × 0.9–1.2m)
BLOOMING PERIOD: Spring to autumn
SOIL: Rich, well-drained but moisture-retentive with plenty of humus.

FRONT

5-10

LATIN NAME: *Helianthemum nummularium* 'Supreme,' syn. 'Red Orient'
COMMON NAME: Sun rose
ALTERNATIVES: 'Ben Hope,' 'Ben More,' 'Fire Dragon'
DESCRIPTION: Evergreen shrub of spreading habit with oval blue-gray leaves which make a superb foil for the scarlet, circular blooms. The flowers are further highlighted by a golden boss of stamens.
HEIGHT AND SPREAD: 9–12 × 18in (23–30 × 45cm)
BLOOMING PERIOD: Late spring and summer
SOIL: Well-drained.

LATIN NAME: *Penstemon* 'Chester Scarlet'
COMMON NAME: Known by Latin name
ALTERNATIVES: 'Garnet,' 'Rubicundus,' 'Firebird' ('Schoenholzeri'), 'Prairie Fire,' 'Scarlet Queen'
DESCRIPTION: Evergreen perennial of bushy habit with upright stems clothed in narrow leaves. Relatively large, tubular, hanging blooms with flared mouths appear in elegant spires.
HEIGHT AND SPREAD: 2 × 1½ft (0.6 × 0.45cm)
BLOOMING PERIOD: Mid-summer to mid-autumn
SOIL: Fertile, well-drained.

8-10

LATIN NAME: *Passiflora mollissima* (syn. *Tacsonia mollissima*)
COMMON NAME: Passion flower, banana passion fruit
ALTERNATIVES: *P. caerulea racemosa*, *P. racemosa*, *P. coccinea*, *P. manicata*
DESCRIPTION: Evergreen tendril climber with woody stems and soft, down-covered leaves with three lobes. Deep crimson-pink petals with a purple-blue center. Large yellow fruit. Fast-growing. Size controlled by pruning.
HEIGHT AND SPREAD: 15 × 15ft (4.5 × 4.5m)
BLOOMING PERIOD: Summer to autumn
SOIL: Well-drained.

● 8-10

❄ 8-10

LATIN NAME: *Escallonia* 'Donard Beauty'
COMMON NAME: Known by Latin name
ALTERNATIVES: 'C. F. Ball,' 'Donard Brilliance,' 'Crimson Spire'
DESCRIPTION: Evergreen shrub of bushy, slightly arching habit with small, dark green, oval-shaped leaves and clusters of bell-shaped crimson flowers. Good seaside plant, avoid severe wind chill.
HEIGHT AND SPREAD: 10 × 13ft (3 × 4m)
BLOOMING PERIOD: Late spring to mid-summer
SOIL: Fertile, well-drained. Very limy soils can cause chlorosis.

LATIN NAME: *Lysimachia atropurpurea*
COMMON NAME: Known by Latin name
ALTERNATIVES: None
DESCRIPTION: Herbaceous perennial with slender, upright stems and grayish green narrow leaves. The long spikes of deep purplish red open to a paler crimson.
HEIGHT AND SPREAD: 3 × 1ft (90 × 30cm)
BLOOMING PERIOD: Summer
SOIL: Moisture-retentive to damp.

❄ 6-9

❄ 5-8

LATIN NAME: *Lilium* 'Red Knight' syn. 'Roter Cardinal'
COMMON NAME: Lily
ALTERNATIVES: 'Redruth,' 'Redstart,' 'Firecracker'
DESCRIPTION: Bulb with unbranched stems clothed in narrow leaves. Each stem has a cluster of upward facing buds and flowers. Blooms are maroon-red with black-purple spotting in the throat.
HEIGHT AND SPREAD: 2½ × 3ft (0.75 × 0.9m)
BLOOMING PERIOD: Early summer to mid-summer
SOIL: Fertile, well-drained but moisture-retentive.

❄ 4-8

LATIN NAME: *Berberis thunbergii* 'Kobold'
COMMON NAME: Japanese barberry
ALTERNATIVES: B. 'Atropurpurea Nana' ('Little Favorite')
DESCRIPTION: Dwarf shrub of dense, dome-shaped habit with small, oval to rounded leaves, mid-green, producing rich autumn tints. Small, white, pink-tinged blooms are followed by cylindrical red berries.
HEIGHT AND SPREAD: 1½ × 2½–3ft (0.45 × 0.75–0.9m)
BLOOMING PERIOD: Spring
SOIL: Fertile, well-drained, lime-free.

LATIN NAME: *Salvia splendens* variety
COMMON NAME: Scarlet sage
ALTERNATIVES: 'Lady in Red,' 'Vanguard,' 'Maestro,' 'Scarlet King'
DESCRIPTION: Tender evergreen sub-shrub normally grown as a half-hardy annual bedding plant with fresh green oval leaves and spikes of tubular, bright scarlet blooms. Pinch out seedlings to induce branched habit.
HEIGHT AND SPREAD: 12 × 8–12in (30 × 20–30cm)
BLOOMING PERIOD: Summer to autumn
SOIL: Well-drained.

BACK

5-9

LATIN NAME: *Clematis* 'Niobe'
COMMON NAME: Known by Latin name
ALTERNATIVES: 'Madame Edouard André,' 'Ville de Lyon'
DESCRIPTION: Climber having pinnate leaves with twining leaf stalks. Requires support to enable it to climb. Large blooms consisting of six deep crimson sepals, with a boss of greenish yellow stamens.
HEIGHT AND SPREAD: 6–10 × 3ft (1.8–3 × 0.9m)
BLOOMING PERIOD: Early to late summer
SOIL: Fertile, humus-rich, moisture-retentive. Mulch, shade roots.

LATIN NAME: *Grevillea rosmarinifolia*
COMMON NAME: Known by Latin name
ALTERNATIVES: G. 'Canberra Gem,' G. juniperina, G. wilsonii, G. banksii
DESCRIPTION: Evergreen shrub of rounded habit with well-branched stems covered in narrow leaves reminiscent of rosemary. Clusters of tubular red blooms for most of the year. Provide a warm, sheltered site in cool regions.
HEIGHT AND SPREAD: 3–6 × 3–6ft (0.9–1.8 × 0.9–1.8m)
BLOOMING PERIOD: Spring to summer
SOIL: Well-drained, neutral to acid.

8-10

MIDDLE

9-10

LATIN NAME: *Gladiolus* Grandiflorus Hybrids
COMMON NAME: Gladioli
ALTERNATIVES: Many hybrids so choose by flower color and height.
DESCRIPTION: Plant growing from a corm with sword-shaped leaves and unbranched flower spikes carrying large, funnel-shaped densely-packed blooms. Overwinter corms frost-free.
HEIGHT AND SPREAD: 24–48 × 4–6in (0.6–1.2 × 10–15cm)
BLOOMING PERIOD: Mid-summer to early autumn
SOIL: Well-drained.

4-8

LATIN NAME: *Lobelia* 'Queen Victoria'
COMMON NAME: Cardinal flower
ALTERNATIVES: L. cardinalis, 'Dark Crusader,' 'Cherry Ripe'
DESCRIPTION: Herbaceous perennial, clump-forming, with leafy flower stems rising from a basal rosette of deep purple-black foliage. Scarlet lipped flowers are closely set on erect spikes.
HEIGHT AND SPREAD: 36 × 12in (90 × 30cm)
BLOOMING PERIOD: Late summer to mid-autumn
SOIL: Rich, moist. Mulch heavily to conserve moisture and protect from frost.

FRONT

10

LATIN NAME: *Pelargonium* (zonal cultivar)
COMMON NAME: Zonal geranium
ALTERNATIVES: Century and Video series, 'Ringo Deep Scarlet'
DESCRIPTION: Tender perennial of bushy, upright habit with rounded, scalloped-edged leaves with a darker zone. Flowers in large rounded clusters. Drought-resistant and long-flowered.
HEIGHT AND SPREAD: 12–18 × 9–12in (30–45 × 23–30cm)
BLOOMING PERIOD: Early summer to mid-autumn
SOIL: Any well-drained.

LATIN NAME: *Petunia* × *hybrida*
COMMON NAME: Known by Latin name
ALTERNATIVES: F1 Multiflora and F1 Grandiflora seed strains
DESCRIPTION: Half-hardy annual with branched stems and oval leaves covered in sticky hairs. Funnel-shaped flowers. F1 hybrid Multifloras have smaller flowers but greater weather resistance.
HEIGHT AND SPREAD: 6–18 × 9–12in (15–45 × 23–30cm)
BLOOMING PERIOD: Early summer to mid-autumn
SOIL: Fertile, well-drained and friable, with good moisture-retention.

LATIN NAME: *Rhus typhina*
COMMON NAME: Staghorn sumach
ALTERNATIVES: 'Dissecta' syn. 'Laciniata,' *R. × pulvinata* Autumn Lace Group
DESCRIPTION: Wide-spreading small tree with large pinnate leaves which turn brilliant red, orange and yellow in autumn. Forms suckers. On female trees, the deep red cone-shaped seed heads remain attractive long after leaf drop. Sap can be a severe skin irritant.
HEIGHT AND SPREAD: 15 × 20ft (5 × 6m)
BLOOMING PERIOD: Summer to autumn
SOIL: Any reasonable soil.

3-8

LATIN NAME: *Abutilon megapotamicum* 'Variegatum'
COMMON NAME: Known by Latin name
ALTERNATIVES: *A. megapotamicum*, 'Wisley Red'
DESCRIPTION: Evergreen shrub with slender, weak stems. Tie to support. Long, narrow, pointed leaves have a heart-shaped base and are yellow-mottled. Hanging red and yellow bell flowers.
HEIGHT AND SPREAD: 6 × 6ft (1.8 × 1.8m)
BLOOMING PERIOD: Summer to autumn (from spring in Australia)
SOIL: Prefers rich, moisture-retentive type.

8-10

LATIN NAME: *Lobelia* 'Compliment Scarlet' syn. 'Kompliment Scharlach'
COMMON NAME: Cardinal flower
ALTERNATIVES: *L. cardinalis*, 'Queen Victoria,' 'Dark Crusader,' 'Cherry Ripe'
DESCRIPTION: Herbaceous perennial, clump-forming, with leafy flower stems rising from basal rosette of foliage. Red, lipped flowers closely-set on erect spikes. Mulch to conserve moisture and for frost cover.
HEIGHT AND SPREAD: 36 × 12in (90 × 30cm)
BLOOMING PERIOD: Mid- to late summer
SOIL: Rich, moist.

4-8

3-10

LATIN NAME: *Hemerocallis* 'Stafford'
COMMON NAME: Daylily
ALTERNATIVES: 'Alan,' 'Lusty Leyland,' 'Ed Murray,' 'Berlin Red'
DESCRIPTION: Herbaceous perennial, clump-forming, with narrow leaves. Flower stems bearing buds and flowers at the tip. Flowers open to six broad petals, deep mahogany-red with a greenish throat.
HEIGHT AND SPREAD: 2½ × 2ft (0.75 × 0.60m)
BLOOMING PERIOD: Mid- to late summer
SOIL: Rich, moist.

5-10

10

LATIN NAME: *Knautia macedonica* syn. *Scabiosa rumelica*
COMMON NAME: Known by Latin name
ALTERNATIVES: None
DESCRIPTION: Herbaceous perennial with a basal rosette of deeply divided leaves. Wiry, divided stems. Each branchlet tipped with pin-cushion shaped bloom of deep crimson. Long-flowered.
HEIGHT AND SPREAD: 2 × 2ft (0.6 × 0.6m)
BLOOMING PERIOD: Summer
SOIL: Well-drained.

LATIN NAME: *Solenostemon* cultivar syn. *Coleus blumei*
COMMON NAME: Coleus, flame nettle
ALTERNATIVES: 'Sabre Mixed'
DESCRIPTION: Tender perennial often used as a house or conservatory plant and also as a half-hardy annual for container and bedding displays. Leaves come in a wide range of colors. Remove blooms.
HEIGHT AND SPREAD: 6–18 × 6–12in (15–45 × 15–30cm)
BLOOMING PERIOD: Summer
SOIL: Any fertile, well-drained but retentive soil.

BACK

4-9

Latin name: *Lonicera × brownii*
Common name: Scarlet trumpet honeysuckle
Alternatives: 'Fuchsioides,' 'Dropmore Scarlet,' 'Scarlet Trumpet'
Description: Climber with green leaves having a gray reverse which contrasts well with the terminal clusters of tubular orange-red flowers. Not scented. In colder regions grow against a warm wall. Support.
Height and spread: 14–21 × 14–21ft (4.3–6.4 × 4.3–6.4m)
Blooming period: Early to late summer
Soil: Deep, well-cultivated, fertile and moisture-retentive.

Latin name: *Lobelia tupa*
Common name: Known by Latin name
Alternatives: None
Description: Herbaceous perennial making a striking specimen or massed planting feature. Tall dark stems with unusual tubular red-brown flowers divided at the mouth. Long, pale green down-covered leaves. Support.
Height and spread: 5 × 3ft (1.5 × 0.9m)
Blooming period: Summer
Soil: Deep, moisture-retentive.

8-10

MIDDLE

Latin name: *Rosa* 'Leslie's Dream'
Common name: Bush rose (large-flowered/hybrid tea)
Alternatives: 'Alec's Red,' 'Deep Secret,' 'My Love,' 'Royal William'
Description: Bush rose with upright habit, leathery mid-green foliage with good disease resistance. Blooms well-shaped and good for cutting.
Height and spread: 3 × 2ft (90 × 60cm)
Blooming period: Summer to early autumn
Soil: Prefers rich, moisture-retentive. Does well on heavy soils and clay.

5-9

Latin name: *Rosa* 'Trumpeter'
Common name: Bush rose
Alternatives: 'The Times,' 'Evelyn Fison'
Description: Cluster-flowered or floribunda bush rose with low, shrubby habit suitable for patio planting and low beds of one variety. Orange-red double blooms in large clusters. Little scent. Good disease resistance.
Height and spread: 20 × 18in (50 × 45cm)
Blooming period: Summer to mid-autumn
Soil: Performs best on rich, moisture-retentive. Does well on heavy clay soils.

5-9

FRONT

3-10

Latin name: *Hemerocallis* 'Little Red Hen'
Common name: Daylily
Alternatives: 'Sammy Russel,' 'Pardon Me,' 'Siloam Red Ruby'
Description: Herbaceous perennial with flowers like trumpet lilies produced from cluster of buds at top of stem (each lasts a day). Arching foliage making dense mounds, attractive in spring.
Height and spread: 1½ × 2ft (75 × 60cm)
Blooming period: Summer
Soil: Fertile, moisture-retentive.

5-9

Latin name: *Potentilla* 'Flamenco'
Common name: Cinquefoil
Alternatives: 'Gibson's Scarlet,' 'Volcan'
Description: Herbaceous perennial making mounds of strawberry-like leaves from which sprawling flower stems emerge. 'Flamenco' has larger than usual blooms produced intermittently after the initial flush.
Height and spread: 18 × 24in (45 × 60cm)
Blooming period: Early summer to early autumn
Soil: Fertile, well-drained tolerating dry conditions.

LATIN NAME: *Tropaeolum speciosum*
COMMON NAME: Scotch flame flower
ALTERNATIVES: None
DESCRIPTION: Herbaceous climber with scarlet blooms like miniature nasturtiums with fringed petals. Delicate lobed green leaves and fine, upright stems best encouraged to scramble up a shady hedge or large shrub.
HEIGHT AND SPREAD: 8 × 5ft (2.4 × 1.5m)
BLOOMING PERIOD: Summer to autumn
SOIL: Cool, moisture-retentive, enriched with organic matter.

❄ 7-10

LATIN NAME: *Calycanthus occidentalis*
COMMON NAME: Californian allspice, sweetshrub
ALTERNATIVES: *C. floridus, C. fertilis*
DESCRIPTION: Shrub of roughly rounded habit with broad leaves and sculpted red-brown fragrant flowers. Both foliage and stems release a fruity aroma when bruised.
HEIGHT AND SPREAD: 6–10 × 6–10ft (1.8–3 × 1.8–3m)
BLOOMING PERIOD: Summer
SOIL: Any fertile, well-drained but moisture-retentive.

❄ 6-9

LATIN NAME: *Penstemon* 'Firebird' syn. 'Schoenholzeri'
COMMON NAME: Known by Latin name
ALTERNATIVES: 'Chester Scarlet'
DESCRIPTION: Semi-evergreen herbaceous perennial with upright stems clothed in narrow leaves, each topped with a series of scarlet tubular flowers, flared at the mouth. Easy to propagate from cuttings.
HEIGHT AND SPREAD: 30–36 × 24in (75–90 × 60cm)
BLOOMING PERIOD: Mid-summer to mid-autumn (spring for Australia)
SOIL: Fertile, well-drained. Dislikes winter wet or mulch or leaves on crown.

❄ 8-10

LATIN NAME: *Penstemon* 'Cherry Ripe'
COMMON NAME: Known by Latin name
ALTERNATIVES: 'Rubicundus,' Prairie Fire,' 'Scarlet Queen'
DESCRIPTION: Semi-evergreen herbaceous perennial with upright stems clothed in lanceolate leaves and topped with spikes of tubular flowers with widely flaring mouths. Cut back after initial flush to encourage shoots.
HEIGHT AND SPREAD: 2 × 2ft (60 × 60cm)
BLOOMING PERIOD: Mid-summer to early autumn
SOIL: Fertile, well-drained, dislikes winter wet and leaves or mulch on crown.

❄ 8-10

❄ 5-8

LATIN NAME: *Potentilla* 'Gibson's Scarlet'
COMMON NAME: Cinquefoil
ALTERNATIVES: 'Flamenco,' 'Volcan'
DESCRIPTION: Herbaceous perennial with divided, tooth-edged leaves and many long, sprawling stems carrying the strawberry-like blooms. This variety is particularly long-blooming.
HEIGHT AND SPREAD: 18 × 24in (45 × 60cm)
BLOOMING PERIOD: Early summer to early autumn
SOIL: Fertile, well-drained, tolerating dry conditions.

💧 9-10

LATIN NAME: *Tropaeolum majus* 'Hermine Grashoff'.
COMMON NAME: Nasturtium
ALTERNATIVES: 'Red Wonder,' 'Empress of India,' 'Jewel Red'
DESCRIPTION: Trailing tender perennial with rounded pale green leaves and rich scarlet double blooms. Useful for containers and to cascade over the edge of a raised bed. An annual in cold winter areas.
HEIGHT AND SPREAD: 9 × 18in (23 × 45cm)
BLOOMING PERIOD: Summer to early autumn
SOIL: Well-drained, not too rich.

BACK

LATIN NAME: *Salvia microphylla* var. *microphylla* syn. *S. grahamii*
COMMON NAME: Ornamental sage
ALTERNATIVES: 'Newby Hall,' 'Scott's Red'
DESCRIPTION: Tender sub-shrub with light green lanceolate foliage and bright scarlet tubular hooded flowers produced over a very long period. Needs protection from a warm wall in colder areas.
HEIGHT AND SPREAD: 4 × 3ft (1.2 × 0.9m)
BLOOMING PERIOD: Mid-summer to autumn
SOIL: Well-drained, avoiding winter dampness.

9-10

LATIN NAME: *Alcea rosea*
COMMON NAME: Hollyhock
ALTERNATIVES: Various singles and doubles e.g. 'Chater's Double'
DESCRIPTION: Biennial. Flowers on tall, upright stems above basal clump of lobed leaves. Sow new plants annually to avoid the disease rust which forms orange pustules on the backs of the leaves and weakens growth.
HEIGHT AND SPREAD: 6–9 × 2ft (1.8–2.7 × 0.6m)
BLOOMING PERIOD: Mid-summer to early autumn
SOIL: Prefers heavy, rich soil, moist in summer.

2-10

MIDDLE

5-9

LATIN NAME: *Persicaria amplexicaulis* 'Firetail' syn. *Polygonum*
COMMON NAME: Knotweed
ALTERNATIVES: 'Atrosanguineum'
DESCRIPTION: Herbaceous perennial making a spreading mound of large, rather coarse, deep green leaves from which arise slender, wand-like flower stems. May be invasive under ideal conditions.
HEIGHT AND SPREAD: 4 × 4ft (1.2 × 1.2m)
BLOOMING PERIOD: Mid-summer to autumn
SOIL: Moisture-retentive to damp.

LATIN NAME: *Amaranthus caudatus* variety
COMMON NAME: Love lies bleeding
ALTERNATIVES: 'Crimson'
DESCRIPTION: Hardy annual giving a striking sub-tropical look to low-growing bedding. Large leaves and crimson flowers either in upright, branched spikes or long, drooping tassels depending on variety. Good to cut and dry.
HEIGHT AND SPREAD: 2½ × 2ft (75 × 60cm)
BLOOMING PERIOD: Early summer to early autumn
SOIL: Any well-drained.

FRONT

LATIN NAME: *Iresine herbstii* 'Brilliantissima'
COMMON NAME: Bloodleaf, beefsteak plant
ALTERNATIVES: *I. lindenii*
DESCRIPTION: Tender perennial/sub-shrub with vivid magenta leaves with prominent veining. Good for containers or as foliage contrast in the border. Pinch out tips to promote bushy growth.
HEIGHT AND SPREAD: 24 × 18in (60 × 45cm)
BLOOMING PERIOD: Not relevant
SOIL: Fertile, well-drained.

9-10

LATIN NAME: *Zinnia* variety
COMMON NAME: Known by Latin name
ALTERNATIVES: 'Double Dwarf Mixed'
DESCRIPTION: Half-hardy annual producing stiffly-branched plants with broad, pale green leaves and vibrant flower heads with dense petals. Good for cutting. Performs badly in wet summer.
HEIGHT AND SPREAD: 12–24 × 12in (30–60 × 30cm) as per variety
BLOOMING PERIOD: Mid-summer to early autumn
SOIL: Well-drained, not too rich, tolerates occasional dry conditions.

LATIN NAME: *Berberis thunbergii*
COMMON NAME: Japanese barberry, common barberry
ALTERNATIVES: *B. t. atropurpurea, B. × ottawensis purpurea*
DESCRIPTION: Shrub with small spoon-shaped green leaves developing good autumn color. Tiny cream cup-shaped flowers are followed by glossy red oblong fruits which hang in clusters.
HEIGHT AND SPREAD: 8 × 8ft (2.5 × 2.5m)
BLOOMING PERIOD: Early spring to mid-spring
SOIL: Any reasonably fertile soil avoiding very dry or limey.

5-8

LATIN NAME: *Phytolacca americana*
COMMON NAME: Poke weed, red ink plant
ALTERNATIVES: *P. polyandra.* Neither are commercially available in USA
DESCRIPTION: Herbaceous perennial of upright growth with large, rather coarse leaves. Fluffy white flower spikes on contrasting rich red stems which develop poisonous berries which are first red, deepening to maroon.
HEIGHT AND SPREAD: 4 × 2ft (1.2 × 0.6m)
BLOOMING PERIOD: Late summer
SOIL: Moisture-retentive.

4-9

3-9

LATIN NAME: *Phlox paniculata* 'Starfire'
COMMON NAME: Known by Latin name
ALTERNATIVES: 'Tenor,' 'Border Gem'
DESCRIPTION: Herbaceous perennial forming upright flower stems with slender, deep green leaves topped with rounded flower clusters. Spicy scent noticeable on warm, moist evenings
HEIGHT AND SPREAD: 3 × 2ft (90 × 60cm)
BLOOMING PERIOD: Mid-summer to early autumn
SOIL: Rich, moisture-retentive and humus-rich. Avoid heavy clay.

7-10

LATIN NAME: *Mimulus cardinalis*
COMMON NAME: Monkey musk, monkey flower
ALTERNATIVES: *Mimulus cupreus* 'Red Emperor'
DESCRIPTION: Herbaceous perennial with soft, slightly sticky leaves and many large, open-mouthed flowers in scarlet with a yellow reverse. Cut back in late summer to generate fresh growth.
HEIGHT AND SPREAD: 3 × 2ft (90 × 60cm)
BLOOMING PERIOD: Summer
SOIL: Moist to boggy.

LATIN NAME: *Crocosmia* 'Carmin Brilliant'
COMMON NAME: Montbretia
ALTERNATIVES: 'James Coey,' 'Vulcan,' 'Spitfire'
DESCRIPTION: Bulbous perennial spreading to form dense clumps of grassy foliage and wiry, arching stems carrying sprays of trumpet-shaped blooms which open from the base up. Orange-red deepening to carmine.
HEIGHT AND SPREAD: 24 × 9in (60 × 23cm)
BLOOMING PERIOD: Late summer
SOIL: Moisture-retentive to damp avoiding very heavy clay or boggy ground.

6-9

LATIN NAME: *Fuchsia* 'Lady Thumb'
COMMON NAME: Known by Latin name
ALTERNATIVES: 'Tom Thumb'
DESCRIPTION: Dwarf shrub, very long-blooming with neat foliage and many hanging "bells" of red and white. Useful for front-of-the-border edging to give interest during late summer and early autumn.
HEIGHT AND SPREAD: 16 × 23in (40 × 58cm)
BLOOMING PERIOD: Summer to autumn
SOIL: Well-drained, fertile, moisture-retentive.

8-10

BACK

6-10

LATIN NAME: *Fuchsia magellanica*
COMMON NAME: Hardy fuchsia, lady's eardrops
ALTERNATIVES: 'F. Riccartonii,' F. m. var. gracillis
DESCRIPTION: Shrub with slender, twiggy branches covered in small, lance-shaped leaves. The narrow, pendant flowers have red sepals with a purple "skirt" and are followed by black fruits.
HEIGHT AND SPREAD: 10 × 6ft (3 × 1.8m)
BLOOMING PERIOD: Mid-summer to mid-autumn
SOIL: Fertile, humus-rich, moisture-retentive but well-drained.

LATIN NAME: *Phygelius × rectus* 'Winchester Fanfare'
COMMON NAME: Known by Latin name
ALTERNATIVES: 'African Queen,' P. capensis 'Coccineus'
DESCRIPTION: Evergreen or semi-evergreen subshrub with upright stems clothed in dark green leaves. The brick-red flowers are tubular with a yellow blotch in the throat and hang down from the branches.
HEIGHT AND SPREAD: 5 × 6ft (1.5 × 1.8m)
BLOOMING PERIOD: Mid-summer to early autumn
SOIL: Well-drained but moisture-retentive.

8-10

MIDDLE

5-8

LATIN NAME: *Crocosmia* 'Lucifer'
COMMON NAME: Montbretia
ALTERNATIVES: 'Bressingham Blaze,' 'Mrs. Geoffrey Howard'
DESCRIPTION: Corm of clump-forming habit with handsome, sword-shaped, bright green leaves, which are a feature all summer, and branching flower spikes carrying the red, flared, tubular blooms.
HEIGHT AND SPREAD: 3–4 × 1ft (0.9–1.2 × 0.3m)
BLOOMING PERIOD: Mid-summer
SOIL: Fertile, well-drained.

9-10

LATIN NAME: *Fuchsia* 'Thalia'
COMMON NAME: Known by Latin name
ALTERNATIVES: F. triphylla
DESCRIPTION: Bushy shrub with upright branches and soft, oval leaves tinged deep bronze or maroon. Hanging clusters of long, tubular, brick-red blooms which flare out at the end.
HEIGHT AND SPREAD: 3 × 3ft (0.9 × 0.9m)
BLOOMING PERIOD: Early summer to early autumn
SOIL: Fertile, humus-rich, moisture-retentive but well-drained.

FRONT

9-10

LATIN NAME: *Dahlia* 'Nellie Geerings'
COMMON NAME: Known by Latin name
ALTERNATIVES: Coltness Hybrids, 'Figaro'
DESCRIPTION: Tuberous perennial, tender, with upright, branched stems clothed in divided leaves. Numerous flat, rounded blooms with broad, rounded petals and a prominent golden "eye." Deadhead.
HEIGHT AND SPREAD: 24 × 18in (60 × 45cm)
BLOOMING PERIOD: Mid-summer to mid-autumn
SOIL: Fertile, humus-rich, moisture-retentive but well-drained.

9-10

LATIN NAME: *Dahlia* 'Tally-ho'
COMMON NAME: Known by Latin name
ALTERNATIVES: 'Diablo Mixed,' 'Redskin Mixed'
DESCRIPTION: Tuberous perennial, tender, with upright, branched stems clothed in dark, bronze-flushed leaves. Purple-black stems and buds. Single blooms with rounded petals and a prominent golden "eye."
HEIGHT AND SPREAD: 24 × 18in (60 × 45cm)
BLOOMING PERIOD: Mid-summer to mid-autumn
SOIL: Fertile, humus-rich, moisture-retentive but well-drained.

6-8

6-9

LATIN NAME: *Acer palmatum* 'Senkaki' ('Sango-kaku')
COMMON NAME: Coral bark maple, Japanese maple
ALTERNATIVES: None
DESCRIPTION: Upright shrub or small tree grown principally for the coral-red of its young stems in winter. The palmate leaves are orange-yellow in spring, changing to green, with good autumn tints.
HEIGHT AND SPREAD: 13 × 6ft (4 × 2m)
BLOOMING PERIOD: Early spring
SOIL: Neutral to acid, humus-rich, moisture-retentive, well-drained.

LATIN NAME: *Hydrangea macrophylla* cultivar
COMMON NAME: Mop head or big leaf hydrangea, hortensia
ALTERNATIVES: 'Hamburg,' 'Amy Pasquier,' 'Preziosa'
DESCRIPTION: Rounded shrub with large, broad leaves sometimes tinged red and purple in autumn. Globular flower heads made up of sterile florets which are light green in bud, changing to pinky red.
HEIGHT AND SPREAD: 6–10 × 6–10ft (1.8–3.1 × 1.8–3m)
BLOOMING PERIOD: Mid-summer to mid-autumn
SOIL: Rich, moisture-retentive with plenty of humus.

LATIN NAME: *Dahlia* 'Alva's Doris'
COMMON NAME: Known by Latin name
ALTERNATIVES: 'Apache,' 'Doris Day'
DESCRIPTION: Tuberous perennial, tender, with large leaves divided into jagged leaflets and rich red cactus-type flowers with narrow quilled petals forming a rounded head. Deadhead regularly.
HEIGHT AND SPREAD: 3½–4 × 3ft (108–120 × 90cm)
BLOOMING PERIOD: Mid summer to mid-autumn
SOIL: Fertile, humus-rich, moisture-retentive but well-drained.

9-10

9-10

LATIN NAME: *Dahlia* 'Bishop of Llandaff'
COMMON NAME: Known by Latin name
ALTERNATIVES: 'Laciniata Purpurea'
DESCRIPTION: Tuberous perennial, tender, with large, bronze-purple tinted leaves divided into jagged leaflets and purple-black stems. This makes a superb foil for the deep scarlet-red single blooms.
HEIGHT AND SPREAD: 3 × 3ft (0.9 × 0.9m)
BLOOMING PERIOD: Mid-summer to mid-autumn
SOIL: Fertile, humus-rich, moisture-retentive but well-drained.

6-10

LATIN NAME: *Sedum* 'Ruby Glow'
COMMON NAME: Stonecrop
ALTERNATIVES: 'Sunset Cloud,' 'Bertram Anderson'
DESCRIPTION: Herbaceous perennial with succulent stems and leaves. The foliage is purple-green with a gray bloom and makes a fine complement for the tiny wine-red flowers in dense, flattened heads.
HEIGHT AND SPREAD: 10 × 18in (25 × 45cm)
BLOOMING PERIOD: Mid-summer to early autumn
SOIL: Well-drained.

6-10

LATIN NAME: *Schizostylis coccinea* 'Major'
COMMON NAME: Kaffir lily, crimson flag
ALTERNATIVES: *S. coccinea*
DESCRIPTION: Herbaceous perennial making tufts of broad, grassy leaves with upright spikes of satiny, cup-shaped blooms in rich crimson, reminiscent of gladioli. Must have sufficient moisture in summer to supply developing blooms.
HEIGHT AND SPREAD: 24 × 9in (60 × 23cm)
BLOOMING PERIOD: Early to mid-autumn
SOIL: Well-drained but with plentiful moisture in summer.

BACK

LATIN NAME: *Pyracantha* cultivar
COMMON NAME: Firethorn
ALTERNATIVES: *P. rogersiana,* 'Mohave,' 'Navaho'
DESCRIPTION: Evergreen shrub of upright or arching habit with lance-shaped, dark green foliage and thorny stems. Clustered creamy-white flowers. Red autumn berries. Susceptible to fireblight and scab.
HEIGHT AND SPREAD: 13 × 10ft (4 × 3m)
BLOOMING PERIOD: Early summer
SOIL: Well-drained, moisture-retentive. Good in alkaline conditions.

6-9

LATIN NAME: *Cotoneaster salicifolius* 'Pendulus' syn. C. 'Hybridus Pendulus'
COMMON NAME: Weeping cotoneaster
ALTERNATIVES: *C. salicifolius,* 'Autumn Fire'
DESCRIPTION: Small weeping evergreen, grafted to produce a standard, with willow-like leaves of deep green. Creamy-white blossoms give way to clusters of rich red berries, attractive to birds.
HEIGHT AND SPREAD: 10 × 13ft (3 × 4m)
BLOOMING PERIOD: Early summer
SOIL: Fertile, well-drained. Avoid poor or strongly alkaline.

6-8

MIDDLE

9-10

LATIN NAME: *Dahlia* 'Carol'
COMMON NAME: Known by Latin name
ALTERNATIVES: 'Brunton,' 'Comet'
DESCRIPTION: Tender tuberous perennial with large green leaves divided into jagged leaflets. Produces pompon-like flower heads in red. Deadhead regularly. Lift and store tubers frost-free.
HEIGHT AND SPREAD: 3 × 3ft (0.9 × 0.9m)
BLOOMING PERIOD: Summer to autumn
SOIL: Fertile, humus-rich and moisture-retentive but well-drained.

LATIN NAME: *Dahlia* 'Hillcrest Royal'
COMMON NAME: Known by Latin name
ALTERNATIVES: 'Banker,' 'Mrs Rees'
DESCRIPTION: Tender tuberous perennial with large green leaves divided into jagged leaflets. The large flowers have broad, spine-like petals (so-called cactus type). Deadhead. Provide staking in more exposed sites.
HEIGHT AND SPREAD: 3–4 × 3–4ft (0.9–1.2 × 0.9–1.2m)
BLOOMING PERIOD: Summer to autumn
SOIL: Fertile, humus-rich and moisture-retentive but well-drained.

9-10

FRONT

LATIN NAME: *Schizostylis coccinea* 'Professor Barnard'
COMMON NAME: Kaffir lily, crimson flag
ALTERNATIVES: *S. coccinea,* 'Major'
DESCRIPTION: Herbaceous perennial of clump-forming habit. Sword-shaped leaves and stems bearing large, satiny, cup-shaped blooms of crimson-pink. Ensure plentiful summer moisture. Divide plants regularly.
HEIGHT AND SPREAD: 24 × 9–12in (60 × 23–30cm)
BLOOMING PERIOD: Early to mid-autumn
SOIL: Fertile, moisture-retentive, but well-drained in winter.

6-10

6-10

LATIN NAME: *Dendranthema* 'Belle'
COMMON NAME: Korean chrysanthemum
ALTERNATIVES: 'Brightness,' 'Gloria,' 'Marion,' 'Peggy,' 'Ruby Mound'
DESCRIPTION: Herbaceous perennial of much-branched habit with lobed leaves and bright red single to semi-double flower heads with a prominent yellow central disk. Continues flowering until the frost.
HEIGHT AND SPREAD: 2 × 2ft (0.6 × 0.6m)
BLOOMING PERIOD: Late summer to mid-autumn
SOIL: Fertile, well-drained.

LATIN NAME: *Malus × robusta* 'Red Sentinel'
COMMON NAME: Flowering crab apple
ALTERNATIVES: 'Red Jade,' 'Crittenden,' 'Gorgeous,' 'Veitch's Scarlet'
DESCRIPTION: Tree of rounded habit with oval leaves and deep pink flower buds which combine prettily with the white apple-blossom-like flowers. Deep red, glossy fruits in autumn retained for many weeks.
HEIGHT AND SPREAD: 26 × 19ft (8 × 6m)
BLOOMING PERIOD: Late spring
SOIL: Any reasonable soil, free from winter waterlogging and summer drought.

4-8

LATIN NAME: *Acer palmatum* 'Atropurpureum'
COMMON NAME: Japanese maple
ALTERNATIVES: *A. palmatum*, 'Shinonome'
DESCRIPTION: Small tree of elegant upright or spreading habit with lobed purple leaves which change to shades of red in autumn. Small clusters of insignificant purple-red flowers in spring. Slow-growing.
HEIGHT AND SPREAD: 12–16 × 12–16ft (3.6–5 × 3.6–5m)
BLOOMING PERIOD: Spring
SOIL: Neutral to acid, humus-rich and moisture retentive.

5-8

8-9

LATIN NAME: *Ruscus aculeatus*
COMMON NAME: Butcher's broom, box holly
ALTERNATIVES: 'Wheeler's Variety' and 'Sparkler' are hermaphrodites
DESCRIPTION: Evergreen suckering shrub of the lily family with leaf-like appendages which are flattened stems. These are oval and pointed. Separate male and female plants. Females may produce red berries.
HEIGHT AND SPREAD: 3 × 4ft (0.9 × 1.2m)
BLOOMING PERIOD: Insignificant
SOIL: Any, including very dry beneath trees.

9-10

LATIN NAME: *Dahlia* 'Aylett's Gaiety'
COMMON NAME: Known by Latin name
ALTERNATIVES: 'Bishop of Llandaff'
DESCRIPTION: Tender tuberous perennial with purple foliage divided into jagged leaflets. Contrasting red flowers, flattened semi-double with broad, rounded petals and a center of yellow stamens.
HEIGHT AND SPREAD: 3–4 × 3–4ft (0.9–1.2 × 0.9–1.2m)
BLOOMING PERIOD: Summer to autumn
SOIL: Fertile, moisture-retentive, humus-rich and well-drained.

7-10

LATIN NAME: *Dendranthema* cultivar
COMMON NAME: Bedding chrysanthemum, patio mums
ALTERNATIVES: 'Bravo,' 'Remarkable,' 'Matador'
DESCRIPTION: Herbaceous perennial usually grown from cuttings taken in spring from lifted rootstock. Lobed leaves and upright, branching stems.
HEIGHT AND SPREAD: 15–24 × 15–24in (38–60 × 38–60cm)
BLOOMING PERIOD: Late summer to the first hard frosts
SOIL: Fertile, well-drained.

3-8

LATIN NAME: *Gaultheria procumbens*
COMMON NAME: Creeping wintergreen, partridge berry
ALTERNATIVES: None
DESCRIPTION: Evergreen creeping shrublet with oval, dark green leaves aromatic when crushed. Small pink flowers followed by red berries. Purple-red leaf tints in winter. May be invasive.
HEIGHT AND SPREAD: 2 × 6in (5 × 15cm). Spread indefinite
BLOOMING PERIOD: Summer
SOIL: Acid to neutral, humus-rich and moisture-retentive.

BACK

7-9

LATIN NAME: *Camellia japonica* 'Jupiter'
COMMON NAME: Known by Latin name
ALTERNATIVES: 'Alexander Hunter,' 'Adolphe Audusson,' 'Mars'
DESCRIPTION: Evergreen, upright shrub with lance-shaped leaves of leathery texture. Single, dish-shaped blooms with a boss of stamens. Grow free-standing or by a wall sheltered from early morning sun.
HEIGHT AND SPREAD: 6–10 × 6–10ft (1.8–3 × 1.8–3m)
BLOOMING PERIOD: Late winter to mid to late spring
SOIL: Acid, humus-rich, moisture-retentive but well-drained.

2-7

LATIN NAME: *Cornus alba* 'Sibirica'
COMMON NAME: Red-barked dogwood, tatarian dogwood
ALTERNATIVES: C. a. 'Sibirica Variegata'
DESCRIPTION: Suckering shrub with upright stems clothed in lance-shaped leaves with conspicuous veining. Shortly before leaf-fall the young stems begin to develop their bright red winter coloring. Prune hard in spring.
HEIGHT AND SPREAD: 8 × 13ft (2.4 × 4m)
BLOOMING PERIOD: Late spring to early summer
SOIL: Any soil but particularly moist or damp, even tolerating waterlogging.

MIDDLE

6-9

LATIN NAME: *Gaultheria mucronata* 'Cherry Ripe' syn. *Pernettya mucronata*
COMMON NAME: Known by Latin name
ALTERNATIVES: 'Bell's Seedling,' 'Crimsonia,' 'Mulberry Wine'
DESCRIPTION: Evergreen shrub with red stems covered in prickly leaves. White, bell-shaped flowers are followed by pinkish red berries.
HEIGHT AND SPREAD: 2½ × 4ft (0.75 × 1.2m)
BLOOMING PERIOD: Early summer
SOIL: Neutral to acid, humus-rich, moisture-retentive.

5-8

LATIN NAME: *Rhododendron* hybrid
COMMON NAME: Known by Latin name
ALTERNATIVES: 'Brittania,' 'Cynthia,' 'Kluis Sensation,' 'Lord Roberts'
DESCRIPTION: Evergreen shrub with large, oval, dark green leaves. Showy flower heads of clustered bell-shaped blooms with protruding stamens. Flowers often attractively spotted or blotched.
HEIGHT AND SPREAD: 3–4 × 4ft (0.9–1.2 × 1.2m)
BLOOMING PERIOD: Mid-spring to early summer
SOIL: Acid, humus-rich, moisture-retentive but well-drained.

FRONT

4-8

LATIN NAME: *Cotoneaster salicifolius* 'Gnom'
COMMON NAME: Willowleaf cotoneaster
ALTERNATIVES: 'Autumn Fire,' C. congestus, C. conspicuus 'Decorus'
DESCRIPTION: Evergreen shrub of low, creeping habit, ideal for groundcover. Small, narrowly lance-shaped leaves of glossy green and tiny white blooms followed by clusters of bright red spherical berries. May be wall-trained.
HEIGHT AND SPREAD: 8–24in × 6ft (0.2–0.6 × 1.8m)
BLOOMING PERIOD: Mid-summer
SOIL: Any well-drained.

4-8

LATIN NAME: *Cotoneaster conspicuus* 'Decorus'
COMMON NAME: Wintergreen cotoneaster
ALTERNATIVES: C. salicifolius 'Gnom,' C. congestus
DESCRIPTION: Evergreen shrub of low spreading habit with arching branches covered with very small, dark green leaves. Single, small white flowers in abundance followed by large red berries.
HEIGHT AND SPREAD: 1 × 6–10ft (0.3 × 1.8–3m)
BLOOMING PERIOD: Late spring
SOIL: Any well-drained.

4-8

7-9

LATIN NAME: *Chaenomeles × superba* 'Knap Hill Scarlet'
COMMON NAME: Flowering quince, japonica
ALTERNATIVES: 'Fire Dance,' 'Etna,' 'Elly Mossel'
DESCRIPTION: Shrub with twiggy growth and oval-shaped leaves. The single, bright red blooms have a boss of golden stamens and grow in clusters on the branches. Small, yellowish green aromatic fruits.
HEIGHT AND SPREAD: 5 × 10ft (1.5 × 3m)
BLOOMING PERIOD: Early to mid-spring
SOIL: Any, avoiding strongly alkaline as this leads to chlorosis.

LATIN NAME: *Camellia japonica* cultivars
COMMON NAME: Known by Latin name
ALTERNATIVES: *C. × williamsii* cultivars
DESCRIPTION: Upright or spreading evergreen shrub, often trained as a wall-shrub. Oval to lance-shaped, dark green foliage. Blooms single, dish-shaped to double, anemone-centered and peony-flowered.
HEIGHT AND SPREAD: 6–10 × 6–10ft (1.8–3 × 1.8–3m)
BLOOMING PERIOD: Late winter to mid-late spring
SOIL: Acid, humus-rich and moisture-retentive but well-drained.

8-10

LATIN NAME: *Phormium* tenax 'Dazzler'
COMMON NAME: New Zealand flax
ALTERNATIVES: *P. colensoi* 'Maori Queen,' *P. colensoi* 'Tricolor'
DESCRIPTION: Evergreen perennial making a dense clump of slightly arching, strap-shaped leaves broadly striped pinkish-red, bronze and green. Tall flower stems produced on mature plants.
HEIGHT AND SPREAD: 4 × 5ft (1.2 × 1.5m)
BLOOMING PERIOD: Mid-summer
SOIL: Any well-drained.

8-10

LATIN NAME: *Phormium colensoi* 'Maori Queen'
COMMON NAME: New Zealand flax
ALTERNATIVES: 'Tricolor' *P. tenax* 'Dazzler'
DESCRIPTION: Evergreen perennial making a dense clump of sword-shaped leaves colored tawny-red, pink and bronze. Tall flower stems produced on mature plants.
HEIGHT AND SPREAD: 4 × 5ft (1.2 × 1.5m)
BLOOMING PERIOD: Mid-summer
SOIL: Any well-drained.

4-9

7-9

LATIN NAME: *Trillium sessile*
COMMON NAME: Toad trillium, toadshade, wake-robin
ALTERNATIVES: *T. chloropetalum* forms, *T. erectum*
DESCRIPTION: Herbaceous perennial of clump-forming habit which in spring produces three-lobed leaves, heavily spotted with maroon. Acts as a collar for the three-petalled blooms of deep red-brown.
HEIGHT AND SPREAD: 12–15 × 12–18in (30–38 × 30–45cm)
BLOOMING PERIOD: Spring
SOIL: Neutral to acid, humus-rich, moisture-retentive.

LATIN NAME: *Skimmia japonica* 'Scarlet Dwarf'
COMMON NAME: Known by Latin name
ALTERNATIVES: 'Bowles,' 'Dwarf Female,' 'Veitchii'
DESCRIPTION: Evergreen shrub with oval leaves and cone-shaped white flower clusters in spring followed by clusters of red berries. Females like this best planted with males such as *S. j.* 'Rubella'.
HEIGHT AND SPREAD: 2 × 13ft (0.6 × 0.9m)
BLOOMING PERIOD: Late spring
SOIL: Neutral to acid, humus-rich, moisture-retentive.

WHITE

WHITE IS A COOL COLOR. WHEN SPRINKLED LIGHTLY AMONG OTHER SHADES, IT CAN REFRESH AND ENLIVEN A BORDER WITHOUT DISTURBING THE BALANCE. IN FULL SUN, WHITE FLOWERS CAN DAZZLE WITH THEIR BRILLIANCE - A POINT TO REMEMBER IF YOU'RE TRYING TO CREATE A RESTFUL SCHEME. IN SHADE, WHITE IS UNPARALLELED IN ITS ABILITY TO RAISE A BORDER OUT OF THE GLOOM. WHITE GLOWS MAGICALLY IN DEEP SHADE. USE IT GENEROUSLY IN A GARDEN DESIGNED FOR EVENING ENTERTAINMENT OR TO LINE A PATH WALKED AT TWILIGHT.

SINCE WHITE IS SUCH AN ATTENTION-GRABBING SHADE, IT CAN HAVE A DRAMATIC EFFECT ON PERSPECTIVE. WHITE USED AT THE END OF A LONG, NARROW GARDEN WILL FORESHORTEN THE VIEW, JUST AS MISTY BLUES, PURPLES, AND GRAYS WILL LENGTHEN IT. SO, IF YOU WANT TO MAKE THE GARDEN APPEAR LONGER, KEEP WHITE FLOWERS AND FOLIAGE NEARER TO THE HOUSE.

WHITE SPEAKS TO US OF PURITY AND INNOCENCE, BUT IT IS RARELY PURE AND MOST OFTEN TINGED WITH TINY AMOUNTS OF APPLE-GREEN, CREAMY YELLOW, OR BLUSH-PINK. BUT IT IS A MISTAKE TO BE TOO RESTRICTIVE WITH YOUR CHOICE OF PLANTS IN AN ALL-WHITE SCHEME, AS YOU RISK THE END RESULT FEELING RATHER COLD AND LIFELESS. A SMATTERING OF OTHER COLORS WILL ADD WARMTH AND DEPTH WITHOUT SPOILING THE EFFECT. IN A SUNNY BORDER, WHITE FLOWERS WORK WONDERFULLY AGAINST A FOIL OF SILVER, GRAY, AND BLUE FOLIAGE. IN SHADE, CHOOSE RICH GREENS, BUTTER-YELLOWS, AND LIME AS A BACKDROP. MANY GOLD-VARIEGATED AND LIME-GREEN DECIDUOUS SHRUBS AND HERBS ACTUALLY PREFER A POSITION IN COOL SHADE.

LEFT: *Silver and white plants (lantana, petunia, cineraria, salvia, and helichrysum) make an elegant display.*

BACK

LATIN NAME: *Symphoricarpos albus*
COMMON NAME: Snowberry
ALTERNATIVES: 'White Hedge'
DESCRIPTION: Vigorous suckering shrub, which may become invasive. Makes a good informal hedge. Dense, twiggy habit with slender stems carrying rounded leaves. Tiny pink flower clusters and large white berries.
HEIGHT AND SPREAD: 3–6 × 6ft (0.9–1.8 × 1.8m)
BLOOMING PERIOD: Summer
SOIL: Any.

3-7

LATIN NAME: *Rubus cockburnianus*
COMMON NAME: White-stemmed bramble
ALTERNATIVES: *R. biflorus, R. thibetanus*
DESCRIPTION: Suckering shrub with prickly branches covered in a white bloom, upright at first then spreading. Dark green, pinnate leaves and small purple flowers. Black fruits. Best against a plain, dark background.
HEIGHT AND SPREAD: 8 × 8ft (2.5 × 2.5m)
BLOOMING PERIOD: Summer
SOIL: Fertile, well-drained.

6-9

MIDDLE

6-9

LATIN NAME: *Skimmia japonica* 'Wakehurst White' syn. 'Fructu Albo'
COMMON NAME: Japanese skimmia
ALTERNATIVES: 'Kew White'
DESCRIPTION: Evergreen shrub of bushy habit with glossy, oval leaves of light green and spherical white berries. Slower-growing than red-berried forms. Grow alongside a male such as *S. j.* 'Rubella.'
HEIGHT AND SPREAD: 3 × 3ft (0.9 × 0.9m)
BLOOMING PERIOD: Late spring
SOIL: Acid to neutral, humus-rich, moisture-retentive.

8-10

LATIN NAME: *Cassinia retorta* 'Ward's Silver'
COMMON NAME: Known by Latin name
ALTERNATIVES: *Cassinia vauvilliersii* var. *albida*
DESCRIPTION: Evergreen shrub with tufted stems covered in gray-white, needle/scale-like leaves. Small, creamy white terminal flowers. Avoid cold, exposed positions.
HEIGHT AND SPREAD: 4–6 × 4–6ft (1.2–1.8 × 1.2–1.8m)
BLOOMING PERIOD: Summer
SOIL: Fertile, well-drained.

FRONT

LATIN NAME: *Viola* × *wittrockiana* cultivar
COMMON NAME: Pansy
ALTERNATIVES: 'Ultima' and 'Universal' series
DESCRIPTION: Short-lived perennial with dark green, rounded to heart-shaped, toothed-edged leaves and slender stalks bearing flat blooms with an almost circular outline.
HEIGHT AND SPREAD: 6–9 × 9–12in (15–23 × 23–30cm)
BLOOMING PERIOD: Winter and early spring
SOIL: Fertile, humus-rich, moisture retentive.

3-9

LATIN NAME: *Helleborus niger*
COMMON NAME: Christmas rose
ALTERNATIVES: 'Potter's Wheel,' *H. orientalis* (white forms)
DESCRIPTION: Evergreen perennial forming a clump of large, leathery, divided leaves and white, cup-shaped blooms on stout stems. At the center is a boss of golden stamens. Some cultivars are spotted.
HEIGHT AND SPREAD: 12 × 18in (30 × 45cm)
BLOOMING PERIOD: Winter to early spring
SOIL: Humus-rich, moisture-retentive. Benefits from organic mulch.

WHITE

BACK

7-9

LATIN NAME: *Rhamnus alaternus* 'Argentovariegata'
COMMON NAME: Buckthorn
ALTERNATIVES: *Euonymus fortunei* 'Silver Queen'
DESCRIPTION: Evergreen shrub with small, oval, gray-green leaves with an irregular creamy white margin. Growth dense; if unclipped, forms an attractive cone-shaped shrub. Somewhat tender. Red berries.
HEIGHT AND SPREAD: 12 × 6ft (3.5 × 2m)
BLOOMING PERIOD: Early summer
SOIL: Any reasonably well-drained.

4-10

LATIN NAME: *Lonicera × purpusii*
COMMON NAME: Winter-flowering honeysuckle, shrubby honeysuckle
ALTERNATIVES: 'Winter Beauty,' *L. fragrantissima, L. standishii*
DESCRIPTION: Dense, twiggy, rounded shrub which may be wall-trained on a sheltered wall to promote flowering. Small, creamy-white flowers produced during mild spells throughout winter. Well scented.
HEIGHT AND SPREAD: 10 × 13ft (3 × 4m)
BLOOMING PERIOD: Late autumn to mid-spring
SOIL: Any well-drained, tolerating dry conditions once established.

6-9

LATIN NAME: *Sarcococca confusa*
COMMON NAME: Sweet box, Christmas box
ALTERNATIVES: *S. hookeriana, S. h.* var. *digyna*
DESCRIPTION: Evergreen shrub of low, rounded habit with oval, dark green tapering leaves and clusters of tiny, highly fragrant, white flowers in the leaf axils. Black berries.
HEIGHT AND SPREAD: 3 × 3ft (0.9 × 0.9m)
BLOOMING PERIOD: Winter
SOIL: Well-drained, humus-rich, moisture-retentive.

4-8

MIDDLE

LATIN NAME: *Daphne mezereum* f. *alba*
COMMON NAME: February daphne
ALTERNATIVES: *D. blagayana*
DESCRIPTION: Shrub of upright habit with bare branches smothered in clusters of tiny, four-petalled blooms, which are highly fragrant. Small, rounded to lance-shaped leaves and poisonous red berries. May die suddenly from virus.
HEIGHT AND SPREAD: 2½ × 3ft (0.75 × 0.9m)
BLOOMING PERIOD: Late winter to early spring
SOIL: Rich, deeply cultivated, with plentiful humus. Tolerates alkalinity.

4-7

LATIN NAME: *Galanthus elwesii*
COMMON NAME: Snowdrop
ALTERNATIVES: *G. nivalis, G. n.* 'Flore Pleno'
DESCRIPTION: Small bulb with narrow, strap-shaped leaves and slender stems bearing the dropper-like white buds which open to reveal the inner tube of petals. Faint honey scent.
HEIGHT AND SPREAD: 4–12 × 2–3in (10–30 × 5–8cm)
BLOOMING PERIOD: Late winter to early spring
SOIL: Humus-rich, moisture-retentive to moist.

3-9

FRONT

LATIN NAME: *Leucojum vernum*
COMMON NAME: Spring snowflake
ALTERNATIVES: *Galanthus nivalis, G. elwesii*
DESCRIPTION: Small bulb with narrow, upright, dark green leaves and nodding white flowers, each petal marked with green. Looks rather like a double-flowered snowdrop.
HEIGHT AND SPREAD: 4–6 × 3–4in (10–15 × 8–10cm)
BLOOMING PERIOD: Spring
SOIL: Humus-rich, moisture-retentive to moist.

103

WHITE

6-10

LATIN NAME: *Viburnum tinus*
COMMON NAME: Laurustinus
ALTERNATIVES: 'Eve Price,' 'Spring Bouquet,' 'Variegatum'
DESCRIPTION: Evergreen shrub of upright to rounded habit, well-branched with dense leaf coverage. Foliage dark green, oval, pointed. Clusters of red flower buds open to white-tinged pink.
HEIGHT AND SPREAD: 12 × 12ft (3.5 × 3.5m)
BLOOMING PERIOD: Late autumn to late spring
SOIL: Any reasonable soil.

6-9

LATIN NAME: *Prunus incisa* 'Praecox'
COMMON NAME: Fuji cherry
ALTERNATIVES: *P. incisa*
DESCRIPTION: Large shrub or small tree grown for its early blossoms. Small, toothed-edged leaves with good autumn color. Buds tinged pink opening to white blooms.
HEIGHT AND SPREAD: 23 × 20ft (7 × 6m)
BLOOMING PERIOD: Mid-winter
SOIL: Any reasonable soil.

9-10

LATIN NAME: *Coleonema album* syn. *Diosma ericoides*
COMMON NAME: Diosma, breath of heaven
ALTERNATIVES: None
DESCRIPTION: Evergreen shrub with light yellow-green, aromatic foliage similar in appearance to the needle-like leaves of heathers. Small, white, five-petalled blooms.
HEIGHT AND SPREAD: 3 × 3ft (1 × 1m)
BLOOMING PERIOD: Winter to spring
SOIL: Neutral to acid, well-drained.

LATIN NAME: *Rosmarinus officinalis* 'Alba'
COMMON NAME: Rosemary
ALTERNATIVES: None
DESCRIPTION: Evergreen shrub of gaunt, upright habit, becoming woody and sparse at the base if not cut back periodically. Requires a warm, sheltered spot. Strongly aromatic, needle-like leaves and white, lipped blooms.
HEIGHT AND SPREAD: 4 × 5ft (1.2 × 1.5m)
BLOOMING PERIOD: Late spring to early summer
SOIL: Light, well-drained, preferably neutral to acid.

7-9

3-7

LATIN NAME: *Galanthus nivalis* 'Pusey Green Tip'
COMMON NAME: Common snowdrop (double form)
ALTERNATIVES: 'Flore Pleno'
DESCRIPTION: Bulbous plant with strap-shaped leaves and double, nodding blooms with many green-tipped petals, some of irregular length. Well worth looking at closely and good for picking.
HEIGHT AND SPREAD: 4–6 × 2–3in (10–15 × 5–8cm)
BLOOMING PERIOD: Late winter to early spring
SOIL: Moisture-retentive to moist.

3-10

LATIN NAME: *Helleborus orientalis*
COMMON NAME: Lenten rose, *hellebore*
ALTERNATIVES: *H. niger* and forms
DESCRIPTION: Evergreen perennial with large, divided leaves of leathery texture. These are best removed when ragged. Cup-shaped, slightly nodding blooms with a boss of yellow stamens.
HEIGHT AND SPREAD: 18 × 18in (45 × 45cm)
BLOOMING PERIOD: Winter to early spring
SOIL: Humus-rich, moisture-retentive to moist.

LATIN NAME: *Erica arborea*
COMMON NAME: Tree heath
ALTERNATIVES: 'Mr. Robert,' *E. a.* var. *alpina*
DESCRIPTION: Evergreen shrub of strongly upright habit. Branches covered in bright green, needle-like leaves in bunches. Masses of tiny, scented blooms on the branch tips.
HEIGHT AND SPREAD: 13 × 7ft (4 × 2.2m)
BLOOMING PERIOD: Mid- to late spring (from winter in mild areas)
SOIL: Acid to neutral, humus-rich, well-drained.

7-9

4-6

LATIN NAME: *Pieris floribunda*
COMMON NAME: Andromeda, mountain pieris
ALTERNATIVES: *Pieris japonica cultivars*, e.g., 'Grayswood'
DESCRIPTION: Evergreen shrub with erect panicles of white, fragrant, bell-shaped blooms opening from greenish white buds that are attractive all winter. Some new red leaf growth in spring.
HEIGHT AND SPREAD: 7 × 10ft (2.2 × 3m)
BLOOMING PERIOD: Early to mid-spring
SOIL: Acid, humus-rich, moisture-retentive to moist.

8-9

LATIN NAME: *Erica lusitanica* 'George Hunt'
COMMON NAME: Portuguese heath
ALTERNATIVES: *E. arborea* 'Albert's Gold,' 'Estrella Gold'
DESCRIPTION: Upright, evergreen shrub with golden yellow, needle-like leaves and masses of tiny, scented, bell-shaped blooms. One of the so-called tree heaths. Needs a sheltered position.
HEIGHT AND SPREAD: 4–5 × 3ft (1.2–1.5 × 0.9m)
BLOOMING PERIOD: Late autumn to late spring
SOIL: Acid, humus-rich.

4-8

LATIN NAME: *Pieris japonica* 'Little Heath'
COMMON NAME: Andromeda, pieris
ALTERNATIVES: 'White Rum,' 'Variegata,' 'Flaming Silver'
DESCRIPTION: Low, dense, evergreen shrub with creamy white-edged leaves and new shoots pink-tinged. This cultivar seldom produces the characteristic bell-shaped blooms and is mainly grown for foliage.
HEIGHT AND SPREAD: 24–30 × 36in (60–75 × 90cm)
BLOOMING PERIOD: Spring
SOIL: Acid, humus-rich, moisture-retentive.

6-9

LATIN NAME: *Erica × darleyensis* 'White Glow'
COMMON NAME: Known by Latin name
ALTERNATIVES: 'White Perfection,' 'Silberschmelze'
DESCRIPTION: Evergreen, low, bushy shrublet with needle-like leaves. Tiny white blooms are produced all along the stems for several weeks. Lime-tolerant but best on neutral to acid soils.
HEIGHT AND SPREAD: 12 × 24in (30 × 60cm)
BLOOMING PERIOD: Early winter to late spring
SOIL: Humus-rich, neutral to acid, moist but well-drained.

5-9

LATIN NAME: *Erica carnea* 'Springwood White'
COMMON NAME: Winter-flowering heath or heather
ALTERNATIVES: *E. × darleyensis* 'White Perfection,' 'Silberschmelze'
DESCRIPTION: Low-growing evergreen shrublet grown for its prolific flower display in winter and early spring. Needle-like leaves of deep green and tiny white blooms. Tolerates some lime.
HEIGHT AND SPREAD: 1½ × 3ft (0.45 × 0.9m)
BLOOMING PERIOD: Mid-winter to early spring
SOIL: Humus-rich, moisture-retentive but well-drained.

BACK

4-9

LATIN NAME: *Amelanchier lamarckii*
COMMON NAME: Shadblow, snowy mespilus, Allegheny serviceberry
ALTERNATIVES: 'Ballerina,' *A. canadensis*
DESCRIPTION: Large suckering shrub with two seasons of interest. The oval leaves are often red-tinged, but also produce brilliant autumn color. White blossoms on bare branches are followed by red fruits.
HEIGHT AND SPREAD: 20 × 20ft (6 × 6m)
BLOOMING PERIOD: Late spring
SOIL: Any reasonable soil.

LATIN NAME: *Magnolia stellata*
COMMON NAME: Star magnolia
ALTERNATIVES: 'Royal Star,' 'Waterlily,' *M. × loebneri* 'Merrill'
DESCRIPTION: Slow-growing, dense, rounded shrub which produces starry, white, fragrant blooms with strap-shaped petals on bare branches in spring. The deep green leaves are narrowly ovate.
HEIGHT AND SPREAD: 9 × 12ft (2.7 × 3.6m)
BLOOMING PERIOD: Early to mid-spring (from late winter in mild areas)
SOIL: Fertile, humus-rich, moisture-retentive. Avoid extreme alkalinity.

4-9

MIDDLE

3-10

LATIN NAME: *Dicentra spectabilis* 'Alba'
COMMON NAME: Bleeding heart, lyre flower, lady's locket
ALTERNATIVES: None
DESCRIPTION: Herbaceous perennial forming a leafy clump of fern-like foliage, above which arching sprays of heart-shaped "lockets" appear in pure white. Lights up a shady border.
HEIGHT AND SPREAD: 24 × 18in (60 × 45cm)
BLOOMING PERIOD: Mid-spring to early summer
SOIL: Fertile, humus-rich, moisture-retentive.

LATIN NAME: *Rhododendron* 'Bric-a-Brac'
COMMON NAME: Known by Latin name
ALTERNATIVES: 'Cowbell,' 'Girard Pleasant White,' 'Molly Fordham'
DESCRIPTION: Compact evergreen shrub with deep green, leathery leaves and large, rounded flower clusters consisting of funnel-shaped, milk white blooms with contrasting dark brown anthers.
HEIGHT AND SPREAD: 3 × 5ft (0.9 × 1.5m)
BLOOMING PERIOD: Early to mid-spring (from winter in warm areas)
SOIL: Acid, humus-rich, moisture-retentive.

8-9

FRONT

3-8

LATIN NAME: *Crocus vernus* 'Joan d'Arc'
COMMON NAME: Crocus
ALTERNATIVES: *Crocus chrysanthus* 'Snow Bunting'
DESCRIPTION: Corm producing clumps of fine, grassy foliage and naked stems topped with rounded blooms which open fully in sun. The bright orange, frilly stigma contrasts with the white petals.
HEIGHT AND SPREAD: 4 × 1–3in (10 × 2.5–8cm)
BLOOMING PERIOD: Spring
SOIL: Any well-drained. May be naturalized in a lawn.

LATIN NAME: *Anemone blanda* 'White Splendour'
COMMON NAME: Greek windflower
ALTERNATIVES: *A. nemorosa* and forms
DESCRIPTION: Tuberous-rooted perennial with lobed leaves and fine-stalked, daisy-like blooms which open out fully in sunshine. The blooms are larger and more showy than those of *A. nemorosa*.
HEIGHT AND SPREAD: 2–4 × 4–6in (5–10 × 10–15cm)
BLOOMING PERIOD: Early spring
SOIL: Well-drained, humus-rich.

4-10

LATIN NAME: *Ribes sanguineum* 'Tydeman's White'

COMMON NAME: Flowering currant

ALTERNATIVES: None

DESCRIPTION: Rounded shrub with rounded, deep green, lobed leaves and hanging branches of tiny white blooms in late spring. The flowering currants are tough plants, tolerating a wide range of conditions.

HEIGHT AND SPREAD: 8 × 8ft (2.5 × 2.5m)

BLOOMING PERIOD: Mid- to late spring

SOIL: Any reasonable soil.

5-7

LATIN NAME: *Magnolia kobus*

COMMON NAME: Kobus magnolia, northern Japanese magnolia

ALTERNATIVES: M. *stellata*, M. × *loebneri* and forms

DESCRIPTION: Unfortunately, this beautiful magnolia only produces its fragrant white blooms some 10–15 years after planting! M. × *loebneri* and its forms all flower from an early age and are a better choice.

HEIGHT AND SPREAD: 40 × 25ft (12 × 7.6m)

BLOOMING PERIOD: Mid-spring (from winter in mild areas)

SOIL: Fertile, well-drained, humus-rich and moisture-retentive.

4-8

4-10

2-10

LATIN NAME: *Polygonatum × hybridum* syn. *P. multiflorum*

COMMON NAME: Soloman's seal

ALTERNATIVES: 'Variegatum,' *P. odoratum* 'Flore Pleno'

DESCRIPTION: Herbaceous perennial with gracefully arching stems of oval, prominently veined leaves. Ivory flowers, tipped with green, hang in clusters from the underside of the stems.

HEIGHT AND SPREAD: 3 × 1ft (0.9 × 0.3m)

BLOOMING PERIOD: Late spring

SOIL: Well-drained but humus-rich and moisture-retentive.

LATIN NAME: *Paeonia* 'Baroness Schröder

COMMON NAME: Peony

ALTERNATIVES: 'Duchesse de Nemours,' 'Festiva Maxima'

DESCRIPTION: Herbaceous perennial forming a bushy plant with large, divided leaves often red-tinted in spring and again in autumn. This cultivar has large, double, white blooms with a blush tint.

HEIGHT AND SPREAD: 3 × 3ft (0.9 × 0.9m)

BLOOMING PERIOD: Late spring to early summer

SOIL: Rich, with a high humus content, well-drained.

3-7

3-9

LATIN NAME: *Hyacinthus orientalis* 'L'Innocence'

COMMON NAME: Hyacinth

ALTERNATIVES: 'White Pearl'

DESCRIPTION: Bulb producing a ring of stiffly upright leaves that later extend and fall outwards. A stout flower stalk bears the close-packed, tubular, highly fragrant, white blooms.

HEIGHT AND SPREAD: 4–8 × 2½–4in (10–20 × 6–10cm)

BLOOMING PERIOD: Spring

SOIL: Any well-drained.

LATIN NAME: *Anemone sylvestris*

COMMON NAME: Snowdrop windflower

ALTERNATIVES: A. *blanda* 'White Splendour,' A. *nemorosa* and forms

DESCRIPTION: Carpet-forming perennial with jagged, lobed leaves and delicate flower stems bearing bowl-shaped blooms of white with a yellow center. This plant may become invasive.

HEIGHT AND SPREAD: 12 × 12in (30 × 30cm)

BLOOMING PERIOD: Spring to early summer

SOIL: Well-drained, humus-rich.

BACK

5-9

LATIN NAME: *Kalmia latifolia* 'Carousel'
COMMON NAME: Mountain laurel, calico bush
ALTERNATIVES: 'Silver Dollar,' 'Snowdrift'
DESCRIPTION: Evergreen shrub producing large clusters of waxy blooms. Flower buds distinctively ridged. May take several years to begin flowering freely.
HEIGHT AND SPREAD: 10 × 10ft (3 × 3m)
BLOOMING PERIOD: Early summer
SOIL: Needs acid conditions. Deep soil with lots of organic matter.

8-9

LATIN NAME: *Carpenteria californica*
COMMON NAME: Known by Latin name
ALTERNATIVES: 'Ladham's Variety'
DESCRIPTION: Evergreen shrub with narrow pointed leaves and large, circular flowers centered with a boss of stamens. In colder areas grow in the shelter of a warm wall.
HEIGHT AND SPREAD: 5 × 5ft (1.5 × 1.5m)
BLOOMING PERIOD: Early summer
SOIL: Deep loam, but tolerant of acid or alkaline conditions.

MIDDLE

4-10

LATIN NAME: *Nectaroscordum siculum bulgaricum*
COMMON NAME: Known by Latin name
ALTERNATIVES: None
DESCRIPTION: Bulb related to allium producing upright stems topped with drooping bells in greenish-cream shaded with purple. Highly decorative seed heads. Stoloniferous bulbs may spread into other plantings.
HEIGHT AND SPREAD: 4 × 1–1½ft (1.2 × 0.3–0.45cm)
BLOOMING PERIOD: Late spring
SOIL: Light but moisture-retentive.

4-10

LATIN NAME: *Leucanthemum × superbum* 'Wirral Supreme'
COMMON NAME: Shasta daisy, chrysanthemum
ALTERNATIVES: 'T. E. Killin,' 'Cobham Gold,' 'Fiona Coghill,' 'Everest'
DESCRIPTION: Perennial with stout, upright stems topped with large double daisy flowers with a broad tuft of short petals at the center. Divide and replant every two years to keep flowering performance.
HEIGHT AND SPREAD: 3 × 1½ft (90 × 45cm)
BLOOMING PERIOD: Early summer to early autumn
SOIL: Any fertile soil provided it is well-drained.

FRONT

8-10

LATIN NAME: *Hebe pinguifolia* 'Pagei'
COMMON NAME: Disc-leaved hebe
ALTERNATIVES: 'Sutherlandii,' *H. cantaburiensis*
DESCRIPTION: Evergreen shrub with prostrate stems which root where they touch making excellent, non-invasive groundcover. Tiny white flowers produced early in the season. Becomes thin if overgrown by plants.
HEIGHT AND SPREAD: 6–12 × 24–36in (15–30 × 60–90cm)
BLOOMING PERIOD: Early summer
SOIL: Any well-drained but not overly dry.

8-10

LATIN NAME: *Cistus × hybridus* syn. *C. × corbariensis*
COMMON NAME: Rock-rose
ALTERNATIVES: *C. salviifolius*, *C. s.* 'Prostratus'
DESCRIPTION: Evergreen shrub forming a low, spreading hummock of dark, wrinkled, green foliage. Small white circular flowers with a central boss of stamens open from contrasting red buds.
HEIGHT AND SPREAD: 2 × 4½ft (0.6 × 1.3m)
BLOOMING PERIOD: Late spring to early summer
SOIL: Any well-drained including those with reasonably high alkalinity.

LATIN NAME: *Philadelphus coronarius* 'Variegatus'
COMMON NAME: Variegated mock orange
ALTERNATIVES: 'Innocence'
DESCRIPTION: Shrub with brightly variegated foliage (leaves have a broad, irregular white margin). The creamy-white flowers are very sweetly scented. Excellent in dappled shade – leaves tend to scorch in full sun.
HEIGHT AND SPREAD: 8 × 6ft (2.5 × 2m)
BLOOMING PERIOD: Early summer
SOIL: Any fertile soil including heavy clay, provided this is not waterlogged.

5-8

LATIN NAME: *Philadelpus × lemoinei*
COMMON NAME: Mock orange
ALTERNATIVES: 'Avalanche,' 'Belle Etoile,' 'Sybille'
DESCRIPTION: Shrub with stems upright at first then arching toward the tip. Tresses of perfumed, four-petalled flowers each with a boss of golden stamens. Remove ⅓ of old wood after flowering.
HEIGHT AND SPREAD: 6 × 7ft (1.8 × 2.15m)
BLOOMING PERIOD: Early to mid-summer
SOIL: Any fertile soil including heavy clay provided not waterlogged.

5-8

LATIN NAME: *Leucanthemum × superbum* 'Phyllis Smith'
COMMON NAME: Shasta daisy, chrysanthemum
ALTERNATIVES: 'Bishopstone'
DESCRIPTION: Perennial with stout, upright stems topped with daisy-like flowers with long fringed petals and yellow centers. Divide and replant every two years to maintain flowering performance.
HEIGHT AND SPREAD: 3 × 1½ft (90 × 45cm)
BLOOMING PERIOD: Early summer to early autumn
SOIL: Any fertile soil provided it is well-drained.

4-10

LATIN NAME: *Gaura lindheimeri*
COMMON NAME: White gaura
ALTERNATIVES: 'The Bride,' 'Whirling Butterflies'
DESCRIPTION: Perennial with open, branched habit. The wiry flower stems carry an abundance of tiny butterfly-like flowers which are white tinged pink. Excellent "filler" between flowers of more substance.
HEIGHT AND SPREAD: 4 × 3ft (1.2 × 0.9m)
BLOOMING PERIOD: Early summer to mid-autumn
SOIL: Well-drained. Tolerates drought.

6-10

4-10

LATIN NAME: *Geranium sanguineum* 'Album'
COMMON NAME: Bloody cranesbill
ALTERNATIVES: *G. clarkei* 'Kashmir White,' *G. macrorrhizum* 'Album'
DESCRIPTION: Perennial with open branching habit. Stems clothed in deeply divided dark green leaves. Very floriferous. In hot climates, plant in partial shade to prolong flowering.
HEIGHT AND SPREAD: 2 × 1½ft (60 × 45cm)
BLOOMING PERIOD: Mid-spring to late summer
SOIL: Any fertile, well-drained.

LATIN NAME: *Lamium maculatum* 'White Nancy'
COMMON NAME: Spotted deadnettle
ALTERNATIVES: *L. m. album*, *L. galeobdolon* 'Herman's Pride'
DESCRIPTION: Semi-evergreen perennial forming a mat of silver-white heart-shaped leaves. Clusters of hooded flowers. Does well in containers and hanging baskets for shade when fed and watered.
HEIGHT AND SPREAD: 6 × 36in (15 × 90cm)
BLOOMING PERIOD: Late spring and summer
SOIL: Moist, humus-rich soil not prone to drying out.

3-10

BACK

6-9

LATIN NAME: *Weigela* 'Candida'
COMMON NAME: Known by Latin name
ALTERNATIVES: *W. florida* 'Bristol Snowflake,' 'Mont Blanc,' 'Snowflake'
DESCRIPTION: Shrub blooming on second year wood. Tubular flowers flared at the mouth. To maximize flowering and maintain habit, prune established plants immediately after flowering.
HEIGHT AND SPREAD: 7 × 7ft (2.2 × 2.2m)
BLOOMING PERIOD: Late spring to early summer
SOIL: Thrives on a wide range of soil types including heavy clay.

LATIN NAME: *Spiraea nipponica* 'Snowmound'
COMMON NAME: Nippon spiraea
ALTERNATIVES: *S. nipponica, S. 'Arguta,' S. × vanhouttei*
DESCRIPTION: Shrub with elegant arching habit, clusters of tiny white flowers and narrow light green leaves. Prune immediately after flowering removing about a third of the oldest stems.
HEIGHT AND SPREAD: 6 × 6ft (1.8 × 1.8m)
BLOOMING PERIOD: Early summer
SOIL: Most soil types but avoid extremely alkaline conditions.

4-9

MIDDLE

4-10

LATIN NAME: *Digitalis purpurea albiflora*
COMMON NAME: Common foxglove
ALTERNATIVES: Excelsior White Group, 'Cloud'
DESCRIPTION: Biennial or short-lived perennial with a basal rosette of leaves topped by a tall spire. Tubular flowers flared at mouth and speckled inside. Seed comes true if isolated from common pink form.
HEIGHT AND SPREAD: 3–5 × 2ft (90–150 × 60cm)
BLOOMING PERIOD: Early to mid-summer
SOIL: Best on moisture-retentive soils with plenty of organic matter.

4-9

LATIN NAME: *Papaver orientale* cultivar
COMMON NAME: Oriental poppy
ALTERNATIVES: 'Perry's White,' 'Black and White'
DESCRIPTION: Perennial with bowl-shaped blooms and petals like tissue-paper. Black or deep maroon centers contrast well. Divided leaves, stems and buds hairy. Foliage dies by mid-summer.
HEIGHT AND SPREAD: 3–4 × 1–3ft (90–120 × 30–90cm)
BLOOMING PERIOD: Late spring to early summer
SOIL: Any fertile loam.

FRONT

3-10

LATIN NAME: *Dicentra eximia* 'Snowdrift'
COMMON NAME: Fringed bleeding heart
ALTERNATIVES: *D. formosa* 'Alba,' *D. f.* 'Silver Smith,' *D. spectabilis* 'Alba'
DESCRIPTION: Perennial with pale, gray-green leaves making ferny hummock above which are held arching sprays of heart shaped flowers. An excellent plant for the shaded garden and under trees.
HEIGHT AND SPREAD: 12 × 18in (30 × 45cm)
BLOOMING PERIOD: Late spring to early summer
SOIL: Humus rich, moisture-retentive but well-drained.

3-10

LATIN NAME: *Cerastium tomentosum*
COMMON NAME: Snow-in-summer
ALTERNATIVES: Species only
DESCRIPTION: Evergreen perennial groundcover with narrow silver, felted leaves and a profusion of starry white flowers. Suitable as groundcover beneath established shrubs in a sunny border or as edging. Invasive.
HEIGHT AND SPREAD: 3in × indefinite (8cm × indefinite)
BLOOMING PERIOD: Late spring to summer
SOIL: Well-drained.

LATIN NAME: *Wisteria sinensis* 'Alba' syn. 'Shiro-capital'
COMMON NAME: Known by Latin name
ALTERNATIVES: *W. floribunda* 'Alba,' *W. f.* 'Snow Showers'
DESCRIPTION: Woody climber with 2ft (60cm) long scented racemes and pea-like blooms. Light green pinnate leaves. Climbs via tendrils. Prune to control size and promote flowering. Buy named, grafted specimens.
HEIGHT AND SPREAD: 30 × 30ft (9 × 9m)
BLOOMING PERIOD: Early summer and at later intervals
SOIL: Prefers moisture-retentive. Avoid strongly alkaline conditions.

5-9

8-10

LATIN NAME: *Choisya ternata*
COMMON NAME: Mexican orange blossom
ALTERNATIVES: 'Sundance,' 'Aztec Pearl'
DESCRIPTION: Evergreen shrub with glossy three-lobed leaves and clusters of fragrant blooms. After initial flowering will bloom on and off until autumn. In cold areas grow against a warm wall.
HEIGHT AND SPREAD: 6 × 5½ft (1.8 × 1.6m)
BLOOMING PERIOD: Late spring and intermittently through the year
SOIL: Most, avoiding waterlogged or extremely alkaline.

LATIN NAME: *Lupinus* cultivar
COMMON NAME: Lupin
ALTERNATIVES: Russell Hybrids, including 'Blushing Bride'
DESCRIPTION: Perennial which produces a mound of compound leaves topped by several stout, tapering flower spikes. Sweetly scented. Relatively short-lived. Remove faded flowers before pods form.
HEIGHT AND SPREAD: 4 × 1½ft (120 × 45cm)
BLOOMING PERIOD: Early summer
SOIL: Prefers well-drained alkaline conditions.

4-9

LATIN NAME: *Hesperis matronalis albiflora*
COMMON NAME: Sweet rocket, damask or dame's violet
ALTERNATIVES: 'Alba Plena' (a double white form)
DESCRIPTION: Biennial or short-lived perennial. Sweetly fragrant especially in the evening. Blooms four-petalled, clustered at top of stems. Leaves pointed, narrowly oval. Self-sows abundantly. Can be invasive.
HEIGHT AND SPREAD: 2½ × 2ft (75 × 60cm)
BLOOMING PERIOD: Late spring to mid-summer
SOIL: Prefers moisture-retentive conditions. Tolerates heavy and poor soil.

4-9

LATIN NAME: *Convolvulus cneorum*
COMMON NAME: Known by Latin name
ALTERNATIVES: Species only
DESCRIPTION: Evergreen shrub forming a mound of silver, silky-textured leaves. Trumpet-shaped flowers in white tinged pink. Good plant for a larger rock garden or gravel bed. In cold areas grow at the foot of a warm wall.
HEIGHT AND SPREAD: 1½ × 2½ft (45 × 75cm)
BLOOMING PERIOD: Late spring to mid-summer
SOIL: Well-drained. Tolerates lime.

8-10

6-10

LATIN NAME: *Viola cornuta* Alba Group
COMMON NAME: Horned violet or tufted pansy
ALTERNATIVES: 'Alba Minor,' *V. odorata* 'Alba'
DESCRIPTION: Evergreen perennial, spreading via rhizomes and making good groundcover. Abundant flowers like mini-pansies. To promote secondary flowering, cut back after first flush and water well.
HEIGHT AND SPREAD: 1 × 2ft (30 × 60cm)
BLOOMING PERIOD: Early to late summer
SOIL: Moisture-retentive but well-drained.

BACK

LATIN NAME: *Philadelphus coronarius*
COMMON NAME: Mock orange
ALTERNATIVES: *P.* 'Beauclerk,' *P.* 'Virginal'
DESCRIPTION: Shrub with dense, suckering habit, the upright stems arching toward the tips. Creamy-white fragrant flowers open to a boss of yellow stamens. Foliage is light green and well-veined.
HEIGHT AND SPREAD: 8 × 5ft (2.5 × 1.5m)
BLOOMING PERIOD: Early summer
SOIL: Any fertile soil including heavy clay but not waterlogged.

5-8

LATIN NAME: *Viburnum opulus*
COMMON NAME: Guelder rose
ALTERNATIVES: 'Notcutt's Variety,' 'Xanthocarpum'
DESCRIPTION: Shrub of large stature and broad, jagged-edged leaves. Tiny fertile flowers clustered in flat, circular heads with an outer ring of showy sterile bracts. Translucent berries, red or yellow and good autumn color.
HEIGHT AND SPREAD: 12 × 12ft (3.6 × 3.6m)
BLOOMING PERIOD: Late spring to early summer
SOIL: Prefers moist, even boggy conditions and tolerates lime.

4-8

MIDDLE

LATIN NAME: *Chrysanthemum carinatum* 'Polar Star'
COMMON NAME: Annual chrysanthemum or painted daisy
ALTERNATIVES: None
DESCRIPTION: Feathery gray-green leaves and masses of daisy flowers with yellow central band and dark eye. Quick-growing with stiff, straight stems, ideal for filling gaps in the border or for cutting.
HEIGHT AND SPREAD: 18–36 × 18in (45–90 × 45cm)
BLOOMING PERIOD: Early summer to early autumn or first frosts
SOIL: Any well-drained.

8-10

LATIN NAME: *Zantedeschia aethiopica*
COMMON NAME: Arum lily, lily of the Nile
ALTERNATIVES: 'Crowborough,' 'Giant White'
DESCRIPTION: Perennial with tuberous roots. Large arrow-shaped leaves and white flowers. Protect young plants with deep mulch or grow in shallow water for frost protection.
HEIGHT AND SPREAD: 18–36 × 14–18in (45–90 × 35–45cm)
BLOOMING PERIOD: Summer
SOIL: Moisture-retentive to submerged 6–12in (15–30cm) of water.

FRONT

LATIN NAME: *Lavatera trimestris* 'Mont Blanc'
COMMON NAME: Annual tree mallow
ALTERNATIVES: 'Parade Hybrids,' 'White Beauty'
DESCRIPTION: Bushy, upright growth and large lobed leaves, with abundant large funnel-shaped flowers resembling hibiscus. Allow sufficient spacing between seedlings for proper development.
HEIGHT AND SPREAD: 24 × 18in (60 × 45cm)
BLOOMING PERIOD: Summer to early autumn or first frosts
SOIL: Any well-drained.

LATIN NAME: *Polemonium caeruleum* var. *lacteum*
COMMON NAME: Jacob's ladder
ALTERNATIVES: None
DESCRIPTION: Perennial making a basal clump of divided leaves. The leaflets are opposite like a ladder giving rise to the common name. Fine, upright flower stems with clusters of open, bell-shaped flowers with golden stamens.
HEIGHT AND SPREAD: 18–24 × 18–24in (45–60 × 45–60cm)
BLOOMING PERIOD: Summer
SOIL: Any reasonably fertile, moisture-retentive soil.

3-9

Latin name: *Delphinium* cultivar
Common name: Known by Latin name
Alternatives: Pacific Giants Hybrids, Galahad Hybrids
Description: Perennial producing tall spires of single, semi-double or double flowers often with a contrasting eye or "bee." Handsome, deeply divided foliage. Staking essential. Renew from cuttings every 3 years.
Height and spread: 4−8 × 3ft (1.2−2.5 × 0.9m)
Blooming period: Early to mid-summer
Soil: Rich, deep, moisture-retentive.

3-10

8-10

Latin name: *Cistus ladanifer*
Common name: Gum rock-rose
Alternatives: 'Albiflorus,' Palhinhae Group, 'Pat,' 'Blanche'
Description: Evergreen shrub with flowers up to 4in (10cm) in diameter and petals marked at base with maroon blotch. On hot, sunny days, the gum-exuding foliage releases a pleasant aroma.
Height and spread: 5 × 4½ft (1.5 × 1.37m)
Blooming period: Early to mid-summer
Soil: Any well-drained including those with reasonably high alkalinity.

5-9

5-9

Latin name: *Rosa* 'Iceberg' syn. 'Schneewittchen'
Common name: Rose
Alternatives: 'Grace Abounding,' 'Elizabeth Philip,' 'Margaret Merril'
Description: Floribunda or cluster-flowered bush rose with open habit and rather thin, branched growth. Produces an abundance of double white blooms with slight scent. Light green glossy foliage.
Height and spread: 4 × 3ft (1.2 × 0.9m)
Blooming period: Late spring to late autumn
Soil: Fertile, moisture-retentive soil. Avoid extreme alkalinity.

Latin name: *Rosa* 'Margaret Merril'
Common name: Rose
Alternatives: 'Grace Abounding,' 'Elizabeth Philip,' 'Iceberg'
Description: Floribunda or cluster-flowered bush rose with upright habit and nicely shaped individual blooms held singly or in clusters – white blushed with pink. Good fragrance indoors as a cut flower.
Height and spread: 3 × 2ft (90 × 60cm)
Blooming period: Late spring to late autumn
Soil: Fertile, moisture-retentive soil. Avoid extreme alkalinity.

4-10

Latin name: *Artemisia stelleriana*
Common name: Dusty miller
Alternatives: 'Boughton Silver,' 'Silver Brocade'
Description: Evergreen sub-shrub with felted light gray foliage. The beautiful leaves are deeply divided. Insignificant yellow flowers produced on gray-white stems covered in leaflets.
Height and spread: 1−2 × 2−3ft (30−60 × 60−90cm)
Blooming period: Summer
Soil: A light, well-drained soil to prevent plants from rotting off.

Latin name: *Lobularia maritima*
Common name: Sweet alyssum
Alternatives: 'Snow Crystals,' 'Snow Carpet,' 'Snowdrift'
Description: Hardy annual making low, spreading hummocks smothered in honey-scented blooms which obscure the foliage. Tend to stop flowering if conditions become too hot and dry. Readily self-seeds.
Height and spread: 3−6 × 9in (7−15 × 23cm)
Blooming period: Early summer to early autumn
Soil: Well-drained but not too dry. Avoid very rich soil.

BACK

4-9

LATIN NAME: *Clematis* 'Marie Boisselot' syn. 'Madame Le Coultre'
COMMON NAME: Known by Latin name
ALTERNATIVES: 'Henryi,' 'Jackmanii Alba'
DESCRIPTION: Climber with large white blooms. Prune lightly in early spring cutting stems back to strong leaf-axil buds and removing thin and damaged stems.
HEIGHT AND SPREAD: 10 × 3ft (3 × 1m)+
BLOOMING PERIOD: Early summer to early autumn
SOIL: Fertile, moisture-retentive and humus-rich.

2-8

LATIN NAME: *Cornus alba* 'Elegantissima'
COMMON NAME: Red-barked dogwood
ALTERNATIVES: None
DESCRIPTION: Shrub with gray-green leaves edged white and many upright stems which color up crimson-red after leaf fall. For larger leaves, remove a few of the oldest stems in early spring. White berries may follow flowers.
HEIGHT AND SPREAD: 6 × 7ft (1.8 × 2.1m)
BLOOMING PERIOD: Late spring to early summer
SOIL: Fertile, moisture-retentive, including heavy clay prone to waterlogging.

MIDDLE

LATIN NAME: *Cosmos* 'Purity'
COMMON NAME: Known by Latin name
ALTERNATIVES: 'Sensation' series, 'Sonata' series
DESCRIPTION: Half-hardy annual with very fine, ferny foliage and large daisy-like flowers on long, stems. Excellent for cutting, works well among herbaceous perennials or in gaps in mixed border.
HEIGHT AND SPREAD: 3 × 1–1½ft (90 × 30–45cm)
BLOOMING PERIOD: Mid-summer to mid-autumn or first frosts
SOIL: Well-drained. Does well on relatively poor soils.

6-9

LATIN NAME: *Crambe maritima*
COMMON NAME: Sea kale
ALTERNATIVES: 'Lily White'
DESCRIPTION: Perennial producing a basal clump of large blue-gray wavy-edged leaves with a waxy texture. Clusters of small white flowers on branching stems above the foliage. Good for seaside gardens.
HEIGHT AND SPREAD: 2 × 2ft (60 × 60cm)
BLOOMING PERIOD: Early summer
SOIL: Any well-drained including sand or stony.

FRONT

7-9

LATIN NAME: *Ballota pseudodictamnus*
COMMON NAME: Known by Latin name
ALTERNATIVES: *B. acetabulosa*
DESCRIPTION: Sub-shrub forming a low mound of gray-green foliage. Rounded leaves and stems covered with white "wool." Pink flowers in whorls, almost hidden by green calyces. Cut to ground in spring.
HEIGHT AND SPREAD: 2 × 3ft (60 × 90cm)
BLOOMING PERIOD: Early to mid-summer
SOIL: Average, well-drained.

8-10

LATIN NAME: *Hebe* 'Pewter Dome'
COMMON NAME: Hebe
ALTERNATIVES: *Hebe pinguifolia* 'Pagei'
DESCRIPTION: Evergreen shrub making a neat, dense dome of small, gray-green, waxy leaves. White fluffy flower spikes. Architectural form contrasts with columns, cones and plants with sword-shaped leaves.
HEIGHT AND SPREAD: 1½ × 3ft (45 × 90cm)
BLOOMING PERIOD: Early summer
SOIL: Well-drained but moisture-retentive.

BACK

LATIN NAME: *Viburnum opulus* 'Roseum' syn. 'Sterile'
COMMON NAME: Snowball tree, Whitsun boss
ALTERNATIVES: None
DESCRIPTION: Shrub with large, jagged-edged leaves and spherical, creamy-white blooms. Unlike the species, this plant is sterile and does not produce berries. Good autumn color.
HEIGHT AND SPREAD: 10 × 10ft (3 × 3m)
BLOOMING PERIOD: Early to mid-summer
SOIL: Fertile, moisture-retentive. Tolerates waterlogging and lime.

4-8

LATIN NAME: *Miscanthus sinensis* 'Variegatus'
COMMON NAME: Eulalia grass, Japanese silver grass
ALTERNATIVES: None
DESCRIPTION: Ornamental grass forming a tall column of parallel stems arching toward the tips. The ribbon-like leaves are brightly white-variegated. Plumes of flowers are produced in early autumn.
HEIGHT AND SPREAD: 6 × 2ft (1.8 × 0.6m)
BLOOMING PERIOD: Mid- to late autumn
SOIL: Fertile, moisture-retentive. Avoid dry conditions.

5-10

LATIN NAME: *Datura innoxia* 'Alba' syn. *D. meteloides*
COMMON NAME: Datura
ALTERNATIVES: None
DESCRIPTION: Short-lived perennial grown as an annual. Large, coarse leaves and trumpet-shaped flowers having a wonderful perfume. Unusual plant for the patio. Start seeds under heat in early spring.
HEIGHT AND SPREAD: 3 × 2½ft (90 × 75cm)
BLOOMING PERIOD: Summer to frosts
SOIL: Any fertile well-drained but moisture-retentive soil.

MIDDLE

4-9

LATIN NAME: *Lilium candidum*
COMMON NAME: Madonna lily
ALTERNATIVES: None
DESCRIPTION: Bulb producing long stems topped with a cluster of large, trumpet-shaped perfumed flowers. Overwinters with a basal rosette of leaves. Dislikes disturbance and prone to mildew. Plant shallowly.
HEIGHT AND SPREAD: 3–5 × 1ft (0.9–1.50 × 0.3m)
BLOOMING PERIOD: Mid-summer
SOIL: Average soil, slightly alkaline.

8-10

LATIN NAME: *Cistus salviifolius*
COMMON NAME: Rock-rose
ALTERNATIVES: 'Prostratus'
DESCRIPTION: Shrub making a low mound of downy leaves. Small white, yellow-centered flowers produced in abundance. 'Prostratus' is lower growing and said to be more hardy.
HEIGHT AND SPREAD: 1½ × 2½ft (45 × 75cm)
BLOOMING PERIOD: Summer
SOIL: Poor sandy soil to prevent lush growth which is prone to frost.

FRONT

9-10

LATIN NAME: *Artemisia arborescens*
COMMON NAME: Known by Latin name
ALTERNATIVES: 'Faith Raven,' *A. absinthium* 'Lambrook Giant'
DESCRIPTION: Semi-evergreen sub-shrub with gray-white dissected foliage giving beautiful lacey effect. Tiny yellow flowers. Not reliably hardy. Best at foot of warm wall. 'Faith Raven' is sturdier.
HEIGHT AND SPREAD: 2–3 × 2ft (0.6–0.9 × 0.6m)
BLOOMING PERIOD: Mid to late summer
SOIL: Overwinters best when growing on quite poor, dry soils.

WHITE

BACK

LATIN NAME: *Lathyrus odoratus* variety
COMMON NAME: Sweet pea
ALTERNATIVES: 'Lillie Langtry,' 'Swan Lake,' 'Royal Wedding,' 'Rembrandt'
DESCRIPTION: Annual climber with pea-like flowers and foliage climbing by tendrils. Needs a framework of support. Alternatively grow over an established shrub. Excellent cut flower. Very fragrant.
HEIGHT AND SPREAD: 9 × 3ft (2.7 × 0.9m)
BLOOMING PERIOD: Mid-summer to early autumn (spring in Australia)
SOIL: Well dug incorporating plenty of organic matter.

4-9

LATIN NAME: *Hydrangea arborescens* 'Annabelle'
COMMON NAME: Smooth hydrangea
ALTERNATIVES: 'Grandiflora'
DESCRIPTION: Shrub of rounded habit with broad, pointed leaves and very large creamy-white rounded flower heads. Flowers attractive in bud and when faded to biscuit color in autumn. Increase by suckers.
HEIGHT AND SPREAD: 6 × 8ft (1.8 × 2.4m)
BLOOMING PERIOD: Mid-summer to early autumn
SOIL: Rich, moisture-retentive. Best neutral to acid, tolerant of lime.

MIDDLE

LATIN NAME: *Malva moschata alba*
COMMON NAME: Musk mallow
ALTERNATIVES: None
DESCRIPTION: Perennial with pretty "fingered" leaves forming a bush smothered in summer with bowl-shaped blooms. Comes true from seed and self-seeds readily. This is useful as young plants tend to flower best.
HEIGHT AND SPREAD: 3 × 2ft (90 × 60cm)
BLOOMING PERIOD: Early to mid-summer
SOIL: Any fertile soil provided it is well-drained. Tolerates lime.

3-10

LATIN NAME: *Verbascum lychnitis*
COMMON NAME: White mullein
ALTERNATIVES: *Verbascum chaixii* 'Album'
DESCRIPTION: Biennial forming an evergreen mound of large gray-green leaves and in its second year, a tall, upright branching flower stem covered in small blooms.
HEIGHT AND SPREAD: 2–3 × 2ft (60–90 × 60cm)
BLOOMING PERIOD: Early to mid-summer
SOIL: Any well-drained.

5-10

FRONT

LATIN NAME: *Artemisia arborescens* 'Porquerolles'
COMMON NAME: Tree wormwood
ALTERNATIVES: 'Faith Raven,' 'Powis Castle'
DESCRIPTION: Evergreen shrub. A compact-growing form of the species with lacey, silver-gray foliage. Flowers insignificant. Hardiest against a warm wall on fairly poor soil.
HEIGHT AND SPREAD: 2 × 3ft (60 × 90cm)
BLOOMING PERIOD: Summer to autumn
SOIL: Well-drained to dry.

9-10

5-10

LATIN NAME: *Artemisia absinthium* 'Lambrook Silver'
COMMON NAME: Wormwood, absinth
ALTERNATIVES: *A. absinthium*
DESCRIPTION: Evergreen perennial with aromatic, finely divided lustrous silver-gray foliage. The tiny yellow-gray flowers appear on long, delicate, branched spikes.
HEIGHT AND SPREAD: 2½ × 2ft (75 × 60cm)
BLOOMING PERIOD: Early summer to early autumn
SOIL: Any well-drained.

8-10

LATIN NAME: *Jasminum officinale*
COMMON NAME: Common jasmine, jessamine
ALTERNATIVES: *J .o. affine, J. o. 'Argenteovariegatum.' J. o. 'Fiona Sunrise'*
DESCRIPTION: Climber with perfumed star-shaped blooms produced in clusters along the stems. Attractive pinnate foliage adds to the airy appearance. Growth best left unchecked to cover large area.
HEIGHT AND SPREAD: 24 × 24ft (7.3 × 7.3m)
BLOOMING PERIOD: Early to late summer
SOIL: Average, well-drained.

LATIN NAME: *Aruncus dioicus*
COMMON NAME: Goat's beard
ALTERNATIVES: 'Glasnevin'
DESCRIPTION: Perennial forming 4ft (1.2m) high hummocks of large, fern-like leaves. The creamy-white flower plumes are more showy in the males, but female plants carry long-lasting ornamental seed heads.
HEIGHT AND SPREAD: 6–7 × 4ft (1.8–2.1 × 1.2m)
BLOOMING PERIOD: Early to mid-summer
SOIL: Any reasonably fertile. Growth more luxuriant on moist soil.

3-9

3-10

LATIN NAME: *Echinacea purpurea 'White Swan'*
COMMON NAME: Coneflower
ALTERNATIVES: 'White Lustre,' 'White Star'
DESCRIPTION: Perennial with stiff, upright flower stems bearing large, daisy-like flowers. At the center of each is a raised dome of glowing ginger-brown. *E. purpurea* is an important medicinal herb.
HEIGHT AND SPREAD: 48 × 18in (1.2 × 0.45m)
BLOOMING PERIOD: Summer
SOIL: Rich, well-drained but with plenty of organic matter.

3-9

LATIN NAME: *Phlox paniculata* cultivar
COMMON NAME: Border phlox
ALTERNATIVES: 'Fujiyama,' 'Europa,' 'White Admiral'
DESCRIPTION: Perennial forming clumps of upright stems clothed in willow-like leaves and topped by clusters of fragrant rounded flowers. May suffer from mildew in hot, dry conditions.
HEIGHT AND SPREAD: 4 × 2ft (1.2 × 0.6m)
BLOOMING PERIOD: Mid-summer to mid-autumn depending on variety
SOIL: Rich, moisture-retentive, humus-rich. Avoid heavy clay.

LATIN NAME: *Hosta undulata*
COMMON NAME: Hosta, plantain lily, funkia, giboshi
ALTERNATIVES: *H. u. univittata, H. u. albomarginata* syn. 'Thomas Hogg'
DESCRIPTION: Perennial making a mound of rich, dark green leaves with a broad central creamy-white zone. The leaves are undulating and sometimes spirally twisted. Lilac bells on tall stems.
HEIGHT AND SPREAD: 18 × 12in (45 × 30cm)
BLOOMING PERIOD: Early summer
SOIL: Fertile, moisture-retentive soil. Thrives in dry conditions in shade.

3-9

LATIN NAME: *Antirrhinum majus* variety
COMMON NAME: Snapdragon
ALTERNATIVES: 'White Wonder,' 'Coronette' series, 'Monarch' series
DESCRIPTION: Annual with stems branching from the base clothed in small, narrow dark green leaves. Grouped according to flower type e.g. penstemon, or hyacinth, but all produce spikes of tubular, lipped flowers.
HEIGHT AND SPREAD: 1–2 × 1ft (30–60 × 30cm)
BLOOMING PERIOD: Early summer to mid-autumn
SOIL: Lighter soils preferred.

117

BACK

6-9

LATIN NAME: *Rubus cockburnianus* 'Golden Vale'
COMMON NAME: White-stemmed bramble
ALTERNATIVES: *R. tibetanus* syn. *R. t.* 'Silver Fern'
DESCRIPTION: Shrub. New cultivar with deep purple, white-washed stems, upright at first then arching over. Yellow leaves, three-lobed. Small, dish-shaped flowers. Cut hard back in spring. Invasive.
HEIGHT AND SPREAD: 6 × 6ft (1.8 × 1.8m)
BLOOMING PERIOD: Late summer to early autumn
SOIL: Most, avoiding very dry or wet.

6-8

LATIN NAME: *Onopordum acanthium*
COMMON NAME: Scotch thistle, cotton thistle
ALTERNATIVES: None
DESCRIPTION: Biennial. A plant for the border like a giant thistle with silver-gray, deeply divided leaves (protect from slugs and snails) and a tall flower stem producing purple-pink thistles.
HEIGHT AND SPREAD: 6 × 3ft (1.8 × 0.9m)
BLOOMING PERIOD: Summer
SOIL: Fertile, well-drained.

MIDDLE

LATIN NAME: *Veronicastrum virginicum album*
COMMON NAME: Culver's root
ALTERNATIVES: None
DESCRIPTION: Perennial with many straight, upright stems clothed in whorls of pointed leaves and topped with narrow spikes. Useful vertical backdrop to foreground planting.
HEIGHT AND SPREAD: 4 × 1½ft (1.2 × 0.45cm)
BLOOMING PERIOD: Late summer
SOIL: Any fertile, preferably moderately acidic.

3-10

5-10

LATIN NAME: *Eryngium giganteum*
COMMON NAME: Miss Willmott's Ghost, sea holly
ALTERNATIVES: None
DESCRIPTION: Biennial or short-lived perennial forming a basal rosette of heart shaped leaves. Tall, silvery flower stems have many blue thimble-shaped heads each with a broad, spiny, silver collar.
HEIGHT AND SPREAD: 3–4 × 2½ft (0.9–1.2 × 0.75cm)
BLOOMING PERIOD: Late summer
SOIL: Any fertile, well-drained.

FRONT

8-10

LATIN NAME: *Hebe rakaiensis* syn. *Veronica subalpina*
COMMON NAME: Hebe
ALTERNATIVES: None
DESCRIPTION: Evergreen shrub with dense, dome-shaped habit. Light, pea-green foliage, especially good in winter contrasting with darker-leaved evergreens. Short fluffy spikes of flower.
HEIGHT AND SPREAD: 3 × 4ft (0.9 × 1.2m)
BLOOMING PERIOD: Early to mid-summer
SOIL: Well-drained but not overly dry.

4-10

LATIN NAME: *Stachys byzantina* syn. *S. lanata*
COMMON NAME: Lamb's tongue, Lamb's ears
ALTERNATIVES: 'Silver Carpet' (non-flowering)
DESCRIPTION: Evergreen perennial with oval leaves covered in a dense silken felt of silvery hairs. Upright flower stems have cerise blooms nearly hidden by silvery wool. Prone to mildew later in season.
HEIGHT AND SPREAD: 18 × 12in (45 × 30cm)
BLOOMING PERIOD: Summer
SOIL: Any avoiding winter wet.

LATIN NAME: *Clematis recta*

COMMON NAME: Herbaceous clematis

ALTERNATIVES: 'Purpurea,' 'Grandiflora'

DESCRIPTION: Perennial with green or purple foliage depending on variety and tall stems carrying a frothy mass of white scented blooms. Needs support. Attractive silvery seed heads.

HEIGHT AND SPREAD: 5–6 × 2ft (1.5–1.8 × 0.6m)

BLOOMING PERIOD: Early to mid-summer

SOIL: Fertile, well-drained, preferably slightly alkaline.

3-9

5-9

LATIN NAME: *Rosa filipes* 'Kiftsgate'

COMMON NAME: Kiftsgate rose

ALTERNATIVES: 'Rambling Rector,' 'Seagull,' 'Wedding Day'

DESCRIPTION: Climber making rampant, cascading growth. Suitable for training up into mature trees. Leaflets small, glossy green. Large clusters of small white single blooms. Some scent.

HEIGHT AND SPREAD: 30 × 20ft+ (9 × 6m)+

BLOOMING PERIOD: Late summer

SOIL: Any well-drained but moisture-retentive including clay.

7-10

LATIN NAME: *Crinum* × *powellii* 'Album'

COMMON NAME: Crinum lily

ALTERNATIVES: None

DESCRIPTION: Bulb with long, arching leaves and stout flower stems topped by large, trumpet-shaped blooms. Lovely fragrance. Tender so in cold areas provide protection of a warm wall.

HEIGHT AND SPREAD: 4 × 2ft (1.2 × 0.6m)

BLOOMING PERIOD: Summer

SOIL: Deep, rich, moisture-retentive. Mulch with organic matter.

8-10

LATIN NAME: *Agapanthus campanulatus* var. *albidus*

COMMON NAME: Lily-of-the-Nile, African lily

ALTERNATIVES: A. 'Rancho White,' 'White Christmas'

DESCRIPTION: Perennial with tuberous roots producing a bold clump of handsome strap-like leaves and arching flower stems topped with ball-shaped clusters of blooms. Stunningly architectural in bold drifts.

HEIGHT AND SPREAD: 2–4 × 1½ft (0.6 × 0.45m)

BLOOMING PERIOD: Late summer

SOIL: Fertile, moisture-retentive but not poorly drained.

LATIN NAME: *Iberis umbellata* 'White Pinnacle'

COMMON NAME: Candytuft

ALTERNATIVES: 'Iceberg,' 'White Empress,' 'Giant Hyacinth-flowered'

DESCRIPTION: Hardy annual producing domed heads of fragrant flowers like miniature hyacinths. Sow direct in autumn or spring in flowering position or in trays under glass for planting in late spring.

HEIGHT AND SPREAD: 12–15 × 9in (30–38 × 23cm)

BLOOMING PERIOD: Late spring to early autumn

SOIL: Any well-drained.

4-10

LATIN NAME: *Lychnis coronaria* Alba

COMMON NAME: Dusty miller, Rose campion

ALTERNATIVES: L. c. 'Oculata'

DESCRIPTION: Short-lived perennial with a basal clump of gray, felted leaves and silvery-gray branched upright flower stems. Flowers flat, rounded. Will self-seed, especially into gravel areas. May be treated as a biennial.

HEIGHT AND SPREAD: 3 × 1½ft (90 × 45cm)

BLOOMING PERIOD: Mid- to late summer

SOIL: Well-drained even dry and poor.

BACK

LATIN NAME: *Clethra alnifolia*
COMMON NAME: Sweet pepper bush
ALTERNATIVES: 'Paniculata,' C. tomentosa
DESCRIPTION: Shrub spreading by suckers producing lance-shaped leaves and narrow fluffy spires of flower. Prefers light shade and will produce good, yellow autumn color.
HEIGHT AND SPREAD: 4 × 6 ft (1.2 × 1.8m)
BLOOMING PERIOD: Late summer to mid-autumn
SOIL: Requires neutral to acid, moist conditions.

4-9

LATIN NAME: *Brugmansia* 'Variegata Sunset' syn. *Datura*
COMMON NAME: Angel's trumpets
ALTERNATIVES: B. suaveolens, B. s. 'Plena'
DESCRIPTION: Shrub with large soft leaves and hanging trumpet-shaped fragrant blooms. Leaves white-variegated. Flowers soft peach. All parts of plant are poisonous.
HEIGHT AND SPREAD: 6–8 × 6–8ft (1.8–2.4 × 1.8–2.4m)
BLOOMING PERIOD: Summer to autumn
SOIL: Average fertile. Overfeeding means poor flowering.

9-10

MIDDLE

LATIN NAME: *Physostegia virginiana* 'Summer Snow'
COMMON NAME: Obedient plant, false dragonhead
ALTERNATIVES: 'Alba,' 'Crown of Snow' syn. 'Schneekrone'
DESCRIPTION: Perennial with a spreading rootstock. Invasive in ideal conditions. Upright spikes of tubular flowers. The blooms stay in the position you bend them, hence the common name.
HEIGHT AND SPREAD: 3 × 2ft (90 × 60cm)
BLOOMING PERIOD: Mid-summer to early autumn
SOIL: Average, fertile, but moisture-retentive.

3-10

3-10

LATIN NAME: *Lysimachia clethroides*
COMMON NAME: Gooseneck loosestrife
ALTERNATIVES: L. barystachys, L. fortunei
DESCRIPTION: Perennial with long tapering flower heads which bend over at the tip and gradually straighten out as the flowers open. Invasive. Suitable for the wild garden.
HEIGHT AND SPREAD: 3 × 2ft (90 × 60cm)
BLOOMING PERIOD: Late summer
SOIL: Fertile, moist.

FRONT

LATIN NAME: *Begonia semperflorens*
COMMON NAME: Fibrous-rooted begonia
ALTERNATIVES: F1 hybrids
DESCRIPTION: Tender perennial usually grown as annual bedding. Rounded, fleshy leaves in green or bronze and round-petalled flowers in dense clusters. Grow from leaf cuttings or buy seedlings in spring.
HEIGHT AND SPREAD: 4–12 × 6–12in (10–30 × 15–30cm)
BLOOMING PERIOD: Early summer to mid-autumn
SOIL: Well-drained but moisture-retentive.

LATIN NAME: *Nicotiana* 'Domino Series' F1
COMMON NAME: Flowering tobacco
ALTERNATIVES: Starship Series, *Nicotiana alata* syn. *N. affinis*
DESCRIPTION: Annual bedding plant with basal rosette of leaves and upright flower stems producing a succession of blooms. May overwinter in mild areas. Some scent.
HEIGHT AND SPREAD: 1–1½ × 1ft (30–45 × 30cm)
BLOOMING PERIOD: Mid-summer to mid-autumn
SOIL: Any well-drained.

LATIN NAME: *Rosa 'Sanders' White Rambler'*
COMMON NAME: Rose
ALTERNATIVES: 'Rambling Rector,' 'Seagull,' 'Wedding Day'
DESCRIPTION: Climber with rampant growth arching at the tips. Neat, glossy fresh green leaflets and a mass of small double rosette-like flowers. Only flowers once.
HEIGHT AND SPREAD: 12 × 12ft (3.7 × 3.7m)
BLOOMING PERIOD: Late summer
SOIL: Rich, moisture-retentive, including heavy clay.

5-9

8-10

LATIN NAME: *Escallonia 'Iveyi'*
COMMON NAME: Known by Latin name
ALTERNATIVES: *E. bifida*
DESCRIPTION: Evergreen shrub with dark green, glossy leaves. White waxy blooms in clusters at ends of shoots. Attractive to butterflies. Grow by warm wall in cooler climes. Good seaside plant.
HEIGHT AND SPREAD: 10 × 10ft (3 × 3m)
BLOOMING PERIOD: Late summer to early autumn
SOIL: Average, fertile, well-drained.

LATIN NAME: *Anemone × hybrida 'Luise Uhink'*
COMMON NAME: Japanese anemone
ALTERNATIVES: 'Honorine Jobert,' 'Whirlwind,' 'Geant des Blanches'
DESCRIPTION: Perennial with a basal clump of three-lobed leaves and slender, upright flower stems carrying bowl-shaped blooms with a central boss of yellow stamens. May become invasive. Excellent in the shrub border.
HEIGHT AND SPREAD: 4 × 2ft (120 × 60cm)
BLOOMING PERIOD: Late summer to mid-autumn
SOIL: Well-drained but preferably moisture-retentive.

6-10

LATIN NAME: *Yucca flaccida*
COMMON NAME: Yucca
ALTERNATIVES: 'Golden Sword' (variegated), 'Ivory,' *Y. flaccida major*
DESCRIPTION: Evergreen perennial with a rosette of narrow, sword-shaped leaves bent over at the tips. Gray-green in color. The central branched flower spike covered in down carries rounded flowers almost horizontally.
HEIGHT AND SPREAD: 3 × 2½ft (90 × 75cm)
BLOOMING PERIOD: Mid- to late summer
SOIL: Any well-drained.

4-10

3-9

LATIN NAME: *Anaphalis margaritacea* syn. *A. yedoensis*
COMMON NAME: Pearly everlasting
ALTERNATIVES: *A. m. cinnamomea, A. m. yedoensis*
DESCRIPTION: Perennial with gray-green lance-shaped leaves, silver edged with a silver felted reverse. Tight clusters of papery flowers at the top of erect flower stems. Flowers dry well for winter decoration.
HEIGHT AND SPREAD: 2–2½ × 2ft (60–75 × 60cm)
BLOOMING PERIOD: Late summer to early autumn
SOIL: Well-drained but moisture-retentive.

5-8

LATIN NAME: *Daboecia cantabrica 'Alba'*
COMMON NAME: St. Dabeoc's heath
ALTERNATIVES: 'Snowdrift'
DESCRIPTION: Evergreen shrublet forming low, spreading hummocks with light green needle-like foliage and clusters of small, bell-shaped flowers. Responds well to heavy clipping in spring.
HEIGHT AND SPREAD: 18 × 24in (45 × 60cm)
BLOOMING PERIOD: Late spring to mid-autumn
SOIL: Acid, moisture-retentive.

BACK

5-9

6-10

LATIN NAME: *Clematis 'Alba Luxurians'*
COMMON NAME: Known by Latin name
ALTERNATIVES: None
DESCRIPTION: Climber with ovate leaflets and nodding four-petalled flowers giving a delicate effect. May be cut back hard in winter/early spring. Grow over spring-flowering shrubs for later interest.
HEIGHT AND SPREAD: 12 × 12ft (3.6 × 3.6m)
BLOOMING PERIOD: Mid-summer to early autumn
SOIL: Moisture-retentive with plenty of organic matter.

LATIN NAME: *Romneya coulteri*
COMMON NAME: Matilija poppy
ALTERNATIVES: 'White Cloud,' R. trichocalyx
DESCRIPTION: Perennial with woody-based stems clothed in deeply divided gray-green leaves. Large blooms with petals like tissue paper and golden yellow boss of stamens. Fragrant. May be invasive.
HEIGHT AND SPREAD: 6 × 6ft (2 × 2m)
BLOOMING PERIOD: Late summer to early autumn
SOIL: Deep, fertile, moisture-retentive.

MIDDLE

LATIN NAME: *Galtonia candicans*
COMMON NAME: Cape hyacinth, spire lily, summer hyacinth
ALTERNATIVES: None
DESCRIPTION: Bulb with drooping, strap-like leaves and tall, upright flower stems topped with showy, pendulous bells. The seed pods are attractive, but self-sown seedlings may become a nuisance.
HEIGHT AND SPREAD: 4 × 2ft (1.2 × 0.6m)
BLOOMING PERIOD: Late summer
SOIL: Best on deep, rich, well-cultivated ground. Avoid thin, sandy soils.

6-9

LATIN NAME: *Yucca flaccida 'Ivory'*
COMMON NAME: Yucca
ALTERNATIVES: Y. flaccida 'Golden Sword,' Y. flaccida major
DESCRIPTION: Evergreen perennial with a rosette of narrow, sword-shaped, gray-green leaves. The central branched flower spike carries the rounded flowers almost horizontally. 'Ivory' is a free-flowering clone of the species.
HEIGHT AND SPREAD: 3 × 2½ft (90 × 75cm)
BLOOMING PERIOD: Mid- to late summer
SOIL: Any well-drained.

4-10

FRONT

4-10

4-10

LATIN NAME: *Tanacetum parthenium (Chrysanthemum parthenium)*
COMMON NAME: Feverfew
ALTERNATIVES: 'Aureum,' 'Rowallane,' 'White Bonnet'
DESCRIPTION: Evergreen aromatic herb with finely divided foliage. Short-lived but self-seeds. Prolific display of white daisy-like blooms. Cut hard back to promote attractive mounds of overwintering foliage.
HEIGHT AND SPREAD: 8–18 × 8–18in (20–45 × 20–45cm)
BLOOMING PERIOD: Summer to early autumn
SOIL: Any reasonably drained soil.

LATIN NAME: *Liriope spicata 'Alba'*
COMMON NAME: Lily turf
ALTERNATIVES: L. muscari 'Monroe White'
DESCRIPTION: Evergreen perennial spreading via underground rhizomes. The broad grassy leaves form dense tufts from which the spikes of tiny, bell flowers appear. Attractive winter foliage.
HEIGHT AND SPREAD: 12 × 12–16in (30 × 30–40cm)
BLOOMING PERIOD: Late summer
SOIL: Well-drained.

8-10

LATIN NAME: *Olearia* 'Talbot de Malahide' syn. *O. albida*
COMMON NAME: Daisy bush
ALTERNATIVES: *O. avicenniifolia, O. a.* 'White confusion,' *O. × haastii*
DESCRIPTION: Evergreen shrub of dense, rounded habit, excellent in mild areas and windswept seaside locations. Gray-green, wavy-edged leaves, white beneath, and fragrant, off-white flowers.
HEIGHT AND SPREAD: 10 × 15ft (3 × 5m)
BLOOMING PERIOD: Late summer
SOIL: Any well-drained.

LATIN NAME: *Buddleia davidii* cultivar
COMMON NAME: Buddleia, butterfly bush
ALTERNATIVES: 'Peace,' 'White Profusion,' 'White Bouquet,' *B. fallowiana* var. *alba*
DESCRIPTION: Shrub with upright stems clothed in large, gray-green, tapering leaves and terminal spikes of honey-scented flowers. Attractive to butterflies. Cut back hard to a framework of strong branches each spring.
HEIGHT AND SPREAD: 13 × 13ft (4 × 4m) if not cut back
BLOOMING PERIOD: Mid-summer to late summer
SOIL: Well-drained. Flowers best on rather poor soil.

5-9

9-10

LATIN NAME: *Argyranthemum frutescens* (*Chrysanthemum frutescens*)
COMMON NAME: Marguerite, Paris daisy
ALTERNATIVES: 'Chelsea Girl,' 'Edelweiss,' 'Qinta White,' 'Royal Haze'
DESCRIPTION: Sub shrub or tender evergreen perennial with a bushy, well-branched habit and finely divided gray-green foliage. The delicate white daisy flowers have a yellow center.
HEIGHT AND SPREAD: 3 × 3ft (0.9 × 0.9m)
BLOOMING PERIOD: Spring to autumn
SOIL: Well-drained.

LATIN NAME: *Hebe salicifolia*
COMMON NAME: Known by Latin name
ALTERNATIVES: *H. × kirkii, H.* 'White Gem'
DESCRIPTION: Evergreen shrub with long narrow, willow-like leaves of bright glossy green and tapering flower spikes of white or palest mauve. Trim with shears or pruners in spring to promote compact habit. Good seaside plant.
HEIGHT AND SPREAD: 4 × 6ft (1.2 × 1.8m)
BLOOMING PERIOD: Summer to early autumn
SOIL: Well-drained.

7-10

4-10

LATIN NAME: *Tanacetum parthenium* 'White Gem' syn. *Matricaria* 'White Gem'
COMMON NAME: Double-flowered feverfew
ALTERNATIVES: 'Snow Puffs,' 'Rowallane,' 'White Bonnet'
DESCRIPTION: Evergreen aromatic herb, usually raised as a half-hardy annual, with finely divided leaves and button-shaped flower heads.
HEIGHT AND SPREAD: 12 × 12in (30 × 30cm)
BLOOMING PERIOD: Early summer to mid-autumn
SOIL: Well-drained.

LATIN NAME: *Limonium sinuatum* strain
COMMON NAME: Statice, sea lavender
ALTERNATIVES: 'Fortress' strain
DESCRIPTION: Perennial usually grown as a half-hardy annual. Flowers often used for dried arrangements. Dark green, lance-shaped, wavy-edged leaves and dense heads of papery blooms.
HEIGHT AND SPREAD: 24 × 12in (60 × 30cm)
BLOOMING PERIOD: Summer to mid-autumn
SOIL: Well-drained.

BACK

5-9

LATIN NAME: *Abelia × grandiflora*
COMMON NAME: Known by Latin name
ALTERNATIVES: *A. × g.* 'Francis Mason'
DESCRIPTION: Evergreen to deciduous shrub, depending on minimum temperature, densely clothed in small, glossy leaves and clusters of bell-shaped flowers, pink in bud. Stems brittle, so avoid windy sites.
HEIGHT AND SPREAD: 5+ × 6+ft (1.5+ × 1.8+m)
BLOOMING PERIOD: Summer to autumn
SOIL: Any fertile, well-drained, avoiding extremely dry or alkaline.

6-7

LATIN NAME: *Sorbaria tomentosa* var. *angustifolia* syn. *S. aitchinsonii*
COMMON NAME: Tree spiraea
ALTERNATIVES: *S. sorbifolia*
DESCRIPTION: Shrub producing stout upright stems with large, pinnate leaves and frothy, creamy white flower plumes. Best suited to large and wild gardens. May become invasive in ideal conditions.
HEIGHT AND SPREAD: 10 × 13+ft (3 × 4+m)
BLOOMING PERIOD: Late summer to early autumn
SOIL: Fairly tolerant but best on deep, rich, moisture-retentive soils.

MIDDLE

3-10

LATIN NAME: *Campanula persicifolia* 'Alba'
COMMON NAME: Peach-leaved bellflower
ALTERNATIVES: 'Hampstead White,' 'White Knight,' 'Wedgwood White'
DESCRIPTION: Perennial making an evergreen rosette of lance-shaped leaves and sending up slender, upright stems bearing large, nodding, bell-shaped blooms of pure white. Self-seeds readily.
HEIGHT AND SPREAD: 3 × 1ft (0.9 × 0.3m)
BLOOMING PERIOD: Summer
SOIL: Fertile, well-drained.

7-9

LATIN NAME: *Senecio smithii*
COMMON NAME: Known by Latin name
ALTERNATIVES: None
DESCRIPTION: Perennial with broad, glossy leaves of gray-green making a coarse clump topped with large heads of white daisy flowers with yellow centers. Best in cool-summer climates.
HEIGHT AND SPREAD: 4 × 2ft (1.2 × 0.6m)
BLOOMING PERIOD: Summer
SOIL: Rich, moist.

FRONT

LATIN NAME: *Euphorbia marginata*
COMMON NAME: Snow-on-the-mountain (Warning – irritant sap)
ALTERNATIVES: 'Summer Icicle'
DESCRIPTION: Half-hardy annual of bushy, upright habit producing whorls of brightly variegated green and white leaves and insignificant flowers. May be cut for flower arranging but seal stems with a flame.
HEIGHT AND SPREAD: 24 × 12in (60 × 30cm)
BLOOMING PERIOD: Summer
SOIL: Well-drained.

10

LATIN NAME: *Pelargonium* Regal cultivar
COMMON NAME: Regal geranium
ALTERNATIVES: 'La Paloma'
DESCRIPTION: Tender evergreen perennial with large, rounded leaves which have a deeply serrated edge. Funnel-shaped blooms often with darker throat markings and contrasting stigma and stamens.
HEIGHT AND SPREAD: 12–18 × 12in (30–45 × 30cm)
BLOOMING PERIOD: Summer (spring in Australia)
SOIL: Well-drained.

LATIN NAME: *Pileostegia viburnoides* syn. *Schizophragma viburnoides*
COMMON NAME: Tanglehead, climbing viburnum
ALTERNATIVES: *Schizophragma hydrangeoides*
DESCRIPTION: Evergreen climber attaching itself to walls or tree trunks via aerial roots. Elegant pointed leaves, leathery in texture, and lacy heads of creamy white flowers. Provide support for young plants. Growth initially slow.
HEIGHT AND SPREAD: 18 × 18ft (5.5 × 5.5m)
BLOOMING PERIOD: Late summer to autumn
SOIL: Any moisture-retentive.

6-10

LATIN NAME: *Hydrangea quercifolia*
COMMON NAME: Oak-leaf hydrangea
ALTERNATIVES: 'Snowflake,' 'Snow Queen'
DESCRIPTION: Shrub with spreading, down-covered branches and handsome lobed leaves. Flowers in loose pyramid-shaped heads become pink-tinged late in the season.
HEIGHT AND SPREAD: 5 × 6ft (1.5 × 1.8m)
BLOOMING PERIOD: Mid-summer to early autumn
SOIL: Tolerant of a wide range of conditions.

5-9

5-8

LATIN NAME: *Lilium* 'Olivia'
COMMON NAME: Hybrid lily
ALTERNATIVES: 'Casa Blanca,' 'Sterling Silver'
DESCRIPTION: Bulbous plant producing long stems with lance-shaped leaves. Large, upward-facing blooms have six ruffled and reflexed petals of white with a yellow stripe and dark brown contrasting anthers.
HEIGHT AND SPREAD: 3 × 4ft (0.9 × 1.2m)
BLOOMING PERIOD: Early summer
SOIL: Well-drained but moisture-retentive and humus-rich.

5-9

LATIN NAME: *Lilium longiflorum*
COMMON NAME: Easter lily, Bermuda lily
ALTERNATIVES: *L. candidum, L. regale*
DESCRIPTION: Bulbous plant producing long stems with lance-shaped leaves topped by outward-facing trumpet-shaped blooms of pure white with orange anthers. Highly fragrant. Easy from seed.
HEIGHT AND SPREAD: 1–3ft (0.3–0.9m)
BLOOMING PERIOD: Spring or summer
SOIL: Well-drained, moisture-retentive, humus-rich.

LATIN NAME: *Petunia hybrida*
COMMON NAME: Petunia
ALTERNATIVES: Multiflora and Floribunda types
DESCRIPTION: Half-hardy annual with upright bushy to spreading, dome-shaped habit with oval to lance-shaped "sticky" foliage and a profusion of trumpet-shaped blooms. Deadhead.
HEIGHT AND SPREAD: 9–18 × 9–12in (23–45 × 23–30cm)
BLOOMING PERIOD: Summer to early autumn
SOIL: Well-drained. Dislikes heavy rain but needs moisture.

LATIN NAME: *Salvia argentea*
COMMON NAME: Silver sage
ALTERNATIVES: None
DESCRIPTION: Short-lived perennial usually grown as a biennial for its rosette of large, felted, silver-white leaves. Sage-like flowers are white tinged purple on tall, branched stems.
HEIGHT AND SPREAD: 15–18 × 15–18in (38–45 × 38–45cm)
BLOOMING PERIOD: Mid- to late summer
SOIL: Well-drained.

6-8

BACK

6-9

6-9

LATIN NAME: *Hydrangea macrophylla* cultivar
COMMON NAME: Lacecap hydrangea
ALTERNATIVES: 'Veitchii,' 'White Wave,' 'Lanarth White'
DESCRIPTION: Shrub with a rounded habit producing lush, broad leaves and domed heads of tiny fertile flowers (pink on alkaline soils, blue on acid) surrounded by showy white sterile flowers.
HEIGHT AND SPREAD: 5½ × 6ft (1.6 × 1.8m)
BLOOMING PERIOD: Late summer to early autumn
SOIL: Deep, rich, moisture-retentive.

LATIN NAME: *Hibiscus syriacus* 'Red Heart'
COMMON NAME: Rose of Sharon, tree hollyhock, shrub althea
ALTERNATIVES: 'Jeanne d'Arc,' 'William R. Smith'
DESCRIPTION: Shrub with upright stems, forming a globe-shaped bush. Does not come to leaf until early summer. Large flowers with showy stamens. Deep red blotch at base of each petal.
HEIGHT AND SPREAD: 5 × 5ft (1.5 × 1.5m)
BLOOMING PERIOD: Late summer to mid-autumn
SOIL: Well-drained, friable soil, acid to slightly alkaline.

MIDDLE

2-9

LATIN NAME: *Actaea alba* syn. *A. pachypoda*
COMMON NAME: White baneberry
ALTERNATIVES: None
DESCRIPTION: Perennial with fern-like foliage and spikes of white flowers followed by white or pink tinged poisonous berries. Excellent for the wild or woodland garden.
HEIGHT AND SPREAD: 3 × 1½ft (0.9 × 0.45m)
BLOOMING PERIOD: Late spring to early summer. Berries late summer
SOIL: Humus-rich, acid.

LATIN NAME: *Cimicifuga simplex* 'Elstead'
COMMON NAME: Bugbane
ALTERNATIVES: *C. simplex* and *C. s.* Atropurpurea Group, *C. s.* 'White Pearl'
DESCRIPTION: Herbaceous perennial with ferny foliage and wiry, arching stems carrying fragrant, wand-like flowers. One of the latest to bloom. Taller species to 7ft (2.1m) are available but none require staking.
HEIGHT AND SPREAD: 4 × 2ft (1.2 × 0.6m)
BLOOMING PERIOD: Mid-autumn
SOIL: Moisture-retentive to damp.

3-9

FRONT

5-9

LATIN NAME: *Dendranthema* cultivar
COMMON NAME: Korean chrysanthemum
ALTERNATIVES: 'White Gloss,' 'Wedding Day'
DESCRIPTION: Herbaceous perennial with daisy-like flowers varying in form and lobed leaves. Stems good for cutting. Protect from winter cold by mulching or lift crowns and store in potting compost.
HEIGHT AND SPREAD: 1½–2+ × 1½ft (45–60+ × 45cm)
BLOOMING PERIOD: Late summer to mid-autumn
SOIL: Any well-drained, fertile.

LATIN NAME: *Sedum spectabile* 'Stardust'
COMMON NAME: Ice-plant, showy sedum
ALTERNATIVES: 'Iceberg'
DESCRIPTION: Perennial with fleshy rounded gray-green leaves and domed heads of tight green buds in summer developing color as they age. Foliage and flower from bud to faded blooms is highly architectural.
HEIGHT AND SPREAD: 18 × 18in (45 × 45cm)
BLOOMING PERIOD: Late summer to late autumn
SOIL: Well-drained, even poor and dry.

4-10

4-8

LATIN NAME: *Hydrangea paniculata* cultivar
COMMON NAME: Panicle hydrangea
ALTERNATIVES: 'Unique,' 'Floribunda,' 'Grandiflora,' 'Praecox,' 'Kyushu'
DESCRIPTION: Shrub with upright branches ending in cone-shaped flowers with tiny fertile florets and large, showy sterile bracts. May be cut back to a framework each spring to promote fewer, larger flowers.
HEIGHT AND SPREAD: 10 × 10ft (3 × 3m)
BLOOMING PERIOD: Mid-summer to late summer
SOIL: Fertile, moisture-retentive. Avoid markedly alkaline soils.

LATIN NAME: *Yucca gloriosa* 'Nobilis'
COMMON NAME: Spanish dagger, moundlily yucca
ALTERNATIVES: *Y. gloriosa, Y. g.* 'Variegata'
DESCRIPTION: Shrub forming a rosette of dark-green, sword-shaped leaves with sharp points. A stout flower stem bears pink-tinted buds which open creamy-white. 'Nobilis' opens earlier than the species, avoiding frost damage.
HEIGHT AND SPREAD: 6 × 6ft (1.8 × 1.8m)
BLOOMING PERIOD: Late summer
SOIL: Well-drained, even dry.

7-10

3-10

LATIN NAME: *Aster ericoides* cultivar
COMMON NAME: Heath aster
ALTERNATIVES: 'White Heather'
DESCRIPTION: Perennial with fine stems and tiny daisy flowers. Small, lance-shaped leaves attractive in summer. Do not cut down until spring as faded flower stems make a valuable contribution.
HEIGHT AND SPREAD: 2½ × 1½ft (75 × 45cm)
BLOOMING PERIOD: Mid-summer to mid-autumn
SOIL: Any well-drained, even poor.

8-9

LATIN NAME: *Gaultheria mucronata* 'Snow White'
COMMON NAME: Chilean pernettya
ALTERNATIVES: 'White Pearl,' 'Alba'
DESCRIPTION: Evergreen shrub with small, dark green prickly leaves and clusters of bell-shaped flowers during early summer followed in females and hermaphrodites by berries. Suckering habit.
HEIGHT AND SPREAD: 2½ × 4ft (75 × 120cm) Taller in shade
BLOOMING PERIOD: Early summer. Berries late summer and winter.
SOIL: Neutral to acid, humus rich.

3-9

LATIN NAME: *Hosta plantaginea*
COMMON NAME: Hosta, plantain lily, funkia, giboshi
ALTERNATIVES: 'Aphrodite' (a double), 'Royal Standard'
DESCRIPTION: Perennial forming a mound of large, glossy, bright green, heart-shaped leaves and tall flower stems carrying fragrant trumpet-shaped flowers opening in evening. Best in warm spot.
HEIGHT AND SPREAD: 2 × 2ft (60 × 60cm)
BLOOMING PERIOD: Late summer to early autumn
SOIL: Moisture-retentive and humus rich.

5-8

LATIN NAME: *Colchicum speciosum* 'Album'
COMMON NAME: Showy autumn-flowering crocus
ALTERNATIVES: *C. autumnale* 'Alboplenum,' *C. a.* 'Album'
DESCRIPTION: Corm producing bare flower stems topped by large, cup-shaped blooms which are very weather-resistant. In late winter or early spring, large, upright leaves develop. Very poisonous.
HEIGHT AND SPREAD: 6–8 × 6–8in (15–20 × 15–20cm)
BLOOMING PERIOD: Early to mid-autumn
SOIL: Any well-drained.

Blue

TRUE BLUE IS QUITE RARE IN THE WORLD OF GARDEN PLANTS. YOU'RE FAR MORE LIKELY TO COME ACROSS A PURPLE-TINGED VARIANT OR A STEELY GRAY-BLUE THAN PURE ELECTRIC- OR SKY-BLUE. SO WHEN YOU DO CATCH SIGHT OF A PURE BLUE FLOWER OR BERRY, YOU TEND TO NOTICE IT. HOWEVER, BLUE IS RARELY A SHOW-STOPPING COLOR LIKE RED OR WHITE. PLANTINGS OF SOFT MAUVE-BLUES AND SMOKY GRAYS EVOKE DISTANT HILLS SHROUDED IN MIST. IF YOU USE THESE COLORS FARTHER AWAY FROM THE HOUSE, IT HAS THE EFFECT OF VISUALLY EXTENDING THE GARDEN, MAKING IT APPEAR LONGER.

COLOR SCHEMES WHICH USE NOTHING OTHER THAN SHADES OF BLUE ARE DIFFICULT TO DESIGN BECAUSE THERE ARE RELATIVELY FEW PLANTS TO CHOOSE FROM THAT GIVE CONTINUITY FOR MUCH OF THE SEASON.

ADDED TO THIS IS THE FACT THAT ALL-BLUE SCHEMES OFTEN END UP LOOKING FLAT AND UNINTERESTING. IF YOU BROADEN YOUR SELECTION TO INCLUDE FLOWERS OF PURPLE-BLUE WITH HIGHLIGHTS OF WHITE, SOFT PINK, CRIMSON-RED, CERISE, AND VELVET-PURPLE, YOU WILL HAVE A MUCH RICHER AND MORE SATISFYING SCHEME, WHICH WILL BE COOL AND CALMING. FOR FOLIAGE INTEREST HERE, TRY MIXING IN WHITE-VARIEGATED, SILVER, GRAY, AND PURPLE-LEAVED PLANTS. TRUE BLUES LOOK STUNNING WITH THE YELLOW, GOLD, AND RED SHADES OF AUTUMN AND FORTUNATELY THERE ARE QUITE A NUMBER OF SUITABLE PLANTS TO CHOOSE FROM AT THIS TIME OF THE YEAR. IN SUMMER, IT'S EASY TO MAKE A BRIGHT BLUE AND ORANGE OR LEMON-YELLOW SCHEME USING ANNUALS.

LEFT: *Classic cottage garden planting with tall blue delphiniums, roses, campanulas, and erigerons.*

BACK

LATIN NAME: *Ceanothus impressus*
COMMON NAME: Santa ceanothus, California lilac
ALTERNATIVES: 'Puget Blue,' 'Concha,' 'Dark Star'
DESCRIPTION: Evergreen shrub. Quick growing with a spreading habit. Crinkled, dark green leaves and short panicles of blue flowers, deeper in bud. Grow against a sheltered sunny wall in colder areas.
HEIGHT AND SPREAD: 6 × 9ft (1.8 × 2.7m)
BLOOMING PERIOD: Mid-spring to early summer
SOIL: Rich, deep, well-drained.

8-10

LATIN NAME: *Ceanothus* cultivar
COMMON NAME: California lilac
ALTERNATIVES: 'A. T. Johnson,' 'Burkwoodii,' 'Cascade,' 'Southmead,' 'Delight'
DESCRIPTION: Evergreen shrub with small, dark glossy leaves and a profusion of light to mid-blue flowers which smother the bush. Vigorous and quick-maturing in the right spot. May be scorched by cold spring winds.
HEIGHT AND SPREAD: 10–13 × 10–13ft (3–4 × 3–4m)
BLOOMING PERIOD: Late spring to early summer
SOIL: Rich, deep, well-drained.

8-10

MIDDLE

LATIN NAME: *Borago officinalis*
COMMON NAME: Borage, star flower
ALTERNATIVES: None
DESCRIPTION: Annual herb with large, coarse, hairy leaves (irritant) and clusters of pendulous star-shaped, deep blue flowers used for garnishing salads and drinks. Self-seeds.
HEIGHT AND SPREAD: 3 × 1ft (90 × 30cm)
BLOOMING PERIOD: Summer to early autumn
SOIL: Well-drained.

LATIN NAME: *Cerinthe major* 'Purpurascens'
COMMON NAME: Honeywort
ALTERNATIVES: None
DESCRIPTION: Herbaceous perennial, easily raised from seed. Member of the borage family. Distinctive blue-green foliage and arching flower heads with prominent blue-purple bracts and pale purple blooms.
HEIGHT AND SPREAD: 12–24 × 18in (30–60 × 45cm)
BLOOMING PERIOD: Summer
SOIL: Well-drained. Essential for plant's survival to avoid winter wet at roots.

8-10

FRONT

4-8

LATIN NAME: *Muscari armeniacum*
COMMON NAME: Armenian grape hyacinth
ALTERNATIVES: 'Blue Spike,' 'Early Giant,' 'Heavenly Blue'
DESCRIPTION: Bulbs with persistent grass-like foliage making good groundcover or border edging. Clumps send up numerous stems topped with deep blue spikes of tiny bells. Honey scented.
HEIGHT AND SPREAD: 6–8 × 3–4in (15–20 × 8–10cm)
BLOOMING PERIOD: Mid- to late spring
SOIL: Well-drained.

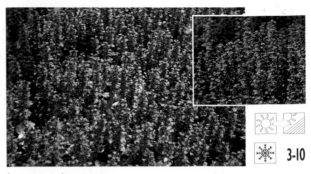

3-10

LATIN NAME: *Ajuga reptans*
COMMON NAME: Bugle, ajuga
ALTERNATIVES: 'Atropurpurea,' 'Braunherz,' 'Catlin's Giant'
DESCRIPTION: Herbaceous perennial groundcover. Semi-evergreen foliage in rosettes. Runners with new rosettes after flowering. Short spikes of blue-lipped flowers. Dry conditions promote mildew.
HEIGHT AND SPREAD: 6 × 36in (15 × 90cm)
BLOOMING PERIOD: Mid-spring
SOIL: Any moisture-retentive.

LATIN NAME: *Baptisia australis*
COMMON NAME: Blue wild indigo
ALTERNATIVES: 'Exaltata'
DESCRIPTION: Herbaceous perennial, member of the pea family, with attractive blue-green pinnate leaves and spires of indigo blue, lupin-like flowers. Plants are cut back to ground level by the first frost. Dislikes disturbance.
HEIGHT AND SPREAD: 4 × 2ft (1.2 × 0.6m)
BLOOMING PERIOD: Late spring to early summer
SOIL: Rich, deep, not too dry.

3-10

LATIN NAME: *Cichorium intybus*
COMMON NAME: Chicory
ALTERNATIVES: None
DESCRIPTION: Herbaceous perennial, naturalized along roadsides in parts of the United States and Australia. Slender upright growth with clusters of sky blue daisy flowers which close after midday. Basal rosette of leaves.
HEIGHT AND SPREAD: 4 × 1½ft (1.2 × 0.45cm)
BLOOMING PERIOD: Early summer to autumn
SOIL: Any well-drained, especially limey.

3-10

LATIN NAME: *Iris pallida*
COMMON NAME: Sweet iris, Dalmatian iris
ALTERNATIVES: *I. p.* 'Variegata,' *I. p.* 'Argentea Variegata'
DESCRIPTION: Herbaceous perennial with spreading rhizomes producing fans of blue-green, sword-shaped foliage. Soft blue fragrant flowers on stout, branching stems. Good yellow and white-variegated forms available.
HEIGHT AND SPREAD: 28–36in (70–90cm)
BLOOMING PERIOD: Late spring to early summer
SOIL: Rich, well-drained. Tolerates lime.

3-10

LATIN NAME: *Iris sibirica*
COMMON NAME: Siberian iris
ALTERNATIVES: 'Heavenly Blue,' 'Cambridge,' 'Sea Shadows'
DESCRIPTION: Herbaceous perennial spreading by underground rhizomes to form dense clumps of narrow foliage. Slender flower stems and pointed buds. Unlike some, does not need frequent division. Attractive seed pods.
HEIGHT AND SPREAD: 20–48in × indefinite (50–120cm × indefinite)
BLOOMING PERIOD: Late spring to early summer
SOIL: Tolerates a wide range but best in moisture-retentive to boggy.

4-10

6-10

LATIN NAME: *Viola* 'Belmont Blue' syn. 'Boughton Blue'
COMMON NAME: Horned violet, tufted pansy
ALTERNATIVES: 'Lilacina,' 'Maggie Mott'
DESCRIPTION: Herbaceous perennial with small heart-shaped leaves and upright stems forming low mounds of foliage. Small, pale-blue fragrant flowers. Clip over to promote new growth.
HEIGHT AND SPREAD: 3–6 × 12in (7–15 × 30cm)
BLOOMING PERIOD: Mid-spring to early autumn
SOIL: Well-drained but moisture-retentive.

LATIN NAME: *Viola wittrockiana* variety
COMMON NAME: Pansy
ALTERNATIVES: 'Joker Light Blue' F2, 'Ullswater Blue'
DESCRIPTION: Annual or short-lived perennial with heart-shaped leaves and large disk-shaped, honey-scented flowers. Deadhead to prolong flowering and keep well-watered in dry spells.
HEIGHT AND SPREAD: 6–9 × 9–12in (15–22.5 × 30cm)
BLOOMING PERIOD: Most of the year depending on the strain
SOIL: Well-drained but moisture-retentive.

BACK

LATIN NAME: *Delphinium* cultivar
COMMON NAME: Known by Latin name
ALTERNATIVES: 'Lord Butler,' 'Chelsea Star,' 'Blue Nile,' 'Bluebird,' 'Summer Skies'
DESCRIPTION: Herbaceous perennial with deeply divided leaves forming a rounded basal clump, from which several upright flower stems arise bearing spikes of blue, open flowers, each with a prominent white eye.
HEIGHT AND SPREAD: 5–6 × 2½–3ft (1.5–1.8 × 0.75–0.9m)
BLOOMING PERIOD: Summer
SOIL: Fertile, humus-rich, moisture-retentive.

3-10

LATIN NAME: *Delphinium* 'Blue Dawn'
COMMON NAME: Known by Latin name
ALTERNATIVES: 'Galahad,' 'King Arthur,' 'Dreaming Spires'
DESCRIPTION: Herbaceous perennial with deeply divided leaves forming a rounded basal clump, from which several upright flower stems arise bearing spikes of blue, open flowers, each with a prominent dark brown eye.
HEIGHT AND SPREAD: 6–7 × 2½–3ft (1.8–2.2 × 0.75–0.9m)
BLOOMING PERIOD: Summer
SOIL: Fertile, humus-rich, moisture-retentive.

3-10

MIDDLE

8-10

LATIN NAME: *Ceanothus thrysiflorus* var. *repens*
COMMON NAME: California lilac, creeping blue blossom
ALTERNATIVES: *C. griseus* var. *horizontalis* 'Yankee Point'
DESCRIPTION: Evergreen shrub of spreading to mound-forming habit with deep green, glossy, oval leaves and thimble-shaped flower heads of powder-blue.
HEIGHT AND SPREAD: 3–4 × 6–10ft (0.9–1.2 × 1.8–3m)
BLOOMING PERIOD: Early summer
SOIL: Well-drained.

4-10

LATIN NAME: *Catananche caerulea*
COMMON NAME: Cupid's dart
ALTERNATIVES: 'Major'
DESCRIPTION: Herbaceous perennial, which tends to be short-lived. It has branching, wiry stems with long, narrow, gray-green leaves and a profusion of clear blue daisy flowers which close around midday.
HEIGHT AND SPREAD: 18–24 × 24in (0.45–0.6 × 0.6m)
BLOOMING PERIOD: Summer
SOIL: Light, well-drained, even poor.

FRONT

6-9

LATIN NAME: *Scilla peruviana*
COMMON NAME: Cuban lily
ALTERNATIVES: *Brodiaea coronaria*
DESCRIPTION: Bulb producing a cluster of narrow leaves from which arise flower stems bearing broad, conical-shaped heads of tiny, purple-blue blooms. Does well in raised beds.
HEIGHT AND SPREAD: 4–10 × 6–8in (10–25 × 15–20cm)
BLOOMING PERIOD: Early summer (from late spring in mild areas)
SOIL: Well-drained.

3-10

LATIN NAME: *Veronica chamaedrys*
COMMON NAME: Germander speedwell
ALTERNATIVES: *V. prostrata* and cultivars
DESCRIPTION: Carpeting perennial which naturalizes well in grass. The small, oval leaves are scallop-edged. Fine reddish stems bear bright blue, white-centered flowers. Good for the wild garden.
HEIGHT AND SPREAD: 1 × 12in (2.5 × 30cm)
BLOOMING PERIOD: Early summer
SOIL: Any well-drained.

BACK

3-10

LATIN NAME: *Delphinium* 'Centurion Sky Blue'
COMMON NAME: Known by Latin name
ALTERNATIVES: 'Galahad,' 'King Arthur,' 'Dreaming Spires'
DESCRIPTION: Herbaceous perennial with divided leaves forming a rounded basal clump, from which several upright stems arise bearing spikes of blue, open flowers, each with a paler blue eye.
HEIGHT AND SPREAD: 5–6 × 2½–3ft (1.5–1.8 × 0.75–0.9m)
BLOOMING PERIOD: Summer
SOIL: Fertile, humus-rich, moisture-retentive.

LATIN NAME: *Passiflora caerulea*
COMMON NAME: Passion flower
ALTERNATIVES: 'Constance Elliot'
DESCRIPTION: Evergreen or semi-evergreen climber, with palmate leaves and tendrils, which produces large blooms of intricate beauty, sometimes followed by yellow, egg-shaped fruits.
HEIGHT AND SPREAD: 20 × 20ft (6 × 6m)
BLOOMING PERIOD: Mid- to late summer
SOIL: Well-drained.

7-10

LATIN NAME: *Lupinus* cultivar
COMMON NAME: Lupine, lupin
ALTERNATIVES: Russel Hybrids, Gallery Series
DESCRIPTION: Herbaceous perennial forming a large mound of handsome palmate leaves with narrow leaflets. Stout flower stems bear spikes of pea-like blooms, which are often bicolored or two-toned. Susceptible to aphids.
HEIGHT AND SPREAD: 3–4 × 1½ft (0.9–1.2 × 0.45m)
BLOOMING PERIOD: Summer
SOIL: Fertile, well-drained.

4-9

MIDDLE

6-10

LATIN NAME: *Campanula lactiflora*
COMMON NAME: Bellflower
ALTERNATIVES: 'Prichard's Variety'
DESCRIPTION: Herbaceous perennial whose top-heavy stems need support, especially in windy sites. Stout stems with lance-shaped leaves and branched heads of lilac-blue, bell-shaped blooms.
HEIGHT AND SPREAD: 4–5 × 2ft (1.2–1.5 × 0.6m)
BLOOMING PERIOD: Early summer to late autumn
SOIL: Fertile, well-drained.

FRONT

4-10

LATIN NAME: *Geranium himalayense* 'Gravetye'
COMMON NAME: Hardy geranium, cranesbill
ALTERNATIVES: 'Irish Blue,' 'Gravetye,' G. 'Johnson's Blue'
DESCRIPTION: Herbaceous perennial which produces finely cut palmate foliage that often colors well in autumn. The bowl-shaped blooms are an intense violet-blue with prominent veining.
HEIGHT AND SPREAD: 1 × 2ft (0.3 × 0.6m)
BLOOMING PERIOD: Early summer
SOIL: Well-drained.

LATIN NAME: *Echium* 'Blue Ball'
COMMON NAME: Annual borage, viper's bugloss
ALTERNATIVES: 'Blue Bedder'
DESCRIPTION: Hardy annual with narrow, lance-shaped leaves and feathery bracts surmounting the upward-facing, bell-shaped blooms of rich blue. These are especially attractive to bees.
HEIGHT AND SPREAD: 9–12 × 9in (23–30 × 23cm)
BLOOMING PERIOD: Summer
SOIL: Light, well-drained.

BACK

LATIN NAME: *Plumbago auriculata* syn. *P. capensis*
COMMON NAME: Cape leadwort, plumbago
ALTERNATIVES: None
DESCRIPTION: Evergreen climber with a scrambling habit. The vigorous green shoots clothed in small, lance-shaped leaves become woody with age. Light blue, five-petalled blooms in domed clusters.
HEIGHT AND SPREAD: 10–16 × 10–16ft (3–4.9 × 3–4.9m)
BLOOMING PERIOD: Mid-spring to late autumn
SOIL: Well-drained.

9-10

LATIN NAME: *Ceanothus arboreus*
COMMON NAME: California lilac, feltleaf ceanothus
ALTERNATIVES: 'Trewithen Blue'
DESCRIPTION: A very large evergreen shrub or small tree. Large, rich-green, oval leaves with a downy underside and clusters of thimble-shaped flower heads in soft blue.
HEIGHT AND SPREAD: 20 × 25ft (6 × 8m)
BLOOMING PERIOD: Late spring and again in summer
SOIL: Well drained.

8-10

MIDDLE

LATIN NAME: *Campanula* 'Kent Belle'
COMMON NAME: Bellflower
ALTERNATIVES: *C. persicifolia* and forms
DESCRIPTION: Herbaceous perennial with lance-shaped leaves and long, upright stems bearing a series of tubular to bell-shaped blooms of rich purple-blue.
HEIGHT AND SPREAD: 48 × 24in (120 × 60cm)
BLOOMING PERIOD: Early to mid-summer
SOIL: Fertile, well-drained.

3-10

LATIN NAME: *Nicandra physalodes*
COMMON NAME: Apple of Peru, shoe-fly. May be danger to stock.
ALTERNATIVES: None
DESCRIPTION: Annual of branching, upright habit having oval leaves and large, bell-shaped, violet-blue flowers with a white throat, which last a day. Green spherical fruits with purple bracts. Self-seeds.
HEIGHT AND SPREAD: 3 × 1ft (0.9 × 0.3m)
BLOOMING PERIOD: Summer to early autumn
SOIL: Fertile, well-drained.

FRONT

LATIN NAME: *Veronica austriaca* subsp. *teucrium* syn. *V. teucrium*
COMMON NAME: Austrian speedwell
ALTERNATIVES: 'Crater Lake Blue,' 'Royal Blue'
DESCRIPTION: Carpet-forming perennial with slender, upright spikes of deep, vivid blue blooms and small, gray-green, divided leaves. Several improved forms available.
HEIGHT AND SPREAD: 12–24 × 12–24in (30–60 × 30–60cm)
BLOOMING PERIOD: Early to mid-summer
SOIL: Any well-drained.

4-7

LATIN NAME: *Nigella damascena*
COMMON NAME: Love-in-a-mist
ALTERNATIVES: 'Miss Jekyll'
DESCRIPTION: Hardy annual with bright green leaves divided into hair-like segments. The sky-blue blooms are followed by balloon-like seed pods in green turning brown, good for drying.
HEIGHT AND SPREAD: 24 × 8in (60 × 20cm)
BLOOMING PERIOD: Summer (spring to summer in Australia)
SOIL: Well-drained.

6-9

LATIN NAME: *Hydrangea macrophylla* 'Blue Wave'
COMMON NAME: Lacecap hydrangea
ALTERNATIVES: 'Teller Blau,' *H. serrata* 'Bluebird,' *H.* 'Blue Deckle'
DESCRIPTION: Large, dome-shaped shrub with large, oval, pointed leaves and domed heads of tiny fertile florets surrounded by larger, showy sterile bracts. Flowers are pink on neutral to alkaline soils.
HEIGHT AND SPREAD: 5½ × 12ft (1.8 × 3.5m)
BLOOMING PERIOD: Mid-summer to early autumn
SOIL: Fertile, humus-rich, moisture-retentive. Blue on acid soils.

LATIN NAME: *Hydrangea* 'Blue Deckle'
COMMON NAME: Lacecap hydrangea
ALTERNATIVES: *H. m.* 'Teller Blau,' *H. m.* 'Blue Wave,' *H. serrata* 'Bluebird'
DESCRIPTION: Large, dome-shaped shrub with broad, lance-shaped leaves developing red tints later in the year. Domed heads of tiny fertile florets surrounded by larger, showy sterile bracts with a "pinked" edge.
HEIGHT AND SPREAD: 5½ × 12ft (1.8 × 3.5m)
BLOOMING PERIOD: Mid-summer to early autumn
SOIL: Fertile, humus-rich, moisture-retentive.

4-10

3-10

LATIN NAME: *Eryngium bourgatii*
COMMON NAME: Sea holly
ALTERNATIVES: *E. alpinum, E. × tripartitum*
DESCRIPTION: Herbaceous perennial grown as much for its marbled foliage as its flowers. Rosette of gray-green foliage with white veins and narrow stems carrying clusters of blue-green thistle-like blooms.
HEIGHT AND SPREAD: 24 × 12in (60 × 30cm)
BLOOMING PERIOD: Mid- to late summer
SOIL: Fertile, well-drained, but tolerating poor, stony soil.

LATIN NAME: *Eryngium alpinum*
COMMON NAME: Sea holly
ALTERNATIVES: *E. × oliverianum, E. × zabelii* and forms e.g. 'Violetta'
DESCRIPTION: Herbaceous perennial with leathery, rounded to heart-shaped, toothed-edged basal leaves and wiry blue stems, supporting large thimble flower heads of lilac-blue each with a ruff of bracts.
HEIGHT AND SPREAD: 2½–3 × 2ft (0.75–0.9 × 0.6cm)
BLOOMING PERIOD: Summer
SOIL: Fertile, well-drained.

3-10

LATIN NAME: *Lobelia erinus* 'Crystal Palace'
COMMON NAME: Edging lobelia
ALTERNATIVES: Royal Hybrids, 'Blue Moon'
DESCRIPTION: Half-hardy annual with a mound-forming habit with small oval to lance-shaped bronzy-green leaves and small but profuse, deep blue flowers. Must have moisture to perform well.
HEIGHT AND SPREAD: 4 –8 × 4–6in (10–20 × 10–15cm)
BLOOMING PERIOD: Summer to autumn
SOIL: Fertile, moisture-retentive.

LATIN NAME: *Campanula carpatica*
COMMON NAME: Carpathian bellflower
ALTERNATIVES: 'Jewel,' 'Blue Clips,' 'Blue Carpet'
DESCRIPTION: Clump-forming perennial making a spreading dome of oval, toothed-edged leaves smothered at flowering time with open, bell-shaped blooms.
HEIGHT AND SPREAD: 3–4 × 12in (8–10 × 30cm)
BLOOMING PERIOD: Mid- to late summer (from spring in Australia)
SOIL: Fertile, well-drained.

BACK

LATIN NAME: *Ipomoea indica* syn. *I. acuminata, I. learii*
COMMON NAME: Blue dawn flower
ALTERNATIVES: *I. tricolor* 'Heavenly Blue,' *Thunbergia grandiflora*
DESCRIPTION: Shrubby climber with large heart-shaped or rounded leaves and funnel-shaped blooms of intense blue deepening to magenta and lasting just a day. An invasive weed in warm climates.
HEIGHT AND SPREAD: 13–16ft (4–5m)
BLOOMING PERIOD: Early summer to late autumn
SOIL: Humus-rich, well-drained.

9-10

LATIN NAME: Aconitum 'Newry Blue' (Warning – deadly poisonous if eaten)
COMMON NAME: Monkshood, wolf's bane, helmet flower
ALTERNATIVES: A. 'Bressingham Spire,' A. carmichaelii 'Barker's Variety'
DESCRIPTION: Herbaceous perennial of clump-forming habit with upright stems bearing deeply divided, glossy, dark green leaves. The unbranched spires carry deep blue-purple blooms.
HEIGHT AND SPREAD: 4–5 × 1½ft (1.2–1.5 × 0.45m)
BLOOMING PERIOD: Summer
SOIL: Fertile, humus-rich, moisture-retentive but well drained.

2-9

MIDDLE

LATIN NAME: *Centaurea annua*
COMMON NAME: Cornflower, bluebottle, bachelor's buttons
ALTERNATIVES: None
DESCRIPTION: Hardy annual with narrow lance-shaped leaves on upright, branched stems topped with double, daisy-like heads of rich blue. Good for cutting. Self-sows freely.
HEIGHT AND SPREAD: 3 × 1ft (90 × 0.3cm)
BLOOMING PERIOD: Spring or summer to autumn
SOIL: Well-drained but not dry.

LATIN NAME: *Aconitum × cammarum* 'Bicolor' (Warning – deadly poisonous if eaten)
COMMON NAME: Monkswood, wolf's bane, helmet flower
ALTERNATIVES: 'Eleonara,' 'Blue Sceptre'
DESCRIPTION: Herbaceous perennial of clump-forming habit with deeply-divided, glossy green leaves and branched, upright flower stems carrying hooded flowers of blue flushed white.
HEIGHT AND SPREAD: 3–4 × 1½ft (0.9–1.2 × 0.45m)
BLOOMING PERIOD: Mid- to late summer
SOIL: Humus-rich, moisture-retentive but well-drained.

3-9

FRONT

LATIN NAME: *Nigella hispanica*
COMMON NAME: Love-in-a-mist
ALTERNATIVES: *N. damascena* and varieties
DESCRIPTION: Hardy annual with very finely cut foliage and branched stems bearing large blue flower heads with deep maroon centers and red stamens. Deadhead regularly. Attractive seed pods.
HEIGHT AND SPREAD: 18–24 × 9in (45–60 × 23cm)
BLOOMING PERIOD: Summer (spring and early summer in Australia)
SOIL: Humus-rich, well-drained but moisture-retentive.

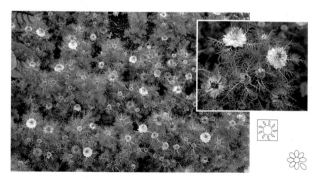

LATIN NAME: *Nigella damascena* 'Moody Blue'
COMMON NAME: Love-in-a-mist
ALTERNATIVES: 'Persian Jewels,' 'Miss Jekyll'
DESCRIPTION: Hardy annual with very finely cut foliage and branched stems bearing blooms which begin deep violet-blue and fade to pale sky-blue, giving a range of shades. Attractive seed pods.
HEIGHT AND SPREAD: 15 × 9in (38 × 23cm)
BLOOMING PERIOD: Summer (spring and early summer in Australia)
SOIL: Humus-rich, moisture-retentive but well-drained.

LATIN NAME: *Clematis 'Perle d'Azur'*
COMMON NAME: Known by Latin name
ALTERNATIVES: 'Beauty of Worcester,' 'Elsa Späeth,' 'Lasurstern,' 'Mrs. Cholmondeley'
DESCRIPTION: Climber with pinnate leaves and twining leaf stems, or petioles, requiring a framework of fine support wires. Abundant flowers with six light blue sepals flushed purple at the center and greenish stamens.
HEIGHT AND SPREAD: 10 × 3ft (3 × 0.9m)
BLOOMING PERIOD: Summer
SOIL: Humus-rich, moisture-retentive, well-drained.

5-9

7-10

LATIN NAME: *Ceanothus × delileanus 'Gloire de Versailles'*
COMMON NAME: California lilac, ceanothus
ALTERNATIVES: 'Indigo,' 'Henri Desfosse,' 'Topaz'
DESCRIPTION: Shrub of vigorous, upright, bushy growth with oval, mid-green leaves and masses of thimble-shaped, fluffy flower heads in soft powder blue. Very long-flowered and fragrant.
HEIGHT AND SPREAD: 5 × 5ft (1.5 × 1.5m)
BLOOMING PERIOD: Mid-summer to early autumn
SOIL: Well-drained.

LATIN NAME: *Malva sylvestris 'Primley Blue'*
COMMON NAME: Common mallow, blue mallow, high mallow
ALTERNATIVES: None
DESCRIPTION: Biennial or short-lived perennial with upright or lax stems covered in lobed leaves and bearing single flat blooms with five pale blue-gray petals with darker stripes. Stake to maintain upright habit.
HEIGHT AND SPREAD: 3–4 × 1½ft (0.9–1.2 × 0.45m)
BLOOMING PERIOD: Summer to early autumn
SOIL: Any well-drained.

3-9

3-10

LATIN NAME: *Scabiosa caucasica*
COMMON NAME: Scabious, pincushion flower
ALTERNATIVES: 'Clive Greaves,' 'Moerheim Blue'
DESCRIPTION: Herbaceous perennial of clump-forming habit with lobed stem leaves and long flower stalks topped with large, disk-shaped flowers with pincushion centers.
HEIGHT AND SPREAD: 2–2½ × 2ft (0.6–0.75cm × 0.6m)
BLOOMING PERIOD: Spring (Australia) to late summer
SOIL: Fertile, well-drained. Prefers alkaline conditions.

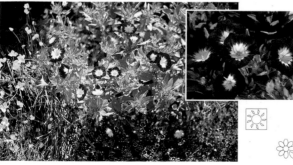

LATIN NAME: *Convolvulus tricolor 'Blue Ensign'*
COMMON NAME: Dwarf morning glory
ALTERNATIVES: 'Royal Ensign,' *C. sabatius*
DESCRIPTION: Hardy annual, but sow seed individually in pots under glass in spring for planting out after frosts. Forms a bushy, dome-shaped plant covered with trumpet-shaped flowers with a white center.
HEIGHT AND SPREAD: 12 × 9in (30 × 23cm)
BLOOMING PERIOD: Mid-summer to early autumn
SOIL: Any well-drained soil provided it is not too fertile.

LATIN NAME: *Anchusa capensis 'Blue Angel'*
COMMON NAME: Bugloss
ALTERNATIVES: 'Blue Bird,' 'Bedding Blue'
DESCRIPTION: Hardy annual making small, bushy hummocks with narrow, hairy leaves and masses of tiny vivid blue blooms. Excellent for border edging and pots. Clip back after first flush of bloom.
HEIGHT AND SPREAD: 9 × 9in (23 × 23cm)
BLOOMING PERIOD: Early summer to early autumn
SOIL: Well-drained, but not too dry or very rich.

BLUE

BACK

LATIN NAME: *Ipomoea tricolor* 'Heavenly Blue'
COMMON NAME: Morning glory
ALTERNATIVES: *I. purpurea*
DESCRIPTION: Half-hardy annual climber needing support for its twining stems. The light green leaves are large and heart-shaped and the almost circular blue blooms have a white throat. Flowers close in the afternoon.
HEIGHT AND SPREAD: 10ft (3m)
BLOOMING PERIOD: Early summer to early autumn
SOIL: Well-drained, humus-rich.

LATIN NAME: *Aconitum napellus*
COMMON NAME: Monkswood, helmet flower, wolf's bane (Highly poisonous.)
ALTERNATIVES: *A. cammarum* 'Bicolor,' *A.* 'Newry Blue'
DESCRIPTION: Herbaceous perennial with tall, strongly upright stems topped with spires of hooded, indigo-blue blooms. Handsome, deeply cut foliage forms a basal clump.
HEIGHT AND SPREAD: 5 × 1ft (1.5 × 0.3m)
BLOOMING PERIOD: Late summer
SOIL: Well drained but humus-rich and moisture-retentive.

2-9

MIDDLE

LATIN NAME: *Agapanthus* 'Headbourne Hybrids'
COMMON NAME: Blue African lily, agapanthus
ALTERNATIVES: *A. campanulatus* and forms
DESCRIPTION: Clump-forming perennials with handsome, arching, strap-shaped foliage and, arising from the center, leafless stems carrying umbels of mid-blue tubular flowers. Protect with mulch in cold climates.
HEIGHT AND SPREAD: 2½ × 1½ft (0.75 × 0.45cm)
BLOOMING PERIOD: Late summer
SOIL: Well-drained but moisture-retentive.

8-10

3-10

LATIN NAME: *Echinops ritro*
COMMON NAME: Globe thistle
ALTERNATIVES: 'Veitch's Blue,' 'Taplow Blue,' *E. ruthenicus*
DESCRIPTION: Herbaceous perennial of architectural value in the border, having large, jagged-edged leaves with a gray reverse and tall, silver-gray stems bearing spherical, blue flower heads.
HEIGHT AND SPREAD: 4 × 2ft (1.2 × 0.6m)
BLOOMING PERIOD: Late summer
SOIL: Well-drained.

FRONT

LATIN NAME: *Salvia farinacea* 'Strata'
COMMON NAME: Ornamental sage
ALTERNATIVES: 'Blue and White,' 'Victoria,' 'Blue Bedder'
DESCRIPTION: Half-hardy annual of bushy, upright habit with stiff stems clothed in small, lance-shaped leaves and white-stemmed spikes bearing white buds which open to deep blue, giving a two-tone effect.
HEIGHT AND SPREAD: 18–24 × 18in (0.45 × 0.6m)
BLOOMING PERIOD: Summer to autumn
SOIL: Well-drained.

9-10

LATIN NAME: *Felicia amelloides*
COMMON NAME: Blue marguerite, kingfisher daisy
ALTERNATIVES: 'Santa Anita,' 'Variegata,' *F. bergeriana*
DESCRIPTION: Tender perennial of bushy, domed habit with small, lance-shaped leaves and wiry stems bearing spherical buds, which open to sky-blue daisies with yellow centers.
HEIGHT AND SPREAD: 1–2 × 1–2ft (0.3–0.6 × 0.3–0.6m)
BLOOMING PERIOD: Late spring to autumn
SOIL: Well drained.

LATIN NAME: *Clematis × durandii*

COMMON NAME: Known by Latin name

ALTERNATIVES: None

DESCRIPTION: Herbaceous perennial with long, flopping stems which can either be allowed to trail or be trained over a support. Divided leaves with large oval leaflets and nodding, four-petalled, deep purple-blue blooms.

HEIGHT AND SPREAD: 6 × 3ft (1.8 × 0.9m)

BLOOMING PERIOD: Mid- to late summer

SOIL: Fertile, humus-rich, moisture-retentive.

5-10

8-10

LATIN NAME: *Eucalyptus gunnii*

COMMON NAME: Gum tree, eucalyptus, cider gum

ALTERNATIVES: *E. pauciflora* subsp. *niphophila*

DESCRIPTION: Slender evergreen tree if unchecked, but often cut back annually to near ground level to promote juvenile foliage with silvery blue, rounded leaves. Adult foliage sickle-shaped.

HEIGHT AND SPREAD: 5–6 × 3–4ft (1.5–1.8 × 0.9–1.2m)

BLOOMING PERIOD: Mid- to late summer

SOIL: Light, well-drained.

3-10

LATIN NAME: *Clematis heracleifolia* var. *davidiana*

COMMON NAME: Known by Latin name

ALTERNATIVES: 'Wyvale,' 'Campanile,' 'Côte d'Azur'

DESCRIPTION: Perennial with a woody base sending up many soft, leafy upright shoots bearing clusters of open, four-petalled, scented blooms of light blue followed by fluffy, silvery seed heads.

HEIGHT AND SPREAD: 3 × 2½ft (0.9 × 0.75m)

BLOOMING PERIOD: Late summer

SOIL: Fertile, humus-rich, moisture-retentive. Mulch to keep moist.

8-10

LATIN NAME: *Agapanthus* 'Lilliput'

COMMON NAME: Blue African lily, agapanthus

ALTERNATIVES: 'Blue Imp,' 'Baby Blue'

DESCRIPTION: A dwarf form of agapanthus with arching, grassy leaves forming a clump above which the almost spherical flower clusters are held on smooth, leafless stems.

HEIGHT AND SPREAD: 24 × 9in (0.6 × 0.23m)

BLOOMING PERIOD: Late summer

SOIL: Well-drained but not dry.

LATIN NAME: *Viola × wittrockiana* variety

COMMON NAME: Pansy

ALTERNATIVES: F1 hybrids

DESCRIPTION: Short-lived perennial usually grown as an annual when used for bedding. Dark green, heart-shaped, toothed-edged leaves and large, deep blue, almost circular blooms. Deadhead.

HEIGHT AND SPREAD: 6–9 × 9–12in (0.15–0.23 × 0.23–0.30cm)

BLOOMING PERIOD: Spring to mid-autumn; winter in mild climates

SOIL: Fertile, well-drained but moisture-retentive.

6-10

LATIN NAME: *Geranium wallichianum* 'Buxton's Variety'

COMMON NAME: Hardy geranium, cranesbill

ALTERNATIVES: G. 'Johnson's Blue'

DESCRIPTION: Herbaceous perennial with a spreading habit and deeply cut palmate leaves. The flowers are relatively small but numerous, clear blue with a white center and dark stamens.

HEIGHT AND SPREAD: 1 × 3ft (0.3 × 0.9m)

BLOOMING PERIOD: Mid-summer to autumn

SOIL: Fertile, well-drained.

BACK

❄ **6-9**

LATIN NAME: *Hydrangea macrophylla* 'Générale Vicomtesse de Vibraye'
COMMON NAME: Hortensia, mop-head hydrangea, big leaf hydrangea
ALTERNATIVES: 'Blue Deckle,' 'Altona'
DESCRIPTION: Shrub with broad leaves, pointed at the tip and rounded heads of sterile florets. On acid soil develops sky blue turning greenish blue in autumn; alkaline soil causes pink flowers.
HEIGHT AND SPREAD: 5 × 5ft (1.5 × 1.5m)
BLOOMING PERIOD: Mid-summer to early autumn
SOIL: Fertile, humus-rich, moisture-retentive but not waterlogged.

❄ **6-9**

LATIN NAME: *Hydrangea macrophylla* cultivar
COMMON NAME: Hortensia, mop-head hydrangea, big leaf hydrangea
ALTERNATIVES: 'Blue Deckle,' 'Altona'
DESCRIPTION: Shrub of rounded habit with broad leaves, pointed at the tip and large rounded heads made up mainly of showy, sterile florets. On acid soil becomes blue; alkaline soil results in pink flowers.
HEIGHT AND SPREAD: 5 × 5ft (1.5 × 1.5m)
BLOOMING PERIOD: Mid-summer to early autumn
SOIL: Fertile, humus-rich, moisture-retentive but not waterlogged.

MIDDLE

LATIN NAME: *Caryopteris × clandonensis*
COMMON NAME: Bluebeard, blue spirea, blue-mist shrub
ALTERNATIVES: 'Heavenly Blue,' 'Kew Blue,' 'Ferndown,' 'Arthur Simmonds'
DESCRIPTION: Shrub forming a dome of radiating stems covered in gray-green aromatic leaves. Flower clusters appear in the leaf axils. Cut back to a low framework of branches just before growth begins.
HEIGHT AND SPREAD: 2¼ × 2½ft (70 × 80cm)
BLOOMING PERIOD: Late summer to early autumn
SOIL: Well-drained, does well on alkaline soils.

❄ **6-9**

LATIN NAME: *Perovskia atriplicifolia*
COMMON NAME: Russian sage
ALTERNATIVES: 'Blue spire'
DESCRIPTION: Sub-shrub with many upright stems, gray-white in color. Gray-green aromatic leaves and airy spires of lavender-blue. Stems remain attractive through winter. Cut back to ground level each spring.
HEIGHT AND SPREAD: 4 × 1¼ft (1.2 × 0.45cm)
BLOOMING PERIOD: Late summer to early autumn
SOIL: Any well-drained but not too rich.

❄ **5-10**

FRONT

LATIN NAME: *Ceratostigma willmottianum*
COMMON NAME: Shrubby plumbago, Wilmott blue leadwort
ALTERNATIVES: *C. griffithii, C. plumbaginoides*
DESCRIPTION: Shrub making a low mound of twiggy stems covered in pointed leaves and bearing small gentian-blue flowers late in the season. Good autumn color. May die back over winter but regrows well.
HEIGHT AND SPREAD: 2 × 2ft (60 × 60cm)
BLOOMING PERIOD: Late summer to autumn
SOIL: Fertile, deeply cultivated, well-drained.

❄ **7-10**

LATIN NAME: *Ceratostigma plumbaginoides*
COMMON NAME: Plumbago, leadwort
ALTERNATIVES: *C. willmottianum, C. griffithii*
DESCRIPTION: Sub-shrub which usually dies down to ground level in winter. Makes excellent late-flowering groundcover but may be invasive in some situations. Red-purple autumn leaf color shows the flowers off well.
HEIGHT AND SPREAD: 1 × 1½ft (30 × 45cm)
BLOOMING PERIOD: Autumn
SOIL: Fertile, deeply cultivated, well-drained.

❄ **5-10**

5-8

LATIN NAME: *Hibiscus syriacus* 'Oiseau Blue' syn. 'Bluebird'
COMMON NAME: Rose-of-Sharon, tree hollyhock, flower of an hour
ALTERNATIVES: None
DESCRIPTION: Shrub of upright, goblet-shaped habit with lobed leaves and hibiscus-like flowers. In poor dry soils, growth is weak and chlorotic. Mulch in spring, water in dry spells, feed regularly.
HEIGHT AND SPREAD: 5–6 × 5–6ft (1.5–1.8 × 1.5–1.8m)
BLOOMING PERIOD: Late summer to mid-autumn
SOIL: Rich, moisture-retentive. Mulch with compost.

LATIN NAME: *Salvia guaranitica* 'Blue Enigma'
COMMON NAME: Ornamental sage
ALTERNATIVES: *Salvia uliginosa, S. azurea*
DESCRIPTION: Sub-shrub with upright stems clothed in dark green leaves. Produces a very late display of intense blue hooded flowers with darker calyces. Requires a warm, sheltered site to overwinter successfully.
HEIGHT AND SPREAD: 5 × 3ft (1.5 × 0.9m)
BLOOMING PERIOD: Early to mid-autumn
SOIL: Well-drained.

9-10

LATIN NAME: *Gentiana asclepiadea*
COMMON NAME: Willow gentian
ALTERNATIVES: 'Knightshayes,' 'Phyllis'
DESCRIPTION: Herbaceous perennial with arching stems and willow-like leaves. Trumpet-shaped flowers in leaf axils. Best left undisturbed and does well in a cool position.
HEIGHT AND SPREAD: 3 × 2ft (90 × 60cm)
BLOOMING PERIOD: Early autumn
SOIL: Moisture-retentive and humus-rich. Tolerates lime.

5-9

3-9

LATIN NAME: *Clematis heracleifolia*
COMMON NAME: Known by Latin name
ALTERNATIVES: 'Campanile,' 'Côte d'Azur,' *C. h. var. davidiana*
DESCRIPTION: Herbaceous perennial forming a clump of upright stems with divided leaves and topped by clusters of fragrant flowers. Silvery seed heads provide further interest.
HEIGHT AND SPREAD: 3 × 5ft (0.9 × 1.5m)
BLOOMING PERIOD: Late summer
SOIL: Fertile, well-drained. Good on limey soils.

6-9

LATIN NAME: *Gentiana sino-ornata*
COMMON NAME: Gentian
ALTERNATIVES: 'Angel Wings,' 'Edelstein Blue'
DESCRIPTION: Alpine making a low carpet of stems clothed in narrow leaves. Large, trumpet-shaped blooms of vivid blue. Divide and re-plant every three years or so to keep plants vigorous.
HEIGHT AND SPREAD: 2–6 × 12–15in (5–15 × 30–38cm)
BLOOMING PERIOD: Autumn
SOIL: Acidic, peaty and moist.

8-10

LATIN NAME: *Convolvulus sabatius* syn. *C. mauritanicus*
COMMON NAME: Ground morning glory
ALTERNATIVES: *C. s.* dark form
DESCRIPTION: Evergreen perennial with trailing stems and gray-green leaves. Lilac-blue, trumpet-shaped flowers which close in cloudy weather. Loose groundcover. Cut back hard in late winter.
HEIGHT AND SPREAD: 6–8 × 12in (15–20 × 30cm)
BLOOMING PERIOD: Summer to early autumn
SOIL: Any well-drained, especially over winter.

Yellow

There are cool and warm yellows, ranging from acid-yellow (mixed with plenty of green but no red) to gold (with red, but not so much that you begin to distinguish it as orange). Just as with other colors, these two ends of the scale rarely sit well with one another. Yellow is also mixed with white to give a wide variety of cream shades, and these softer colors are perfect for lifting heavy schemes of purple and deep blue.

Yellow reminds us of sunshine and so is particularly effective at livening up dull and shady spots in the garden - try a zingy scheme of yellows with touches of white, lime-green, and sharp orange.

Citrus shades of yellow, orange, and terracotta add a Mediterranean feel to a hot, sunny border. Use a backdrop of blue-painted trellis or stand a couple of rich, blue-glazed pots among the flowers for a truly stunning effect.

An all-yellow border is easy to create because there is a wide range of flowers and foliage available throughout the year. But, as with most colors, you can have too much of a good thing. In full sun, the effect can be overwhelming. For contrast and to cool the scheme down, use deep blue-purple and cerise-red blooms and rich green and glaucous foliage. Or raise the temperature with flame-red, orange, and bronze.

LEFT: *A trio of yellow plants (Mount Etna broom, foxtail lily, golden marjoram) make a striking composition.*

BACK

6-8

LATIN NAME: *Corylopsis sinensis var. calvescens* syn. *C. platypetala*
COMMON NAME: Winter hazel
ALTERNATIVES: 'Spring Purple,' *C. spicata*, *C. pauciflora*
DESCRIPTION: A round-topped shrub, often slow to establish and flower well, but making a choice specimen for a woodland garden. Rounded leaves and pale yellow, fragrant catkin-like flowers.
HEIGHT AND SPREAD: 12 × 12ft (4 × 4m)
BLOOMING PERIOD: Early to mid-spring
SOIL: Acid, fertile, humus-rich, moisture-retentive.

6-8

LATIN NAME: *Corylopsis pauciflora*
COMMON NAME: Winter hazel
ALTERNATIVES: *C. sinensis* and forms, *C. spicata*
DESCRIPTION: Shrub with fragrant, bell-shaped blooms of pale yellow produced in profusion on bare stems. The leaves are oval-shaped and toothed-edged and give good autumn color.
HEIGHT AND SPREAD: 6 × 6ft (1.8 × 1.8m)
BLOOMING PERIOD: Mid-spring
SOIL: Acid, fertile, humus-rich, moisture-retentive.

MIDDLE

LATIN NAME: *Lysichiton americanus*
COMMON NAME: Western skunk cabbage, bog arum
ALTERNATIVES: None
DESCRIPTION: Herbaceous perennial thriving in boggy or stream-side positions, which produces giant arum-lily spathes of bright yellow and handsome leaves. Flowers give off an unpleasant smell.
HEIGHT AND SPREAD: 4 × 6ft (1.2 × 1.8m)
BLOOMING PERIOD: Early spring
SOIL: Moist to boggy.

5-8

5-8

LATIN NAME: *Mahonia aquifolium*
COMMON NAME: Oregon grape holly
ALTERNATIVES: 'Apollo,' 'Atropurpurea'
DESCRIPTION: Evergreen, suckering shrub with glossy, deep green pinnate, prickly leaves and dense rounded clusters of tiny yellow flowers, followed by blue-black berries.
HEIGHT AND SPREAD: 3 × 10ft (0.9 × 3m)
BLOOMING PERIOD: Early spring
SOIL: Any well-drained but moderately moisture-retentive.

FRONT

3-7

LATIN NAME: *Eranthis hyemalis*
COMMON NAME: Winter aconite
ALTERNATIVES: *E. h. Tubergenii* Group 'Guinea Gold'
DESCRIPTION: Tuberous perennial with golden yellow cup-shaped blooms surmounted by a ruff of divided light green bracts. Will self-seed in undisturbed ground beneath deciduous shrubs.
HEIGHT AND SPREAD: 2–4 × 3–4in (5–10 × 8–10cm)
BLOOMING PERIOD: Late winter
SOIL: Humus-rich, moisture-retentive but well-drained.

3-7

LATIN NAME: *Eranthis hyemalis* Tubergenii Group 'Guinea Gold'
COMMON NAME: Winter aconite
ALTERNATIVES: *E. hyemalis*
DESCRIPTION: Tuberous perennial slowly forming spreading clumps. May be divided immediately after flowering. Golden yellow blooms are larger and more showy than those of *E. hyemalis*.
HEIGHT AND SPREAD: 3–4 × 3–4in (8–10 × 8–10cm)
BLOOMING PERIOD: Late winter
SOIL: Humus-rich, moisture-retentive but well-drained.

Latin name: *Taxus baccata* 'Standishii'
Common name: Yew, English yew
Alternatives: 'Fastigiata Aurea'
Description: Evergreen shrub (poisonous) with a strongly upright, narrow habit and, when grown in full sun, bright golden yellow foliage. Spherical red fruits.
Height and spread: 4–5 × 1ft (1.2–1.5 × 0.3m)
Blooming period: Not significant
Soil: Well-drained.

6-7

8-10

Latin name: *Acacia pravissima*
Common name: Oven's wattle
Alternatives: *A. baileyana, A. longifolia*
Description: Evergreen, arching to spreading shrub with triangular "leaves" crowding the stems, giving them a tooth-edged appearance, and fluffy, mimosa-like flowers.
Height and spread: 15 × 15ft (4.5 × 4.5m)
Blooming period: Late winter to early spring
Soil: Well-drained.

Latin name: *Yucca filamentosa* 'Variegata'
Common name: Adam's needle yucca
Alternatives: 'Bright Edge,' *Y. flaccida* 'Golden Sword,' *Y. gloriosa* 'Variegata'
Description: Evergreen perennial making a rosette of sharp-pointed, sword-shaped leaves, broadly margined creamy yellow, with wispy, curling threads. The stout, upright flower stem, to 6ft (1.8m), carries bell-shaped white flowers.
Height and spread: 6 × 5ft (1.8 × 1.5m)
Blooming period: Mid- to late summer
Soil: Well-drained.

4-10

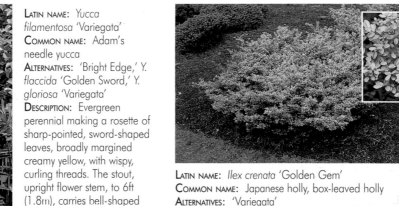

5-8

Latin name: *Ilex crenata* 'Golden Gem'
Common name: Japanese holly, box-leaved holly
Alternatives: 'Variegata'
Description: Evergreen shrub of low, spreading habit with small golden-green leaves, densely packed on the branches. May be clipped to produce a neater outline. Flowers inconspicuous.
Height and spread: 2½ × 4ft (0.75 × 1.2m)
Blooming period: Late spring to early summer
Soil: Rich, moisture-retentive, well-drained.

Latin name: *Narcissus cyclamineus*
Common name: Miniature daffodil
Alternatives: 'February Gold,' 'Peeping Tom,' 'Tête a Tête,' 'Jumblie'
Description: Dwarf bulb with golden yellow, downward-pointing blooms consisting of a narrow tube and swept-back petals. Clumps of narrow, grassy leaves.
Height and spread: 6in (15cm)
Blooming period: Late winter to early spring
Soil: Moist, acid, humus-rich, well-drained.

5-7

3-9

Latin name: *Primula polyantha* Rainbow Series 'Cream Shades'
Common name: Polyanthus
Alternatives: 'Crescendo' seed strains
Description: Short-lived perennial usually grown as a biennial for winter/spring bedding. Makes rosettes of crinkled green leaves from the center of which stout stems carrying stalked circular blooms arise.
Height and spread: 9–12 × 12in (23–30 × 30cm)
Blooming period: Late winter to late spring
Soil: Moisture-retentive but well-drained.

BACK

5-8

LATIN NAME: *Rhododendron* 'Champagne'
COMMON NAME: Known by Latin name
ALTERNATIVES: 'Virginia Richards,' 'Unique,' 'Crest,' 'Ode Wright'
DESCRIPTION: Evergreen shrub of bushy, slightly spreading habit with oblong, pointed leaves of deep green and large terminal clusters of pale, creamy yellow, funnel-shaped blooms.
HEIGHT AND SPREAD: 10 × 12ft (3 × 3.7m)
BLOOMING PERIOD: Early summer (spring in Australia)
SOIL: Acid, humus-rich, moisture-retentive but well-drained.

LATIN NAME: *Hedera helix* 'Goldheart' syn. 'Oro di Bogliasco'
COMMON NAME: Gold heart ivy
ALTERNATIVES: *H. colchica* 'Sulphur Heart,' *H.* 'Buttercup'
DESCRIPTION: Self-clinging climber, shown here in its adult leaf form, having glossy, deep green leaves with a large, irregular, golden-yellow center. Full sun develops color.
HEIGHT AND SPREAD: 25 × 20ft (7.6 × 6m)
BLOOMING PERIOD: Autumn to spring
SOIL: Well-drained but moisture-retentive.

5-10

MIDDLE

4-9

LATIN NAME: *Doronicum plantagineum*
COMMON NAME: Leopard's bane
ALTERNATIVES: 'Excelsum,' 'Harpur Crewe'
DESCRIPTION: Herbaceous perennial making a mound of bright, mid-green, heart-shaped leaves and producing several leafless flower stems bearing large, golden yellow daisy blooms.
HEIGHT AND SPREAD: 30 × 12in (75 × 30cm)
BLOOMING PERIOD: Spring
SOIL: Well-drained and moisture-retentive but tolerates dry shade.

2-7

LATIN NAME: *Ribes alpinum* 'Aureum'
COMMON NAME: Mountain currant
ALTERNATIVES: *R. sanguineum, R. odoratum*
DESCRIPTION: Low, spreading shrub with lobed foliage that is bright yellow in spring, greenish in summer, and yellow in autumn. Small hanging flower clusters in spring. Females bear red fruits.
HEIGHT AND SPREAD: 3–4 × 5ft (0.9–1.2 × 1.5m)
BLOOMING PERIOD: Early spring
SOIL: Any reasonably fertile, well-drained.

FRONT

4-8

LATIN NAME: *Crocus × luteus* 'Golden Yellow' syn. 'Dutch Yellow'
COMMON NAME: Known by Latin name
ALTERNATIVES: *Crocus chrysanthus* cultivars
DESCRIPTION: Corm of robust nature which naturalizes easily in grass and produces its large, bright yellow, weather-resistant blooms in early spring. Narrow grassy foliage.
HEIGHT AND SPREAD: 3–4in (8–10cm)
BLOOMING PERIOD: Early spring
SOIL: Well-drained.

9-10

LATIN NAME: *Freesia* cultivar
COMMON NAME: Known by Latin name
ALTERNATIVES: 'Bergunden Yellow,' 'Yellow River,' *F. armstrongii*
DESCRIPTION: Bulbous plant with narrow, sword-shaped leaves and slender stems bearing arching sprays of highly fragrant, funnel-shaped blooms. May need support of twiggy sticks or slender canes.
HEIGHT AND SPREAD: 12 × 1½–2½in (30 × 4–6cm)
BLOOMING PERIOD: Winter/spring, depending on planting time
SOIL: Well-drained.

LATIN NAME: *Forsythia 'Beatrix Farrand'*
COMMON NAME: Known by Latin name
ALTERNATIVES: *F. × intermedia* cultivars
DESCRIPTION: Shrub of bushy, upright to somewhat arching habit, which flowers on the bare brown stems in early spring. Light green oval leaves. Good yellow autumn color. Larger than usual deep yellow blooms.
HEIGHT AND SPREAD: 7 × 7ft (2.2 × 2.2m)
BLOOMING PERIOD: Early to mid-spring
SOIL: Any reasonably well-drained, including clay.

4-9

LATIN NAME: *Forsythia × intermedia 'Lynwood'*
COMMON NAME: Known by Latin name
ALTERNATIVES: *F. × intermedia* cultivars, e.g, 'Spectabilis'
DESCRIPTION: Shrub of bushy, upright to somewhat arching habit, which flowers on the bare brown stems in early spring. Light green oval leaves. Some autumn color. A larger cultivar with a profusion of blooms.
HEIGHT AND SPREAD: 13 × 12ft (4 × 3.5m)
BLOOMING PERIOD: Early to mid-spring
SOIL: Any well-drained.

4-9

8-10

LATIN NAME: *Phormium cookianum 'Cream Delight'*
COMMON NAME: New Zealand flax
ALTERNATIVES: *P. 'Yellow Wave'*
DESCRIPTION: Perennial forming a clump of broad, arching, strap-shaped leaves with a wide, creamy yellow central stripe. Tall flower stems bear orange-yellow, tubular blooms rich in nectar.
HEIGHT AND SPREAD: 3 × 3ft (0.9 × 0.9m)
BLOOMING PERIOD: Mid-summer
SOIL: Well-drained.

5-7

LATIN NAME: *Fritillaria imperialis 'Lutea Maxima'*
COMMON NAME: Crown imperial
ALTERNATIVES: None
DESCRIPTION: Bulb with tall, upright stems clothed in whorls of lance-shaped leaves and topped with heads of up to five hanging bells with protruding stamens. Each cluster has a "crown" of leaves at the center.
HEIGHT AND SPREAD: 4–5 × 1ft (1.2–1.5 × 0.9m)
BLOOMING PERIOD: Spring
SOIL: Well-drained.

4-8

LATIN NAME: *Narcissus 'Rip van Winkle'* syn. *N. pumilus 'Plenus'*
COMMON NAME: Daffodil
ALTERNATIVES: None
DESCRIPTION: Bulb with narrow, strap-shaped leaves forming a clump from which the leafless flower stems arise bearing unusual, many-petalled blooms of golden yellow.
HEIGHT AND SPREAD: 6in (15cm)
BLOOMING PERIOD: Early spring
SOIL: Well-drained but moisture-retentive.

4-9

LATIN NAME: *Narcissus 'Peeping Tom'*
COMMON NAME: Daffodil
ALTERNATIVES: 'February Gold,' 'Jetfire,' 'Little Witch'
DESCRIPTION: Bulb with narrow, strap-shaped leaves forming a clump over which the golden yellow blooms are produced. These have reflexed petals and an unusually long, narrow tube when fully developed.
HEIGHT AND SPREAD: 15in (38cm)
BLOOMING PERIOD: Early spring
SOIL: Well-drained but moisture-retentive.

YELLOW

LATIN NAME: *Jasminum mesnyi* syn. *J. primulinum*
COMMON NAME: Primrose jasmine
ALTERNATIVES: *J. fruticans, J. humile revolutum*
DESCRIPTION: Evergreen shrub with long, lax stems and green trifoliate leaves. Grow trained against a warm wall for added protection and to ripen wood to encourage flowering. Large single or semi-double blooms.
HEIGHT AND SPREAD: 6–10 × 6–10ft (1.8–3 × 1.8–3m)
BLOOMING PERIOD: Late spring
SOIL: Any well-drained including quite poor soils.

8-10

LATIN NAME: *Azara serrata*
COMMON NAME: Known by Latin name
ALTERNATIVES: *A. microphylla, A. dentata, A. lanceolata, A. petiolaris*
DESCRIPTION: Evergreen shrub with small, glossy, serrated edged leaves and fluffy flowers which smell sweetly of vanilla. May be grown against a warm wall for added protection in cold areas.
HEIGHT AND SPREAD: 8–12 × 8–12ft (2.4–3.6 × 2.4–3.6m)
BLOOMING PERIOD: Spring
SOIL: Any fertile, well-drained and well-cultivated.

8-10

3-10

LATIN NAME: *Paeonia mlokosewitschii*
COMMON NAME: Peony 'Mollie-the-Witch'
ALTERNATIVES: None
DESCRIPTION: Herbaceous perennial with pinky-red new shoots. Divided gray-green leaves with bowl-shaped blooms. Very early flowering. Dislikes disturbance. Young growth susceptible to frost.
HEIGHT AND SPREAD: 3 × 2ft (90 × 60cm)
BLOOMING PERIOD: Mid-spring
SOIL: Well-drained, fertile, moisture-retentive. Tolerates lime.

10

LATIN NAME: *Euryops pectinatus*
COMMON NAME: Known by Latin name
ALTERNATIVES: *E. chrysanthemoides*
DESCRIPTION: Tender perennial/sub-shrub of upright, branched habit with finely divided gray-green foliage. Yellow daisy flowers. Prune hard in spring to generate good, bushy habit and prevent leginess.
HEIGHT AND SPREAD: 3 × 2ft (90 × 60cm)
BLOOMING PERIOD: Late spring to mid-autumn
SOIL: Any well-drained.

4-9

LATIN NAME: *Narcissus* 'Cheerfulness'
COMMON NAME: Double daffodil
ALTERNATIVES: 'Yellow Cheerfulness,' 'Tahiti,' 'Unique'
DESCRIPTION: Bulb with narrow strap-like leaves on upright stems topped with buds which open to double, pale yellow scented blooms. Deadhead once faded. Leave stems and leaves to die down.
HEIGHT AND SPREAD: 15in (38cm)
BLOOMING PERIOD: Mid-spring
SOIL: Moisture-retentive.

4-9

LATIN NAME: *Meconopsis cambrica*
COMMON NAME: Welsh poppy
ALTERNATIVES: 'Flore Pleno'
DESCRIPTION: Herbaceous perennial (short-lived) with a woody tap root. Foliage fresh green, fern-like. Slender stems bear bowl-shaped blooms (yellow or orange). Self-seeds readily even in deep shade.
HEIGHT AND SPREAD: 18 × 12in (45 × 30cm)
BLOOMING PERIOD: Late spring
SOIL: Humus-rich, moisture-retentive.

LATIN NAME: *Piptanthus nepalensis* syn. *P. laburnifolius*
COMMON NAME: Evergreen laburnum
ALTERNATIVES: None
DESCRIPTION: Evergreen to deciduous shrub with upright, sparsely branched habit and large trifoliate leaves, glossy above and matte gray-green beneath. Pea-like flowers. Some autumn color. If frosted, may re-grow from base.
HEIGHT AND SPREAD: 10 × 8ft (3 × 2.4m)
BLOOMING PERIOD: Mid- to late spring
SOIL: Fertile, well-drained. Tolerates high alkalinity.

8-9

5-9

LATIN NAME: *Rosa* 'Canary Bird'
COMMON NAME: Shrub rose
ALTERNATIVES: 'Helen Knight,' 'Cantabrigiensis'
DESCRIPTION: Shrub with arching stems covered with ferny foliage and in spring puts on a spectacular display of small, fragrant, single yellow blooms similar in shape to those of a wild rose.
HEIGHT AND SPREAD: 9 × 12ft (2.7 × 3.6m)
BLOOMING PERIOD: Spring
SOIL: Fertile, humus-rich but well drained.

4-8

LATIN NAME: *Berberis thunbergii* 'Aurea'
COMMON NAME: Golden common or Japanese barberry
ALTERNATIVES: None
DESCRIPTION: Shrub of twiggy habit with thorny stems. Small, spoon-shaped leaves, bright lime-green to pale yellow in spring, darker through the season. Prone to scorching in full sun. Autumn color.
HEIGHT AND SPREAD: 3 × 4ft (0.9 × 1.2m)
BLOOMING PERIOD: Early spring to mid-spring
SOIL: Any fertile, avoiding very dry conditions or waterlogging.

4-9

LATIN NAME: *Lysimachia punctata*
COMMON NAME: Yellow loosestrife
ALTERNATIVES: *L. ciliata*
DESCRIPTION: Herbaceous perennial with spreading rootstock. Invasive. Many upright stems with lanceolate, mid-green leaves and spires of bright yellow. Lovely massed in a wild or water garden.
HEIGHT AND SPREAD: 3 × 2ft (90 × 60cm)
BLOOMING PERIOD: Early summer to mid-summer
SOIL: Any moisture-retentive.

LATIN NAME: *Tulipa* 'Golden Memory'
COMMON NAME: Tulip
ALTERNATIVES: 'Bellona,' 'Sunray,' Golden Apeldoorn,' 'Mamasa,' 'West Point'
DESCRIPTION: Bulb with broad, strap-like leaves and upright stems bearing a single cone-shaped bud which opens to a bowl-shape in full sun. Deadhead but leave the stems and leaves to die down to build bulb reserves.
HEIGHT AND SPREAD: 20 × 24in (50 × 60cm)
BLOOMING PERIOD: Mid-spring to late spring
SOIL: Any well-drained.

3-9

7-9

LATIN NAME: *Genista lydia*
COMMON NAME: Broom
ALTERNATIVES: *Cytisus procumbens, Cytisus* × *kewensis*
DESCRIPTION: Shrub with evergreen, wiry arching branches of gray-green coloring producing a cascade effect, especially useful in winter. Bright yellow pea flowers along length of stem. Sparse foliage.
HEIGHT AND SPREAD: 1–2 × 6ft (0.3–0.6 × 1.8m)
BLOOMING PERIOD: Late spring to early summer
SOIL: Well-drained, acid or alkaline.

YELLOW

BACK

8-9

LATIN NAME: *Cytisus battandieri*
COMMON NAME: Pineapple broom, Moroccan broom
ALTERNATIVES: 'Yellow Tail'
DESCRIPTION: Semi-evergreen shrub with silvery-green leaves covered in soft hairs and short, upright spikes of fruity-scented flowers. May be wall-trained for extra protection or grown free-standing.
HEIGHT AND SPREAD: 16 × 13ft (4.9 × 4m)
BLOOMING PERIOD: Early summer to mid-summer
SOIL: Tolerates all but poorly drained soils and extreme alkalinity.

LATIN NAME: *Robinia pseudoacacia* 'Frisia'
COMMON NAME: Golden acacia, black locust
ALTERNATIVES: *Gleditsia triacanthos* 'Sunburst'
DESCRIPTION: Small tree, late into leaf, with glowing yellow-green pinnate foliage, especially bright in spring. White "pea" flowers. Good yellow autumn color. Brittle-stemmed so avoid windy sites.
HEIGHT AND SPREAD: 20+ × 13ft (6+ × 4m)
BLOOMING PERIOD: Mid-summer
SOIL: Rich, moisture-retentive. Avoid poor and extreme alkalinity.

3-9

MIDDLE

3-10

LATIN NAME: *Digitalis grandiflora* (syn. *D. ambigua*)
COMMON NAME: Foxglove
ALTERNATIVES: 'Temple Bells,' *D. lanata, D. lutea, D. davisiana*
DESCRIPTION: Short-lived perennial making a basal clump of evergreen deeply veined leaves and sending up slender spires of tubular flowers, flared at the mouth.
HEIGHT AND SPREAD: 30 × 12in (76 × 30cm)
BLOOMING PERIOD: Early summer
SOIL: Fertile, humus-rich.

LATIN NAME: *Brachyglottis* 'Sunshine' (syn. *Senecio*)
COMMON NAME: Shrubby ragwort
ALTERNATIVES: *B. greyi, B. laxifolia*
DESCRIPTION: Evergreen silver-gray leaved shrub of low spreading habit. Yellow daisy flowers produced in clusters on second-year wood. Prune out some of these older branches at ground level in spring. Good seaside plant.
HEIGHT AND SPREAD: 3 × 5ft (90 × 152cm)
BLOOMING PERIOD: Early summer
SOIL: Any well-drained.

8-10

FRONT

7-10

LATIN NAME: *Iris* (Xiphium type)
COMMON NAME: Dutch iris
ALTERNATIVES: 'Golden Harvest'
DESCRIPTION: Bulbous iris with stout flower stems bearing one or two blooms. The foliage is long and narrow. Plant in groups between lower-growing herbaceous and shrubs for early summer display.
HEIGHT AND SPREAD: 32 × 6in (80 × 15cm)
BLOOMING PERIOD: Late spring to early summer
SOIL: Well-drained, good on alkaline soils.

LATIN NAME: *Allium moly*
COMMON NAME: Lily leek, golden garlic
ALTERNATIVES: 'Jeannine'
DESCRIPTION: Bulbous, clump-forming perennial with grassy, gray-green foliage and flower stems bearing dome-shaped heads of up to 40 starry flowers.
HEIGHT AND SPREAD: 4–14 × 4–5in (10–35 × 10–12cm)
BLOOMING PERIOD: Early summer
SOIL: Well-drained.

3-9

6-8

LATIN NAME: Lonicera × tellmanniana
COMMON NAME: Honeysuckle
ALTERNATIVES: L. tragophylla, L. japonica 'Halliana'
DESCRIPTION: Climber with long twining stems and green oval leaves. Large clusters of deep yellow tubular blooms shaded orange. No scent. Requires a cool root run, shaded by foreground shrubs.
HEIGHT AND SPREAD: 12–15 × 12–15ft (3.6–4.6 × 3.6–4.6m)
BLOOMING PERIOD: Summer
SOIL: Fertile, moisture-retentive, with a deep organic mulch.

LATIN NAME: Lonicera tragophylla
COMMON NAME: Honeysuckle, Chinese woodbine
ALTERNATIVES: L. × tellmanniana, L. japonica 'Halliana'
DESCRIPTION: Large, vigorous climber with long twining stems and large clusters of bright yellow blooms set off by the bronzed leaves and gray reverse. May be invasive.
HEIGHT AND SPREAD: 30–40 × 20–30ft (9–12 × 6–9m)
BLOOMING PERIOD: Early summer to mid-summer
SOIL: Fertile, moisture-retentive.

6-9

LATIN NAME: Phlomis fruticosa
COMMON NAME: Jerusalem sage
ALTERNATIVES: 'Edward Bowles'
DESCRIPTION: Evergreen shrub with gray "wool" covering leaves and stems. Leaves almost white beneath. Whorls of hooded flowers followed by long-lasting, attractive seed heads.
HEIGHT AND SPREAD: 3 × 4ft (90 × 120cm)
BLOOMING PERIOD: Early summer to mid-summer
SOIL: Best on light, open, well-drained, especially in cooler regions.

8-10

3-10

LATIN NAME: Hemerocallis 'Wind Song'
COMMON NAME: Daylily
ALTERNATIVES: 'Whichford,' 'Marion Vaughn,' 'Favorite Things'
DESCRIPTION: Herbaceous perennial with large, widely flared trumpet flowers with ruffled petals produced from cluster of buds at top of stem (each lasts a day). Arching grassy foliage makes dense mounds.
HEIGHT AND SPREAD: 28 × 30in (71 × 76cm)
BLOOMING PERIOD: Mid-summer
SOIL: Fertile, moisture-retentive. Avoid very dry or very wet sites.

3-10

LATIN NAME: Hemerocallis 'Corky'
COMMON NAME: Daylily
ALTERNATIVES: 'Stella de Oro,' 'Happy Returns,' H. dumortieri
DESCRIPTION: Herbaceous perennial with flowers like trumpet lilies produced from cluster of buds at top of stem (each lasts a day). Contrasting dark stems and red-tinged buds. Attractive grassy foliage.
HEIGHT AND SPREAD: 18 × 18in (45 × 45cm)
BLOOMING PERIOD: Late spring to early summer
SOIL: Fertile, moisture-retentive. Avoid very dry or very wet sites.

5-10

LATIN NAME: Helianthemum 'Wisley Primrose'
COMMON NAME: Rock rose, sun rose
ALTERNATIVES: 'Amy Baring,' 'Ben Nevis,' 'Jubilee'
DESCRIPTION: Evergreen shrub with neat, gray-green leaves. Rounded flowers open from clusters of nodding buds. Clip over lightly after flowering. Must have good drainage and best in full sun.
HEIGHT AND SPREAD: 8 × 36in (20 × 90cm)
BLOOMING PERIOD: Early summer to mid-summer
SOIL: Well-drained to dry including poor, stony ground. Avoid strong alkaline.

YELLOW

BACK

5-9

LATIN NAME: *Rosa* 'Golden Wings'
COMMON NAME: Shrub rose
ALTERNATIVES: None
DESCRIPTION: Shrub having a bushy habit and light green pinnate foliage with large, single, cup-shaped blooms of pale yellow and a central boss of darker golden stamens. Moderate fragrance.
HEIGHT AND SPREAD: 6 × 4½ft (2 × 1.35m)
BLOOMING PERIOD: Summer to autumn (beginning spring in Australia)
SOIL: Rich, well-drained but moisture-retentive.

LATIN NAME: *Cytisus scoparius* f. *andreanus*
COMMON NAME: Broom
ALTERNATIVES: 'Cornish Cream,' 'Golden Cascade,' 'Gold Finch,' 'Moonlight'
DESCRIPTION: Shrub with evergreen whip-like branches and upright habit bearing small, sparsely-spaced trifoliate leaves and masses of pea-like blooms with golden yellow "wings" and brown "keels."
HEIGHT AND SPREAD: 10 × 8ft (3 × 2.5m)
BLOOMING PERIOD: Spring to early summer
SOIL: Well-drained, preferably neutral to acid.

5-8

MIDDLE

9-10

LATIN NAME: *Coronilla valentina* subsp. *glauca* syn. *C. glauca*
COMMON NAME: Daffodil bush
ALTERNATIVES: 'Citrina,' 'Variegata'
DESCRIPTION: Evergreen, bushy, rounded shrub with blue-gray leaves which make a perfect foil for the sweetly scented, golden yellow pea-like blooms. Seldom without some flowers through the year.
HEIGHT AND SPREAD: 3 × 3ft (0.9 × 0.9m)
BLOOMING PERIOD: Spring through summer into autumn
SOIL: Well-drained.

LATIN NAME: *Alstroemeria* 'Cyprus'
COMMON NAME: Peruvian lily
ALTERNATIVES: Butterfly Hybrids, Princess Series, Ligtu hybrids
DESCRIPTION: Tuberous-rooted perennial with orchid-like blooms of pale pinkish white, heavily marked and suffused yellow with a deeper yellow blotch. Narrow, lance-shaped leaves. Stems good for cutting.
HEIGHT AND SPREAD: 3–4 × 2–3ft (0.9–1.2 × 0.6–0.9m)
BLOOMING PERIOD: Summer
SOIL: Well-drained. Protect crowns from winter cold with an organic mulch.

7-10

FRONT

9-10

LATIN NAME: *Clivia miniata* var. *citrina*
COMMON NAME: Known by Latin name
ALTERNATIVES: *C. miniata* hybrids
DESCRIPTION: Evergreen perennial, clump-forming from an underground rhizome. Broad, strap-shaped, arching leaves. Large funnel-shaped blooms clustered into a bold head.
HEIGHT AND SPREAD: 16 × 12–24ft (40 × 30–60cm)
BLOOMING PERIOD: Autumn, winter, or spring
SOIL: Well-drained.

4-10

LATIN NAME: *Sedum aizoon*
COMMON NAME: Stonecrop
ALTERNATIVES: 'Aurantiacum' ('Euphorbioides')
DESCRIPTION: Evergreen perennial with upright stems covered in fleshy, bright green, lance-shaped leaves with a serrated edge. Flattened heads of tiny, golden-yellow, star-shaped blooms.
HEIGHT AND SPREAD: 18 × 18in (45 × 45cm)
BLOOMING PERIOD: Summer
SOIL: Well-drained to dry.

BACK

LATIN NAME: *Lonicera nitida* 'Baggesen's Gold'
COMMON NAME: Boxleaf honeysuckle, poor man's box
ALTERNATIVES: None
DESCRIPTION: Evergreen shrub of upright to arching habit with very small, densely packed, golden yellow leaves. Avoid dry soil and exposure to full sun as this can lead to bleaching and scorching. Responds well to clipping.
HEIGHT AND SPREAD: 4 × 5ft (1.2 × 1.5m)
BLOOMING PERIOD: Insignificant
SOIL: Well-drained, avoiding dry or waterlogged.

7-9

LATIN NAME: *Metrosideros excelsa* 'Aureus'
COMMON NAME: Known by Latin name
ALTERNATIVES: 'Moon Maiden'
DESCRIPTION: Evergreen shrub with glossy, dark green, oval leaves, white felted beneath, and terminal clusters of tufted creamy yellow blooms consisting mainly of stamens.
HEIGHT AND SPREAD: 26 × 20ft (8 × 6m)
BLOOMING PERIOD: Summer
SOIL: Fertile, well-drained.

9-10

MIDDLE

3-10

3-10

LATIN NAME: *Hemerocallis* 'Dubloon'
COMMON NAME: Day lily
ALTERNATIVES: 'Corky,' 'Golden Chimes,' 'Favorite Things'
DESCRIPTION: Herbaceous perennial making a clump of long, narrow leaves which are particularly bright and attractive in spring. Slender stems bear clusters of buds and star-like blooms with narrow petals.
HEIGHT AND SPREAD: 2½ × 1½ft (0.75 × 0.45m)
BLOOMING PERIOD: Summer
SOIL: Well-drained but moisture-retentive.

LATIN NAME: *Hemerocallis* 'Azur'
COMMON NAME: Daylily
ALTERNATIVES: 'Golden Chimes,' 'Corky,' 'Favorite Things'
DESCRIPTION: Herbaceous perennial making a clump of long, narrow leaves which are particularly attractive in spring. Slender stems bear clusters of buds and blooms with broad, slightly ruffled petals.
HEIGHT AND SPREAD: 3 × 2ft (0.9 × 0.6m)
BLOOMING PERIOD: Summer
SOIL: Well-drained but moisture-retentive.

FRONT

3-9

LATIN NAME: *Viola* × *wittrockiana* Universal Series F1
COMMON NAME: Pansy
ALTERNATIVES: F1 hybrid series
DESCRIPTION: Biennial often grown as annual, used for bedding and containers with rounded to heart-shaped, toothed-edged leaves and large, flat, almost circular blooms, often sweetly scented.
HEIGHT AND SPREAD: 6–9 × 9–12in (15–23 × 23–30cm)
BLOOMING PERIOD: Depends on variety and time of sowing.
SOIL: Well-drained but moisture-retentive.

LATIN NAME: *Lysimachia nummularia* 'Aurea'
COMMON NAME: Golden creeping Jenny, moneywort
ALTERNATIVES: *L. nummularia*
DESCRIPTION: Creeping perennial with branched stems rooting into the ground. Pairs of small, circular leaves of buttery yellow, and golden yellow, cup-shaped blooms. Good groundcover in moist shade.
HEIGHT AND SPREAD: 1–2in × indefinite (2.5–5cm × indefinite)
BLOOMING PERIOD: Summer
SOIL: Moisture-retentive to damp.

BACK

LATIN NAME: *Verbascum bombyciferum*
COMMON NAME: Mullein
ALTERNATIVES: V. 'Gainsborough'
DESCRIPTION: Evergreen biennial with broad silver-green leaves in a clump at the base and up the flower stems. Solid spires of yellow blooms set in silvery-white "wool." May self-seed especially into gravel mulch.
HEIGHT AND SPREAD: 4–6 × 2ft (1.2–1.8 × 0.6m)
BLOOMING PERIOD: Summer
SOIL: Well-drained.

5-9

LATIN NAME: *Lilium* hybrid
COMMON NAME: Hybrid lily
ALTERNATIVES: Golden Splendor strain, Aurelian hybrids
DESCRIPTION: Bulb producing tall stems clothed in narrow leaves and topped by large, trumpet-shaped blooms. Plant in groups between lower-growing shrubs and herbaceous plants in the mixed border.
HEIGHT AND SPREAD: 4–7 × 1ft (1.2–2.1 × 0.3m)
BLOOMING PERIOD: Summer
SOIL: Fertile, friable, well-drained but humus-rich.

4-9

MIDDLE

LATIN NAME: *Zantedeschia elliottiana*
COMMON NAME: Golden arum lily
ALTERNATIVES: New Zealand Hybrids
DESCRIPTION: Evergreen tuberous plant making a clump of broad, arrow-shaped leaves in green spotted with silver. Large waxy "sculpted" blooms (spathes) surrounding the poker-like spadix. Numerous named cultivars.
HEIGHT AND SPREAD: 2–3 × 1½–2ft (60–90 × 45–60cm)
BLOOMING PERIOD: Summer
SOIL: Well-drained but moisture-retentive.

10

LATIN NAME: *Solidago* 'Laurin'
COMMON NAME: Goldenrod
ALTERNATIVES: 'Goldenmosa,' 'Citronella'
DESCRIPTION: Herbaceous perennial making a spreading clump of upright stems clothed in narrow green leaves. Branched, downward facing heads of tiny yellow flowers. Some varieties highly invasive.
HEIGHT AND SPREAD: 2–2½ × 1½ft (60–75 × 45cm)
BLOOMING PERIOD: Late summer
SOIL: Any reasonably well cultivated.

3-10

FRONT

6-9

LATIN NAME: *Santolina rosmarinifolia* (syn. *S. virens*) 'Primrose Gem'
COMMON NAME: Holy flax, green lavender cotton, green santolina
ALTERNATIVES: *S. rosmarinifolia*, *S. chamaecyparissus*
DESCRIPTION: Evergreen shrub making a dome-shape with densely-packed dark green stems arising from a woody base. Highly dissected leaves. Flowers like very small, rounded buttons.
HEIGHT AND SPREAD: 2 × 3ft (60 × 90cm)
BLOOMING PERIOD: Summer
SOIL: Well-drained, not too rich or habit is spoiled.

6-9

LATIN NAME: *Santolina pinnata* ssp. *neapolitana* 'Sulphurea'
COMMON NAME: Lavender cotton, santolina
ALTERNATIVES: *S. rosmarinifolia*, 'Primrose Gem,' *S. chamaecyparissus*
DESCRIPTION: Evergreen aromatic shrub with a dome-shaped habit and grayish green dissected leaves. Pale yellow button-shaped flowers. May be cut back hard in spring to keep dense habit.
HEIGHT AND SPREAD: 2 × 3ft (60 × 90cm)
BLOOMING PERIOD: Mid-summer
SOIL: Well-drained, not too rich or habit is spoiled.

LATIN NAME: *Ligularia stenocephala*
COMMON NAME: Known by Latin name
ALTERNATIVES: *L. przewalskii,* 'The Rocket'
DESCRIPTION: Herbaceous perennial with jagged-edge broadly rounded foliage making a large mound. Tall, purple-tinged stems bearing spires of orange-yellow daisy-like flowers. Protect against slugs and snails in spring.
HEIGHT AND SPREAD: 4 × 2ft (1.2 × 0.6m)
BLOOMING PERIOD: Mid- to late summer
SOIL: Moisture-retentive to wet.

4-10

LATIN NAME: *Fremontodendron* 'California Glory'
COMMON NAME: Fremontia
ALTERNATIVES: *F. californicum*
DESCRIPTION: Evergreen to semi-evergreen shrub. Short-lived. Lobed leaves and large waxy blooms. Train to cover a large sunny wall or in frost-free conditions grow as a free-standing shrub. Irritant hairs.
HEIGHT AND SPREAD: 20 × 18ft (6 × 5.4m)
BLOOMING PERIOD: Late spring to mid-autumn
SOIL: Well-drained, not too rich to avoid soft growth which is less hardy.

8-10

3-10

LATIN NAME: *Coreopsis verticillata*
COMMON NAME: Threadleaf coreopsis, tickseed
ALTERNATIVES: 'Golden Shower,' 'Zagreb,' 'Moonbeam'
DESCRIPTION: Herbaceous perennial with thread-like leaves and a profusion of starry, golden yellow blooms. Stems are self-supporting. Divide and re-plant in spring to keep plants vigorous.
HEIGHT AND SPREAD: 2–2½ × 1½ft (60–75 × 45cm)
BLOOMING PERIOD: Summer to mid-autumn
SOIL: Fertile, well-drained.

5-9

LATIN NAME: *Rosa* 'Peaudouce' syn. 'Elina,' 'Dicjana'
COMMON NAME: Large-flowered (hybrid tea) bush rose
ALTERNATIVES: 'King's Ransom,' 'Sunblest,' 'Grandpa Dickson'
DESCRIPTION: Bush rose of vigorous, upright habit with attractive dark green foliage and very large double blooms which are creamy-white deepening to lemon yellow at the center. Some scent.
HEIGHT AND SPREAD: 42 × 30in (106 × 75cm)
BLOOMING PERIOD: Spring to autumn
SOIL: Fertile, moisture-retentive and humus-rich. Avoid thin, limey.

LATIN NAME: *Calendula officinalis*
COMMON NAME: Pot marigold, calendula
ALTERNATIVES: 'Lemon Queen'
DESCRIPTION: Hardy annual with a bushy habit, light green, pungent-smelling leaves and single or double circular flower heads in shades of yellow or orange depending on the variety. Deadhead regularly.
HEIGHT AND SPREAD: 12–24 × 9–12in (30–60 × 22–30cm)
BLOOMING PERIOD: Summer to early autumn (spring in warm areas)
SOIL: Well-drained.

LATIN NAME: *Antirrhinum majus* variety
COMMON NAME: Snapdragon
ALTERNATIVES: Coronet series, 'Golden Monarch'
DESCRIPTION: Half-hardy annual making bushy plants clothed in small narrow leaves. Flowers in branched spikes – remove main spike when faded to encourage flowering side shoots. Pinch out seedlings to promote bushiness.
HEIGHT AND SPREAD: 1–2 × 1ft (30–60 × 30cm)
BLOOMING PERIOD: Early summer through autumn
SOIL: Well-drained, avoiding very heavy, poorly-drained ground.

BACK

LATIN NAME: *Helianthus annuus*
COMMON NAME: Sunflower
ALTERNATIVES: 'Lemon Queen,' 'Titan,' 'Mammoth Russian'
DESCRIPTION: Hardy annual making a single stem culminating in a giant flower with a central disk and surrounding circle of petals. The sunflower seeds which develop are attractive to birds in the autumn.
HEIGHT AND SPREAD: 4–5 × 1½ft (1.2–1.5 × 0.4m)
BLOOMING PERIOD: Summer
SOIL: Well-drained.

LATIN NAME: *Helianthus annuus* 'Moonwalker'
COMMON NAME: Sunflower
ALTERNATIVES: 'Lemon Queen'
DESCRIPTION: Half-hardy annual. Sunflower unusual for producing several large flowers on a single stem. Pale lemon yellow petals and dark brown centers.
HEIGHT AND SPREAD: 4–5 × 1½ft (1.2–1.5 × 0.45m)
BLOOMING PERIOD: Summer
SOIL: Any well-drained.

MIDDLE

LATIN NAME: *Anthemis tinctoria* 'E. C. Buxton'
COMMON NAME: Golden marguerite
ALTERNATIVES: 'Sauce Hollandaise,' 'Wargrave'
DESCRIPTION: Hardy perennial with finely divided leaves and producing many cool lemon-yellow daisies over the summer months. Paler and deeper cultivars are available.
HEIGHT AND SPREAD: 30 × 18in (75 × 45cm)
BLOOMING PERIOD: Summer
SOIL: Well-drained.

❄ 3-10

❄ 4-8

LATIN NAME: *Lilium* 'Destiny'
COMMON NAME: Lily
ALTERNATIVES: 'Concorde,' 'Connecticut King,' 'Sun Ray'
DESCRIPTION: Bulb producing long upright stems with narrow, lanceolate leaves and upward-facing, cup-shaped flowers with reflexed petals and a speckled throat. Contrasting brown anthers.
HEIGHT AND SPREAD: 3 × 4ft (90 × 120cm)
BLOOMING PERIOD: Early summer to mid-summer
SOIL: Fertile, well-drained but moisture-retentive and humus-rich.

FRONT

LATIN NAME: *Helianthus annuus* variety
COMMON NAME: Dwarf sunflower
ALTERNATIVES: 'Big Smile,' 'Music Box Mixed,' 'Sunspot,' 'Teddy Bear'
DESCRIPTION: Half-hardy annual producing single very large flowers on bushy plants. May be grown individually in pots or to add substance to a planting of more diaphanous annuals. Excellent for cutting.
HEIGHT AND SPREAD: 18–28 × 18in (45–71 × 45cm)
BLOOMING PERIOD: Summer
SOIL: Any well-drained.

LATIN NAME: *Chrysanthemum coronarium* 'Primrose Gem'
COMMON NAME: Annual chrysanthemum
ALTERNATIVES: 'Golden Gem'
DESCRIPTION: Hardy annual making bushy plants with finely divided foliage and many semi-double, pale primrose yellow flowers with a deeper center. 'Golden Gem' is a slightly darker shade.
HEIGHT AND SPREAD: 12–18 × 12in (30–45 × 30cm)
BLOOMING PERIOD: Summer
SOIL: Any well-drained.

LATIN NAME: *Lonicera periclymenum* 'Graham Thomas'
COMMON NAME: Woodbine, honeysuckle
ALTERNATIVES: *L. periclymenum*
DESCRIPTION: Climber with twining stems and paired grayish-green leaves. Climbs to the top of its support before spreading out. Some varieties have pink and purple-flushed flowers. Very fragrant in the evening.
HEIGHT AND SPREAD: 12–20 × 12–20ft (3.6–6 × 3.6–6m)
BLOOMING PERIOD: Summer to autumn
SOIL: Moisture-retentive. Thin, dry soils increase the risk of mildew.

4-8

LATIN NAME: *Spartium junceum*
COMMON NAME: Spanish broom
ALTERNATIVES: None
DESCRIPTION: Shrub with upright habit and long, green whip-like branches with very sparse foliage. Branchlets carry a profusion of pea-like flowers. Excellent seaside plant for windy sites. Trim lightly in spring.
HEIGHT AND SPREAD: 10 × 6ft (3 × 1.8m)
BLOOMING PERIOD: Summer to autumn
SOIL: Well-drained. Good on alkaline soils.

8-10

7-10

LATIN NAME: *Alstroemeria aurea*
COMMON NAME: Peruvian lily
ALTERNATIVES: *Alstroemeria* hybrids e.g. 'Princess Sophie'
DESCRIPTION: Herbaceous perennial with tall stems carrying narrow leaves and clusters of lily-like blooms which are streaked and spotted. May be invasive. Mulch the more tender hybrids against frost.
HEIGHT AND SPREAD: 3 × 1ft (90 × 30cm)
BLOOMING PERIOD: Summer
SOIL: Light, well-drained but moisture-retentive.

3-9

LATIN NAME: *Centaurea macrocephala*
COMMON NAME: Golden knapweed, globe centaurea
ALTERNATIVES: *C. ruthenica*
DESCRIPTION: Herbaceous perennial with coarse leaves and large, thistle-like heads with papery brown bracts and a tuft of yellow petals. Good for drying once petals have faded.
HEIGHT AND SPREAD: 3 4 × 2ft (90–120 × 60cm)
BLOOMING PERIOD: Summer
SOIL: Any well-drained soil but especially stony, lime-rich ground.

LATIN NAME: *Rudbeckia* 'Toto'
COMMON NAME: Coneflower
ALTERNATIVES: 'Nutmeg,' 'Goldilocks,' 'Becky,' 'Sonora'
DESCRIPTION: Half-hardy annual. Dwarf rudbeckia make bushy plants with large, golden daisy flowers opening fully to virtually circular blooms with a prominent dark brown central dome.
HEIGHT AND SPREAD: 8–12 × 12in (20–30 × 30cm)
BLOOMING PERIOD: Mid-summer to autumn
SOIL: Any well-drained, but moisture-retentive.

LATIN NAME: *Oenothera fruticosa glauca* syn. *O. tetragona*
COMMON NAME: Evening primrose, common sundrops
ALTERNATIVES: 'Yellow River,' 'Fireworks' ('Fyrverkeri')
DESCRIPTION: Herbaceous perennial making mounds of dark foliage over which the yellow, cup-shaped flowers emerge from red-tinged buds. 'Fireworks' has foliage flushed purple-red.
HEIGHT AND SPREAD: 18 × 12in (45 × 30cm)
BLOOMING PERIOD: Early to mid-summer
SOIL: Any well-drained.

4-10

BACK

LATIN NAME: *Cestrum aurantiacum*
COMMON NAME: Known by Latin name
ALTERNATIVES: *C. parqui, C. diurnum*
DESCRIPTION: Evergreen to deciduous scrambler which may be grown as a shrub if cut back each year. Broad, oval green leaves and clusters of tubular yellowish orange blooms with star-shaped petals. Needs a sheltered aspect.
HEIGHT AND SPREAD: 6½ × 6½ft (2 × 2m)
BLOOMING PERIOD: Summer
SOIL: Fertile, well-drained.

9-10

LATIN NAME: *Grevillea juniperina f. sulphurea*
COMMON NAME: Known by Latin name
ALTERNATIVES: None
DESCRIPTION: Evergreen shrub with very narrow, needle-like leaves and terminal clusters of tubular, pale yellow blooms which have long curling styles giving a spidery appearance. Must have lime-free soil.
HEIGHT AND SPREAD: 4 × 4ft (1.2 × 1.2m)
BLOOMING PERIOD: Spring to summer
SOIL: Well-drained, neutral to acid.

9-10

MIDDLE

LATIN NAME: *Rosa* 'Peer Gynt'
COMMON NAME: Bush rose – large-flowered or hybrid tea type
ALTERNATIVES: 'Sunblest,' 'King's Ransom,' 'Grandpa Dickson,' 'Freedom'
DESCRIPTION: Bush rose with attractive rich green foliage and large blooms which are yellow with reddish tinges. These are held singly or in clusters.
HEIGHT AND SPREAD: 32 × 24in (80 × 60cm)
BLOOMING PERIOD: Late spring to mid-autumn
SOIL: Rich, moisture-retentive. Does well on fertile, clay loam.

5-9

6-9

LATIN NAME: *Primula florindae*
COMMON NAME: Giant cowslip, Tibetan primrose
ALTERNATIVES: *P. sikkimensis*
DESCRIPTION: Herbaceous perennial making a clump of spear-shaped leaves from which flower stems arise topped by clusters of drooping, clear yellow, fragrant bells. Stems are covered with a white powder.
HEIGHT AND SPREAD: 2–3 × 1–2ft (0.6–0.9 × 0.3–0.6m)
BLOOMING PERIOD: Summer
SOIL: Moisture-retentive to moist, humus-rich soil.

FRONT

LATIN NAME: *Eschscholzia californica*
COMMON NAME: California poppy
ALTERNATIVES: 'Golden Values,' *E. lobbii* 'Moonlight,' *E. caespitosa* 'Sundew'
DESCRIPTION: Hardy annual with finely cut fern-like foliage of blue-gray coloring and simple flowers with petals like tissue-paper. Deadhead regularly to prolong display. Self-seeds readily. Drought resistant.
HEIGHT AND SPREAD: 12 × 6in (30 × 15cm)
BLOOMING PERIOD: Early summer to early autumn
SOIL: Any well-drained.

LATIN NAME: *Limonium sinuatum variety*
COMMON NAME: Statice, sea lavender
ALTERNATIVES: 'Forever Gold,' 'Gold Coast'
DESCRIPTION: Hardy annual with arching flower sprays. The tiny "everlasting" flowers are made up of paper petals. Upright, "winged" stems arise from a basal rosette of leaves.
HEIGHT AND SPREAD: 1–2 × 1ft (0.3–0.6 × 0.3m)
BLOOMING PERIOD: Mid-summer to mid-autumn
SOIL: Well-drained.

LATIN NAME: *Aucuba japonica* 'Crotonifolia'
COMMON NAME: Spotted laurel, Japanese aucuba
ALTERNATIVES: 'Variegata'
DESCRIPTION: Evergreen shrub with large leaves of leathery texture, variegated with bold, golden-yellow markings. 'Crotonifolia' is a female cultivar so red berries may appear in autumn.
HEIGHT AND SPREAD: 10 × 10ft (3 × 3m)
BLOOMING PERIOD: Insignificant
SOIL: Fertile, well-drained. Mature plants drought-tolerant in shade.

7-10

LATIN NAME: *Allamanda cathartica* 'Hendersonii'
COMMON NAME: Known by Latin name
ALTERNATIVES: None
DESCRIPTION: Evergreen, woody-stemmed climber with distinct whorls of lance-shaped green leaves and large, trumpet-shaped blooms of bright yellow.
HEIGHT AND SPREAD: 16ft (4.8m)
BLOOMING PERIOD: Summer to autumn
SOIL: Well-drained but moisture-retentive, neutral to acid preferred.

10

LATIN NAME: *Hemerocallis* 'Golden Chimes'
COMMON NAME: Daylily
ALTERNATIVES: 'Marion Vaughn,' 'Hyperion,' 'Brocaded Gown'
DESCRIPTION: Herbaceous perennial with a clump of long leaves above which are dark, slender flower stems with buds which open to golden-yellow, bronze-backed, trumpet-shaped blooms.
HEIGHT AND SPREAD: 2½ × 2ft (0.75 × 0.6m)
BLOOMING PERIOD: Early to mid-summer
SOIL: Fertile, moisture-retentive to moist.

3-10

LATIN NAME: *Achillea* 'Coronation Gold'
COMMON NAME: Yarrow
ALTERNATIVES: *A. filipendulina* 'Gold Plate,' *A. millefolium* 'Hoffnung'
DESCRIPTION: Herbaceous perennial with finely cut gray-green leaves making a basal clump which persists through winter. Upright stems carry flat, plate-like heads of flowers. Good for cutting and drying.
HEIGHT AND SPREAD: 3 × 1½ft (90 × 45cm)
BLOOMING PERIOD: Early to mid-summer
SOIL: Any well-drained but moisture-retentive.

3-10

LATIN NAME: *Tagetes patula* variety
COMMON NAME: French marigold
ALTERNATIVES: 'Yellow Jacket,' 'Hero,' 'Safari' and 'Petite Boy' Series
DESCRIPTION: Half-hardy annual of bushy habit with aromatic, divided foliage and numerous single or double blooms. Remove faded blooms regularly to prolong flowering and protect from slugs and snails.
HEIGHT AND SPREAD: 10 × 10in (25 × 25cm)
BLOOMING PERIOD: Summer to mid-autumn
SOIL: Well-drained.

LATIN NAME: × *Solidaster luteus* syn. × *S. hybridus*
COMMON NAME: Known by Latin name
ALTERNATIVES: 'Lemore'
DESCRIPTION: Herbaceous perennial of clump-forming habit with narrow leaves and bright starry flowers carried in dense heads on slender, wiry stems. Long flowering period. Susceptible to mildew.
HEIGHT AND SPREAD: 24 × 30in (60 × 75cm)
BLOOMING PERIOD: Mid-summer to autumn
SOIL: Rich, well-drained.

4-10

BACK

8-10

LATIN NAME: *Choisya ternata* 'Sundance'
COMMON NAME: Golden Mexican orange blossom
ALTERNATIVES: None
DESCRIPTION: Evergreen shrub with aromatic trifoliate leaves, bright yellow-green in spring becoming golden-green. Clusters of white orange-blossom-like flowers. Young leaves prone to frost damage.
HEIGHT AND SPREAD: 4 × 4ft (1.2 × 1.2m)
BLOOMING PERIOD: Late spring to early summer
SOIL: Fertile, moisture-retentive but well-drained. Avoid alkalinity.

7-10

LATIN NAME: *Elaeagnus pungens* 'Frederici'
COMMON NAME: Thorny elaeagnus
ALTERNATIVES: 'Maculata,' 'Dicksonii'
DESCRIPTION: Evergreen shrub of dense, twiggy habit with narrowly pointed leaves and bold, creamy-yellow variegation. Tiny pale yellow, sweetly scented flowers born in autumn.
HEIGHT AND SPREAD: 6–10 × 6–10ft (1.8–3 × 1.8–3m)
BLOOMING PERIOD: Mid- to late autumn
SOIL: Any well-drained but avoid very dry or highly alkaline conditions.

MIDDLE

4-9

LATIN NAME: *Inula hookeri*
COMMON NAME: Known by Latin name
ALTERNATIVES: None
DESCRIPTION: Herbaceous perennial with a spreading rootstock and mounds of broad foliage producing in late summer furry buds which open to daisy-like flowers with fine petals of unusual greenish yellow.
HEIGHT AND SPREAD: 2½ × 2ft (75 × 60cm)
BLOOMING PERIOD: Late summer
SOIL: Fertile, moisture-retentive to damp.

4-9

LATIN NAME: *Spiraea japonica* 'Goldflame'
COMMON NAME: Japanese spiraea
ALTERNATIVES: 'Golden Princess'
DESCRIPTION: Shrub of dense twiggy growth forming a mound of golden-yellow foliage. New growth orange-red tinted. Fluffy flat heads of deep pink flowers in summer. Cut to ground in early spring.
HEIGHT AND SPREAD: 2½ × 2½ft (75 × 75cm)
BLOOMING PERIOD: Early summer to mid-summer
SOIL: Fertile, moisture-retentive. Dislikes thin, poor, dry soils.

FRONT

9-10

LATIN NAME: *Gazania* 'Dorothy'
COMMON NAME: Known by Latin name
ALTERNATIVES: 'Mini-star Yellow,' *G. uniflora* 'Royal Gold,' 'Gold Rush'
DESCRIPTION: Tender perennial normally treated as a half-hardy annual making carpets of green lanceolate leaves. Large daisy flowers which only open on bright days and close in the evening.
HEIGHT AND SPREAD: 9 × 8–12in (22 × 20–30cm)
BLOOMING PERIOD: Early summer to mid-autumn
SOIL: Any well-drained. Performs well on poor, dry soil and near sea.

9-10

LATIN NAME: *Gazania* 'Silvery Beauty'
COMMON NAME: Known by Latin name
ALTERNATIVES: 'Lemon Beauty,' 'Mini-Star Yellow,' 'Dorothy,' *G. uniflora*
DESCRIPTION: Tender perennial normally treated as a half-hardy annual. Makes carpets of silver-gray foliage topped with large yellow daisies with a dark central ring. Flowers close on dull days.
HEIGHT AND SPREAD: 9 × 8–12in (22 × 20–30cm)
BLOOMING PERIOD: Early summer to mid-autumn
SOIL: Any well-drained. Performs well on poor, dry soil and near sea.

3-10

LATIN NAME: *Achillea filipendulina* 'Gold Plate'
COMMON NAME: Fernleaf yarrow
ALTERNATIVES: 'Parker's Variety,' 'Cloth of Gold'
DESCRIPTION: Herbaceous perennial with feathery green foliage and upright stems carrying large, flat heads of golden yellow. Long-lasting in water especially if leaves are stripped. Good for drying.
HEIGHT AND SPREAD: 4 × 1½ft (120 × 45cm)
BLOOMING PERIOD: Early summer to mid-summer
SOIL: Any well-drained but moisture-retentive.

LATIN NAME: *Inula magnifica*
COMMON NAME: Known by Latin name
ALTERNATIVES: *I. helenium*
DESCRIPTION: Herbaceous perennial of giant stature with broad, coarse foliage and stout stems carrying glowing yellow daisy flowers with very long, fine ray petals which droop slightly. Good for the wild or bog garden. Needs shelter.
HEIGHT AND SPREAD: 6–8 × 3ft (1.8–2.4 × 0.9m)
BLOOMING PERIOD: Late summer to early autumn
SOIL: Moisture-retentive to damp.

4-9

3-7

LATIN NAME: *Potentilla fruticosa* 'Primrose Beauty'
COMMON NAME: Shrubby cinquefoil
ALTERNATIVES: 'Moonlight,' 'Goldfinger,' 'Klondike'
DESCRIPTION: Shrub with dense twiggy growth forming a rounded bush covered in very small, pinnate gray-green leaves. Small flat rounded flowers produced in flushes.
HEIGHT AND SPREAD: 4× 4ft (1.2 × 1.2m)
BLOOMING PERIOD: Early summer to early autumn
SOIL: Any well-drained. Avoid waterlogged or very dry soils.

9-10

LATIN NAME: *Argyranthemum frutescens* 'Jamaica Primrose'
COMMON NAME: Marguerite, Paris daisy
ALTERNATIVES: 'Lemon Meringue,' 'Penny,' 'Yellow Star' ('Etoile d'Or')
DESCRIPTION: Perennial/sub-shrub of bushy habit with long-stemmed daisy flowers. Take stem cuttings in autumn or keep plants at between 7–10°C (44–50°F) to overwinter. Watch for leaf miner.
HEIGHT AND SPREAD: 3 × 3ft (90 × 90cm)
BLOOMING PERIOD: Mid-summer to mid-autumn
SOIL: Fertile, well-drained.

LATIN NAME: *Tagetes* 'Lemon Gem'
COMMON NAME: Dwarf marigold
ALTERNATIVES: 'Golden Gem,' 'Ursula'
DESCRIPTION: Half-hardy annual making spreading domes of filigree foliage almost completely smothered by a profusion of little "marigold" flowers. Excellent summer edging plant for paths.
HEIGHT AND SPREAD: 6–9× 9in (15–22 × 22cm)
BLOOMING PERIOD: Early summer to mid-autumn
SOIL: Fertile, well-drained.

LATIN NAME: *Tropaeolum majus* 'Tip Top Alaska Gold'
COMMON NAME: Nasturtium
ALTERNATIVES: 'Tip Top Gold,' 'Peach Melba,' 'Jewel Series Golden or Primrose'
DESCRIPTION: Hardy annual with bushy habit. Unusual white-marbled leaves and open-mouthed spurred flowers. Rich soils cause overproduction of leaf to flower. Prone to aphids and caterpillars.
HEIGHT AND SPREAD: 8–12 × 12in (20–30 × 30cm)
BLOOMING PERIOD: Early summer to mid-autumn
SOIL: Well-drained, performing best on somewhat poor soil.

BACK

4-7

LATIN NAME: *Hypericum* 'Hidcote'
COMMON NAME: St. John's wort
ALTERNATIVES: 'Rowallane'
DESCRIPTION: Semi-evergreen shrub of rounded habit with mid-green lanceolate leaves and dish-shaped blooms with a boss of golden-yellow stamens. Tough landscaping plant for towns and cities.
HEIGHT AND SPREAD: 4 × 4ft (1.2 × 1.2m)
BLOOMING PERIOD: Early summer to late autumn
SOIL: Any well-drained but moisture-retentive.

3-10

LATIN NAME: *Rudbeckia laciniata*
COMMON NAME: Coneflower
ALTERNATIVES: 'Hortensia' R. subtomentosa, R. maxima, 'Herbstsonne'
DESCRIPTION: Herbaceous perennial with deeply divided leaves and tall, upright stems carrying large yellow daisies with unusual green central cones. 'Herbstsonne' has an even more pronounced cone.
HEIGHT AND SPREAD: 6–7 × 2ft (1.8–2.1 × 0.6m)
BLOOMING PERIOD: Mid-summer to late summer
SOIL: Fertile, well-drained but moisture-retentive.

MIDDLE

6-10

LATIN NAME: *Kniphofia* 'Gold Else'
COMMON NAME: Red hot poker, torch lily, *tritoma*
ALTERNATIVES: 'Buttercup,' 'Candlelight,' 'Sunningdale Yellow,' 'Gold Mine,' 'Ada'
DESCRIPTION: Herbaceous perennial making small clumps of grassy leaves and erect, bare-stemmed spikes of soft yellow downward-facing tubular flowers. Protect roots from frost with a deep mulch.
HEIGHT AND SPREAD: 2½ × 1½ft (75 × 45cm)
BLOOMING PERIOD: Mid-summer
SOIL: Any well-drained, especially during winter.

7-10

LATIN NAME: *Dendranthema* 'Sea Urchin'
COMMON NAME: Spray chrysanthemum
ALTERNATIVES: 'Yellow Triumph,' 'Golden Mound'
DESCRIPTION: Herbaceous perennial best grown from cuttings taken in spring from last year's rootstocks which have been overwintered under protection. Needs staking and regular feeding and watering.
HEIGHT AND SPREAD: 4 × 2–2½ft (1.2 × 0.60–0.75cm)
BLOOMING PERIOD: Late summer to mid-autumn
SOIL: Light, well-drained but moisture-retentive.

FRONT

LATIN NAME: *Cladanthus arabicus*
COMMON NAME: Known by Latin name
ALTERNATIVES: None
DESCRIPTION: Hardy annual making hummocks of ferny aromatic foliage and scented daisy-like flowers. Sow outdoors in spring or prick out into divided seed trays to avoid root disturbance.
HEIGHT AND SPREAD: 24 × 12in (60 × 30cm)
BLOOMING PERIOD: Summer to early autumn
SOIL: Very well-drained.

6-10

LATIN NAME: *Kniphofia* 'Little Maid'
COMMON NAME: Red hot poker, torch lily, *tritoma*
ALTERNATIVES: 'Goldelse,' 'Buttercup,' 'Candlelight'
DESCRIPTION: Herbaceous perennial with grassy clumps of foliage and slender wands of palest yellow tubular flowers which are green in bud. Continues to produce a succession of blooms well into autumn. Mulch to protect crowns.
HEIGHT AND SPREAD: 24 × 18in (60 × 45cm)
BLOOMING PERIOD: Late summer to mid-autumn
SOIL: Well-drained.

BACK

8-10

4-9

LATIN NAME: *Genista aetnensis*
COMMON NAME: Mount Etna broom
ALTERNATIVES: None
DESCRIPTION: Shrub or small tree of airy habit with whip-like pendulous evergreen branches and sparse foliage. In mid-summer the plant is smothered in fragrant pea-like flowers.
HEIGHT AND SPREAD: 12–14 × 12–14ft (3.6–4.2 × 3.6–4.2m)
BLOOMING PERIOD: Mid-summer
SOIL: Any well drained.

LATIN NAME: *Heliopsis helianthoides* 'Light of Loddon'
COMMON NAME: Known by Latin name
ALTERNATIVES: 'Sommersonne' ('Summer Sun'), 'Sonnenglut'
DESCRIPTION: Herbaceous perennial with tall, self-supporting stems. Coarse foliage and many large, orange-yellow double daisy flowers. Care needed as this plant may be invasive.
HEIGHT AND SPREAD: 4–5 × 2ft (1.2–1.5 × 0.6m)
BLOOMING PERIOD: Mid-summer to late summer
SOIL: Any fertile soil.

LATIN NAME: *Kniphofia* 'Candlelight'
COMMON NAME: Red hot poker, torch lily, *tritoma*
ALTERNATIVES: 'Buttercup,' 'Gold Else'
DESCRIPTION: Herbaceous perennial making small clumps of grassy leaves and erect, bare-stemmed spikes of soft yellow downward-facing tubular flowers. Protect roots from frost with a deep mulch.
HEIGHT AND SPREAD: 3 × 1½ft (90 × 45cm)
BLOOMING PERIOD: Mid-summer
SOIL: Any well-drained, especially during winter months.

6-10

MIDDLE

3-10

LATIN NAME: *Hemerocallis* cultivar
COMMON NAME: Day lily
ALTERNATIVES: 'Whichford,' 'Golden Chimes,' 'Golden Scroll'
DESCRIPTION: Herbaceous perennial making a clump of long narrow leaves with tall stems carrying fragrant, trumpet-shaped blooms which open in succession from a cluster of buds and only last a day.
HEIGHT AND SPREAD: 2½–3 × 2½ft (75 90 × 75cm)
BLOOMING PERIOD: Mid-summer
SOIL: Moisture-retentive to damp.

9-10

FRONT

8-10

LATIN NAME: *Osteospermum* 'Buttermilk'
COMMON NAME: Known by Latin name
ALTERNATIVES: 'Anglia Yellow,' 'Zulu'
DESCRIPTION: Tender perennial with large daisy-like flowers with dark centers on long stems arising from a basal clump of toothed-edge leaves. Take cuttings in late summer or overwinter whole plants.
HEIGHT AND SPREAD: 24 × 12in (60 × 30cm)
BLOOMING PERIOD: Spring to autumn
SOIL: Well-drained.

LATIN NAME: *Bidens ferulifolia*
COMMON NAME: Known by Latin name
ALTERNATIVES: 'Golden Goddess,' B. aurea
DESCRIPTION: Tender perennial for front of the border and container work. Vigorous, sprawling habit. Long stems covered in ferny foliage and a profusion of honey-scented flowers. Good drought recovery.
HEIGHT AND SPREAD: 1½–2 × 1–1½ft (45–60 × 30–45cm)
BLOOMING PERIOD: Summer to autumn
SOIL: Fertile, well-drained.

BACK

LATIN NAME: *Bupleurum fruticosum*
COMMON NAME: Known by Latin name
ALTERNATIVES: None
DESCRIPTION: Evergreen shrub useful as a neutral backdrop for other flowers. Airy greenish yellow umbels and handsome gray-green leaves. Good for exposed, seaside gardens.
HEIGHT AND SPREAD: 5 × 5ft (1.5 × 1.5m)
BLOOMING PERIOD: Mid-summer to early autumn
SOIL: Tolerates a wide range of conditions.

7-10

LATIN NAME: *Pyracantha rogersiana* 'Flava'
COMMON NAME: Pyracantha, firethorn
ALTERNATIVES: 'Golden Charmer,' 'Soleil d'Or'
DESCRIPTION: Evergreen to semi-evergreen shrub for a wall or to grow free-standing. Arching stems with small, dark green leaves. Creamy-white blossom. Clusters of bright yellow fruits early autumn to mid-winter.
HEIGHT AND SPREAD: 12 × 6ft (3.6 × 1.8m)
BLOOMING PERIOD: Early summer
SOIL: Dislikes extreme alkalinity.

7-9

MIDDLE

5-9

LATIN NAME: *Rosa* 'Korresia' syn. 'Friesia'
COMMON NAME: Rose
ALTERNATIVES: Many e.g., 'Zonta Rose,' 'Chinatown,' 'Mountbatten'
DESCRIPTION: Cluster-flowered bush with highly fragrant, deep yellow blooms. Wavy petals. Upright, bushy habit and healthy, attractive foliage.
HEIGHT AND SPREAD: 2½ × 2ft (75 × 60cm)
BLOOMING PERIOD: Early summer to late autumn
SOIL: Fertile, humus-rich, moisture-retentive. Avoid highly alkaline.

LATIN NAME: *Phygelius aequalis* 'Yellow Trumpet'
COMMON NAME: Known by Latin name
ALTERNATIVES: 'Moonraker'
DESCRIPTION: Perennial with creamy yellow tubular flowers in clusters at the top of the stems. Best in a sheltered position e.g. at the base of a sunny wall. Evergreen to semi-evergreen in frost-free conditions.
HEIGHT AND SPREAD: 3 × 1½ft (90 × 45cm)
BLOOMING PERIOD: Mid-summer to mid-autumn
SOIL: Fertile, well-drained but moisture-retentive, water well in summer.

7-10

FRONT

9-10

LATIN NAME: *Dahlia* 'Yellow Hammer'
COMMON NAME: Dahlia
ALTERNATIVES: Many cultivars with differing flower forms
DESCRIPTION: Tuberous-rooted plant producing large single flowers or rich yellow with a distinctive fragrance. Attractive dark purple-green foliage. Lift and store tubers for winter unless in a frost-free area.
HEIGHT AND SPREAD: 12–18 × 12–18in (30–40 × 30–40cm)
BLOOMING PERIOD: Mid-summer to early autumn
SOIL: Rich, moisture-retentive but well-drained.

5-9

LATIN NAME: *Dendranthema* cultivar
COMMON NAME: Korean hybrid chrysanthemum
ALTERNATIVES: 'Yellow Delight,' 'Yellow Daphne,' 'Golden Bowl'
DESCRIPTION: Herbaceous perennial with daisy-like flowers varying in form with lobed leaves. Stems good for cutting. Protect from winter cold by mulching or lift crowns and store in potting compost.
HEIGHT AND SPREAD: 1½–2+ × 1½ft (45–60+ × 45cm)
BLOOMING PERIOD: Late summer to mid-autumn
SOIL: Any well-drained, fertile.

BACK

LATIN NAME: *Mahonia × media* 'Charity'
COMMON NAME: Oregon grape holly
ALTERNATIVES: 'Buckland,' 'Lionel Fortescue,' 'Winter Sun,' 'Underway'
DESCRIPTION: Evergreen shrub or small tree of upright habit. Stems topped with curving racemes of bright yellow fragrant flowers. The large pinnate leaves are a dark, glossy green.
HEIGHT AND SPREAD: 10 × 5½ft (3 × 1.8m)
BLOOMING PERIOD: Late autumn to mid-winter
SOIL: Open-textured, humus-rich. Avoid dry, strongly alkaline.

7-9

LATIN NAME: *Clematis rehderiana*
COMMON NAME: Known by Latin name
ALTERNATIVES: None
DESCRIPTION: Vigorous climber to cover walls and fences or to ramble through large shrubs. Creamy-yellow bell-shaped flowers. Elegant foliage. Sheltered site. Tie stems onto wire supports.
HEIGHT AND SPREAD: 12 × 12ft (3.6 × 3.6m)
BLOOMING PERIOD: Late summer to mid-autumn
SOIL: Humus-rich and moisture-retentive.

6-9

MIDDLE

LATIN NAME: *Solidago* 'Goldenmosa'
COMMON NAME: Goldenrod
ALTERNATIVES: 'Cloth of Gold,' 'Golden Dwarf'
DESCRIPTION: Compact perennial with fluffy, mimosa-like flower sprays in rich yellow at the ends of upright, unbranched stems. Leaves narrow, yellowish green. Some varieties are invasive.
HEIGHT AND SPREAD: 3 × 2ft (90 × 60cm)
BLOOMING PERIOD: Late summer to early autumn
SOIL: Any provided it is well-drained.

4-10

LATIN NAME: *Kniphofia* 'Percy's Pride'
COMMON NAME: Red hot poker, torch lily
ALTERNATIVES: 'Primrose Yellow,' 'Goldmine,' 'Ada,' 'Yellow Hammer'
DESCRIPTION: Perennial with poker-like flower spikes of creamy-yellow tinged with green. Basal clumps of stiff, grassy foliage. Dislikes winter wet and cold so protect crowns with a mulch before the cold weather arrives.
HEIGHT AND SPREAD: 36 × 18–20in (90 × 45–50cm)
BLOOMING PERIOD: Late summer to mid-autumn
SOIL: Well-drained, especially in winter.

6-10

FRONT

LATIN NAME: *Sternbergia lutea*
COMMON NAME: Autumn daffodil
ALTERNATIVES: None
DESCRIPTION: Bulb producing bright yellow, crocus-like flowers with grassy leaves. If conditions are suitable and bulbs are left undisturbed, clumps steadily increase in size.
HEIGHT AND SPREAD: 1–6 × 3–4in (2.5–15 × 7.6–10cm)
BLOOMING PERIOD: Early to mid-autumn
SOIL: Well-drained.

6-9

3-10

LATIN NAME: *Achillea* 'Moonshine'
COMMON NAME: Yarrow
ALTERNATIVES: 'Taygetea' is very similar
DESCRIPTION: Perennial with flat heads of sulphur-yellow flowers over soft gray-green divided foliage. Evergreen to semi-evergreen. Unlike taller varieties, 'Moonshine' does not need staking.
HEIGHT AND SPREAD: 24 × 20in (60 × 50cm)
BLOOMING PERIOD: Early summer to early autumn
SOIL: Any provided fertile and well-drained.

BACK

4-9

LATIN NAME: *Heliopsis helianthoides* 'Hohlspiegel'
COMMON NAME: Known by Latin name
ALTERNATIVES: 'Sonnenglut,' 'Light of Loddon,' 'Goldgefieder'
DESCRIPTION: Herbaceous perennial with coarse foliage and tall upright stems topped by double golden-yellow blooms. A tough, easily-grown plant which does not require staking.
HEIGHT AND SPREAD: 4 × 2ft (1.2 × 0.6m)
BLOOMING PERIOD: Late summer
SOIL: Any fertile soil.

5-9

LATIN NAME: *Clematis tangutica*
COMMON NAME: Golden clematis
ALTERNATIVES: *C. orientalis,* 'Bill MacKenzie,' 'Aureolin'
DESCRIPTION: Climber with light green ferny foliage and many deep yellow nodding bells followed by attractive silvery seed heads. Plant with roots in shade with support. May be cut back hard in spring.
HEIGHT AND SPREAD: 12–18 × 12–18ft (3.6–5.4 × 3.6–5.4m)
BLOOMING PERIOD: Mid-summer to late autumn
SOIL: Moisture-retentive and humus-rich.

MIDDLE

8-10

LATIN NAME: *Pleioblastus auricoma* syn. *P. viridistriatus*
COMMON NAME: Variegated bamboo
ALTERNATIVES: None
DESCRIPTION: Evergreen bamboo with upright canes arising from a spreading roots. Oblong leaves tapering to a point, boldly striped with yellow. Cut to ground after winter for fresh new growth.
HEIGHT AND SPREAD: 4ft × indefinite (1.2m × indefinite)
BLOOMING PERIOD: Not applicable
SOIL: Moisture-retentive to damp.

7-9

LATIN NAME: *Hypericum × inodorum* 'Elstead'
COMMON NAME: St. John's wort
ALTERNATIVES: 'Ysella' (a gold-leaved form), H. forrestii
DESCRIPTION: Semi-evergreen shrub of upright habit with paired, mid-green leaves and shoot tips culminating in small yellow flowers with prominent stamens. Cone-shaped fruits of pale pink to scarlet.
HEIGHT AND SPREAD: 3 × 3ft (90 × 90cm)
BLOOMING PERIOD: Late summer
SOIL: Any reasonably fertile. Avoid dry soils.

FRONT

LATIN NAME: *Zinnia elegans*
COMMON NAME: Zinnia
ALTERNATIVES: 'Sun Bow Mixed,' Short Stuff Gold,' 'Peter Pan Gold'
DESCRIPTION: Annual with large, vividly colored blooms, often pompon-shaped, produced at the ends of stiff, branching stems. Perform best in hot, dry summers. Susceptible to mildew.
HEIGHT AND SPREAD: 8–24 × 8–24in (20–60 × 20–60cm)
BLOOMING PERIOD: Mid-summer to early autumn
SOIL: Fertile and well-drained but moisture-retentive. Avoid poor soils.

LATIN NAME: *Helichrysum bracteatum*
COMMON NAME: Strawflower, immortelle, everlasting flower
ALTERNATIVES: 'Bright Bikini'
DESCRIPTION: Hardy annual used for cutting and dry arrangements but providing long-lasting color late in the season. Sow indoors in autumn or spring.
HEIGHT AND SPREAD: 12–15 × 12in (30–38 × 30cm)
BLOOMING PERIOD: Mid-summer to mid-autumn
SOIL: Well-drained.

BACK

LATIN NAME: *Coronilla valentina* ssp. *glauca* 'Variegata'
COMMON NAME: Known by Latin name
ALTERNATIVES: 'Citrina,' *C. v.* ssp. *glauca*
DESCRIPTION: Shrub with gray-green leaflets variegated creamy-white. Small, pea-like flowers, sweetly-fragrant, produced over a very long period, with the main flush in spring. The plain-leaved form is slightly hardier.
HEIGHT AND SPREAD: 6 × 6ft (1.8 × 1.8m)
BLOOMING PERIOD: Spring to autumn
SOIL: Well-drained. Tolerates quite high alkalinity.

8-9

LATIN NAME: *Sinacalia tangutica* (syn. *Senecio tanguticus*)
COMMON NAME: Known by Latin name
ALTERNATIVES: None
DESCRIPTION: Herbaceous perennial with invasive roots. Deeply divided foliage and tall stems topped with tapering plumes of tiny daisy flowers. Elegant, pale, fluffy seed heads give late season interest.
HEIGHT AND SPREAD: 5 × 2ft (1.5 × 0.6m)
BLOOMING PERIOD: Late summer to early autumn
SOIL: Moisture-retentive to damp, humus-rich.

6-9

MIDDLE

5-8

LATIN NAME: *Kirengeshoma palmata*
COMMON NAME: Known by Latin name
ALTERNATIVES: Koreana group
DESCRIPTION: Herbaceous perennial with foliage lobed with tapering points. Arching stems with large rounded buds in loose clusters. Tubular blooms with pointed, fleshy petals, flared at the mouth.
HEIGHT AND SPREAD: 3 × 2ft (90 × 60cm)
BLOOMING PERIOD: Late summer to early autumn
SOIL: Moisture-retentive, humus-rich, acidic.

LATIN NAME: *Helichrysum splendidum*
COMMON NAME: Known by Latin name
ALTERNATIVES: *Helichrysum italicum*
DESCRIPTION: Evergreen sub-shrub with dense, silver-gray foliage. Makes a neat dome. Small golden-yellow flowers appear above the foliage unless hard-pruned in spring.
HEIGHT AND SPREAD: 4 × 4ft (1.2 × 1.2m)
BLOOMING PERIOD: Mid-summer to autumn
SOIL: Well-drained. Tolerates high alkalinity.

8-10

FRONT

7-9

LATIN NAME: *Sanvitalia procumbens*
COMMON NAME: Creeping zinnia
ALTERNATIVES: 'Yellow Carpet,' 'Gold Braid'
DESCRIPTION: Hardy annual with creeping/trailing habit making low groundcover. Lanceolate leaves and daisy flowers with broad, dark central disk. Sun-loving but performing well even in wet summers.
HEIGHT AND SPREAD: 6 × 12–18in (15 × 30–45cm)
BLOOMING PERIOD: Mid-summer to mid-autumn
SOIL: Any fertile, well-drained.

LATIN NAME: *Crocosmia × crocosmiiflora* 'Solfaterre'
COMMON NAME: Montbretia
ALTERNATIVES: 'Citronella'
DESCRIPTION: Bulbous plant with broad, grassy bronze-tinted leaves. Arching flower stems carry sprays of funnel-shaped blooms, soft yellow-tinged apricot.
HEIGHT AND SPREAD: 24 × 19in (60 × 48cm)
BLOOMING PERIOD: Mid-summer to mid-autumn
SOIL: Fertile, moisture-retentive.

BACK

9-10

LATIN NAME: *Citrus limon × meyeri* syn. *Citrus meyeri*
COMMON NAME: Meyers lemon
ALTERNATIVES: *Citrus limon* cultivars
DESCRIPTION: Evergreen shrub with dark, glossy foliage with strong lemon aroma when crushed. This is a compact variety which flowers and fruits almost continuously, producing medium-sized lemons.
HEIGHT AND SPREAD: 23 × 10ft (7 × 3m)
BLOOMING PERIOD: Year-round
SOIL: Well-drained. Water well during fruit production.

LATIN NAME: *Chimonanthus praecox* var. *luteus* (syn. C. p. 'Luteus')
COMMON NAME: Wintersweet
ALTERNATIVES: *C. praecox, C. p.* 'Grandiflorus'
DESCRIPTION: Shrub of sparsely branched, upright habit, which flowers on the bare branches, producing fragrant, waxy, bell-shaped blooms. This variety has yellow flowers and is more showy than the species.
HEIGHT AND SPREAD: 8 × 8ft (2.5 × 2.5m)
BLOOMING PERIOD: Late winter
SOIL: Any, especially alkaline.

6-9

MIDDLE

10

7-9

LATIN NAME: *Senecio grandifolius* (*Telanthophora grandifolia*)
COMMON NAME: Known by Latin name
ALTERNATIVES: None
DESCRIPTION: Evergreen shrub with stout, upright branches bearing large oval leaves with toothed edges and prominent venation. The terminal flower heads are golden yellow, broad, dome-shaped.
HEIGHT AND SPREAD: 10–15 × 6–10ft (3–5 × 2–3m)
BLOOMING PERIOD: Winter to spring
SOIL: Well-drained.

LATIN NAME: *Cedrus deodara* 'Aurea'
COMMON NAME: Deodar
ALTERNATIVES: None
DESCRIPTION: Conifer grown for its golden yellow foliage and elegant pendulous branch tips. Will eventually form quite a large shrub, but leaders may be pruned to keep growth low and dome-shaped.
HEIGHT AND SPREAD: 4 × 4ft (1.2 × 1.2m)
BLOOMING PERIOD: Insignificant
SOIL: Well-drained, moisture-retentive.

FRONT

4-9

9-10

LATIN NAME: *Primula veris* hybrid
COMMON NAME: Cowslip
ALTERNATIVES: *Primula vulgaris*
DESCRIPTION: Herbaceous perennial forming a rosette of oval leaves and, from the center, an upright stem bearing long-stalked five-petalled flowers in shades of yellow tinged pink or orange.
HEIGHT AND SPREAD: 6–8 × 6–8in (15–20 × 15–20cm)
BLOOMING PERIOD: Spring
SOIL: Humus-rich, moisture-retentive but well-drained.

LATIN NAME: *Primula × kewensis* 'Mountain Spring'
COMMON NAME: Known by Latin name
ALTERNATIVES: *P. × kewensis*
DESCRIPTION: Tender herbaceous perennial forming clumps of leaves dusted powdery white. Flower stems bear clusters of fragrant, deep yellow, tubular blooms.
HEIGHT AND SPREAD: 12 × 6–12in (30 × 15–30cm)
BLOOMING PERIOD: Winter to early spring
SOIL: Well-drained with fine gravel added.

5-8

LATIN NAME: *Hamamelis × intermedia* 'Pallida'
COMMON NAME: Witch hazel
ALTERNATIVES: 'Arnold Promise,' *H. mollis*
DESCRIPTION: Shrub with an open, spreading habit, flowering on bare wood through the winter. 'Pallida' has broad, oval leaves producing good autumn color and fragrant, pale yellow, "spidery" blooms.
HEIGHT AND SPREAD: 16 × 20ft (5 × 6m)
BLOOMING PERIOD: Winter to early spring
SOIL: Neutral to acid, humus-rich, moisture-retentive.

6-10

LATIN NAME: *Jasminum nudiflorum*
COMMON NAME: Winter-flowering jasmine
ALTERNATIVES: None
DESCRIPTION: Shrub with lax stems most often trained as a wall shrub. The deep yellow flowers appear on the leafless green stems during any mild period in winter. Small, glossy, three-lobed leaves.
HEIGHT AND SPREAD: 10 × 10ft (3 × 3m)
BLOOMING PERIOD: Early winter to early spring
SOIL: Any moderately well-drained.

5-8

LATIN NAME: *Rhododendron* Golden Oriole Group
COMMON NAME: Knap Hill rhododendron
ALTERNATIVES: 'Talavera,' 'Crest,' 'Buttermint,' 'Eldorado,' 'Hotei'
DESCRIPTION: Evergreen shrub with oblong leaves rounded at the tips in dark green. The soft yellow, bell-shaped blooms are produced in clusters and are highlighted by the dark brown anthers.
HEIGHT AND SPREAD: 3 × 3ft (0.9 × 0.9m)
BLOOMING PERIOD: Early spring
SOIL: Acid, humus-rich, moisture-retentive but well-drained.

7-8

LATIN NAME: *Mahonia × wagneri* 'Moseri'
COMMON NAME: Known by Latin name
ALTERNATIVES: *M. aquifolium* 'Apollo'
DESCRIPTION: Slow-growing evergreen shrub, grown for its colorful large pinnate leaves. These begin yellowish green in spring and become pinky orange before darkening. Good yellow flower clusters.
HEIGHT AND SPREAD: 4 × 4ft (1.2 × 1.2m)
BLOOMING PERIOD: Spring
SOIL: Any well-drained but moisture-retentive.

3-7

LATIN NAME: *Ranunculus ficaria* 'Brazen Hussy'
COMMON NAME: Lesser celandine
ALTERNATIVES: *R. ficaria* cultivars
DESCRIPTION: Tuberous-rooted perennial forming mats of bronze-purple, heart-shaped leaves in spring and golden yellow, cup-shaped blooms. Foliage dies away in late spring. Good in the wild garden.
HEIGHT AND SPREAD: 2 × 8in (5 × 20cm)
BLOOMING PERIOD: Early spring
SOIL: Moisture-retentive but well-drained.

3-9

LATIN NAME: *Uvularia grandiflora*
COMMON NAME: Merrybells, bellwort
ALTERNATIVES: 'Pallida,' *U. perfoliata*
DESCRIPTION: Herbaceous perennial, producing bare upright stems which arch over at the tip. Beneath downward-facing, lance-shaped green leaves hang pale yellow, lily-like flowers.
HEIGHT AND SPREAD: 24 × 9in (60 × 23cm)
BLOOMING PERIOD: Spring
SOIL: Acid, humus-rich, moisture-retentive but well-drained.

Purple

PURPLE RANGES FROM ALMOST BLACK THROUGH DEEP MAROON TO PALE MAUVE AND LILAC. THERE ARE WARM RED-PURPLES AND COOL BLUE-PURPLES. HAPPILY, THE DIFFERENT COLORS TEND TO BE QUITE EASY TO COMBINE, ESPECIALLY WHEN MIXED WITH PURPLE-GREEN OR BRONZE-PURPLE FOLIAGE. DEEP PURPLE FLOWERS AND FOLIAGE BLENDED WITH OTHER RICH COLORS LIKE SCARLET, CRIMSON-RED, AND DEEP BLUE CAN CREATE BROODING AND PASSIONATE SCHEMES FULL OF DRAMA, ESPECIALLY IN DAPPLED SHADE. ADD FILIGREE SILVER AND SCATTERINGS OF CREAMY YELLOW OR WHITE TO LIGHTEN THE SCHEME AND MAKE IT MORE ROMANTIC.

YOU CAN CREATE STUNNING, THEATRICAL SCHEMES USING BLACK-PURPLE VARIETIES OF FLOWERS LIKE TULIPS, BEARDED IRIS, DAHLIAS, AND VIOLAS MIXED WITH WHITE, SILVER, OR BRIGHT LIME-GREEN FLOWERS AND FOLIAGE. DEEP, GLOWING PURPLES ALSO CONTRAST WELL WITH CLEAR ORANGE FLOWERS, LEMON, AND GOLDEN YELLOWS.

PASTEL PURPLES CREATE RESTFUL SCHEMES WITH SILVER AND GRAY-LEAVED PLANTS BUT BENEFIT FROM DOTTINGS OF MORE INTENSE PURPLE-REDS WHICH WILL ENLIVEN THE SCENE. IN A BORDER WHERE YELLOWS PREDOMINATE, SOFT PURPLE FLOWERS AND PURPLE-GREEN OR BRONZE FOLIAGE PLANTS MAKE THE IDEAL FOIL.

PURPLE BULBS, BERRIES, SHRUBS, AND HERBACEOUS PERENNIALS COME INTO THEIR OWN IN AUTUMN WHEN THE GOLDEN AND FLAME-ORANGE LEAVES MAKE A MARVELOUS BACKDROP. YOU CAN CREATE A SIMILAR BUT LESS SUBTLE EFFECT IN SPRING AND SUMMER BY WEAVING IN GOLD-LEAVED OR YELLOW-VARIEGATED SHRUBS AND PERENNIALS.

LEFT: *Purple foliage and flowers mingle to give dark and dramatic results - alliums, purple sage, bronze fennel, and lavender.*

BACK

5-8

LATIN NAME: *Rhododendron mucronulatum*
COMMON NAME: Korean rhododendron, azalea
ALTERNATIVES: 'Nana'
DESCRIPTION: Semi-evergreen or deciduous shrub with clusters of single, bright rose-purple blooms with prominent stamens. Flowers appear just as the new leaves are sprouting. Good autumn color.
HEIGHT AND SPREAD: 6 × 5ft (1.8 × 1.5m)
BLOOMING PERIOD: Early spring
SOIL: Acid, humus-rich, moisture-retentive.

5-8

LATIN NAME: *Rhododendron* 'Seta'
COMMON NAME: Known by Latin name
ALTERNATIVES: 'Fastuosum Flore Pleno,' 'Gomer Waterer,' 'Susan'
DESCRIPTION: Evergreen shrub of upright habit with small, dark green leaves and single, trumpet-shaped blooms in large clusters. Shading from white at the throat to pinkish-purple at the rim. Dark anthers.
HEIGHT AND SPREAD: 5 × 6ft (1.5 × 1.8m)
BLOOMING PERIOD: Early to mid-spring
SOIL: Acid, moisture-retentive, humus-rich.

MIDDLE

8-10

LATIN NAME: *Euphorbia characias* ssp. *wulfenii* 'Purple and Gold'
COMMON NAME: Milkweed, Spurge (Warning – Irritant)
ALTERNATIVES: None
DESCRIPTION: Evergreen perennial forming a clump of upright branches from a central stem. Leaves flushed purple-bronze and lime green flower bracts. Cut stems once flowers have faded.
HEIGHT AND SPREAD: 3–4 × 4ft (90–120 × 120cm)
BLOOMING PERIOD: Early spring
SOIL: Fertile, well-drained.

5-8

LATIN NAME: *Rhododendron* (dwarf cultivar)
COMMON NAME: Dwarf rhododendron
ALTERNATIVES: 'Gristede,' 'Blue Diamond,' 'Blue Tit'
DESCRIPTION: Dwarf, evergreen shrub with glossy leaves and dome-shaped habit. Tight clusters of single, light purple blooms. Best in sheltered spot in part shade, but tolerates full sun.
HEIGHT AND SPREAD: 2½–3 × 3–4ft (75–90 × 90–120cm)
BLOOMING PERIOD: Mid- to late spring
SOIL: Acid, moisture-retentive, humus-rich.

FRONT

5-8

LATIN NAME: *Rhododendron* 'Bluebird'
COMMON NAME: Dwarf rhododendron
ALTERNATIVES: 'Blue Tit,' 'Blue Diamond'
DESCRIPTION: Evergreen shrub with small, dark green glossy leaves and tight clusters of single pale lavender blooms. Does best sheltered from cold winds and in light shade. Excellent for planting *en masse*.
HEIGHT AND SPREAD: 2–2½ × 3ft (60–75 × 90cm)
BLOOMING PERIOD: Mid- to late spring
SOIL: Acid, moisture-retentive, humus-rich.

3-10

LATIN NAME: *Ajuga reptans* 'Burgundy Glow'
COMMON NAME: Bugle, bugleweed, carpet bugle
ALTERNATIVES: 'Multicolor'
DESCRIPTION: Evergreen to semi-evergreen carpeting perennial forming rosettes of purple, pink and cream variegated leaves. Runners with new plantlets produced at flowering time. Short, upright spikes of blue flowers.
HEIGHT AND SPREAD: 6 × 18in (15 × 45cm)
BLOOMING PERIOD: Late spring to early summer
SOIL: Fertile, moisture-retentive. Dry soils encourage mildew.

3-7

4-8

LATIN NAME: *Syringa vulgaris* 'Volcan' syn. 'Vulcan'
COMMON NAME: Common lilac, pipe tree
ALTERNATIVES: 'Charles Joly,' 'Mrs. Edward Harding'
DESCRIPTION: Shrub or small tree with attractive, heart-shaped leaves of mid-green coloring and narrow, dense heads of rich purple-pink. Deadheading improves performance. Remove suckers.
HEIGHT AND SPREAD: 8–16 × 5–10ft (2.4–5 × 1.5–3m)
BLOOMING PERIOD: Mid to late spring
SOIL: Well-drained.

LATIN NAME: *Berberis thunbergii* var. *atropurpurea* 'Rose Glow'
COMMON NAME: Red-leafed barberry
ALTERNATIVES: 'Harlequin'
DESCRIPTION: Shrub with deep purple, spoon-shaped leaves. New growth variegated and as season progresses becomes splashed with pink and cream. Red autumn berries sometimes produced.
HEIGHT AND SPREAD: 8 × 10ft (2.4 × 3m)
BLOOMING PERIOD: Early to mid-spring
SOIL: Any well-drained but not dry soil.

4-10

LATIN NAME: *Thalictrum aquilegiifolium*
COMMON NAME: Meadow rue
ALTERNATIVES: 'Thundercloud,' 'Purpureum'
DESCRIPTION: Herbaceous perennial with foliage very like that of columbine. Light mauve fluffy flowers followed by attractive seed heads. Avoid over fertility, which produces weak stems.
HEIGHT AND SPREAD: 3 × 2ft (90 × 60cm)
BLOOMING PERIOD: Early summer
SOIL: Any reasonable fertile soil.

5-10

LATIN NAME: *Weigela florida* 'Foliis Purpureis'
COMMON NAME: Known by Latin name
ALTERNATIVES: 'Victoria'
DESCRIPTION: Shrub with purple-tinged leaves on upright stems and tubular pale mauve-pink blooms produced in abundance. Foliage a good complement for early-flowering roses and silver-leaved plants.
HEIGHT AND SPREAD: 3–4 × 3–4ft (90–120 × 90–120cm)
BLOOMING PERIOD: Spring to early summer
SOIL: Any reasonably fertile soil. Does well on clay.

4-10

4-8

LATIN NAME: *Allium christophii*
COMMON NAME: Stars of Persia, downy onion
ALTERNATIVES: None
DESCRIPTION: Bulbous plant, best planted in early autumn in groups to come up through low planting. Broad leaves die away before the large, light purple heads appear. Good for drying.
HEIGHT AND SPREAD: 2 × 1½ft (60 × 75cm)
BLOOMING PERIOD: Spring to early summer
SOIL: Fertile, well-drained.

LATIN NAME: *Pulsatilla vulgaris*
COMMON NAME: Pasque flower
ALTERNATIVES: Heiler Hybrids, 'Violet Bells'
DESCRIPTION: Herbaceous perennial/alpine with finely dissected leaves covered in silky hairs. Large, nodding mauve-purple single blooms with boss of golden-yellow stamens followed by feathery seed heads.
HEIGHT AND SPREAD: 6–9 × 6–9in (15–22 × 15–22cm)
BLOOMING PERIOD: Spring
SOIL: Fertile, very well-drained.

BACK

4-8

LATIN NAME: *Corylus maxima* 'Purpurea'
COMMON NAME: Purple-leaf filbert, purple giant filbert
ALTERNATIVES: None
DESCRIPTION: Shrub with large, rounded dark purple leaves. Purple catkins appear on the bare branches in early spring and purple hazel nuts sometimes produced. Best cut to ground level every 4–5 years.
HEIGHT AND SPREAD: 10–13 × 10–16ft (3–4 × 3–5m)
BLOOMING PERIOD: Early to late spring
SOIL: Any reasonable soil.

5-8

LATIN NAME: *Rhododendron* cultivar
COMMON NAME: Known by Latin name
ALTERNATIVES: 'Purple Splendor', 'Old Port'
DESCRIPTION: Evergreen shrub with dark green, leathery leaves and large, dome-shaped heads of flowers. Best sheltered from strong, cold winds in part shade or sun but with plenty of moisture.
HEIGHT AND SPREAD: 10 × 10ft (3 × 3m)
BLOOMING PERIOD: Late spring to early summer
SOIL: Acid, moisture-retentive and humus-rich.

MIDDLE

2-9

LATIN NAME: *Dictamnus albus* var. *purpureus* syn. *D. fraxinella*
COMMON NAME: Gas plant, Burning bush, fraxinella, dittany, dictamnus
ALTERNATIVES: None
DESCRIPTION: Herbaceous perennial, long-lived and not needing frequent division to keep it flowering well. Elegant flowers with protruding stamens. Volatile oils from seed pods may be ignited hence the common name.
HEIGHT AND SPREAD: 3 × 2ft (90 × 60cm)
BLOOMING PERIOD: Early summer
SOIL: Well-drained.

3-10

LATIN NAME: *Campanula persicifolia*
COMMON NAME: Peach-leaved bellflower
ALTERNATIVES: 'Blue Gardenia,' 'Grandiflora'
DESCRIPTION: Herbaceous perennial making a basal rosette of slender evergreen leaves from which arise flower stems with bell-shaped blooms of lilac-blue. Long in flower and a good self-seeder.
HEIGHT AND SPREAD: 3 × 1ft (90 × 30cm)
BLOOMING PERIOD: Early to late summer
SOIL: Any fertile, well-drained.

FRONT

4-9

LATIN NAME: *Aubrieta* 'Greencourt Purple'
COMMON NAME: Known by Latin name
ALTERNATIVES: 'Dr. Mules,' 'Gurgedyke'
DESCRIPTION: Evergreen perennial/alpine with small gray-green leaves forming a mat of foliage which at flowering time is studded with rich purple semi-double blooms. Cut back hard after flowering.
HEIGHT AND SPREAD: 3–4 × 12in (8–10 × 30cm)
BLOOMING PERIOD: Spring
SOIL: Very well-drained. Tolerates lime.

4-9

LATIN NAME: *Vinca minor* 'Aureovariegata'
COMMON NAME: Lesser Periwinkle, vinca
ALTERNATIVES: 'Atropurpurea,' 'Bowles Variety' ('La Graveana'), 'Multiplex'
DESCRIPTION: Evergreen sub-shrub with long trails of pointed, yellow-variegated leaves in pairs. Stems root where they touch the ground so forming good groundcover. Purple-blue flowers.
HEIGHT AND SPREAD: 6 × 36+in (15 × 90+cm)
BLOOMING PERIOD: Mid-spring to early summer
SOIL: Moisture-retentive.

LATIN NAME: *Phlomis tuberosa*
COMMON NAME: Known by Latin name
ALTERNATIVES: 'Amazone,' *P. italica*
DESCRIPTION: Herbaceous perennial with a basal rosette of somewhat coarse, deep green broad leaves. Upright stems carry whorls of light purple-hooded flowers emerging from reddish calyces.
HEIGHT AND SPREAD: 4–5 × 3ft (120–150 × 90cm)
BLOOMING PERIOD: Late spring to early summer
SOIL: Any well-drained.

5-10

LATIN NAME: *Rhododendron* cultivar
COMMON NAME: Known by Latin name
ALTERNATIVES: 'Blue Peter,' 'Susan'
DESCRIPTION: Evergreen shrub with handsome dark green, leathery leaves and large, dome-shaped heads of flowers. Best given a spot sheltered from strong, cold winds in light shade or sun but with plenty of available moisture.
HEIGHT AND SPREAD: 10–13 × 10–13ft (3–4 × 3–4m)
BLOOMING PERIOD: Late spring to early summer
SOIL: Acid, moisture-retentive and humus-rich.

5-8

LATIN NAME: *Lunaria annua*
COMMON NAME: Honesty, dollar plant
ALTERNATIVES: *L. annua* 'Variegata,' *L. rediva*
DESCRIPTION: Biennial with heart-shaped, crinkled leaves and tall stems carrying light mauve to deep purple fragrant blooms. A cottage garden plant, ideal for filling shady corners. Attractive silvery seed pods. Self-seeds and may become invasive.
HEIGHT AND SPREAD: 30 × 12in (75 × 30cm)
BLOOMING PERIOD: Spring to early summer
SOIL: Any well-drained.

6-9

4-9

LATIN NAME: *Geranium psilostemon* syn. *G. armenum*
COMMON NAME: Cranesbill, hardy geranium
ALTERNATIVES: None
DESCRIPTION: Herbaceous perennial with divided, jagged-edged foliage and magenta-purple blooms with a prominent black eye. Support by way of twiggy sticks. Good autumn leaf color.
HEIGHT AND SPREAD: 4 × 4ft (1.2 × 1.2m)
BLOOMING PERIOD: Early to mid-summer
SOIL: Deep, rich, moisture-retentive.

6-9

LATIN NAME: *Euphorbia dulcis* 'Chameleon'
COMMON NAME: Spurge, milkweed
ALTERNATIVES: *E. amygdaloides* 'Purpurea'
DESCRIPTION: Herbaceous perennial grown for its bright purple-red foliage. Small, yellowish-green flowers in mid- to late spring. May spread and become a nuisance when established. Irritant sap.
HEIGHT AND SPREAD: 2 × 1½ft (60 × 75cm)
BLOOMING PERIOD: Mid- to late spring
SOIL: Well-drained.

8-9

LATIN NAME: *Iris* Californian Hybrid (syn. Pacific Coast Hybrid)
COMMON NAME: Pacific Coast hybrid
ALTERNATIVES: *I. douglasii*, *I. missouriensis*, *I. tenax* plus many more
DESCRIPTION: A group of herbaceous or evergreen rhizomatous iris in the "beardless" section, making spreading clumps of arching, grassy leaves above which the blooms appear.
HEIGHT AND SPREAD: 10–28in × indefinite (25–70cm × indefinite)
BLOOMING PERIOD: Late spring to early summer
SOIL: Humus-rich, drained but moisture-retentive, acid to neutral.

BACK

5-9

5-8

LATIN NAME: *Buddleja alternifolia* (syn. *Buddleia alternifolia*)
COMMON NAME: Fountain buddleia
ALTERNATIVES: 'Argentea'
DESCRIPTION: Shrub of large stature needing room to show off its spectacular cascading branches. Narrow, gray-green leaves and globular clusters of fragrant flowers. May be fan-trained on a wall.
HEIGHT AND SPREAD: 10–13 × 10–13ft (3–4 × 3–4m)
BLOOMING PERIOD: Late spring and summer
SOIL: Deep, rich soil but will tolerate a variety of conditions.

LATIN NAME: *Acer palmatum* 'Dissectum Atropurpureum'
COMMON NAME: Japanese maple
ALTERNATIVES: A. p. 'Bloodgood,' A. p. d. 'Crimson Queen'
DESCRIPTION: Shrub or small tree which develops beautiful sinuous branches and a canopy of finely-cut leaves of deep purple which turn rich oranges and reds in autumn. Needs shelter and good soil.
HEIGHT AND SPREAD: 12 × 12ft (3.6 × 3.6m)
BLOOMING PERIOD: Spring (insignificant)
SOIL: Neutral to acid, deep, humus-rich, moisture-retentive.

MIDDLE

3-9

LATIN NAME: *Papaver orientale* 'Hadspen'
COMMON NAME: Oriental poppy
ALTERNATIVES: 'Blue Moon,' 'Patty's Plum,' 'Lavender Glory'
DESCRIPTION: Herbaceous perennial with deeply-divided leaves and stems with large, rounded flower buds opening to bowl-shaped blooms with "tissue-paper" petals. Unusual dusky-purple coloring.
HEIGHT AND SPREAD: 3 × 2ft (90 × 60cm)
BLOOMING PERIOD: Early summer
SOIL: Fertile, well-drained.

3-10

LATIN NAME: *Iris cultivar*
COMMON NAME: Tall bearded iris
ALTERNATIVES: 'Sable,' 'Matinata,' 'Mary Frances'
DESCRIPTION: Herbaceous perennial spreading by thick, fleshy rhizomes. Bold, sword-shaped glaucous-green leaves, and flower stems carrying several large, velvet-textured blooms. Some cultivars need staking at flowering time.
HEIGHT AND SPREAD: 3ft × indefinite (90cm × indefinite)
BLOOMING PERIOD: Spring to early summer
SOIL: Preferably alkaline to neutral, rich, well-drained.

FRONT

5-9

5-9

LATIN NAME: *Lavandula angustifolia* 'Munstead'
COMMON NAME: Dwarf lavender
ALTERNATIVES: 'Hidcote,' 'Twickle Purple,' 'Royal Purple'
DESCRIPTION: Evergreen shrub of bushy habit with gray-green aromatic foliage and slender stems carrying short fragrant spikes. Clip over lightly.
HEIGHT AND SPREAD: 1½–2½ × 2–2½ft (18–75 × 60–75cm)
BLOOMING PERIOD: Mid-summer
SOIL: Well drained. Does well on limy soils.

LATIN NAME: *Lavandula* 'Hidcote'
COMMON NAME: Dwarf lavender
ALTERNATIVES: 'Munstead,' 'Twickle Purple,' 'Royal Purple'
DESCRIPTION: Evergreen shrub of bushy, spreading habit with narrow, gray-green aromatic foliage and flower stems carrying short fragrant spikes of rich purple. Clip over lightly immediately after flowering.
HEIGHT AND SPREAD: 1½–2½ × 2–2½ft (18–75 × 60–75cm)
BLOOMING PERIOD: Mid-summer
SOIL: Well drained. Does well on limy soils.

LATIN NAME: *Rosa glauca*
COMMON NAME: Redleaf rose
ALTERNATIVES: None
DESCRIPTION: Shrub with deep purple-red arching stems and pinnate leaves which have a blue-gray bloom – more pronounced in sun. The small, dog-rose type flowers are white shading to cerise pink. Red hips in autumn.
HEIGHT AND SPREAD: 6 × 5ft (1.8 × 1.5m)
BLOOMING PERIOD: Early summer
SOIL: Fertile. Unlike many roses, this prefers a light, well-drained soil.

2-8

8-10

LATIN NAME: *Fabiana imbricata* 'Violacea'
COMMON NAME: Known by Latin name
ALTERNATIVES: None
DESCRIPTION: Evergreen shrub with small, scale-like leaves giving the appearance of a tree heather. Tubular blooms smother the bush at flowering time. Needs a warm, sheltered spot in cooler climates.
HEIGHT AND SPREAD: 6½ × 6½ft (2 × 2m)
BLOOMING PERIOD: Late spring to early summer
SOIL: Acid soil essential. Fertile, humus-rich, but well-drained.

8-10

LATIN NAME: *Hebe* 'E. A. Bowles'
COMMON NAME: Hebe, shrubby veronica
ALTERNATIVES: 'Autumn Glory,' 'Mrs. Winder,' 'Bowles Hybrid'
DESCRIPTION: Evergreen bushy shrub of rounded habit with small leaves and slender flower spikes produced over a long period. Best in warm, sheltered site in cooler climates. Good for coastal gardens.
HEIGHT AND SPREAD: 2½ × 4ft (0.75 × 1.2m)
BLOOMING PERIOD: Mid-summer to late autumn
SOIL: Well-drained.

3-10

LATIN NAME: *Geranium wlassovianum*
COMMON NAME: Cranesbill, hardy geranium
ALTERNATIVES: *G. pratense* 'Plenum Violaceum,' *G. maderense*
DESCRIPTION: Herbaceous perennial making a mound of velvety stems and foliage. The attractively-cut leaves are deep green and make an excellent foil for the rich purple blooms with deeper veining.
HEIGHT AND SPREAD: 2 × 2ft (60 × 60cm)
BLOOMING PERIOD: Early summer
SOIL: Well-drained, moisture-retentive soil. Dislikes waterlogging.

LATIN NAME: *Brachycome multifida*
COMMON NAME: Swan River daisy
ALTERNATIVES: 'Blue Mist,' *B. iberidifolia* 'Purple Splendor,' *B. i.* 'Blue Star'
DESCRIPTION: Tender perennial making carpets of mossy foliage covered for a long period with small, lilac-blue daisies. The annual, *B. iberidifolia* is easily raised from seed and comes in many varieties.
HEIGHT AND SPREAD: 20 × 36in (50 × 90cm)
BLOOMING PERIOD: Spring to autumn
SOIL: Fertile, well-drained but moisture-retentive.

8-10

9-10

LATIN NAME: *Scaevola aemula* 'Blue Fan'
COMMON NAME: Known by Latin name
ALTERNATIVES: 'Blue Wonder,' 'Purple Fanfare'
DESCRIPTION: Tender perennial with leathery, jagged-edged leaves and stiff spreading/trailing habit. Unusual blooms with a "fan" of petals carried along the length of the flower stem.
HEIGHT AND SPREAD: 12 × 9–12in (30 × 22–30cm)
BLOOMING PERIOD: Summer to autumn
SOIL: Any reasonable, well-drained.

BACK

LATIN NAME: *Monarda* 'Aquarius'

COMMON NAME: Bee balm, bergamot, Oswego tea

ALTERNATIVES: 'Blaustrumpf,' 'Capricorn,' 'Mahogany,' 'Mohawk,' 'Scorpion,' 'Donnervolke,' 'Kardinal'

DESCRIPTION: Herbaceous perennial with a clump-forming rootstock producing many upright stems clothed in aromatic leaves similar to mint. Whorls of hooded blooms. May be invasive due to spreading roots.

HEIGHT AND SPREAD: 50 × 18–24in (127 × 45–60cm)

BLOOMING PERIOD: Summer

SOIL: Rich, moisture-retentive. Tolerates lime.

4-10

LATIN NAME: *Clematis* 'Etoile Violette'

COMMON NAME: Known by Latin name

ALTERNATIVES: 'Royal Velours,' 'Purpurea Plena Elegans'

DESCRIPTION: Climber. A cultivar of *C. viticella* but with larger, almost spherical, deep purple blooms with cream anthers. Best cut down each spring to about 12in (30cm). Quick-growing, ideal for training over spring-flowering shrubs.

HEIGHT AND SPREAD: 10–12 × 5ft (3–4 × 1.5m)

BLOOMING PERIOD: Summer to early autumn

SOIL: Deep, rich, moisture-retentive.

6-9

MIDDLE

8-10

LATIN NAME: *Fuchsia* 'Lena'

COMMON NAME: Known by Latin name

ALTERNATIVES: 'Dollar Princess,' 'Estelle Marie'

DESCRIPTION: Frost-hardy shrub with lax stems and green foliage which flowers over a long period. Blooms are two-toned, light pink and deep violet-purple with protruding stamens.

HEIGHT AND SPREAD: 3 × 3ft (90 × 90cm)

BLOOMING PERIOD: Summer to autumn

SOIL: Rich, moisture-retentive.

3-10

LATIN NAME: *Lysimachia ciliata* 'Firecracker'

COMMON NAME: Fringed loosestrife

ALTERNATIVES: 'Purpurea,' 'Atropurpurea'

DESCRIPTION: Herbaceous perennial with deep bronze-purple lanceolate leaves and small, bright yellow flowers in summer. A relatively new variety making a foil for vibrantly colored flowers.

HEIGHT AND SPREAD: 2–3 × 1½–2ft (60–90 × 45–60cm)

BLOOMING PERIOD: Early to mid-summer

SOIL: Rich, moisture-retentive but well-drained.

FRONT

5-10

LATIN NAME: *Stokesia laevis*

COMMON NAME: Known by Latin name

ALTERNATIVES: 'Wyoming'

DESCRIPTION: Herbaceous perennial forming an evergreen basal rosette of narrow leaves. Stems carrying large purple-blue blooms rather like cornflowers.

HEIGHT AND SPREAD: 12–18 × 12–18in (30–45 × 30–45cm)

BLOOMING PERIOD: Summer

SOIL: Well-drained.

6-10

LATIN NAME: *Roscoea purpurea*

COMMON NAME: Known by Latin name

ALTERNATIVES: *R. humeana, R. auriculata*

DESCRIPTION: Tuberous perennial. Member of ginger family with lance-shaped leaves and flowers with an upper, hooded petal and double-lobed lower lip like orchids. Mulch in winter for frost protection.

HEIGHT AND SPREAD: 12 × 12in (30 × 30cm)

BLOOMING PERIOD: Late summer

SOIL: Humus-rich, moisture-retentive but tolerant of lime.

6-9

3-10

LATIN NAME: *Clematis* 'Vyvyan Pennell'
COMMON NAME: Known by Latin name
ALTERNATIVES: 'Beauty of Worcester,' 'Countess of Lovelace'
DESCRIPTION: Climber with double, richly-colored blooms of lavender-purple tinged red. Late summer blooms are single. Tolerates moderate shade. Prune one third of previous season's growth in early spring.
HEIGHT AND SPREAD: 6–10 × 3ft (1.8–3 × 0.9m)
BLOOMING PERIOD: Late spring to late summer
SOIL: Deep, rich, moisture-retentive.

LATIN NAME: *Delphinium* cultivar
COMMON NAME: Known by Latin name
ALTERNATIVES: 'Black Knight,' 'Astolat,' 'Bruce,' 'Fanfare'
DESCRIPTION: Herbaceous perennial with a clump-forming rootstock producing tall stems clothed in deeply-divided leaves ending in long, solid spires of spurred flowers. Needs staking. Poisonous if eaten.
HEIGHT AND SPREAD: 4–8 × 3ft (1.2–2.4 × 0.9m)
BLOOMING PERIOD: Early to mid-summer
SOIL: Rich, moisture-retentive but well-drained.

4-10

LATIN NAME: *Ligularia dentata* 'Desdemona'
COMMON NAME: Known by Latin name
ALTERNATIVES: 'Othello'
DESCRIPTION: Herbaceous perennial with large rounded to heart-shaped leaves, bronze-green above, rich mahogany-purple below. Orange-yellow daisies. Protect new growth from slugs.
HEIGHT AND SPREAD: 3 × 2ft (90 × 60cm)
BLOOMING PERIOD: Mid to late summer
SOIL: Rich, moist to damp, to support lush summer growth.

LATIN NAME: *Cleome hassleriana* syn. *C. spinosa*
COMMON NAME: Spider flower
ALTERNATIVES: 'Color Fountains Mixed,' 'Violet Queen'
DESCRIPTION: Half-hardy annual of bushy, upright growth with fingered leaves and exotic-looking blooms with long-protruding stamens. May need support in windy sites. Fragrant. Self-seeds abundantly.
HEIGHT AND SPREAD: 2–4 × 1½–2½ft (0.6–1.2 × 0.45–0.75cm)
BLOOMING PERIOD: Early summer to mid-autumn
SOIL: Fertile, well-drained.

8-10

LATIN NAME: *Dorotheanthus bellidiformis* syn. *Mesembryanthemum criniflorum*
COMMON NAME: Livingstone daisy, ice plant
ALTERNATIVES: 'Magic Carpet Mixed'
DESCRIPTION: Half-hardy annual with fleshy leaves and stems bearing large, daisy flowers with glistening petals.
HEIGHT AND SPREAD: 4–6 × 8in (10–15 × 20cm)
BLOOMING PERIOD: Mid-summer to early autumn (may be longer)
SOIL: Well-drained. Thrives on sand, tolerant of poor conditions.

LATIN NAME: *Verbena rigida* syn. *V. venosa*
COMMON NAME: Known by Latin name
ALTERNATIVES: 'Lilacina'
DESCRIPTION: Tender, tuberous-rooted perennial which may survive through winter in mild gardens. Stiff, upright leafy growth topped with small clusters of pale purple flowers.
HEIGHT AND SPREAD: 18–24 × 12in (45–60 × 30cm)
BLOOMING PERIOD: Mid-summer to autumn
SOIL: Any well-drained.

BACK

LATIN NAME: *Solanum crispum*
COMMON NAME: Climbing potato, Chilean potato tree
ALTERNATIVES: 'Glasnevin,' S. jasminoides, S. wendlandii
DESCRIPTION: Climber/wall-shrub with lance-shaped foliage and starry flowers in clusters. The central boss of golden yellow stamens stands out well against the mauve-blue petals. Tie stems onto supports.
HEIGHT AND SPREAD: 12 × 12ft (3.6 × 3.6m)
BLOOMING PERIOD: Early summer to early autumn
SOIL: Well-drained but not dry. Dislikes extreme alkalinity.

❄ 8-10

LATIN NAME: *Lathyrus odoratus*
COMMON NAME: Sweet pea
ALTERNATIVES: Continental Hybrids, Old Spice Hybrids, Mammoth Hybrids
DESCRIPTION: Annual climber with light gray-green pinnate foliage and branched tendrils. Fragrant, winged flowers in clusters. Remove blooms as they fade or cut regularly to encourage flowering. Best in areas with long, cool spring.
HEIGHT AND SPREAD: 9 × 3ft (2.7 × 0.9m)
BLOOMING PERIOD: Summer to autumn (winter to spring in Australia)
SOIL: Fertile, well-drained and moisture-retentive.

MIDDLE

❄ 3-9

LATIN NAME: *Malva sylvestris*
COMMON NAME: Common mallow, blue mallow, high mallow
ALTERNATIVES: M. s. 'Brave Heart,' 'Zebrina'
DESCRIPTION: Herbaceous perennial which seeds freely and often hybridizes with other garden mallows. Traditional herb with coarse lobed leaves and pale mauve blooms with lobed, striped petals.
HEIGHT AND SPREAD: 18–36 × 24–36in (45–90 × 60–90cm)
BLOOMING PERIOD: Early summer to autumn
SOIL: Any well-drained.

❄ 7-10

LATIN NAME: *Dierama pulcherrimum*
COMMON NAME: Wand flower, Venus' or Angel's fishing rod
ALTERNATIVES: Slieve Donard hybrids, dwarf forms
DESCRIPTION: Bulbous perennial with a clump of long, grassy evergreen leaves from which tall, arching flower stems arise carrying many bell flowers in mauve-pink. Seeds freely with color variations.
HEIGHT AND SPREAD: 4–5 × 1ft (1.2–1.5 × 0.3m)
BLOOMING PERIOD: Late summer
SOIL: Moisture-retentive to damp. Humus-rich.

FRONT

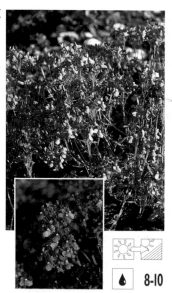

LATIN NAME: *Nemesia caerulea* 'Elliott's Variety'
COMMON NAME: Known by Latin name
ALTERNATIVES: N. caerulea, N. fruticans, 'Joan Wilder, N. 'Woodcote'
DESCRIPTION: Tender perennial quite unlike the normal bedding nemesia, having very small, pale lilac-purple blooms on wiry stems. Small, lance-shaped leaves. Much more drought-tolerant and longer in flower.
HEIGHT AND SPREAD: 9–12 × 9–12in (22–30 × 22–30cm)
BLOOMING PERIOD: Summer to early autumn
SOIL: Fertile, well-drained but moisture-retentive.

💧 8-10

LATIN NAME: *Petunia × hybrida*
COMMON NAME: Known by Latin name
ALTERNATIVES: Carpet Series, 'Daddy Blue,' 'Heavenly Lavender'
DESCRIPTION: Half-hardy annual with rounded to lance-shaped leaves covered in sticky hairs. Large blooms often sweetly fragrant. Protect from slugs and snails and deadhead to promote flowering.
HEIGHT AND SPREAD: 6–12 × 12in (15–30 × 30cm)
BLOOMING PERIOD: Summer to autumn
SOIL: Rich, moisture-retentive.

4-8

LATIN NAME: *Lathyrus odoratus*
COMMON NAME: Sweet pea
ALTERNATIVES: Same as dark shade (left)
DESCRIPTION: Climber with gray-green pinnate foliage and branched tendrils. Fragrant, winged flowers in clusters. Remove blooms as they fade or cut regularly. Best in areas with long, cool spring.
HEIGHT AND SPREAD: 9 × 3ft (2.7 × 0.9m)
BLOOMING PERIOD: Summer to autumn
SOIL: Fertile, well-drained and moisture-retentive.

LATIN NAME: *Berberis thunbergii* var. *atropurpurea*
COMMON NAME: Red-leafed barberry
ALTERNATIVES: *B.* × *ottawensis* 'Purpurea'
DESCRIPTION: Shrub with very dark purple-red stems and foliage. Leaves small, spoon-shaped. Clusters of small, cup-shaped blooms, white with a pink tinge. Red berries and good autumn leaf tints.
HEIGHT AND SPREAD: 9 × 10ft (2.8 × 3m)
BLOOMING PERIOD: Early to mid-spring
SOIL: Any, provided not too dry otherwise growth is poor.

LATIN NAME: *Amaranthus hypochondriacus* 'Erythrostachys'
COMMON NAME: Prince's feather
ALTERNATIVES: None
DESCRIPTION: Half-hardy annual making statuesque plant with broad bronzy-purple leaves and upright, branched panicles of deep red-purple. Best in a warm, sheltered site. Good "dot" plant for bedding displays.
HEIGHT AND SPREAD: 4 × 1½ft (1.2 × 0.45m)
BLOOMING PERIOD: Summer to autumn
SOIL: Rich, well-drained but moisture-retentive.

4-8

LATIN NAME: *Lobelia* × *gerardii* 'Vedrariensis'
COMMON NAME: Known by Latin name
ALTERNATIVES: Lobelia hybrids (not usually as hardy) e.g. 'Compliment Purple'
DESCRIPTION: Herbaceous perennial with lance-shaped, deep green leaves, bearing strong, upright flower stems, covered for much of their length with rich purple blooms.
HEIGHT AND SPREAD: 36 × 12in (92 × 30cm)
BLOOMING PERIOD: Late summer
SOIL: Fertile, humus-rich, moisture-retentive to damp.

9-10

LATIN NAME: *Petunia* × *hybrida*
COMMON NAME: Known by Latin name
ALTERNATIVES: Carpet Series F1, 'Midnight Dreams,' 'Pirouette Purple'
DESCRIPTION: Half-hardy annual with rounded to lance-shaped leaves covered in sticky hairs. Large blooms often sweetly fragrant. Protect from slugs and snails. Deadhead to promote flowering.
HEIGHT AND SPREAD: 6–12 × 12in (15–30 × 30cm)
BLOOMING PERIOD: Summer to autumn
SOIL: Rich, moisture-retentive.

LATIN NAME: *Osteospermum* 'Sunny Lady'
COMMON NAME: Known by Latin name
ALTERNATIVES: 'Port Wine,' 'Tresco Purple' and many others
DESCRIPTION: Tender perennial with toothed leaves and wiry stems bearing daisy flowers. Blooms with paler reverse and contrasting 'eye'. Closed in shade.
HEIGHT AND SPREAD: 18–24 × 12in (45–60 × 30cm)
BLOOMING PERIOD: Summer to autumn
SOIL: Well-drained.

BACK

LATIN NAME: *Salvia sclarea*
COMMON NAME: Clary sage
ALTERNATIVES: *S. s. var. turkestanica*
DESCRIPTION: Hardy biennial, often grown as an annual with a basal clump of broad leaves and upright or sprawling stems bearing spikes of small, lipped flowers surmounted by persistent bracts. Whole plant strongly aromatic.
HEIGHT AND SPREAD: 4–5 × 1½ft (1.2–1.5 × 0.45m)
BLOOMING PERIOD: Summer
SOIL: Any well-drained.

6-9

LATIN NAME: *Thalictrum delavayi*
COMMON NAME: Yunnan meadow rue
ALTERNATIVES: 'Hewitt's Double'
DESCRIPTION: Herbaceous perennial with dainty, columbine-like leaflets and airy branched heads carrying tiny mauve-petalled flowers with prominent cream stamens. Needs shelter and deep, rich soil to do well. Stake stems.
HEIGHT AND SPREAD: 5 × 2ft (1.5 × 0.6m)
BLOOMING PERIOD: Summer
SOIL: Deep, rich, moisture-retentive soil.

5-10

MIDDLE

LATIN NAME: *Centaurea cyanus* 'Black Ball'
COMMON NAME: Annual cornflower, bachelor's-buttons
ALTERNATIVES: None
DESCRIPTION: Hardy annual with deep maroon-purple ball-shaped heads carried on slender, branched flower stems. Lance-shaped, gray-green leaves. Plants susceptible to mildew in hot, dry conditions.
HEIGHT AND SPREAD: 2½ × 1ft (75 × 30cm)
BLOOMING PERIOD: Early summer to early autumn
SOIL: Any well-drained.

4-8

LATIN NAME: *Lilium* 'Black Beauty'
COMMON NAME: Hybrid lily
ALTERNATIVES: Lily hybrid strains, including Black Dragon Hybrids
DESCRIPTION: Bulb with tall, purple-black stems carrying spectacular blooms. The petals are deep red-purple, strongly recurved and edged in white. Plant in groups to rise up between lower plantings.
HEIGHT AND SPREAD: 4–6ft (1.2–1.8m)
BLOOMING PERIOD: Mid-summer
SOIL: Rich, well-drained but moisture-retentive.

FRONT

5-10

LATIN NAME: *Erigeron* hybrids
COMMON NAME: Fleabane
ALTERNATIVES: 'Dignity,' 'Quakeress,' 'Meer' syn. ('Black Sea')
DESCRIPTION: Herbaceous perennial, making low carpets of foliage studded with medium-sized daisy flowers. Taller varieties may need support in the form of twiggy sticks. Excellent seaside plant.
HEIGHT AND SPREAD: 18–24 × 24in (45–60 × 60cm)
BLOOMING PERIOD: Summer
SOIL: Fertile, well-drained.

5-10

LATIN NAME: *Tradescantia × andersoniana* cultivar
COMMON NAME: Spiderwort
ALTERNATIVES: 'Purple Dome,' 'Bilberry Ice,' 'Pauline'
DESCRIPTION: Herbaceous perennial with untidy, grassy leaves in bold clumps. The small, three-petalled blooms are clustered at the top of the stems. Foreground planting helps camouflage foliage.
HEIGHT AND SPREAD: 24 × 24in (60 × 60cm)
BLOOMING PERIOD: Summer to autumn
SOIL: Fertile, moisture-retentive.

LATIN NAME: *Abutilon × suntense*
COMMON NAME: Known by Latin name
ALTERNATIVES: 'Jermyn's,' 'Ralph Gould,' 'Violetta,' *A. vitifolium*
DESCRIPTION: Frost-hardy shrub making rapid growth and flowering prolifically against a warm wall or in a sheltered border. Light green jagged-edged leaves and dish-shaped mauve flowers. May die off suddenly.
HEIGHT AND SPREAD: 15 × 10ft (5 × 3m)
BLOOMING PERIOD: Late spring to mid-summer
SOIL: Any fertile, well-drained.

8-10

LATIN NAME: *Ipomoea purpurea*
COMMON NAME: Common morning glory
ALTERNATIVES: Ipomoea nil 'Platycodon Purple'
DESCRIPTION: Annual vine with twining stems, heart-shaped leaves and trumpet-shaped blooms. A weed in some parts of the world. Various color forms available.
HEIGHT AND SPREAD: 10–15ft (3–4.5m)
BLOOMING PERIOD: Summer
SOIL: Fertile, well-drained.

LATIN NAME: *Campanula glomerata 'Superba'*
COMMON NAME: Clustered bellflower
ALTERNATIVES: 'Joan Elliott'
DESCRIPTION: Herbaceous perennial with a spreading rootstock which is somewhat invasive. Upright stems carry dense spherical clusters of rich violet-purple bell-shaped blooms.
HEIGHT AND SPREAD: 2½ × 2ft (75 × 60cm)
BLOOMING PERIOD: Early to mid-summer
SOIL: Any well-drained.

3-10

LATIN NAME: *Hemerocallis 'Ed Murray'*
COMMON NAME: Daylily
ALTERNATIVES: 'Starling,' 'Chicago Royal Robe,' 'Persian Shrine'
DESCRIPTION: Herbaceous perennial making a clump of broad grassy leaves, highly attractive in spring when they emerge bright green in color. Stems topped with clusters of black-red trumpet-shaped blooms.
HEIGHT AND SPREAD: 2½ft (0.75m)
BLOOMING PERIOD: Mid-summer
SOIL: Fertile, moisture-retentive.

3-10

LATIN NAME: *Ageratum 'Pacific'*
COMMON NAME: Known by Latin name
ALTERNATIVES: 'Blue Angel,' 'Blue Danube,' 'Bengall,' 'Blue Blazer'
DESCRIPTION: Half-hardy annual making low rosettes of rounded, toothed-edged leaves with solid clusters of tiny, purple-blue fluffy flowers at the center. Deadhead faded clusters to prolong flowering.
HEIGHT AND SPREAD: 6–10 × 6–9in (15–25 × 15–22cm)
BLOOMING PERIOD: Early summer to mid-autumn
SOIL: Any reasonably fertile, moisture-retentive.

LATIN NAME: *Stachys macrantha 'Superba'*
COMMON NAME: Big betony
ALTERNATIVES: 'Robusta,' *Stachys macrantha*
DESCRIPTION: Perennial making a carpet of corrugated, heart-shaped leaves with toothed edges above which short spikes of hooded flowers appear. Makes excellent weed-smothering groundcover.
HEIGHT AND SPREAD: 24 × 9in (60 × 22cm)
BLOOMING PERIOD: Summer
SOIL: Any well-drained.

4-10

BACK

☼ ❄ 5-8

LATIN NAME: *Cotinus coggygria* 'Notcutt's Variety'
COMMON NAME: Smoke bush, Venetian sumach, smoke tree
ALTERNATIVES: 'Royal Purple,' 'Grace'
DESCRIPTION: Shrub with translucent oval leaves in dark purple-red. Fluffy plumes of purple-pink flowers. May be cut back moderately hard in late winter to promote larger leaves at the expense of flowers.
HEIGHT AND SPREAD: 10–16 × 10–16ft (3–4.8 × 3–4.8m)
BLOOMING PERIOD: Mid-summer to autumn
SOIL: Deep, moderately fertile soil preferred.

☼ ❄ 5-8

LATIN NAME: *Cotinus coggygria* 'Royal Purple'
COMMON NAME: Smoke bush, Venetian sumach, smoke tree
ALTERNATIVES: 'Notcutt's Variety,' 'Grace,' 'Velvet Cloak'
DESCRIPTION: Shrub with translucent oval leaves in rich purple-red. Fluffy plumes of purple-red flowers. May be cut back moderately hard in late winter to promote larger leaves at the expense of flowers.
HEIGHT AND SPREAD: 10–16 × 10–16ft (3–4.8 × 3–4.8m)
BLOOMING PERIOD: Mid-summer to autumn
SOIL: Deep, moderately fertile soil preferred.

MIDDLE

☼ ❄ 7-10

LATIN NAME: *Acanthus spinosus*
COMMON NAME: Bear's breeches
ALTERNATIVES: *A. mollis, A. spinosissimus*
DESCRIPTION: Herbaceous perennial of architectural stature with a mound of long, arching, deeply-cut, spiny, glossy leaves. Substantial columns of hooded white flowers with large purple bracts. Spreading root. Self-seeds.
HEIGHT AND SPREAD: 4 × 2ft (1.2 × 0.6m)
BLOOMING PERIOD: Summer
SOIL: Well-drained.

☼ ❄ 8-10

LATIN NAME: *Penstemon* 'Alice Hindley'
COMMON NAME: Known by Latin name
ALTERNATIVES: 'Stapleford Gem,' 'Sour Grapes,' 'Papal Purple,' 'Grape Tart'
DESCRIPTION: Evergreen perennial in mild climates, of bushy habit with many upright stems arising from the base. Stems well-clothed in glossy, narrowly lanceolate leaves. Tubular, flared blooms in pale violet.
HEIGHT AND SPREAD: 3–4 × 2ft (0.9–1.2 × 0.6m)
BLOOMING PERIOD: Summer to early autumn
SOIL: Fertile, well-drained.

FRONT

☼ ● 9-10

LATIN NAME: *Osteospermum* 'Pink Whirls'
COMMON NAME: Known by Latin name
ALTERNATIVES: None
DESCRIPTION: Tender, evergreen perennial of sprawling habit with mauve-pink daisy-like blooms with a darker blue-purple center and reverse. Petals spoon-shaped. Foliage gray-green, toothed edged.
HEIGHT AND SPREAD: 24 × 12–18in (60 × 30–45cm)
BLOOMING PERIOD: Summer to autumn
SOIL: Fertile, well-drained.

☼ ❄ 4-10

LATIN NAME: *Heuchera micrantha* var. *diversifolia* 'Palace Purple'
COMMON NAME: Known by Latin name
ALTERNATIVES: 'Rachel,' 'Pewter Moon'
DESCRIPTION: Clump-forming perennial with evergreen bronzy-purple foliage. Leaves are palmate and jagged-edged. Flower sprays pale pinkish white. Easy to raise from seed. Select darkest seedlings.
HEIGHT AND SPREAD: 18 × 18in (45 × 45cm)
BLOOMING PERIOD: Late spring to mid summer
SOIL: Rich, moisture-retentive.

LATIN NAME: *Buddleja davidii* 'Harlequin' syn. Buddleia davidii 'Harlequin'
COMMON NAME: Buddleia, variegated butterfly bush
ALTERNATIVES: None
DESCRIPTION: Shrub with lanceolate leaves, gray-green edged cream which make an excellent foil for the rich, purple-red tapered flowers. Cut back hard in late winter to generate strong shoots with larger leaves and flowers.
HEIGHT AND SPREAD: 9 × 9ft (2.7 × 2.7m)
BLOOMING PERIOD: Mid- to late summer
SOIL: Any well-drained.

5-9

6-9

LATIN NAME: *Hydrangea macrophylla* cultivars
COMMON NAME: Mop-head hydrangea, hortensia, big leaf hydrangea
ALTERNATIVES: 'Europa,' 'Westfalen,' 'Geoffrey Chadbund'
DESCRIPTION: Shrub with broad leaves tapering to a fine point. Dome-shaped heads mainly of showy sterile florets. Attractive in green bud stage and flowers often color beautifully in autumn.
HEIGHT AND SPREAD: 6–10 × 6–10ft (1.8–3 × 1.8–3m)
BLOOMING PERIOD: Summer to autumn
SOIL: Rich, moisture-retentive. Acid for purple tones in plants listed.

LATIN NAME: *Penstemon* 'Stapleford Gem'
COMMON NAME: Known by Latin name
ALTERNATIVES: 'Alice Hindley,' 'Sour Grapes,' 'Papal Purple,' 'Grape Tart'
DESCRIPTION: Evergreen perennial in mild climates, of bushy habit. Stems clothed in glossy, narrowly lanceolate leaves. Tubular, flared blooms in pale mauve and white.
HEIGHT AND SPREAD: 2½ × 2ft (0.75 × 0.6m)
BLOOMING PERIOD: Summer to mid-autumn
SOIL: Fertile, well-drained. Do not mulch crowns over winter – induces rot.

8-10

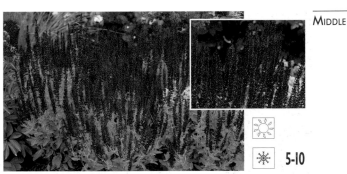

5-10

LATIN NAME: *Salvia × superba* syn. *S. nemorosa* 'Superba'
COMMON NAME: Ornamental sage
ALTERNATIVES: *S. × sylvestris* 'Mainacht' ('May Night')
DESCRIPTION: Herbaceous perennial of bushy habit with lanceolate leaves and stiff spikes of blue lipped flowers and purple-red bracts. Excellent contrast with golden-yellow blooms, especially achilleas.
HEIGHT AND SPREAD: 3 × 1½ft (0.9 × 0.45m)
BLOOMING PERIOD: Summer to early autumn
SOIL: Fertile, well-drained.

10

LATIN NAME: *Aeonium arboreum* 'Atropurpureum'
COMMON NAME: Known by Latin name
ALTERNATIVES: 'Schwarzkopff' syn. 'Zwartkop'
DESCRIPTION: Succulent of upright, loosely-branched habit, each stem terminating in a rosette of very dark purple-red leaves. Golden-yellow pyramidal flower clusters. Stems which have flowered die off.
HEIGHT AND SPREAD: 2 × 3ft (0.6 × 0.9m)
BLOOMING PERIOD: Spring
SOIL: Well-drained.

10

LATIN NAME: *Verbena × hybrida*
COMMON NAME: Known by Latin name
ALTERNATIVES: 'La France,' 'Homestead Purple,' 'Tex Tuf Purple,' Romance Hybrids
DESCRIPTION: Tender perennial with small deep green lance-shaped leaves with serrated edges. Bushy to trailing habit with stiff branching stems. Flowers, flared at the mouth in dome-shaped clusters.
HEIGHT AND SPREAD: 6–12 × 12–18+in (15–30 × 30–45+cm)
BLOOMING PERIOD: Summer to mid-autumn
SOIL: Fertile. Avoid dry conditions.

BACK

LATIN NAME: *Buddleja davidii* 'Empire Blue'
COMMON NAME: Butterfly bush, buddleia
ALTERNATIVES: 'Nanho Purple,' 'Lochinch,' *B. × fallowiana*
DESCRIPTION: Shrub with strong growth and upright habit. Foliage dark gray-green, lanceolate. Tapering, light lavender flower heads produced on new wood. Sweetly fragrant. Cut back hard in late winter.
HEIGHT AND SPREAD: 10–13 × 10–13ft (3–4 × 3–4m)
BLOOMING PERIOD: Mid-summer to early autumn
SOIL: Well-drained.

5-9

LATIN NAME: *Buddleja davidii* 'Dartmoor'
COMMON NAME: Butterfly bush, buddleia
ALTERNATIVES: 'Isle de France,' 'Lochinch,' *B. fallowiana*
DESCRIPTION: Shrub with stong upright habit flowering on new wood. Deep gray-green lanceolate leaves and large, branched flower panicles in deep lilac. Sweetly fragrant. Cut back hard in late winter.
HEIGHT AND SPREAD: 10–13 × 10–13ft (3–4 × 3–4m)
BLOOMING PERIOD: Mid-summer to early autumn
SOIL: Well-drained.

5-9

MIDDLE

LATIN NAME: *Aconitum* 'Spark's Variety' syn. *A. henryi*
COMMON NAME: Monkshood, wolf's bane
ALTERNATIVES: 'Bressingham Spire,' *A. carmichaelii* 'Kelmscott'
DESCRIPTION: Herbaceous perennial with long, deep blue-purple branched flower spikes. Unusual helmet-shaped blooms. Foliage divided into jagged "fingers." Highly poisonous.
HEIGHT AND SPREAD: 4–5 × 1½ft (1.2–1.5 × 0.45m)
BLOOMING PERIOD: Mid-summer to early autumn
SOIL: Fertile, well-drained but moisture-retentive.

2-9

9-10

LATIN NAME: *Hebe × andersonii* 'Variegata'
COMMON NAME: Known by Latin name
ALTERNATIVES: None
DESCRIPTION: Evergreen shrub with leathery, oval leaves, gray-green margined creamy-white. Short spikes of lilac-purple flowers borne over a long period. More tender than the plain-leaved form.
HEIGHT AND SPREAD: 4 × 4ft (1.2 × 1.2m)
BLOOMING PERIOD: Mid-summer to autumn
SOIL: Fertile, well-drained.

FRONT

5-8

LATIN NAME: *Erica cinerea* 'Hookstone Lavender'
COMMON NAME: Bell heather
ALTERNATIVES: 'Cindy,' 'Contrast,' 'Eden Valley,' 'Purple Beauty'
DESCRIPTION: Evergreen shrublet forming a low mound of fine stems covered in needle-like leaves. Tiny, bell-shaped flowers in abundance. After flowering, lightly clip over plants with shears.
HEIGHT AND SPREAD: 12 × 18in (30 × 45cm)
BLOOMING PERIOD: Mid-summer to early autumn
SOIL: Neutral to acid, humus-rich but well drained.

9-10

LATIN NAME: *Heliotropium arborescens* syn. *H. peruvianum* cultivar
COMMON NAME: Heliotrope, cherry pie
ALTERNATIVES: 'Iowa,' 'Black Beauty,' 'Marine'
DESCRIPTION: Tender perennial with attractive, deeply-veined leaves, dark green sometimes overlaid with purple. Bushy habit. Pale lilac to deep purple flower clusters. Sweetly fragrant.
HEIGHT AND SPREAD: 12–18 × 12in (30–45 × 30cm)
BLOOMING PERIOD: Summer to early autumn
SOIL: Fertile, well-drained.

BACK

5-9

LATIN NAME: *Buddleja davidii* 'Black Knight'
COMMON NAME: Butterfly bush, buddleia
ALTERNATIVES: 'Royal Red'
DESCRIPTION: Shrub with strong growth and upright habit. Foliage dark gray-green, lanceolate. Tapering, deep plum-purple fragrant flowers. Cut back hard in late winter. Flower heads give winter interest.
HEIGHT AND SPREAD: 10–13 × 10–13ft (3–4 × 3–4m)
BLOOMING PERIOD: Mid-summer to early autumn
SOIL: Well-drained.

LATIN NAME: *Tibouchina urvilleana* syn. *T. semidecandra*
COMMON NAME: Glory bush
ALTERNATIVES: None
DESCRIPTION: Evergreen shrub of upright, sparsely-branched habit with large leaves, strongly marked with parallel venation and softly hairy. Large, glowing-purple, dish-shaped blooms over a long period.
HEIGHT AND SPREAD: 10 × 6ft (3 × 1.8m)
BLOOMING PERIOD: Summer to early winter
SOIL: Neutral to acid.

10

8-10

LATIN NAME: *Hebe* 'Autumn Glory'
COMMON NAME: Known by Latin name
ALTERNATIVES: 'Amy,' 'Bowles' Hybrid'
DESCRIPTION: Evergreen shrub forming a low mound of shoots. Deep purple-black stems and deep, gray-green leaves with a fine red margin. Short spikes of deep lavender-purple over a long period.
HEIGHT AND SPREAD: 2–3 × 2–3ft (0.6–0.9 × 0.6–0.9m)
BLOOMING PERIOD: Mid-summer to early winter
SOIL: Fertile, well-drained.

MIDDLE

5-10

LATIN NAME: *Aster × frikartii* 'Mönch'
COMMON NAME: Michaelmas daisy
ALTERNATIVES: *A. frikartii,* 'Wonder of Staffa'
DESCRIPTION: Herbaceous perennial with oval, gray-green leaves and branching flower stems bearing rich lavender-purple daisy flowers with yellow centers. Unlike some asters, *A. frikartii* is mildew resistant.
HEIGHT AND SPREAD: 36 × 15in (91 × 38cm)
BLOOMING PERIOD: Mid-summer to mid-autumn
SOIL: Fertile, well-drained.

LATIN NAME: *Nepeta × faassenii*
COMMON NAME: Catmint
ALTERNATIVES: *N.* 'Six Hills Giant'
DESCRIPTION: Herbaceous perennial with a creeping root system making low mounds of soft, gray-green aromatic foliage. Small soft lavender flowers in slender sprays. Attractive to cats hence the common name.
HEIGHT AND SPREAD: 18 × 18in (45 × 45cm)
BLOOMING PERIOD: Early to late summer
SOIL: Any well-drained.

3-10

FRONT

5-10

LATIN NAME: *Tradescantia × andersoniana* 'Purple Dome'
COMMON NAME: Spiderwort
ALTERNATIVES: 'Bilberry Ice,' 'Pauline'
DESCRIPTION: Herbaceous perennial with untidy, grassy leaves in bold clumps. Small, three-petalled blooms are clustered at the top of flowering stems. Foreground planting helps camouflage foliage.
HEIGHT AND SPREAD: 2 × 2ft (0.6 × 0.6m)
BLOOMING PERIOD: Summer to autumn
SOIL: Fertile, moisture-retentive.

PURPLE

BACK

LATIN NAME: *Leycesteria formosa*
COMMON NAME: Himalayan honeysuckle, pheasant berry
ALTERNATIVES: None
DESCRIPTION: Shrub of upright, suckering habit, with bright, evergreen winter stems and dark green, lance-shaped leaves. Hanging strands of small white, bell-shaped blooms with purple-red bracts and purple-black berries.
HEIGHT AND SPREAD: 8 × 12ft (2.5 × 3.5m)
BLOOMING PERIOD: Late summer
SOIL: Any reasonably moisture-retentive but well-drained.

7-9

LATIN NAME: *Elsholtzia stauntonii*
COMMON NAME: Known by Latin name
ALTERNATIVES: None
DESCRIPTION: Sub-shrub with aromatic, toothed-edge leaves and short, fluffy spikes of mauve flowers. In cold climates the plant dies down to ground level each winter.
HEIGHT AND SPREAD: 5 × 7ft (1.5 × 2.2m)
BLOOMING PERIOD: Late summer to early winter
SOIL: Avoid thin, strongly alkaline types.

5-8

MIDDLE

LATIN NAME: *Fuchsia* 'Love's Reward'
COMMON NAME: Known by Latin name
ALTERNATIVES: 'Estelle Marie,' 'Rose of Castile,' 'Berba's Ingrid,' 'Fey'
DESCRIPTION: Tender shrub of bushy habit with mid-green oval, pointed leaves and clusters of bell-shaped hanging blooms with white sepals and white-edged purple petals.
HEIGHT AND SPREAD: 3 × 3ft (0.9 × 0.9m)
BLOOMING PERIOD: Summer to mid-autumn
SOIL: Well-drained, humus-rich, moisture-retentive.

9-10

LATIN NAME: *Hosta* 'Tall Boy'
COMMON NAME: Hosta, plantain lily, funkia
ALTERNATIVES: 'Honeybells,' 'Krossa Regal,' *H. ventricosa*
DESCRIPTION: Herbaceous perennial making bold clumps of handsome, lance-shaped foliage and sending up many strong flower stems, bearing pale purple, trumpet-shaped blooms, up to 5ft (1.5m) in height.
HEIGHT AND SPREAD: 3–5 × 2ft (0.9–1.5 × 0.6m)
BLOOMING PERIOD: Summer
SOIL: Well-drained to damp.

3-9

FRONT

LATIN NAME: *Viola hederacea*
COMMON NAME: Australian, ivy-leaved or trailing violet
ALTERNATIVES: None
DESCRIPTION: Tender evergreen perennial with very small rounded leaves and upright flower stems bearing white violets usually with prominent purple blotches. Good groundcover in warmer climes.
HEIGHT AND SPREAD: 1–2in × indefinite (2.5–5cm × indefinite)
BLOOMING PERIOD: Summer (most of the year in Australia)
SOIL: Well-drained, moisture-retentive.

8-10

LATIN NAME: *Sedum* 'Strawberries and Cream'
COMMON NAME: Stonecrop
ALTERNATIVES: 'Ruby Glow,' 'Vera Jameson'
DESCRIPTION: Herbaceous perennial of bushy, upright habit with deep purple, succulent, oval leaves and domed heads of tightly-packed flowers which are crimson-red in bud opening to cream and pink.
HEIGHT AND SPREAD: 2 × 2ft (0.6 × 0.6m)
BLOOMING PERIOD: Late summer
SOIL: Well-drained to dry.

4-10

LATIN NAME: *Verbena bonariensis* syn. *V. patagonica*
COMMON NAME: Known by Latin name
ALTERNATIVES: None
DESCRIPTION: Tender perennial making a basal clump of dark green leaves. The slender but rigid stems are strongly upright with sparse foliage and bear small but vivid purple flower clusters. Self-seeds.
HEIGHT AND SPREAD: 60 × 20in (150 × 50cm)
BLOOMING PERIOD: Summer to autumn
SOIL: Any well-drained.

7-10

LATIN NAME: *Clematis viticella* 'Little Nell'
COMMON NAME: Known by Latin name
ALTERNATIVES: 'Minuet,' 'Elvan,' 'Royal Velours'
DESCRIPTION: Climber with pinnate leaves and twining leaf stems. Needs support. May also be grown over a shrub to provide late summer color. Cut back to 12in (30cm) in early spring.
HEIGHT AND SPREAD: 12 × 12ft (3.7 × 3.7m)
BLOOMING PERIOD: Late summer
SOIL: Well-drained, humus-rich, moisture-retentive. Mulch.

6-9

LATIN NAME: *Tricyrtis formosana*
COMMON NAME: Toad lily
ALTERNATIVES: *T. hirta*
DESCRIPTION: Herbaceous perennial making slowly spreading clumps with upright stems covered along the length with glossy, dark green leaves. Intriguing speckled flowers in clusters. Water well in hot summer areas.
HEIGHT AND SPREAD: 2–3 × 1½ft (0.6–0.9 × 0.45m)
BLOOMING PERIOD: Early autumn (summer to autumn in Australia)
SOIL: Well-drained but moisture-retentive with plenty of humus.

5-9

LATIN NAME: *Fuchsia* 'Berba's Ingrid'
COMMON NAME: Known by Latin name
ALTERNATIVES: 'Estelle Marie,' 'Rose of Castile,' 'Love's Reward'
DESCRIPTION: Tender shrub of bushy habit with mid-green oval, pointed leaves and clusters of bell-shaped hanging blooms with white, reflexed sepals and purple petals.
HEIGHT AND SPREAD: 3 × 3ft (0.9 × 0.9m)
BLOOMING PERIOD: Summer to mid-autumn
SOIL: Well-drained, humus-rich, moisture-retentive.

9-10

LATIN NAME: *Sedum maximum* 'Atropurpureum'
COMMON NAME: Stonecrop
ALTERNATIVES: *S.* 'Ruby Glow,' *S.* 'Vera Jameson'
DESCRIPTION: Herbaceous perennial with dark maroon-purple succulent foliage covered with a gray-white bloom and dense heads of tiny red star-like blooms.
HEIGHT AND SPREAD: 2 × 2ft (0.6 × 0.6m)
BLOOMING PERIOD: Late summer
SOIL: Well-drained to dry.

4-10

LATIN NAME: *Liatris spicata* syn. *L. callilepis*
COMMON NAME: Blazing star, spike gayfeather
ALTERNATIVES: 'Kobold'
DESCRIPTION: Herbaceous perennial forming a dense clump of arching grassy leaves from which the upright flower stems appear. The bright, rosy mauve flower spikes open from the top down.
HEIGHT AND SPREAD: 2 × 1ft (0.6 × 0.3m)
BLOOMING PERIOD: Late summer
SOIL: Well-drained.

3-10

PURPLE

BACK

5-8

LATIN NAME: *Clematis 'Betty Corning'*
COMMON NAME: Known by Latin name
ALTERNATIVES: *C. v.* 'Little Nell,' *C. v.* 'Venosa Violacea'
DESCRIPTION: Climber with pinnate leaves and fine stems. Requires a framework of support unless allowed to scramble over a shrub. 'Betty Corning' is a hybrid between *C. texensis* and *C. viticella*.
HEIGHT AND SPREAD: 10–12 × 10–12ft (3–3.6 × 3–3.6m)
BLOOMING PERIOD: Mid-summer to early autumn
SOIL: Fertile, humus-rich, moisture-retentive.

5-8

LATIN NAME: *Clematis 'Jackmanii'*
COMMON NAME: Known by Latin name
ALTERNATIVES: 'Superba'
DESCRIPTION: Climber with pinnate leaves. Deep violet-purple blooms with four, petal-like sepals. Cut previous season's growth to 12in (30cm) of its origin in late winter/early spring.
HEIGHT AND SPREAD: 12–15 × 12–15ft (3.7–4.6 × 3.7–4.6m)
BLOOMING PERIOD: Mid-summer to early autumn
SOIL: Fertile, humus-rich, moisture-retentive.

MIDDLE

9-10

LATIN NAME: *Canna cultivar*
COMMON NAME: Indian shot, canna
ALTERNATIVES: 'Black Knight,' *C. indica* 'Purpurea'
DESCRIPTION: Rhizomatous perennial like a small banana plant with large bronzy-green to deep maroon-purple leaves depending on cultivar. Blooms may be plain, speckled or edged in another color.
HEIGHT AND SPREAD: 3–4 × 1½–2ft (90–120 × 45–60cm)
BLOOMING PERIOD: Late summer to autumn
SOIL: Fertile, moisture-retentive to moist.

3-10

LATIN NAME: *Aster ericoides 'Blue Star'*
COMMON NAME: Heath aster
ALTERNATIVES: 'Erlkönig'
DESCRIPTION: Herbaceous perennial, branched and bearing short, narrow leaves. Covered in tiny daisy flowers in autumn. In winter, the plant's skeleton gives a delicate, starry effect.
HEIGHT AND SPREAD: 2½–3 × 1ft (0.6–0.75 × 0.30m)
BLOOMING PERIOD: Autumn
SOIL: Any fertile, well-drained.

FRONT

5-10

LATIN NAME: *Liriope muscari*
COMMON NAME: Big blue lily turf, liriope
ALTERNATIVES: 'Majestic,' 'Big Blue,' 'Variegata,' 'Gold-banded'
DESCRIPTION: Evergreen perennial making spreading clumps of broad, grassy leaves above which solid spikes of violet-purple appear, not unlike those of muscari hence the Latin name. A tough plant useful for edging.
HEIGHT AND SPREAD: 12 × 18in (30 × 45cm)
BLOOMING PERIOD: Autumn
SOIL: Any fertile soil with reasonable drainage.

5-8

LATIN NAME: *Crocus nudiflorus*
COMMON NAME: Autumn-flowering crocus
ALTERNATIVES: *C. vernus, C. medius, C. speciosus*
DESCRIPTION: Corm bearing its tubular, flared flowers with distinctive golden yellow stigma in autumn on bare stems. The narrow, grassy leaves come later in winter and spring and then die away. Good for naturalizing in grass.
HEIGHT AND SPREAD: 4 × 1–3in (10 × 2.5–8cm)
BLOOMING PERIOD: Autumn
SOIL: Any well-drained.

LATIN NAME: *Callicarpa bodinieri var. giraldii 'Profusion'*
COMMON NAME: Beautyberry
ALTERNATIVES: *C. bodiniei, C. japonica, C. americana*
DESCRIPTION: Shrub of open habit. Leaves purple-tinted in autumn. Clusters of lilac flowers in leaf axils on second year wood followed by vivid, violet-purple fruits. Plant in groups for best fruiting.
HEIGHT AND SPREAD: 10–13 × 10–13ft (3–4 × 3–4m)
BLOOMING PERIOD: Late summer
SOIL: Any fertile soil, avoid extreme alkalinity.

❄ 6-8

❄ 5-8

LATIN NAME: *Hibiscus syriacus 'Mauve Queen'*
COMMON NAME: Rose of Sharon, tree hollyhock, flower of an hour
ALTERNATIVES: 'Russian Violet,' 'Coelestis,' 'Carnation Boy'
DESCRIPTION: Shrub with upright branches forming a goblet-shaped bush. Dark green lobed leaves and large, trumpet-shaped flowers with protruding column of stigma and stamens.
HEIGHT AND SPREAD: 5–6 × 5–6ft (1.5–1.8 × 1.5–1.8m)
BLOOMING PERIOD: Summer to mid-autumn
SOIL: Fertile, well-drained. Avoid extreme alkalinity.

LATIN NAME: *Aster turbinellus*
COMMON NAME: Fall aster
ALTERNATIVES: None
DESCRIPTION: Herbaceous perennial with wiry, upright, branched stems covered in small, narrow leaves and producing airy sprays of tiny violet-blue daisy flowers late in the season.
HEIGHT AND SPREAD: 4 × 2ft (1.2 × 0.6m)
BLOOMING PERIOD: Autumn
SOIL: Any fertile, well-drained.

❄ 5-10

LATIN NAME: *Cimicifuga simplex 'Atropurpurea' (C. racemosa 'Atropurpurea')*
COMMON NAME: Bugbane, cimicifuga
ALTERNATIVES: 'Brunette'
DESCRIPTION: Herbaceous perennial with deeply divided glossy, purple-black leaflets and wiry stems carrying "wands" of pinkish white fluffy flowers. Fragrant.
HEIGHT AND SPREAD: 4+ × 2ft (1.2+ × 0.6m)
BLOOMING PERIOD: Early to mid-autumn
SOIL: Rich, moist.

❄ 3-9

❄ 6-8

LATIN NAME: *Daboecia cantabrica 'Atropurpurea'*
COMMON NAME: Connemara heath, St. Daboec's heath, Irish heath
ALTERNATIVES: 'Hookstone Purple,' D. Scotica Group
DESCRIPTION: Evergreen shrublet making a low carpet. Small leaves and upright sprays of hanging bell-shaped blooms. Best in part shade but will stand full sun if ground is moist. Clip over in spring.
HEIGHT AND SPREAD: 8 × 36in (20 × 90cm)
BLOOMING PERIOD: Early summer to late autumn
SOIL: Neutral to acid, humus-rich, moisture retentive.

❄ 7-9

LATIN NAME: *Aster sedifolius 'Nanus'*
COMMON NAME: Fall aster
ALTERNATIVES: None
DESCRIPTION: Herbaceous perennial making a dome of branching stems covered with lanceolate leaves and starry, lavender-blue flowers. 'Nanus' more compact and less likely to "flop" than species.
HEIGHT AND SPREAD: 12–18 × 12–18in (30–45 × 30–45cm)
BLOOMING PERIOD: Late summer to early autumn
SOIL: Fertile, well-drained.

BACK

LATIN NAME: *Strobilanthes atropurpureus*
COMMON NAME: Mexican petunia
ALTERNATIVES: None
DESCRIPTION: Herbaceous perennial with a bushy, upright habit and pointed leaves with a toothed edge. The curious purple blooms are tubular with a flared mouth, appearing in clusters at the shoot tips.
HEIGHT AND SPREAD: 4 × 2ft (1.2 × 0.6m)
BLOOMING PERIOD: Summer to autumn
SOIL: Fertile, well-drained.

6-10

LATIN NAME: *Cordyline australis* 'Atropurpurea'
COMMON NAME: New Zealand cabbage palm
ALTERNATIVES: Purpurea Group
DESCRIPTION: Evergreen tree, slow-growing, of sparsely branched habit with long, strap-shaped leaves in purple-bronze forming rosettes at the top of bare trunks. Sprays of scented white flowers on mature plants.
HEIGHT AND SPREAD: 13+ × 10+ft (4+ × 3+m)
BLOOMING PERIOD: Summer (spring to summer in Australia)
SOIL: Well-drained.

10

MIDDLE

LATIN NAME: *Aster novi-belgii* 'Marie Ballard'
COMMON NAME: Michaelmas daisy, New York aster
ALTERNATIVES: *A. × frikartii* 'Mönch'
DESCRIPTION: Herbaceous perennial with upright stems that may require staking. Small, narrow, dark green leaves and clusters of double, daisy-like blooms at the top of the stems.
HEIGHT AND SPREAD: 3 × 1½ft (0.9 × 0.45m)
BLOOMING PERIOD: Autumn
SOIL: Well-drained but not dry.

4-9

LATIN NAME: *Hypoestes aristata*
COMMON NAME: Known by Latin name
ALTERNATIVES: None
DESCRIPTION: Evergreen bushy perennial or sub-shrub with oval green leaves and terminal spikes of purple tubular flowers in abundance. A frost-tender but showy plant.
HEIGHT AND SPREAD: 3 × 2ft (0.9 × 0.6m)
BLOOMING PERIOD: Late winter
SOIL: Well-drained.

10

FRONT

LATIN NAME: *Phormium* 'Bronze Baby'
COMMON NAME: New Zealand flax
ALTERNATIVES: 'Rubrum,' 'Tiny Tim,' 'Dazzler,' 'Dusky Chief'
DESCRIPTION: Evergreen perennial of dwarf habit making a rosette of arching, strap-shaped leaves of reddish purple with a fine red margin. A useful accent plant for the front of a sunny border.
HEIGHT AND SPREAD: 1½–2 × 2½ft (0.45–0.75 × 0.75m)
BLOOMING PERIOD: Mid-summer
SOIL: Well-drained.

8-10

LATIN NAME: *Ophiopogon planiscapus* 'Nigrescens'
COMMON NAME: Mondo grass, dwarf lilyturf
ALTERNATIVES: None
DESCRIPTION: Evergreen perennial with purple-black, arching, grassy leaves. Spreads via underground runners to make good groundcover. Insignificant light purple blooms and berries.
HEIGHT AND SPREAD: 9 × 12in (23 × 30cm)
BLOOMING PERIOD: Summer
SOIL: Well-drained.

4-10

INDEX OF LATIN NAMES

INDEX OF COMMON NAMES

CREDITS

Key: italicised references refer to close-up inset pictures, all other references refer to main plant pictures

al above left, ar above right, cl centre left, cr centre right, bl below left, br below right

Europa 39cr

Jon Delorme 80

Harry Smith Horticultural Collection 6, 10, 13cr, 18cr, 37al, 37*al*, 37ar, 44al, 44ar, 44ar, 45al, 45*al*, 46, 48al, 49ar, 49ar, 49bl, 49*bl*, 49br, 52al, 52*al*, 52bl, 52*bl*, 52br, 52br, 54ar, 54ar, 55al, 55al, 55ar, 55ar, 55cl, 58ar, 58ar, 64, 66cr, 66*cr*, 67cl, 70cl, 70*cl*, 70cr, 71cl, 71*cl*, 86al, 86*al*, 100, 104cl, 104*cl*, 122bl, 122*bl*, 123cl, 124br, 124*br*, 125bl, 125*bl*, 128, 135al, 135*al*, 135ar, 142, 145cl, 145*cl*, 145cr, 145*cr*, 146cl, 158ar, 159ar, 169cr, 169cr, 170, 189cl, 189*cl*, 192cl, 192*cl*, 192cr, 192cr

All other photographs were taken by Peter Stiles
Index by Kate Robinson

DEDICATION

For Joan and Neil with love